HISTORY IN THE HOUSE

Also by Richard Davenport-Hines

Dudley Docker
Sex, Death and Punishment
The Macmillans
Glaxo
Vice
Auden
Gothic
The Pursuit of Oblivion
A Night at the Majestic
Ettie: The Intimate Life of Lady Desborough
Titanic Lives
An English Affair
Universal Man: The Seven Lives of John Maynard Keynes
Edward VII: The Cosmopolitan King
Enemies Within
John Meade Falkner
Conservative Thinkers from All Souls College Oxford
Picture Perfect

Edited or co-edited

Speculators and Patriots
British Business in Asia since 1860
Hugh Trevor-Roper's Letters from Oxford
Hugh Trevor-Roper's Wartime Journals
Hugh Trevor-Roper's China Journals
One Hundred Letters from Hugh Trevor-Roper

RICHARD DAVENPORT-HINES

History In The House

Some Remarkable Dons and the Teaching of
Politics, Character and Statecraft

**WILLIAM
COLLINS**

William Collins
An imprint of HarperCollins*Publishers*
1 London Bridge Street
London SE1 9GF

WilliamCollinsBooks.com

HarperCollins*Publishers*
Macken House
39/40 Mayor Street Upper
Dublin 1
D01 C9W8, Ireland

First published in Great Britain in 2024 by William Collins

1

A catalogue record for this book is available from the British Library

ISBN 978-0-00-828572-2

Typeset in Minion Pro by Palimpsest Book Production Limited, Falkirk, Stirlingshire

Printed and bound in the UK using 100% renewable electricity at CPI Group (UK) Ltd

This book contains FSC™ certified paper and other controlled sources
to ensure responsible forest management.

For more information visit: www.harpercollins.co.uk/green

For
John Drury
Caroline Elam
Brian Young

Some have only a dark day and a long night from him, snows and white cattle, a miserable life, and a perpetual harvest of catarrhs and consumptions, apoplexies and dead-palsies; but some have splendid fires, and aromatic spices, rich wines, and well digested fruits, great wit and great courage; because they dwell in his eye, and look in his face, and are the Courtiers of the Sun, and wait upon him in his Chambers of the East; just so it is in friendship.

JEREMY TAYLOR

CONTENTS

List of illustrations

Plate Section 1

Thomas Wolsey, portrait by Sampson Strong, 1610 *(By permission of the Governing Body of Christ Church, Oxford)*
Henry VIII, founder of Christ Church
Francesco Guiccardini *(Veneranda Biblioteca Ambrosiana/Mondadori Portfolio/Bridgeman Images)*
William Camden, portrait by Marcus Gheeraerts *(National Portrait Gallery, London)*
Edward Hyde, Earl of Clarendon, portrait after Adriaen Hanneman *(National Portrait Gallery, London)*
John Fell, Richard Allestree and John Dolben, portrait by Peter Lely *(By permission of the Governing Body of Christ Church, Oxford)*
John Locke, portrait after Godfrey Kneller *(By permission of the Governing Body of Christ Church, Oxford)*
Cyril Jackson, portrait by William Owen *(By permission of the Governing Body of Christ Church, Oxford)*
Christ Church cathedral
The choir of Christ Church cathedral

Plate Section 2

Christ Church, as seen from the chaplains' court
Christ Church kitchens
The West front of Christ Church
Henry Halford Vaughan, photograph by Julia Cameron *(National Portrait Gallery, London)*

William Stubbs, photograph by Sarah Acland *(National Portrait Gallery, London)*

Frederick York Powell *(National Portrait Gallery, London)*

Arthur Hassall *(By permission of the Governing Body of Christ Church, Oxford)*

Christ Church undergraduates on the river *(By permission of the Governing Body of Christ Church, Oxford)*

An Edwardian idyll *(By permission of the Governing Body of Christ Church, Oxford)*

An undergraduate room in Tom Quad *(By permission of the Governing Body of Christ Church, Oxford)*

An Edwardian undergraduate's cheaper attic bedroom *(By permission of the Governing Body of Christ Church, Oxford)*

Thomas Banks Strong *(By permission of the Governing Body of Christ Church, Oxford)*

The undergraduate reading-room *(By permission of the Governing Body of Christ Church, Oxford)*

Keith Feiling *(By permission of the Governing Body of Christ Church, Oxford)*

J. C. Masterman *(By permission of the Governing Body of Christ Church, Oxford)*

Roy Harrod *(By permission of the Governing Body of Christ Church, Oxford)*

Patrick Gordon Walker, photograph by Walter Stoneman *(National Portrait Gallery, London)*

Hugh Trevor-Roper *(By permission of the Governing Body of Christ Church, Oxford)*

Robert Blake *(By permission of the Provost and Fellows of the Queen's College, Oxford)*

It is by solidity of criticism more than by the plenitude of erudition, that the study of history strengthens, and straightens, and extends the mind . . . the critic is one who, when he lights on an interesting statement, begins by suspecting it . . . The responsible writer's character, his position, antecedents, and probable motives have to be examined . . . a historian has to be treated as a witness, and not believed unless his sincerity is established. The maxim that a man must be presumed to be innocent until his guilt is proved, is not made for him.

LORD ACTON

History, true or false, speaks to our passions always.

LORD BOLINGBROKE

Reason, by its nature, is not kindly to history, or at least thinks little of arguments from history.

OWEN CHADWICK

New ideas are not nearly as potent as broken habits.

LEWIS NAMIER

Strict argument is interesting only if it is also a working out of an imaginative vision.

STUART HAMPSHIRE

PART ONE

CHAPTER 1

The Historian Needs a Lust for Life

The University of Oxford is six hundred years older than the United Kingdom. Eight monarchical dynasties have ruled England since the university's emergence in Plantagenet times. Little wonder, then, that when Disraeli, in his *Vindication of the English Constitution* of 1835, listed 'those great national institutions . . . which make us as a nation', there sprang foremost to his mind, in due order, 'our Crown, our Church, our Universities, our great municipal and commercial Corporations, our Magistracy'. A lifetime later, Mandell Creighton, Bishop of London, who had been an animating force in the early years of Oxford's School of Modern History, reverted to Disraeli's theme. For many centuries, so he said in 1900, the nation had been moulded by three powers, the State, the Church and the University. 'It still remains an absolute truth', he continued, 'that human life rests on three great primary requirements – order, conduct, knowledge; and these three requisites are still expressed in the forms of the State, the Church, and the University'. Disraeli and Creighton spoke of institutions – of the monarchy, of the Church of England, of the universities – rather than of individual leaders because institutions are stronger than men, and last longer, and better accommodate both continuity and change, and are more impervious to enthusiasm.[1]

When Disraeli referred to 'our universities', he meant England's two ancient universities, Oxford and Cambridge. The third university at Durham was new-born when he wrote, the University of London had not yet been founded, and those in Dublin and Scotland were discounted by him. Creighton was speaking at a ceremony marking the foundation of the first of the non-collegiate civic universities, at Birmingham. Durham, London and Birmingham, though, existed in different spheres from Oxford and Cambridge. Only the two ancient universities stood together, for centuries, as part of the constitutional structure of a kingdom that lacks a formal constitution. Their national status is indivisible from their historic position as repositories, in Bertrand Russell's words, of 'all the labours of the ages, all the devotion, all the inspiration, all the noonday brightness of human genius'.[2]

Big, agglomerative historical volumes already exist about the universities of Oxford and Cambridge. I have not overreached myself by trying to replicate them. The setting of a university is too wide and miscellaneous for my purposes. Instead I have studied a smaller learned community, and the personal subjectivity, the individual influences, the tutorial exchanges, the erudition and imagination, the continuities of ideas and the dissentient reactions that combined to form the intellectual development of that community. This book is confined, moreover, to the methods and purposes of studying modern history, which is the only subject in which I have expertise. Other subjects of the university syllabus, such as classical antiquity, philosophy, European languages and literature, the sciences and mathematics, are left aside.

Each college within the ancient universities is a separate realm of memory, to use Pierre Nora's phrase. I have chosen to study one of the most distinctive of those realms, Christ Church, a college which was projected in July 1524. The closed society of a college enables me to show the interplay of a smallish cast of characters, who work at close quarters in a single institution, meet in the same common rooms, talk at the same tables, walk in the same quadrangles, enjoy the same amenities, are enriched by similar traditions and have cognate aspirations. A college community clarifies the maturing of personal character, the use and impact of articulate sentences, the workings and enduring effects of individual influence on group thinking. (Its distinctiveness was emphasized by the fact that its senior members were not called Fellows, as in other Oxford colleges, but Students.) In part one of this book, with these ends in mind, I concentrate attention on two deans of Christ Church, John Fell and Cyril Jackson, and on Christ Church-educated historians such as William Camden and William Stubbs, in a form that is more focused than a university-wide outrush of facts, names and dates.

There was growing recognition in Tudor England, during the foundation phase of Christ Church, that the study of history improved the minds, enlarged the imaginations and broadened the vicarious experiences of princes, noblemen and administrators. History showed Stuart England, by precept and example, good government and bad, virtue and vice in rulers, and the reasons for the success or failure of states. 'Man without learning and the remembrance of things past falls into a beastly sottishness and his life is no more to be accounted of than to be buried alive,' wrote Sir William Dugdale, who accompanied Charles I when he made Oxford into the royal capital during the 1640s. William Camden was at the forefront of the newly advancing techniques and purposes of historical writing that developed, as I describe in chapter 3, in seventeenth-century England. The belief that the lessons of modern history were a politically moderating influence, and should therefore be part of the educational process, was upheld by David Gregory, who was appointed as Oxford's first Regius Professor of Modern History three hundred years ago in 1724, and as Dean of Christ Church in 1756. Camden, Gregory and their colleagues had no sense that historians should furnish universal truths or provide definitions that would hold true for perpetuity. Historians study piecemeal evidence of events, dates and testimony, and make deductions and discoveries which are not definitive.[3]

Almost all modern historians, until the late nineteenth century, had been educated in classical history at both school and university. They knew that, in ancient Greece and Rome, historians had prided themselves on being astute and accurate witnesses of their own times, and were concerned either exclusively or prevalently with facts and events of the recent past. Thucydides took the contemporary Peloponnesian war as his subject. Xenophon wrote about Sparta and Thebes in his own time. The lost books of Livy were contemporary history. Herodotus studied the Persian wars of the previous generation. Polybius began his narrative with the second Punic war, but brought it forward into his own era. The *Annals* and *Histories* of Tacitus record the Roman Empire in the first century AD, which was the century of his birth. Most ancient historians, according to Arnaldo Momigliano, saw their task as giving instruction in the management of change. The great historians of the sixteenth and seventeenth centuries – notably Guicciardini, Davila, Sarpi, de Thou,

Camden and Clarendon – followed Thucydides, Herodotus and other ancient historians in their contemporary awareness, and in their engagement with current or recent events and trends. They followed them, too, in their insuperable mistrust, in their wholesome pessimism, in their readiness at all times to recognize that everything can go amiss.[4]

The slackening of the dominance of classical studies in Oxford began when the three schools of classics, mathematics and natural sciences were supplemented by a fourth, the joint School of Law and Modern History, in 1853. This new faculty proved too amorphous, and was subdivided into separate schools of law and modern history in 1872. All the early leaders of the School of Modern History had their initial training in the history and culture of classical antiquity. James Froude, who was appointed Regius Professor of Modern History at Oxford in 1892, recalled his reading as an Oriel undergraduate in the 1830s. Aeschylus delighted him: he thrilled at the grandeur of Homer's characters: he took pains to master Pindar. 'Mathematics was distasteful to me as a thing without flesh and blood, but Aristotle laid hold of me, and Plato's dialogues opened a new and boundless world,' Froude recalled. 'Herodotus was as charming as the *Arabian Nights* had been, and the bridled thought and majesty of Thucydides gave me serious thought.' Froude sat up all one night, as an undergraduate at Oriel, reading Sophocles' tragedy *Philoctetes*, written during the Peloponnesian war about events during the Trojan war. When he had finished reading, he wept like a child:

> Philoctetes deserted on his solitary island, crawling for ten years among the rocks, in the intervals of intolerable torments from an envenomed wound, sustaining himself by the wild birds which he can shoot with the bow of Hercules, betrayed at last into the hands of his worst enemy by the treachery of a false friend who steals the bow from him and prepares to leave him to die famished in his misery, is an unrelieved picture of pure human suffering so described as to make the gods party to it, as to exhibit the full triumph of injustice over innocence, and so worked out that before the gods interpose at last, the imagination has been overstrained and the feelings relieve themselves in tears.

The anguish, betrayals, injustice and sorrows of life, as conjured by the writers of classical antiquity, felt palpable to nineteenth-century members of the School of Modern History, and made their minds.[5]

But Frederick York Powell, Arthur Hassall, Keith Feiling and J. C. Masterman, the subjects of chapters 5, 6, 7 and 8, preferred, when they were undergraduates, to study modern history in the new school rather than classical antiquity. Stephen McKenna, who matriculated at Christ Church in 1906, wrote fifteen years later:

> Modern History, in scope and variety, in the volume of reading, in the mental discipline and the practical benefit of knowledge and perspective, excels even the final school of *Literae Humaniores* which has been for so long the peculiar glory of Oxford. Touching the ancient world at one end and modern politics at the other, interlaced with geography, economics, political science, law and modern languages, it does indeed exclude natural science and Asiatic languages, but it excludes little else.[6]

In 1876, soon after the inauguration of the School of Modern History, the Oxford don F. H. Bradley wrote a cardinal text on *The Presuppositions of Critical History*. Bradley argued that every scholarly historical inference is drawn from the historian's own circumstances, presuppositions and sense of the present state of the world. 'To be critical,' he wrote, 'we must stand on our own experience.' All past events are interpreted by historians from their present standpoint, and with their own inflexions. The condition and context of the lives of scholars, if they are not mere mechanical investigators or shy pettifoggers, enriches their research and findings. Historians with any depth or originality in their work allow their own ego history to shape their selection and analysis of evidence. It is by self-awareness that they learn to teach the process and management of change.[7]

The essayist Mary Coleridge listed, in 1893, the absolute necessities for an historian as well-informed imagination, a dash of prejudice and the power of writing one's own biography at the same time. Twenty years later another essayist, Charles Whibley, decried impartiality as a barren aim. 'History is an interpretation of the past as seen through another's temperament,' he argued. Historians who repress their imagination and individuality change themselves 'from a thinking sentient being to a lifeless register of lifeless facts'. Factual neutrality is unattainable, Whibley continued, given the personal subjectivity in the selection, arrangement and ordering of historic evidence, 'which even a man of stone cannot avoid'. The Oxford historian Llewellyn Woodward was of like mind in the 1920s: 'Historical truth is born of skill in selection.' Above all it is 'a public confession of the historian, made after long self-examination, and projected into narrative form. The historian is never passive; he shapes his history out of the riches or poverty of his own mind.' This viewpoint was powerfully sustained by the Oxford philosopher-historian R. G. Collingwood. 'History is . . . the self-knowledge of the living mind,' he said in 1936. 'For history is not contained in books or documents; it lives only, as a present interest and pursuit, in the mind of the historian when he criticizes and interprets those documents, and by doing so relives for himself the states of mind into which he inquires.' 'All history is contemporary history: not in the ordinary sense of the word, where contemporary history means the history of the comparatively recent past, but in the strict sense: the consciousness of one's own activity as one actually performs it.'[8]

The views of these Oxford college men, Bradley, Woodward and Collingwood, resemble those of Marc Bloch, the French patriot and co-founder of the *Annales* School. Historians, Bloch wrote, engage in three battles: against concealment, against common sense and against current opinion. They are foes of diplomatic secrets, business secrets, family secrets. The suppression of truth, like the misdirection of knowledge, provokes them. Their vocation is to collect, exchange and explain information. They break confidentiality, uncover secrets, spot covert actions, identify furtive desires, recognize common sense as the bludgeon wielded by bullies, and reject the 'nonsensical hocus-pocus' of newspaper stories. Bloch liked to recall a visit to Stockholm with Henri Pirenne, the Belgian medievalist. Pirenne wanted to start their sightseeing tour with a visit to the newly built city hall. 'If I were an antiquarian,' he explained, 'I would have eyes only for the old stuff, but I am a historian. I love life.' The scholar who lacks any inclination to observe the people around him, or to chart the workings of perpetual change on their present mental and physical environment, may make a useful anti-quarian; but, said Bloch, 'he would be wise to renounce all claims to [the title] of a historian'.[9]

Pirenne's Stockholm remark delighted the Australian-born Oxford scholar Keith Hancock, and helped him to form his historical priorities. 'Getting closer to people, getting inside situations, is the historian's initial task. *Attachment*, not detachment, is the virtue he must seek first,' Hancock decided. (Hugh Trevor-Roper endorsed this view: detachment, he wrote in 1959, is a 'dreary virtue' in an historian: 'a touch of sympathy, antipathy, or even life would not come amiss'.) Hancock regarded history, when written in a neutral spirit, and drawn from documents alone, as:

> dead stuff, and probably more false than true. The search for records, the criticism of them, the selection of those that have a bearing on a defined problem, the definition and redefinition of that problem, its elucidation in narrative form – all these things belong to the rigorous discipline of history; but this discipline is by itself uncreative. The historian needs also a lust for life.

If historians are too mindful of the limits of their pupils and readers, Hancock warned, they may seek in the past only those ideas and practices that are readily comprehensible to their contemporaries. A worse peril, he continued, is that they may scold the past for not conforming to present standards of value.[10]

The task of historians, according to the Dutch scholar Pieter Geyl, is to draw avowedly personal inferences from the evidence of the past. Each work of history has a component, Geyl argued, 'which gets mixed up with historical truth in an almost untraceable manner, which does not necessarily turn it into falsehood, but which nevertheless transforms it into something different from the simple truth – I mean the opinion, or the sentiment, or the philosophy of life, of the narrator; or in other words the personality of the historian.' It was in accordance with such views that E. H. Carr, the historian of Soviet Russia, enjoined his readers to study the historian before they begin to study the facts. It is erroneous to suppose 'that history is something that exists outside the mind of the historian and independently of it', this janissary of Collingwood declared in a BBC talk of 1951. 'The pattern in history is what is put there by the historian,' Carr said. 'Without pattern there can be no history. Pattern can only be the product of mind – the mind of the historian working on events of the past.' In this spirit, my book scrutinizes the minds of a select and self-regulated group of men who taught modern history at Christ Church. It is a study of the patterns of the past that were made by their masculine imagination and temperament, by their training in all-male communities and by intentions that were manly either by instinct or by conditioning.[11]

Until late in the twentieth century, there seemed no strangeness in men living, thinking and working in an exclusively masculine institution. In every period, and in all contexts, most women and men preferred their own sex for social rather than carnal interaction. There was better understanding, generally, between people of the same gender, readier trust between them and a glad sense of kinship. The experiences, memories, ideas, plans, pleasures and talk of the opposite sex were opaquer and held less interest. 'Friendship's the sweetest joy of human life,' a woman wrote in 1755 of female amity: "Tis that I wish – and not to be a wife.' Of course, companionate same-sex friendships can be easily spoilt. Men and women are equal in their capacity for envy, competitiveness, aggression, mistaken fancies, storms of temper, bad impulses.[12]

Oxford colleges were endowed by women, and scholarships too, from the thirteenth century onwards; but there were no women students in the University of Oxford until the foundation of Somerville College and of Lady Margaret Hall in 1879. Thereafter, for almost a century, women undergraduates lived in enclosed communities in which they found safety, affinities, trust and meaning at the cost of being excluded, marginalized, demeaned in other university institutions. Kenneth Diplock, a scholar of University College in the 1920s who later became a law lord, had no sense of being offensive when he published a manifesto on the future of Oxford in 1929: 'In ninety-nine cases out of a hundred, from the point of view of social or intellectual life, the woman student is no more a part of Oxford than the Morris car-workers.' Not until 1974 were the first women undergraduates admitted to any of the men's colleges in Oxford. Christ Church elected its first woman as a research lecturer in 1978, and its first woman as a Student a year later. The first woman postgraduate was admitted in 1979, and the earliest women undergraduates in 1980.[13]

Groups of men, generation after generation in all-male colleges, remade their own minds and affirmed other people's thinking by talk, and by listening to talk. Talk was the device by which male friends exchanged and adapted opinions, upheld customs, served material purposes, provided the tactical ambition for public careers, incited intellectual curiosity, provided emotional fulfilment and engaged with contradictions. It was the medium of their rivalry, resentment and malice too. Companionate talk between men, and hostile or insincere talk too, is the basis of this book. It is implicit in every section.

In the opening chapters, for example, Camden journeys to Paris to discuss sixteenth-century Anglo-Scottish relations with Jacques-Auguste de Thou. Edward Hyde, Earl of Clarendon attends the Great Tew circle, where shrewd, animated talk is the order of the day. The Students of Christ Church assemble a volume of poetry commemorating Lord Bayning because the dead man's talk had been so lissom, inventive and enjoyable. The Beam Hall congregation, worshipping in Oxford during the 1650s, spend time together, when not at prayer, discussing the state of the university and of the realm under the Protectorate. The decisions taken and the plans laid by the Beam Hall congregants prove crucial to the invigoration and empowerment of Christ Church after the Restoration in 1660. John Fell, whom the monarch appointed Dean, makes a priority of instilling the habit of purposeful talk in young college men. To take phrases from the twentieth-century Christ Church philosopher Gilbert Ryle, 'edified and edifying talk', 'sentences properly delivered and properly received', 'didactic telling, intelligently given and intelligently received', became a fundamental part of successful Christ Church education.[14]

The ordinary speech that people learn in their families, the literalness, the shibboleths, the categories imposed by parents and siblings, the timid instrumentalism that is presented as practicality, are seldom edified and edifying, or intelligently given and intelligently received. The commonsensical talk of domestic households is, as Stuart Hampshire wrote in 1969, 'a mechanism of defence, as often an instrument for disguising one's perceptions, and for simplifying thoughts and for taming the natural movements of self-assertion within the mind'. Collegiate universities are, at their best, refuges where people go to escape from the mental constrictions, emotional hindrances and narrow heritage of their homes. In good colleges they hear, and may learn to say, properly delivered didactic sentences spoken by argumentative people of all ages. Such talk, when uttered by self-aware and purposive people in full control of their words, denies the significance of commonplace thoughts, says Hampshire, wreaks revenge upon the complacent good sense of practical people, confronts the socially approved use of words, unsettles and wilfully disrupts and may indulge in aggressive eccentricity.[15]

In the mid-eighteenth century Dean Gregory emulated Fell in cultivating young Christ Church men with edified and edifying talk. Lord Shelburne, who became the third of the thirteen prime ministers to have attended the House, remembered that Gregory 'conversed familiarly and frequently with me . . . and gave me notions of people and things, which were afterwards useful'. His successors as Dean, especially Cyril Jackson, encouraged their pupils in both studied and spontaneous talk. In the late nineteenth century conclaves such as the Canning Club and the Stubbs Society worked on the same principle of engendering political and historical ideas by free and determined talk. 'Post-prandial fellowship in English history has not seldom been the parent of intellectual discovery,' said the political theorist Harold Laski, who gained first-class honours in modern history at New College in 1914.[16]

Talk reached its acme in the twentieth century. Ronald Knox, J. C. Masterman, J. I. M. Stewart and other Oxford dons wrote novels, with such titles as *Let Dons Delight*, *The Guardians* and *To Teach the Senators Wisdom*, comprising the spirited dialogue between college fellows. Knox, Masterman and Stewart mastered the college idioms, and drew their knowledge of other people's motives and actions, from watching, hearing, interpreting and remembering their own time at Balliol and Trinity, Christ Church and Worcester. Trevor-Roper's wartime journals record the teases, grumbles and playful speculations that he enjoyed with colleagues from the House, including Ayer, Hampshire, Ryle, Stuart. The obituaries of Christ Church men often praise their talk. E. R. Dodds 'showed much wit' in his conversation, 'and ranged over many topics', Hugh Lloyd-Jones recalled: 'he never lost his sympathy with rebellion, and unlike most people understood that different generations need to rebel against different things'.[17]

Feiling had a prudish inhibition about befriending or talking at large with undergraduates; but York Powell, Hassall, Masterman, Harrod, Blake and intermittently Trevor-Roper relished provocative, animated talk with their pupils. The talk between young men mattered immensely, too. W. H. Auden, who was an undergraduate at the House in the 1920s, recalled (in a poem of 1966) the brisk, bold, challenging arguments swapped by Christ Church undergraduates: dogmas and abstractions pitched back and forth in earnest, and yet with a subversive sense of play. It was a similar case with Auden's Christ Church contemporaries Patrick Gordon Walker and John Hampden Jackson. The pair talked, disputed, developed Marxist interpretations, explained historic losses and laid plans to remedy the defects of the present: the historiographical consequences for Gordon Walker as an historian are shown in chapter 10.[18]

Informal, unstructured masculine talk was a power through the centuries. Kenneth Diplock gave the sum of it in 1929: 'To the undergraduate a lecture is, at best, potted knowledge for the examination schools; at worst, it is just a waste of time.' The most intimate and enriching sources of information for undergraduates are found in college rooms:

> in social gatherings that, centring round a cask of beer or cocktail-shaker, last far into the night with small talk and just talk. You will hear much gossip there, for intellectual Oxford is as close a corporation as the élite of any suburb. You will hear cynicism there too; but . . . most of all you will hear conversation (often sparkling) on a variety of topics as wide as the world; prose, poetry, painting, sculpture, philosophy, economics, education, love and life itself, dealt with, perhaps flippantly, perhaps seriously, perhaps superficially, perhaps deeply, but dealt with in a spirit of interest and of genuine criticism.

There is a keener spirit of enquiry in a drinking session of bright Oxford undergraduates slouched in a college room, concluded

Diplock, than in a score of lectures on the core subjects of sylla-buses.[19]

One should rejoice at the liberty of mind, efforts and achievements of the eight twentieth-century middle-class, Christian-educated men in part two of this book. York Powell, Hassall, Feiling, Masterman, Harrod, Gordon Walker, Trevor-Roper and Blake comprise an unruly radical, a staunch legitimist of the Protestant settlement, a Tory, a Whig, a Keynesian, a socialist, a rationalist who enjoyed mischief, and a student of realpolitik. Although they differed in their political loyalties, social doctrines, historical methods and personal alle-giances, they agreed in their first principles. They regarded pure knowledge with piety. They stood for truth. Hassall made rote learning into his life's work, but for the others nothing was manda-tory in their lessons. They enjoined factual precision, a keen critical spirit, well-drawn inferences and a pleasure in seeing continuities and counterpoints. Raw, clamant new doctrines, mystification, freakish originality, windy mysticism did not impress them. With the exception of Feiling, who had a propensity for woolly words and allusive periphrasis, they strove for clarity, directness, neatly marshalled arguments and conclusiveness. Their tenor in college life was learned and liberating.

The study of history was understood to provide lessons in state-craft. Extensions of the parliamentary franchise in 1832 and 1867, and again in 1884–5, 1918 and 1928, resulted in recalculated and intensified efforts by Oxford dons to show pupils the requisite tech-niques of stable government in epochs of enlarged and potentially unstable suffrage. These efforts included the instillation of personal and political responsibility in students, along with the lesson that public actions have consequences that should be anticipated. My octet explored with their Christ Church pupils the wielding of power, the making of choices and the exercise of civil and political respon-sibility. They resembled neither the lazy, supine men whom Edward Gibbon found slanging their pupils in eighteenth-century Oxford nor the early Victorians of 'petty, pottering habits' whom Matthew Arnold met as impediments to knowledge and truth. Instead, in a phrase of J. I. M. Stewart, who was elected as a Student of Christ Church in 1949, they were intelligent, strenuous and 'sufficiently aware of the perplexity and treachery and uncontrollability of things in general. Their study, indeed, was the crimes, follies, misfortunes, incapacity, muddle, disloyalty, animosities and incorrigibility of humankind in every generation.[20]

CHAPTER 2

A College for State Men

Richard Pace was a spy employed in England and Italy by Cardinal Wolsey. In 1515 he found himself talking to a member of the English gentry. 'By the body of God,' exclaimed his interlocutor, who had doubtless heard that Pace had been educated in the universities of Oxford and Padua, 'I would sooner see my son hanged than a bookworm. It is a gentleman's calling to be able to blow the horn, to hunt, and to hawk. He should leave learning to clodhoppers.' The case of Erasmus, the hunting squire added, showed that nothing came of learning except poverty. The squire's fright at what he could not understand and his determination to bluster his fears into insignificance were obvious to Pace. His reply, according to the historian William Camden, was tart. 'Then you and other Noble men must be content that your children may wind their horns and keep their Hawks, while the children of mean men do manage matters of estate.'[1]

Despite the squire's prejudices, royal households had for centuries welcomed noblemen who were literate and cultivated. Medieval literature presented articulacy, charm, comeliness and percipience as worthy masculine attributes alongside military prowess. The fifteenth-century warrior monarch Henry V played the harp, recorder and flute and composed hymns for the Christian mass. Young gentlemen in Plantagenet England were esteemed if they could make music, sing, dance, show their eloquence in official and less formal settings and speak foreign languages. These graces fitted them for secular leadership long before the influence of Italian humanism reached England in the fifteenth century.

After Richard III was killed in battle in 1485, his successors Henry VII and Henry VIII were set on obliterating the remnant attitudes of the recent ruinous civil wars. They wanted to limit the power of baronial toughs and their pugnacious retinues. Instead, they sought sharp, ambitious, articulate, discreet and judicious officials, who could manage contending interests and unravel constricting knots. Although Tudor monarchs trusted their military commanders to learn their skills on campaign, they wanted civilian servants who had already been taught to be winning with their words, adaptable and realistic in their ideas, and tireless. There developed a 'virtue politics' which promoted reflective subtlety and studied civility as techniques in tempering adversaries and stabilizing government. Virtue politics was concerned with statecraft: the inculcation of ethical ideals in college men, and the enrichment of pupils by the beauties of book learning were nugatory considerations. It produced a new caste of 'State Men', as Henry Percy, ninth Earl of Northumberland, later termed them: 'Their ends are employments, by employments to rise, either as negotiators – to term them mannerly – or as Secretaries, or Clerks of Council, or as Ambassadors, or as Councillors, or as Secretaries of State, or to other offices of greatness.'[2]

The new mood of virtue politics prompted Pace's employer, Thomas Wolsey, the Ipswich butcher's son who became Cardinal Archbishop of York and Lord Chancellor of England, to begin to build the Cardinal's College in Oxford. There were twelve Oxford colleges when in 1524 he purposed a thirteenth. It was to be a humanist foundation, akin to Magdalen (where he had once been a Fellow), in which the teaching of Latin, Greek and philosophy would supplement the traditional study of theology and scripture. Twenty-two priories and convents were suppressed, under papal and royal authority, so that their revenues amounting to £2,000 could be diverted to maintain six professors, four lectors, sixty Senior Canons and forty Petty Canons in the new institution. (Canons are clergymen who live alongside other clergymen, often within the precincts of a cathedral.) The size of the endowment and the scale of the buildings were unmatched in Oxford history. Construction was sufficiently advanced in 1528 for Thomas Cromwell to comment that 'the like was never seen for largeness, beauty, sumptuous, curious, and substantial building'.[3]

In 1529 Wolsey lost Henry VIII's favour, and was denuded of

his wealth and power. The monarch's intention to suppress and dismember his college hit him hard: he appealed – as he said, weeping prostrate at the royal feet – for mercy to be shown to Cardinal's College. Months later, in 1530, he died during a journey to the Tower of London. Subsequently, Henry VIII established a drowsy replacement of Cardinal's College, which was named after him as founder. It had a substantial rental income of £666 in 1535. A few years later, in 1541–2, Henry created afresh five provincial bishoprics to invigorate the ecclesiastical structure of his realm. Next, finding that the new diocese of Oxford was poor in income-yielding property, he denoted the church of St Frideswide, which lay within the site of King Henry VIII College, as its cathedral. The college's property and revenues were vested in the cathedral's Dean and chapter, who formed the governing body of the new corporation. Cathedral and college were merged into a hybrid institution which was called the House of Christ, *Aedis Christi*, Christ Church. Appointment to the deanery or to the canonries was by Crown mandate rather than by election or co-option. The duality of the decanal role as head of a cathedral chapter and of a college was unique.

If Wolsey had completed the foundation of Cardinal's College, it would have exceeded New College and Magdalen as the grandest of the late medieval foundations. When it took shape as Christ Church, under Henry VIII's auspices, it became the chief of post-Reformation colleges. Hitherto all Oxford college founders had been churchmen: after the Reformation none were. Despite using Wolsey's cluttered coat of arms as their own, the Students of the college, in the early modern period, tended to emphasize the King and not the Cardinal as their founder: William Strode, a stout Protestant who was appointed Canon there in 1638, wrote of 'Our Christ-Church Pile, / Great Henrie's monument', without a nod at the Catholic primate.[4]

The college was more closely identified with the Crown than its counterparts in the university. Successive monarchs, as the college's hereditary Visitors, held ultimate authority to decide disputes in all aspects of college business. The sumptuous arrangements during Queen Elizabeth's visit in 1592 were a mark of its grandeur. This 'royal and ample foundation', always 'so learned and noble', became, so Robert Burton claimed in the 1620s, 'the most flourishing college in Europe'.[5]

Young men, some from poor origins, had long attended universities as a prelude to taking holy orders and reaching influence or renown in the Church. Ambitious commoner families in Tudor England began to recognize that the universities, with their new lectureships in Latin, Greek, rhetoric and moral philosophy, could fit their sons for positions of authority, influence and enrichment in national governance, even if the young men did not take a degree at the finish. The inculcation of good character, which meant prudence, discretion, responsibility, equity and steadiness in forming decisions, became a primary aim of university education in the sixteenth century, and remained so until the 1960s. In time the gentry and nobility followed commoner families in expecting that a college training would qualify young men to exercise regional or national leadership. By 1573 Sir Humphrey Gilbert, an Oxford-educated member of the Devon gentry, thought 'the best sort are most like to excel in virtue, which in times past knew nothing but to hallow a hound or lure a hawk'. By the 1630s it was axiomatic that 'Learning', as Henry Peacham wrote in his treatise on gentlemanliness, 'is an essential part of Nobility', and that honour 'dependeth on the culture of the mind'. The two English universities professed to provide a culture of virtue which fitted young men for public responsibilities: there was scant interest in producing investigative scholars.[6]

There were two convergent sources for Anglicized humanism. One sprang from Aristotle's theory of citizenship, the other from the Roman orator Cicero, whose name in this period was often 'Englished' as Tully. A commoner of Christ Church, describing his daily schedule of work in 1552, said that he began with an hour's reading of Aristotle's *Politics*. Then, for an hour at midday, 'I read Cicero's *Offices*, a truly golden book, from which I derive a twofold enjoyment, both from the purity of the language and the knowledge of philosophy. From one to three, I exercise my pen, chiefly in writing letters, wherein, as far as possible, I imitate Cicero.' Cicero's *De officiis* was reprinted seven times between 1558 and 1600: the Tudor statesman William Cecil, Lord Burghley, with whom no one vied in length of public service until William Gladstone in the nineteenth century, 'to his dying day, would always carry it about him, either in his bosom or pocket'. As to Cicero's *Epistulae ad Familiares*, with their accounts of factional struggles in the Roman republic, Burghley 'made these letters, his glass, his rule, his Oracle, and ordinary pocket-book'. When Sir Humphrey Gilbert's ship *Squirrel* foundered off the coast of Newfoundland in 1583, he was last seen in the prow trying to look calm by reading Cicero. Generations later, John Locke, who entered Christ Church in 1652, advised that 'a young Lad' need not read any discourse on morality 'till he can read *Tully's Offices* not as a schoolboy to learn *Latin*, but as one that would be informed in the Principles and Precepts of Virtue for the Conduct of his Life'.[7]

'Every Jake would be a gentleman,' the Ciceronian humanist and royal servant Thomas Starkey noted in his treatise on the new educational thinking, which was written in 1529–33. As a broader range of people aspired to public influence and social standing in Tudor England, the study of classical literature at the two universities lifted men of obscure origins to the level of gentlemen. Traditionally a 'gentleman' had been defined as someone whose paternal and maternal family had both borne a coat of arms for three generations. Tudor heralds slackened the old rules not only for the benefit of men who had been enriched by the distribution of confiscated Church property: they also busied themselves accommodating the aspirations of the expanding numbers of university men. The historian and chorographer William Harrison, who took his bachelor's degree at Christ Church in 1560, described the amenability of the College of Arms in 1577: 'Whosoever studies the laws of the realm, whoso abides in the university giving his mind to his book, or professes physic and the liberal sciences . . . and will bear the port, charge, and countenance of a gentleman, he shall for money have a coat of arms bestowed upon him by heralds (who . . . pretend antiquity and service and many gay things).'[8]

In Stuart England, too, university men like to assert their gentility. They continued to pay heralds to grant them coats of arms and, in Robert Burton's words, 'by all means screw themselves into ancient families, falsifying pedigrees, usurping escutcheons'. Although Burton scoffed at college fellows who tried to enhance their status with heraldic 'eagles, lions, serpents, bears, tygers, dogs, crosses, bends, fesses, &c., and such like baubles, which they commonly set up in their galleries, porches, windows, on bowls, platters, coaches, in tombs, churches, men's sleeves', when he published *The Anatomy of Melancholy* under the pseudonym of 'Democritus Junior', he rewarded those who had studied heraldry by displaying his coat of arms on the frontispiece of the third edition of 1628 as an identifier: *azure on a fesse between three talbots' heads or a crescent gules*.[9]

The nobility and gentry of Tudor England were often discouraged from sending their heirs to university. Thomas Starkey certainly urged that the colleges should be reserved for youngsters intended for holy orders. Noblemen should be compelled to enrol their sons in specialist academies where they would be instructed 'not only in virtue and learning but also in all feats of war'. The abbeys of St Albans and Westminster, he added, might be annexed for this use. If young noblemen were put together in an abbey academy, there to be instructed 'not only in virtue & learning' but also in military leadership and the arts of civil government, it would be 'the most noble institution that ever was yet devised'. The abbeys which had been built as privileged places in which monks grew together into higher virtues could be converted into academies from which would spring, wrote Starkey, 'the fountain of all civility and politic rule'. In the reconstituted abbeys young noblemen would be taught their responsibilities and duties, garbed in authority, and given the skills to administer the realm. Starkey expected these pupils to develop a kinship of beliefs, intentions and methods, together with mutually cooperative habits, if they lived communally. Their loyalties and sense of duty would be enlarged if they could be reared outside their fathers' proud and insular households.[10]

The first Elizabethan parliament, which met in 1559, received a legislative proposal which had probably been drafted by the humanist lawyer Nicholas Bacon, whom Queen Elizabeth had recently appointed to preside over the House of Lords as de facto Lord Chancellor. Bacon, as a yeoman's son, was a Jake rather than a gentleman, who knew both the covetousness of his kind and the threat that nobler families faced from parvenu ambitions. His memorandum of 1559 appealed to the old social order to take measures to invigorate itself and to keep the new men boxed. 'The wanton bringing up and ignorance of the nobility forces the Prince to advance new men that can serve, which for the most part neither affecting true honour, because the glory thereof descended not to them, nor yet the common wealth (though coveting to be hastily in wealth and honour), forget their duty and old estate and subvert the noble houses to have their rooms themselves.' Bacon's proposals were threefold. First, the passing of an ordinance that bound the nobility to educate their sons at university from the age of twelve to eighteen. Secondly, 'that none study the laws, temporal or civil, except he be immediately descended from a nobleman or gentleman, for they are the entries to rule and government'. He had long envisaged the creation of a fifth Inn of Court to train the scions of hereditary landowning families in the protection and enlargement of their properties. Thirdly, Bacon proposed that one-third of all free scholarships at the universities be allotted to the sons of poorer gentlemen.[11]

Other humanists thought similarly to Starkey and Bacon. In 1573 Sir Humphrey Gilbert proposed the formation of a discrete school for the wards of the Crown and for other sons of the nobility and gentry. Recalling his own experiences in Oxford before his admission to an Inn of Court, Gilbert condemned university teaching as too abstruse for young nobles and gentry who must 'study matters of action meet for present practize both of peace and war'. He proposed the name of Queen Elizabeth Academy for his training school, but twenty years later the monarch preferred to spend her money on the foundation of Trinity College, Dublin.[12]

Starkey's abbey institute of virtue politics, Bacon's fifth Inn of Court, Gilbert's Queen Elizabeth Academy remained as paper schemes to train young men in the arts and craft of government. Tudor England nevertheless underwent what Sir John Neale called, in 1949, a 'cultural revolution' in parliamentary life. Only three or four members of Henry VIII's Reformation parliament of 1529–36 are known to have attended university at Oxford or Cambridge. In the parliament of 1563 some 67 MPs (out of a total of 420) had studied in one of the universities, and 108 in an Inn of Court: there was an overlap of 36 between these groups. By 1584, when the Commons had 460 members, a total of 219 had higher education (145 had attended university, and 164 the Inns of Court, with an overlap of 90). In the 1593 parliament, 161 members had been to the university, 197 to the Inns of Court: after subtracting the overlap, this means that 252 members (well over half) had higher education. Similarly, the majority of the 825 men who sat in the House of Commons between 1604 and 1629 had attended either Oxford or Cambridge. In consequence, Neale argued, the membership of the House of Commons came to surpass the average ability of the nation.[13]

It is supposed that parliamentary oratory first shone in the reign of Elizabeth, when MPs began to keep records of the choice eloquence that they heard. Yet Burghley's nephew Francis Bacon, who had attended Cambridge and Gray's Inn before studying state-craft and civil law in French and Italian universities, found that the verbal facility of full-going university men ill-fitted them for nego-tiations as State Men. Their training made them 'too curious and irresolute by variety of reading, or too peremptory or positive by strictness of rules and axioms, or too immoderate and overweening by reason of the greatness of the examples'. Bacon's contemporary Thomas Nashe felt that he was living in a 'gowned age', which confused verbiage with eloquence and obscurity with erudition. Every would-be orator, he wrote in an address of 1589 *To the Gentlemen Students of both Universities*, 'abhors the English he was born to'. The new articulacy enlarged vocabulary without improving intelligence. As a result, 'brainless . . . Idlebies' produce 'a confused mass of words without matter, a Chaos of sentences without any profitable sense, resembling drums, which being empty within, sound big without'. In the next generation Robert Burton wrote a Latin comedy, *Philosophaster*, which was performed in Christ Church by its gentleman-commoners, scholars and Students in 1617. *Philosophaster* is a spry satire on 'pseudo-Academicks', those pretentious impostors to scholarship who use polysyllables, periph-rasis and jargon to deceive gullible men into thinking them erudite and wise.[14]

By the close of the Tudor century, it was the acknowledged duty of the two English universities to support monarchical authority in Church affairs and state business. In 1603, the year of King James VI of Scotland's accession to the English throne, Thomas Sackville, Lord Buckhurst, who had been Chancellor of the University of

Oxford since 1591 and had succeeded Burghley as Lord High Treasurer in 1599, reminded an assembly of senior members of the university that they represented a national institution which was always watched by the eyes of the nation. King James (as the first-ever ruler of Scotland, Ireland and England) required the English universities to take a lead in promoting the unity of ideas, intentions and action that he was set on establishing within the British archipelago. It was an acknowledgement of their enhanced importance in his realm that he granted them the right to elect their own representatives in the House of Commons in 1604.[15]

Historically, the universities had trusted the priors and abbots of adjacent religious houses to protect their interests from the jealous and aggressive townsmen of the boroughs of Oxford and Cambridge. But the Henrician dissolution of the monasteries and the flagging authority of bishops during the reign of Elizabeth had led Cambridge in 1566 and Oxford in 1570 to petition for parliamentary enfranchisement so that their university privileges might be defended in the House of Commons. Every shire had its knights in parliament, it was argued, and every incorporated town had its burgesses, but universities had no parliamentary representatives to protect them from encroachment. This view was upheld by the Jacobean Attorney-General, Sir Edward Coke, who had attended Trinity College, Cambridge, likened his university to 'worthy Athens' and extolled it as 'the very eyes and ears of the kingdom'. In 1604 James issued letters patent which authorized the election of two burgesses by the senior members of each university. The universities understood that, although sittings of parliament might be of brief duration, those of the courts – the Royal Court and the law courts – were constant. They chose members of those two omnipresent institutions, the Royal Household and the judiciary, as their burgesses.[16]

From the outset Christ Church was a recognized Jacobean academy for future State Men. Francis Stewart had become a ward of his cousin King James after the murder of his father, the Earl of Moray. In 1604, when the boy was fifteen, the King sent him, with £200 a year, to study in Christ Church. Stewart was (almost certainly) the first Scotsman to matriculate in the University of Oxford. His education there brought him into conformity with the Church of

England, which enabled his naturalization as an Englishman by act of parliament. He was knighted in 1610, soon after he reached his majority, and was appointed to posts in the Royal Household. The favour of the reigning monarch, his Anglicanism and naturalization resulted in his election as MP for Oxford University in 1626. In parliament, even when later he was representing a Cornish constituency, Stewart spoke in defence of his university's interests and precedence.

Stewart, who became a vice-admiral in the navy and a privateer, sat on parliamentary committees inquiring into such subjects as ordnance procurement and the postal system. Evidently, he was a capable negotiator and manager of business. He had none of the slothful tendencies that Christ Church men often remarked in one another. 'Amongst us,' lamented Robert Burton, 'the badge of gentry is idleness: to be of no calling, not to labour (for that's derogatory to their birth), to be a mere spectator, a drone.' Some of these nonentities were sufficiently self-conscious to make a bogus show of being reading men. John Earle, the future Bishop of Salisbury, who matriculated at Christ Church in 1619, soon afterwards penned a character sketch of a 'scholar-mountebank' who is 'tricked out in all the accoutrements of learning' but remains in complacent ignorance. 'His table is spread wide with some classic folio, which . . . hath laid open in the same page this half year.' During ostentatious solitary walks in Christ Church meadow he assumes a meditative pose and holds a book in front of his face. Besides the mountebank-scholar Earle also depicted a type of gentleman-commoner in the 1620s. This youth prefers outdoor exercise, but in foul weather retires to his college rooms, and toys with pretty books decorated with neat silk strings as markers. In other idle moments he loiters in the Bodleian Library, 'where he studies arms and books of honour, and turns a gentleman critic in pedigrees'.[17]

The Great Rebellion marked a new phase in the history of Christ Church. In August 1642 King Charles I directed Thomas Howard, Earl of Berkshire to ensure public safety by securing the university. At this prompting, the college men, bearing such weapons as they had, marched through the streets and drilled in Christ Church quadrangle. At Magdalen bridge a bulwark was erected, and at

Wadham a trench was dug. A month later Samuel Fell, the Dean of
Christ Church, and his family left Oxford ahead of the arrival of
parliamentarian troops commanded by William Fiennes, Viscount
Saye and Sele. Saye's men descended on colleges and churches, burnt
'popish' books and pictures and plundered college plate. At Christ
Church they spent a day trying to force their way into the Treasury
strongroom only to find it empty of all but a single groat. 'Enraged
with that disappointment,' reported the Dean's son John Fell, 'they
went to the deanery, where having ransacked what they thought fit,
they put it altogether in a chamber, locked it up, and retired to their
quarters, intending the next morning to return and dispose of their
prize.' Richard Allestree, a Student who later operated as an under-
cover royalist agent and courier, contrived that the plunderers' booty
was hidden away overnight.[18]

In November 1642, King Charles made Oxford the seat of the
Royal Household and the fortified base of their troops. The city
nominally, and the university in practice, replaced London as the
royalist capital. For four years the monarch lived in state in Christ
Church, where he held his Court. The chapter house there was
converted into the royal council chamber. As John Fell recalled,
'Oxford was then an epitome of the whole nation, and all the business of it; there was here the Court, the garrison, the flower of the
nobility and gentry, lawyers and divines of all England.'[19]

After the New Model Army occupied Oxford in 1646, parliamentary Visitors delated most heads of college, extruded most professors
and expelled some 200 college Fellows, including the most able
Students of Christ Church. All of the rejected men were required
to leave Oxford within three days, 'upon pain of being taken for
spies of war', as John Fell reported. 'Within the compass of a few
weeks an almost general riddance was made of the loyal University
of Oxford; in whose room succeeded an illiterate rabble, swept up
from the plough-tail, from shops and grammar schools, and the
dregs.'[20]

During the interregnum, an intrepid Cavalier Anglican congregation of ejected dons and undergraduate royalists defied the
authorities by meeting for worship at the lodgings of Thomas Willis
in Beam Hall in Merton Street. Willis was a Christ Church man,
who had married Samuel Fell's daughter. His brother-in-law John

Fell, together with his Christ Church friends Allestree and John Dolben, were dominant figures among the Beam Hall congregants. This group proved vital in the swift rally of the University of Oxford following the Restoration in 1660.

Within months of Charles II regaining his throne, Allestree published a summons for Church of England gentlemen to rally to the preservation of the monarchy and of the Established Church. In *The Gentlemans Calling* he admitted that to try to define a 'gentleman' might be 'deemed not only absurd but malicious, a Levelling project, of robbing him of his Birth-right, of degrading him from those privileges which belong to his quality, and of moulding him again into that vulgar Mass, from which divine Providence and humane Laws have distinguished him'. Nevertheless, Allestree persisted in warning that it was no longer good enough for a young gentleman 'to be only a thing of pleasure, sent into the World, as the Leviathan into the deep, to take his pastime therein, and the better to complete the parallel, to devour his underlings too'. In the conditions of the 1660s, the responsibilities, authority and reputation of the gentry must be invigorated for the good of the national polity. Instead of men who reckoned it as a point of breeding to waste time or to lie idle, there was a need of an educational community that taught its pupils how best to negotiate and persuade. Restoration England needed the coming generation to be prudent yet resolute, to be supple in their means yet constant in their ends.[21]

The new monarch had known Christ Church well when it was a royal residence in the 1640s. Accordingly, in July 1660, within two months of regaining the throne, he installed a Cavalier cleric named George Morley as Dean. Morley, who had been a Westminster scholar at Christ Church, entered Oxford in a procession with eighty Students of Christ Church on horseback: as his cavalcade moved from Magdalen bridge to Tom Quad, it was acclaimed by the ringing of bells and the cheering of townsfolk and university men. At the same time the King installed three Beam Hall congregants, Fell, Allestree and Dolben, as Canons occupying the canonries, or adjacent houses, close to the cathedral in Tom Quad. A few months later, in November 1660, after Morley was made Bishop of Worcester, Fell succeeded him as Dean.[22]

Fell's piety was manifest: he attended four public services a day

in the cathedral, and in addition prayed privately twice a day in the
deanery. He had a sharp memory, sound judgement, efficient habits,
imagination, fortitude, clear elocution, a power of persuasion, and
eloquence. He deprecated displays of erudition or glosses to make
for easier reading: an edition of Pliny, published in Oxford in 1677,
which is attributed to him, gives a plain text, without notes, in order
to encourage readers to study with sharper critical attention. He was
sure of the qualities and abilities that were requisite in a model
Student of the post-Restoration college. 'Modern and learned
languages, rhetoric, philosophy, mathematics, history, antiquity,
moral and polemical divinity, all which was not to be pumped up,
or ransacked out of commonplace books, but was ready at hand,' he
wrote in a preface to an edition of Allestree's sermons. Good talkers
were wanted in the revivified community of Christ Church:
thoughtful, articulate and convincing Students who would have sway
with their pupils. They would create the perfect mental atmosphere
for the college, 'a solid and masculine kindness, a perfect coalition
of affections and minds'.[23]

Fell found the House in a parlous state. 'The College of Christ
Church, which was truly the largest and finest . . . was badly
damaged in the war by the parliamentarians,' reported a visiting
Dutchman in 1662. Under Fell's leadership, college buildings were
restored and extended. As Vice-Chancellor of the university from
1666, he took a lead in building the Sheldonian Theatre for occasions of academic pomp, because he wanted the university church
to be reserved for religious ceremonies only. He made an even
greater innovation, the founding of the university printing press,
which enabled the printing of scholarly publications on a reliable
basis for the first time in England. This required a spanking new
building to hold the printing equipment, expert printers, steady
supplies from paper mills, distributors – all of them harder to obtain
than editors with their scholarly annotations. By the mid-1670s his
press was publishing great texts of New Testament criticism
compiled by students of ancient Greek texts who worked under his
patronage. After his enthronement as Bishop of Oxford in 1676, he
initiated the building of Cuddesdon as an episcopal palace.
Throughout the university and the diocese, Fell was a decisive force.
'It was from his personality, his allegiances, his initiatives, and his

industry that so much of the distinctive character and achievements of Restoration Oxford sprang, as Robert Beddard says. The reputation and authority of the university was raised in the life of the nation, and revived too among the scholars of Europe.[24]

By the Act of Uniformity of 1662, the Cavalier parliament in London decreed that access to the university must be confined to Protestants who conformed to the tenets of the state church – the Church of England. Catholics were already debarred from university membership: henceforth nonconformists, non-Christians and non-believers were also excluded. Members of the university, like the bishops, priests and deacons of the Church of England, were compelled to conform to the doctrine and discipline of a revised prayer book. For the next two hundred years, the exclusive Anglicanism of the University of Oxford was 'cherished as the shield and buckler of Protestant orthodoxy', as Beddard has recounted. 'The loyalist university became, at one and the same time, the eager initiator, dedicated upholder, and grateful beneficiary of a remodelled Protestant establishment.' The university acted in concert with the Church of England as a moderating influence, preferring restraint in religious feelings to enthusiasm or zealotry, and opposed to sudden or disruptive change in the life of the nation.[25]

Clergymen who wished to become chaplain to a great nobleman, or to receive a living from any bishop who was Oxford-educated, sought testimonials from Fell. 'He had a hand in all public elections and endeavoured to promote his own men,' his supplicant Anthony Wood noted. 'He had a fond conceit that none could dispute better than a Ch. Ch. man, none could preach better, speech it or anything else.' Fell protected the dignity of his office and the reputation of his house, but was impervious to personal criticism. 'Was in many things very rude,' said Wood, 'yet still aimed at the public good.'[26]

Under Fell's direction, Christ Church became the chief power among the colleges in electing the burgesses for the university seat. For the Cavalier parliament of 1661–79, the university chose two staunch Cavaliers who belonged to Fell's college, Sir Heneage Finch, the Solicitor-General, and Laurence Hyde. Finch was subsequently Lord Keeper, Lord Chancellor and first Earl of Nottingham: the legal historian Sir William Holdsworth reckoned him one of the greatest lord chancellors, both an intellectual and a statesman; a jurist, as well, of rare impartiality, and the patron-friend of learned and literary men. Hyde, too, rose to a high political altitude as Chief Minister and First Lord of the Treasury under Charles II. When Hyde was rewarded with the earldom of Rochester in 1674, the university elected another Christ Church man, Thomas Thynne, later first Viscount Weymouth. Thynne had been a member of the Beam Hall congregation, and was a friend to John Fell and a cousin by marriage to Finch. (Twenty-nine per cent of MPs elected in 1661 had attended Oxford, and 18 per cent Cambridge. For the four parliaments elected in the ten years from October 1679, the Oxford percentage fluctuated between 31 and 33 per cent, and the Cambridge percentage remained steady at 17 per cent.)[27]

Laurence Hyde's father Lord Clarendon, who was elected Chancellor of the university in 1660, knew the pressing need of State Men. A passage in his *History of the Rebellion and Civil Wars in England* describes the lethal disunity among Charles I's councils when Oxford was the royalist capital in the 1640s. 'It were to be wished', Clarendon says, 'that persons of the greatest birth, honour, and fortune, would take care of themselves by education, industry, literature, and a love of virtue, to surpass all other men in knowledge, and all other qualifications, necessary for great actions . . . that princes, out of them, might always choose men fit for all employments, and high trusts.' Clarendon's experiences in the 1640s taught him that the malice and duplicity of factious men always gives them advantages over composed, scrupulous and responsible counsellors.

> Whosoever observes the ill arts, by which these men . . . prevail upon the people in general; their absurd, ridiculous lying, to win the affections, and corrupt the understandings, of the weak; and the bold scandals, to confirm the wilful; the boundless promises they presented to the ambitious; and their gross, abject flatteries, and applications, to the vulgar-spirited, would hardly give himself leave to use those weapons, for the preservation of the three kingdoms.

Clarendon warned politically ambitious men against 'the womanish art of inveighing against persons, when they should be reforming things'. Future governors must understand, by the time they reach university, that 'it is no ill measure in making friendships, to look into, and compare, the power of doing hurt, or doing good'.[28]

Dean Fell was of like mind. After his experience of the civil wars, he determined to serve Church and state by providing a governing caste of composed, rational and scrupulous men that might keep the three kingdoms of England, Scotland and Ireland in peaceful stability. He resolved to make his college into a community that instilled in its pupils the principles of virtuous, steady and patriotic governance. Christ Church would serve as what Starkey and Gilbert might have called an academy for nobles. Fell's coadjutor Allestree described the ideal of the university-bred gentleman in 1660: 'his Discerning faculty is more nimble and agile, can suddenly surround a Proposition, and discover the infirm and feeble parts; and so is not to be imposed upon by such slight Sophisms as captivate whole herds of the Vulgar'. These qualities must be used to promote the national interest. The deportment of a university-bred gentleman should be 'affable and civil, not insolent and imperious', Allestree instructed. 'His Words will be temperate and decent, the product of judgment, not of rage.'[29]

Some historians have treated the revolution of 1688 as the storm flood that brought a cleansing outrush of civility and politeness into English political and literary culture. But the civilizing mission of Christ Church, advanced by Fell's ethos of civility, good conversation and scholarly exactitude, began a generation earlier, and was driven by his unappeasable fear of national disorder which had been aroused in him by the civil wars of 1642–51. He was determined to make Christ Church into a training academy both for the governing classes and for future Anglican authorities.

Parents and guardians in Restoration England liked Fell's recipe: Christ Church matriculations rose every year while he was Dean. State Men, in particular, wanted their stripling sons to acquire the rudiments of statecraft at university: to ponder tactics, to prepare arguments, to read facial expressions and gestures, and thus to fit themselves for their leading parts in political society. 'Be sure', Sir Heneage Finch senior urged his son Daniel in 1663, 'to be present at all disputations in the Hall . . . and study the question beforehand, for one argument of your own choosing, out of those books which write upon the question, which will be better managed by you than any argument which your tutor can put into your head.' The Finches well knew, as one brother told another in 1666, that it is 'the way of Christ's Church, especially of those of that gang who stile themselves the wits, to carpe at and censure all people who will not follow that high degree of debauchery or rather Atheism they are now att'. Accordingly, in another paternal remonstrance, Sir Heneage charged Daniel 'to reverence and defend' the Church of England. 'You will give me but a sad account of your time in the University if you return either factious or indifferent in the point of religion.' He insisted that his sons should recognize the opportunities given by a Christ Church education and reputation: 'you must look upon the University as the way to greater things'. He would be disappointed by a *fainéant* son who shirked authority and responsibility. 'Nothing can make me happy in this world but a prospect of some virtue and industry in you.' As second Earl of Nottingham, Daniel served as Secretary of State under William III, and as Lord President of the Council under George I.[30]

Fell was a tolerant doctrinaire. He commanded the bastion of Anglican orthodoxy with selective leniency. For John Locke, who as Senior Censor of Christ Church in the 1660s had served as a valuable liaison between the Students of the college and the members of the cathedral chapter, he had high esteem, despite his Whiggery. Locke had been a tutor in the family of the Earl of Shaftesbury, who wished to deprive James, Duke of York of his rights of royal succession and favoured the ambitions of the bastard Duke of Monmouth to succeed his father Charles II on the throne. Locke became suspect as an exclusionist, and in 1684 Christ Church reluctantly acceded to a royal mandate ordering that he must be deprived of his college offices. This was done, but his former colleague made redress by setting his *Essay Concerning Human Understanding* to be read by bright youngsters in the House.[31]

Some Thoughts Concerning Education was first published by Locke nine years after his expulsion from Christ Church. It draws on his experience as a Student there as much as on his time as a tutor in Shaftesbury's household, and provides a contextualizing commentary on the hopes and schemes of the better Christ Church men in the century after the Restoration. A gentleman does not need to be an accomplished logician, literary critic, metaphysician, mathematician or historian, wrote Locke. 'But of good Breeding, Knowledge of the World, Virtue, Industry, and a Love of Reputation, he cannot have too much.' It was grievous that universities encouraged young men to be disputatious, and rewarded them for winning an argument by artful articulacy. Respect for the distinctions between truth and lies, or right and wrong, were lost in competitive debates, Locke warned. Ideas lose their value if they are used as a simple means to browbeat opponents.

> Be sure not to let your Son be bred up in the Art and Formality of disputing, either practising it himself, or admiring it in others; unless instead of an able Man, you desire to have him an insignificant Wrangler . . . priding himself in contradicting others; or, which is worse, questioning every Thing, and thinking there is no such Thing as Truth to be sought, but only Victory, in disputing.[32]

It was essential for a tutor to be worldly, said Locke, and to show his pupil 'the Ways, the Humours, the Follies, the Cheats, the Faults of the Age he is fallen into'. If the pupil has intelligence the tutor should 'teach him Skill in Men, and their Manners; pull off the Mask which their several Callings and Pretences cover them with, and make his Pupil discern what lies at the Bottom under such Appearances'. There should be no haste in leading the youth towards maturity of judgement. 'The scene should be gently open'd, and his Entrance made Step by Step, and the Dangers pointed out that attend him from the several Degrees, Tempers, Designs, and Clubs of Men. He should be . . . warn'd who are like to oppose, who to mislead, who to undermine him, and who to serve him.'[33]

The understanding of men and manners, the skills of persuasion and negotiation, wariness of follies and cheats, prudence in pursuing public courses, the imparting of a steady temperament and the maintenance of the Established Church – these were the chief educational aims of Fell's Christ Church. These priorities continued after his death in 1686, but were pursued with diminished energy by the mid-eighteenth century. Then came the Crown appointment of Cyril Jackson as Dean in 1783. Jackson was a sound classical scholar, a botanist, a mathematician, a connoisseur of architecture and a keen appraiser of his pupils' potentials. The exercise of leadership and the taking of decisions were a pleasure to him. Christ Church, during the quarter-century when he held the deanery, was well described as 'an absolute monarchy of the most ultra-Oriental character'. He stood on a par with Fell.[34]

In nineteenth-century language Jackson was an agile lionizer: in twenty-first-century terms he was a nimble networker. By the standards of any age he was intensely political. Disqualified from a parliamentary career by having taken holy orders, he lived vicariously through the public lives of his former pupils. He became set on improving the minds of those Christ Church noblemen and gentleman-commoners likely to become legislators in parliament or to fulfil other public duties. Several nights each week he had six or eight young men of the House to dine at the deanery. He opened conversations, raised topics, asked questions and guided the direction in which his guests were heading. Always he liked to divine what was behind the eyes, and in the heart, of his favoured young men. His hospitality was part of his process for encouraging future governors of the realm to be prudent, shrewd, temperate and steady. Lord Francis Godolphin Osborne, for example, told his father the fifth Duke of Leeds that he would as soon have a seat in the stocks as in the House of Commons; but after three years under Jackson's aegis he was sitting for the family borough of Helston.

The rank of young noblemen in the House was marked by the gold tassel or tuft worn on their trencher caps and by their embroidered gowns: social climbers were accordingly known as tuft hunters. 'Christ Church is so full of noblemen that one's eyes require green spectacles to preserve them from the glare of the golden tufts among these peers,' reported Charles Kirkpatrick Sharpe, who matriculated there in 1798. Some of the noblemen were hopeless material for Jackson. James Harris, afterwards second Earl of Malmesbury, was suspected by Sharpe of being the Missing Link between humankind and monkeys. 'The poor thing is blind of an eye, has one of his fore teeth amissing, and struts on legs like a child's stilts, yet thinks himself absolutely charming.' He had, moreover, as Sharpe noted, 'that frequent accompaniment of folly, extreme ill-nature; and a peevish way of uttering abuse, with much wickedness and no wit'.

Revisiting Christ Church some years later, he found the pre-eminent noblemen to be Augustus FitzGerald, third Duke of Leinster and George Sackville, fourth Duke of Dorset. 'The Irish Duke is much cried up for his beauty,' but Dorset 'is exactly like a sick canary bird in a hard frost'. None of these men distinguished themselves in Jackson's pattern. Malmesbury reached the summit of his abilities as Governor of the Isle of Wight, and Leinster as the leading Freemason in Ireland, while Dorset died young in an accident.[35]

Jackson, like Fell before him, was determined to organize, empower and inspirit the young Christ Church men whom he identified as likely State Men of the future. He wanted his favourite pupils to win glory performing in the Palace of Westminster. Richard Wellesley, the future Marquis Wellesley, who attended Christ Church in 1778–81, was convinced by the Dean that classical oratory, rhetoric and drama gave the requisite foundation for political success. Wellesley accordingly trained himself in public eloquence by declaiming the orations of Demosthenes and Cicero in his rooms. Buttons bearing the initials of Demosthenes and Cicero, together with those of Fox and Pitt, adorned the brown jackets, with velvet collar and cuffs, of a Christ Church debating society founded by Robert Jenkinson, who matriculated at the House in 1787. Twenty-five years later, as Earl of Liverpool, he became the fifth Christ Church Prime Minister (as well as the first Prime Minister of mixed-race English and Indian ancestry). 'I really cannot crouch to young Jenky, whom I have laughed at ever since I have known him': this was how Wellesley referred to Jenkinson.[36]

'Jenky' and George Canning, who was to succeed him as Prime Minister in 1827, were Christ Church contemporaries: 'quarrelling and making up again all day long', as Jackson remembered. For Canning there was a paradisaical purity about his college days. When he returned to Christ Church, at the ripe age of twenty-four, to take his Master's degree, he felt rueful about his own shop-soiled state. 'There is an ingenuousness, a glow, a heart, as it were, in a young man, that . . . a very few years' rubbing and tumbling about in the world, does away.' After university, 'One gets hard and wise and odious – undeceived – or rather . . . désabusé,' he reflected.[37]

Jackson counselled his political acolytes on the requisites for parliamentary advancement. Smart, aspiring young MPs needed, he told Canning, 'quickness, sprightliness, pointedness of language, sometimes with & sometimes without Ideas, fluency of words, wch to have its true merit in the Political life of these days must be capable of being exerted as freely without any knowledge of a subject, as with it'. A novice MP might shine if he had a talent for ridicule or effrontery; and if he mugged up some subject for a parliamentary speech, 'his Party applaud – they must do so – even the leaders of it, who know in their hearts the nothingness of all this'.[38]

'Now, remember what I say,' Jackson urged another of his prized pupils, Robert Peel, the seventh of Christ Church prime ministers, in the course of offering congratulations on Peel's maiden speech in the House of Commons in 1810.

> Give the last high finish to all that you now possess by the continual reading of Homer. Let no day pass without you having him continually in yr hands. Elevate your own mind by the continual meditation of the vastness of his comprehension and the unerring accuracy of all his conceptions. If you will but read him four or five times over every year, over half-a-dozen years, you will have him by heart. And he . . . alone of all *mere men* thoroughly understood the Human mind.

Homer, Jackson told another former pupil, Lord Granville Leveson-Gower, 'serves me on all occasions of hope, fear, grief, or joy', and was 'the best instructor' in human character, motives and conduct that anyone could read.[39]

All this, of course, was conventional Oxford wisdom. Edward Copleston, who was elected Professor of Poetry in 1802, argued that classical literature gave peerless mental training: 'The habit of discrimination, the power of stating a question distinctly, and of arguing with perspicacity, are of much greater importance than the hasty acquisition of miscellaneous knowledge.' The histories of Thucydides and Xenophon deserve a central place 'in all the great business of education', he wrote in 1810. In them students will read of 'the fatal consequences of misrule and anarchy, of wild democracy, of unlimited or unjust power', but without the agitation, prejudice and perversity with which partisans write of recent events. Thucydides and Xenophon provide 'a crowded but not a confused picture of

human affairs, exhibiting all the passions, both in their secret workings and in their fullest energy – all the difficulties and duties of a
true patriot – all the virtues, the vices, the intrigues, the reciprocal
interests, and the diversified fortunes of free states'. Copleston added,
'From no study can an Englishman acquire a better insight into the
mechanism and temper of civil government: from none can he draw
more instructive lessons, both of the danger of turbulent faction,
and of corrupt oligarchy: from none can he better learn how to play
skilfully upon, and how to keep in order, that finely-toned instrument, a free people.' Moreover, the literature of classical antiquity
would train a nation of heroes by inculcating 'a disdain of death in
a good cause, a passionate devotion to the welfare of one's country,
a love of enterprize, and a love of glory'.[40]

Jackson was installed as Dean of Christ Church in the final year
of the American revolutionary war, and presided over the college
throughout the French revolutionary period. The essence of
American and French ideals was liberty based on equality: but, as
Lord Acton said in his lectures on the French revolution, 'the very
essence of the English system was liberty founded on inequality'.
The French and Americans wanted expeditious government unen-
cumbered by any devices of delay. This was the antithesis of 'the
cumbrous forms, the obstacles to prompt action, the contrivances
to favour a minority, and to make opposition nearly equal to government' that characterized, in Acton's summary, the Westminster
system.[41]

The storming of the Bastille and the savagery of its sequel impelled
English university reform. The ancient institutions at Oxford and
Cambridge acquired sudden national importance as well-entrenched
redoubts against the onslaught of the violent revolutionary multitude.
'Our Universities', a preacher told the Lord Mayor of London and
his court of aldermen in 1800, 'are the main pillars, not only of the
learning, and perhaps the science, but of the virtue and piety, whether
seen or unseen, which yet remain among us, and therefore, woe be
to every frantic visionary, and every ruffian scoundrel, who would
raze them from their old and sacred foundations.'[42]

University admissions, which had fallen since mid-century, rose
again in the 1790s as scions of the nobility, gentry, industrial and
other propertied classes were confided in increasing numbers to the

care of colleges. Families felt that, if their sons were to get ideas, it was safer for the family patrimony and national stability that these should be imbibed in the semi-confinement of a hallowed Oxford or Cambridge college. Their heirs would be kept behind walls and gates, under the surveillance of Fellows who were required to be Anglican clergymen or at least candidates for holy orders. There would be few risks of unsupervised speculation.

John Eveleigh, Provost of Oriel, a conservative churchman rather than a liberal reformer, wanted his college to house men with the brains to out-think and out-argue freethinkers, dissenters and subversives. He therefore resolved to lift the intellectual standing of his college by holding competitive examinations before any elections to fellowships. Eveleigh's lead was followed by John Parsons after his election as Master of Balliol in 1798. Parsons was a Tory disciplinarian bent on upholding the Church of England against radical insubordination and lackadaisical thinking. To this end, he introduced public examinations for junior members of Balliol, and insisted on awarding fellowships by competitive examination results. Corpus, Trinity and other colleges followed the lead of Oriel and Balliol.

Eveleigh and Parsons next promoted a new university statute which permitted undergraduates to compete, if they chose, for honours in the BA examination. The lead in framing the statute, and in winning majority support for it, was taken by Cyril Jackson, acting as the confidential adviser of the Duke of Portland, who was the second Prime Minister to have attended Christ Church and had been elected Chancellor of the University in 1792. Jackson judged that the authorities could not expect, in such a restive and unstable epoch, inquisitive undergraduates to keep on sound lines if they had no better object in view than passing the current system of sham or perfunctory examinations. He and his colleagues at Oriel and Balliol feared that if bright young men were not challenged and made to concentrate on their books, they might in their idleness take fire from incendiary agitators.

The new examination statute, which was approved in 1800, saved the university's reputation. Under its terms, candidates underwent an oral test in the elements of religion, as expressed in the Greek New Testament and the Church of England's Thirty-Nine Articles.

The new school of *Literae Humaniores*, indicating humane rather than sacred or divine literature, began with a course in Greek and Latin literature called Classical Moderations (Mods). The undergraduate's proficiency was judged by an oral examination in at least three Greek or Roman authors chosen by the candidate, and an unseen prose translation from English to Latin. Oral tests might be conducted in either Latin or English, but fluency in Latin was indispensable, and knowledge of Greek was requisite. The third year of the course, called Greats, focused on the writings of classical historians and classical philosophers. Kirkpatrick Sharpe of Christ Church described his anxiety at undergoing the new examinations in 1801: 'Six sour Masters of Arts sit at a long table in the middle of the chamber, and ask questions concerning religion, mathematicks, logic, algebra, languages, and heaven knows what, to which the trembling undergraduate answers from the other side of the table.' Although Sharpe felt sure that he would pass the examinations, 'still the Doctors, the Proctors with their horrid wigs and bands, tormented my imagination, and for the whole time previous to the dreadful day I could neither eat not sleep, nor speak, nor scarcely move'.[43]

From 1809 all candidates who wished to read Greats were required to have passed an examination called Responsions, informally known as Little-go, or Smalls. In Responsions, candidates were tested by *viva voce* (oral questions and answering) on works of Greek and Latin, rudimentary logic and Euclid's *Elements*. Robert Lowe, a Fellow of Magdalen in the 1830s, was examining when a friend asked him how the *vivas* were getting on. 'Excellently,' he replied. 'Five men already plucked, and the sixth very shaky.'[44]

The number of young men presenting themselves for degrees doubled over thirty years. In 1807 a separate School of Mathematics and Physics was created. Jackson's protégé Robert Peel brought acclaim to Christ Church by securing the university's earliest double first in classics and mathematics in 1808. In 1809 degrees were subdivided into first, second and third classes. Written question papers were introduced in 1825, and became the most important element of the examination. *Literae Humaniores* was expanded to include ancient history, political philosophy, rhetoric, poetry and moral philosophy. Edward Stanley, afterwards fourteenth Earl of

Derby and intermittently Prime Minister between 1852 and 1868, read nothing at Christ Church in 1817–20 that had been written after the first century. Herodotus, Thucydides, Horace, Aeschylus, Plato, Aristotle, Tacitus, Virgil and Juvenal, together with one term of mathematics, were his fare. Modern history, natural science, foreign languages, literature and economics had no place in any curriculum.[45]

The pre-Christian world predominated in the new syllabus, despite the role of Anglican divines in its formation. Christianity appeared so unassailable within the university that it seemed needless to foreground it in the curriculum or examinations. Extended theological studies were held by Oxford opinion to be unsuitable in an undergraduate course. Jackson preferred that degree examinations should be framed to produce hereditary legislators and men fit for other civil responsibilities rather than parsons. Nothing new, it was indeed thought, could be taught about religion. 'The scheme of Revelation . . . is closed,' Copleston declared in 1810 a few years before succeeding Eveleigh in the provostship of Oriel. 'We expect no new light on earth to break in upon us.' Sound Oxford men had the bounden duty 'to keep strict watch round that sacred citadel', the university, and 'to make our countrymen look to it as a tower of strength, and to defend it against open and secret enemies.'[46]

The examination reforms instigated by Jackson were chiefly responses to the cataclysm in France, but educational advances elsewhere in Europe were also a stimulus. The foundation of the University of Göttingen in 1734 had set higher standards for universities. The failings of English institutions, but not Scottish, became more conspicuous after the start of a new university at Berlin in 1810. Conceived by Wilhelm von Humboldt and backed by the Prussian state, it was the first university to fuse teaching with research. From the outset Berlin's university was associated with the swelling forces of liberalism, industrialization and nationalism. It did not aspire to inculcate gentlemanliness by the provision of a liberal education. It made no effort to instil the principles of leadership into impressionable young minds. The belief that humankind might be advanced and regenerated by knowledgeable mastery of the contemporary world, rather than by studying the philosophy and literature of antiquity, provided the first principle in Berlin. The

Humboldt-inspired universities asserted the primary needs of original research, critical thinking and the freedom to teach and publish unorthodox ideas or new discoveries without fear of expulsion, suspension, ostracism or other penalties for challenging the conventional wisdom. The foundation of the University of Berlin has been hailed as the 'most important caesura in the 800-year tradition of the European universities'.[47]

The wholesome influence of the new century's honours examinations was widely recognized. Edward Nares, the first of five Christ Church men to be appointed Regius Professor of Modern History in the nineteenth century, acknowledged that idle, ignorant and dissipated undergraduates remained in every college; but still felt that the general tone and future prospects of the university were being improved by noblemen, gentry, factory heirs and attorneys' sons striving for first-class honours. He only regretted that *Literae Humaniores* and mathematics were overspecialized subjects: 'perhaps if there were a little more *room* left for general knowledge in the prescribed studies, it might be better'.[48]

Competitive examinations became fetishized. The discipline and striving required to attain first-class honours became more important than the subject under examination, as shown by Macaulay's defence in 1833 of his proposal to fill vacancies in the Indian Civil Service by competitive examination. 'If,' insisted Macaulay, 'instead of learning Greek, we learned Cherokee, the man who understood Cherokee best, who made the most melodious and correct Cherokee verses, who comprehended most accurately the effect of the Cherokee particles, would generally be a superior man to him who was destitute of these accomplishments.' There was an annual drama as 'the flower of youth', as Macaulay called them, 'the most acute, the most industrious, the most ambitious' of Oxford's aspirants to honourable distinctions, broke under the strain of examinations. At Christ Church, Edward Pusey suffered melancholia and excruciating headaches while he read seventeen hours a day before gaining first-class honours in 1822. John Ruskin, at the same college in 1840, worked for his finals from six in the morning until midnight, with, he said, 'no cheerfulness, and no sense of any use in what I read', until he started coughing blood. As Thomas Huxley lamented, 'Students become deteriorated by the constant effort to pass this or that examination, just as we hear of men's brains becoming affected by the daily necessity of catching a train. They work to pass, not to know . . . They do pass, and they don't know.'[49]

Some undergraduates never forgave themselves for doing poorly. Randall Davidson (a future Archbishop of Canterbury) took his fiancée aside, the day after she had accepted his proposal of marriage in 1878, to confess his shame and to give her a chance of retraction: 'I hope you realise that I only got a Third in the Schools at Oxford.' When Harry Tawney gained only second-class honours in Greats in 1903, his father asked him, 'How do you propose to wipe out this disgrace?' Vivian Galbraith felt 'suicidal' when he got a third in Greats in 1913: 'such was the worship of "Firsts" at Balliol that no one would have been surprised if I had cut my throat.'[50]

CHAPTER 3

The Tigers of Old Time

Collingwood, in *The Idea of History*, distinguishes between the chronicler and the historian. Anyone who accepts, without critical scrutiny, the statements of past authorities or the testimony of participants in past events is a chronicler, not a historian, Collingwood says. 'Chronicle is the body of history from which the spirit has gone; the corpse of history.' His contemporary Benedetto Croce held cognate views. History is constituted 'by an act of thought', Croce wrote, thoughts made by scholars whose knowledge, understanding and expert interpretation exist within their perceptions of the contemporary reality around them. His fellow Italian historians, labouring over documentary works, preoccupied with the authenticity of their sources, providing a superficial gloss of acceptance rather than a bold critical spirit, dismayed Croce. He and Collingwood accepted that the collection and preservation of testimony, and the transcription and translation of such testimony, requires scholarly expertise, but regarded these activities as mere pseudo-history. There is no discipline or authenticity in historical work without both the spirit and the process of systematic and searching enquiry for truth. Then comes the synthesis of evidence, which is partly formed by the contemporary perplexities of the historian, and the critical interpretation of that synthesis. People who accumulate knowledge without drawing inferences and making critical judgements derived from their own past experience and present anxieties are not first-rank historians. 'Knowledge, for the sake of knowledge, so far from having anything sublime or aristocratic about it (as some believe), would be an idiotic pastime for idiots, or for the idiotic moments which we all have in us,' Croce wrote. 'Those intellectuals who see salvation in the withdrawal of the artist or the thinker from the world around him, in his deliberate non-participation in vulgar practical contrasts – vulgar in so far as they are practical – do, without knowing it, compass the death of the intellect.'[1]

Cardinal's College evolved into Christ Church during an intermediate phase in the development of English chronicling and historical writing, when Edward Hall was working on his literary compilations. Hall was a former Fellow of King's College, Cambridge turned lawyer of Gray's Inn, who sat in several parliaments during Henry VIII's reign. Beginning in the 1520s he compiled a long, meticulous narrative of English history from the deposition of Richard II in 1399 to the triumphs of the Tudors, which was published in 1558 under the title *The Union of the Two Noble and Illustre families of Lancastre & Yorke. Hall's Chronicle*, as it is generally known, establishes its author as a chronicler and (in Collingwood's terms) pseudo-historian, but a chronicler resolutely fixed on providing humanist instruction. Although Hall mastered French and Latin sources, he chose to write in English (as Thomas Starkey had pointedly done), for he wished to reach readers beyond a small circle of scholars. It was, for him, a matter of pride to write English history, in its native language, in emulation of the French chroniclers John Froissart and Enguerrand de Monstrelet, and of Philippe de Commynes' memoirs, which began to be published in 1524.

Hall's Chronicle opens with the humanist promise that history can help to induce virtue and repress vice. The study of past examples of leadership, even that of men who had been dead for thousands of years, will improve statecraft:

If no man had written [of] the goodness of noble Augustus, nor the pity of merciful Trajan, how should their successors have followed their steps in virtue and princely qualities: on the contrary part, if the cruelty of Nero, the ungracious life of Caligula had not been put in remembrance, young Princes and frail governors might likewise have fallen into a like pit, but by reading their vices and seeing their mischievous end, they be compelled to leave their evil ways, and embrace the good qualities of notable princes and prudent governors.

In Hall's telling, Richard II had neither a bad disposition nor a weak mind: his reign foundered because of his poor choice of advisers and trust in worthless favourites. By contrast, Henry V reformed his life by an act of will on his accession in 1413. The young King, Hall writes, 'put on the shape of a new man', turned 'wavering vice into constant virtue' and made himself into a 'prudent prince and . . . politique governor'. Instead of his former riotous toadies, he surrounded himself with shrewd, disciplined and strenuous men who gave him timely counsel. As a ruler, he evinced 'circumspection, diligence, and constancy', and never acted without first consulting his advisers and assessing possible contingencies (what Hall called 'all the main chances that might happen'). Henry V's counsellors helped 'to ease his charge & pain in supporting the burden of his realm' by offering him 'fruitful persuasions, that he might show himself a singular mirror and manifest example of moral virtues . . . to his common people'. After his enthronement, Henry became 'the mirror of Christendom & the glory of his country', writes Hall, 'a very Paragon'.[2]

Hall's Chronicle had a popular success, but seemed meagre stuff to those Elizabethans who knew the historical writings of the two Florentine contemporaries, Niccolò Machiavelli and Francesco Guicciardini. Sir Philip Sidney, who was educated at Christ Church in the 1570s before spending a year in Italy studying history, caricatured the typical compiler of Hall-like chronicles as 'laden with old Mouse-eaten records, authorising himself (for the most part) upon other histories, whose greatest authorities are built upon the notable foundation of Hearsay; better acquainted with a thousand years ago, than with the present age, and yet better knowing how this world goes, than how his own wit runs'. Given their derivative dullness, Sidney wondered how came it that these pseudo-historians thought themselves superior to anyone else in teaching the manner of virtuous actions.[3]

The cognoscenti of Sidney's generation followed the new paths cut by the Florentines in preference to the worn tracks of the chroniclers. Guicciardini and Machiavelli explained the struggles for power, in their lifetimes, that followed the French invasion of Italy in 1494, and the substitution of republican for Medici rule. Machiavelli's *Florentine Histories* was commissioned by a Medici in 1520 and posthumously published in 1532. Guicciardini's *Istoria d'Italia*, covering the period from the death of Lorenzo the Magnificent in 1492 to that of Pope Clement VII in 1534, became available to readers from 1537. While Machiavelli provided an adjective for the English-speaking world, the name of Guicciardini is virtually unknown, except to Renaissance scholars. 'Yet', as the Oxford historian John Hale noted in 1964, 'he is the greatest historian between Tacitus in the first century and Voltaire and Gibbon in the eighteenth, and he is one of the greatest of all writers of contemporary history.' He taught the craft of politics, and the traits of successful leadership, not high morality. By doing so, he became an essential precursor of the use of modern history to provide lessons in statecraft and character-building for the young students of Christ Church.[4]

For John Addington Symonds, the nineteenth-century scholar of Renaissance Italy, Guicciardini was seldom equalled in any nation or any age for his masterly control of intricate material, philosophic depth of thought and shrewd, proportionate judgement. His candour and dispassion in depicting the politics of sixteenth-century Florence seemed almost scarifying to Symonds. Guicciardini, he wrote,

> never feels enthusiasm for a moment: no character, however great for good or evil, rouses him from the attitude of tranquil disillusioned criticism. He utters but few exclamations of horror or of applause. Faith, religion, conscience, self-subordination to the public good, have no place in his list of human motives; interest, ambition, calculation, envy, are the forces which, according to his experience, move the world. That the strong should trample on the weak, that the wily should circumvent the innocent, that hypocrisy and fraud and dissimulation should triumph, seems to him but natural. His whole theory of humanity is tinged with the sad grey colours of a stolid, cold-eyed, ill-contented, egotistical indifference. He is not angry, desperate, indignant, but phlegmatically prudent.

This was a new temper in historical writing.[5]

Guicciardini's outlook is pithily displayed in his maxims of state or *Ricordi*. Christianity should be prudential and intelligent, he says. 'To have faith means simply to believe firmly – to deem almost a certainty – things that are not reasonable; or, if they are reasonable, to believe them more firmly than reason warrants.' Abstract thinking, if undertaken with too grave a spirit, likely ends in absurdities. 'Philosophers and theologians, and all those who investigate the supernatural and the invisible, say thousands of insane things. As a matter of fact, men are in the dark about such matters, and their investigation serves more to exercise the intellect than to find truth.' Excess is imprudent, even in Christian devotions. 'Too much religion spoils the world, because it makes the mind effeminate, involves men in thousands of errors, and diverts them from many generous and virile enterprises.' Guicciardini recoils from the ignorance of the masses ('To speak of the people is really to speak of a mad animal gorged with a thousand and one errors and confusions, devoid of taste, of pleasure, of stability'), and from the perfidy of individuals and factions: 'Men are so false, so insidious, so deceitful and cunning in their wiles, so avid in their own interest, and so oblivious to other's interests, that you cannot go wrong if you believe little and trust less.'[6]

The first English translations of Guicciardini were published by Sir Robert Dallington in 1613; but the Florentine's influence had reached England earlier through the medium of the histories of the French civil wars of religion by Jacques-Auguste de Thou and Enrico Davila. In particular, de Thou had a strong, wholesome influence on William Camden, and hence on the course of English historiography.

The context and aims of late sixteenth-century French and English historians were similar. The ruling French dynasty of the Valois, like the Tudors of England, was in a terminal phase. Catherine de Medici, the mother of the last three childless kings of the Valois and Queen Consort of their father, was intent on preserving monarchical power from the depredations of political parties and religious factions. Elizabeth I was the last of three childless siblings to reign in England. Thoughtful Frenchmen and Englishmen sought a historic pedigree and intellectual justification for the government of Church and state that stood apart from the legitimacy of the Valois and Tudor dynasties. They preferred pacification by compromise to the settling of quarrels by force of arms. In France those Catholics who had no wish for bloodiness in the cause of religious purity, and preferred to allow liberty of worship to the Protestant Huguenots for the sake of peace, were called *politiques*.[7]

De Thou was 'the intellectual oracle of the *politiques*', in Trevor-Roper's description, 'a Catholic whom the Catholic *dévots* regarded as little better than a Protestant in disguise'. Although de Thou became a Canon of Notre-Dame de Paris, he took only minor holy orders. He counted the Huguenot scholar Joseph Scaliger, whom he had first met studying law at the University of Valence, as one of his most intimate friends. He secured the post of royal librarian for a Protestant friend, Isaac Casaubon, and outraged his co-religionists by revering Erasmus as the glory of his age. In 1595 he became *président à mortier* – that is, a principal magistrate and counsellor to *parlements*. His greatest achievement was the Edict of Nantes (1598), which bestowed a guaranteed legal status on Protestants in France. 'He detested, above all things, intolerance,' Trevor-Roper wrote, 'and he hated the intolerance of his own party, which held power, even more than that of its adversaries, who could only express, not realise, their ferocity.' Aside from his heavy official responsibilities, de Thou dedicated himself to writing an impartial contemporary history, *Historia sui temporis*, which was distinguished by its exact research, discriminating sources and elegant prose.[8]

De Thou had an English counterpart and coeval in William Camden, the first of the great English historians to be trained in Christ Church. Camden, who took his bachelor's degree in 1573, felt enduring gratitude for his college training, and hailed the University of Oxford as 'one of England's stays, the prop and pillar, nay the Sun, the Eye, and the Soule thereof, the very Source and most clear Spring of good Literature and Wisdom: from whence, Religion, Civility and Learning are spread most plenteously into all parts of the Realm'.[9]

As a civil historian and chorographer Camden had, in Trevor-Roper's description, 'a European, not an insular spirit; and that spirit, in historiography, was the new spirit of the French lawyer-historians, of the *politiques*'. He and de Thou, like their contemporaries Enrico Davila and Paolo Sarpi, saw history as a secular study pursued for political and social lessons. They had no truck with the rhetoric, contrivance and moralizing of the humanist tradition, and still less affinity with the churchmen tradition, which lost the subject in a foggy discourse of revelation, prophecy and the workings of Providence. De Thou and Camden wrote in the form of annals, year by year, and used the device of obituaries within those years. The prose of both men had a measured elegance, which was tinged, according to Trevor-Roper, 'with solemn irony'. Camden was as much *politique* as any French lawyer-historian. He sought in history nothing but accurate explanations.[10]

After leaving Christ Church, Camden became Second Master of Westminster School, which Queen Elizabeth had founded in 1560. He became Headmaster in 1593, and tightened the school's connection with Christ Church: for the next four centuries boys from the cloisters of Westminster went every year to those of *Aedes Christi*. Camden's first major work was the outcome of meetings in 1577 with the Antwerp antiquarian, cartographer and geographer Abraham Ortelius. Camden supplied Ortelius with maps, and began work which developed into a topographical survey of England entitled *Britannia*. It was first published in 1586, with a dedication to his patron Burghley: intended for readers in the European republic of letters rather than for his compatriots, it was written in Latin, and did not appear in an English translation until 1610.

Camden's appointment as Clarenceux King of Arms in 1597 relieved him from the chores of schoolmastering, and gave him time both for research and to write his only book in English, *Remains Concerning Britain* (1605). In deference to the newly enthroned Scottish King of England, Camden referred to the isle of Britain in his title, but the subject of *Remains* is England: 'beautified with many populous Cities, fair Boroughs, good Towns, and well-built Villages, strong Munitions, magnificent Palaces of the Prince, stately houses of the Nobility, frequent Hospitals, beautiful Churches, fair Colleges, as well in other places, as in the two Universities, which are comparable to all the rest in Christendom, not only in antiquity, but also in learning, buildings, and endowments'.[11]

Burghley first suggested to Camden that he should write a history of the reign of Elizabeth I. In 1607 King James renewed this proposal in the hope that Camden's findings would dissuade de Thou from accepting the indictment by the great sixteenth-century Franco-Scottish humanist George Buchanan of James's mother in *Detectio Mariæ Reginæ* (1571). James sent his own commentary on his mother's reign, including her relations with her cousin Elizabeth of England, to divert de Thou from giving credence to Buchanan.

'Unfortunately,' as Trevor-Roper recounted, 'de Thou, eager though he was to oblige so great a king, piqued himself upon his own independence of mind and insisted on checking the king's account by reference to other sources.'[12]

This enraged James, who commissioned Camden to write an account which would serve to correct or to refute de Thou. Camden sent a preliminary draft of this work, 'deformed with blots & imperfect places, swarming with errors & patches thrust in' as he said, to de Thou, 'a man most dear unto me', who shocked him by extracting and abridging passages in his work while omitting much else that Camden thought essential to historical correctitude. After this incident, he concentrated his energies in researching and writing his *Annals of Great Britain under Queen Elizabeth*, the first volume of which was published in 1615. 'The study of TRUTH', he declared in its preface, 'hath been the only spur to prick me forward to this Work.' The supreme duty of a civil historian is to establish the truth of events, and to portray the reality of political conditions, and to furnish honest explanations. 'If you take out of History, WHY, HOW, TO WHAT END, and WHAT IS DONE, and whether Actions answer the intents, that which remains is rather a mocking than an instruction.' There was no place in his historical creed for personal grudges, malignity, backbiting or suppression of awkward truths. 'To detract from history [by such malpractices] is nothing else but to pluck out the eyes of a beautiful creature.' Although he followed the chroniclers' method of providing each year with its own chapter, he refused to provide those ornate descriptions of royal spectacle that made *Hall's Chronicle* so vivid. He relied on primary sources, 'Monuments and Records', so as to eliminate ignorance, doubtfulness and falsity. He had not been intimidated by authority: 'I have not feared DANGER, no not from them who by their present power think the Memory of the succeeding Age may be extinguished.' But he was gingerly in his discussions of religion and churchmanship, and almost apologetic for trenching on them. As he explained, 'although I know, that matters military and politique are the proper subjects of a Historian, yet I neither could nor ought to omit Ecclesiastical affairs (for betwixt Religion and policy there can be no divorce).'[13]

Camden endowed a chair of ancient history at Oxford in 1622: its holders have been historians of the Roman period rather than perpetuators of his brand of civil history. It was left to the circle of cultivated and intelligent men who gathered at Lord Falkland's house at Great Tew (ten miles outside Oxford) to renew and strengthen the practice and application of civil history. Civil history – empirical, and a form of knowledge that deductive minds might apply in practice – was summarized in an essay written by a member of the Great Tew circle, John Hales. Hales, who had been elected as a Fellow of Merton in 1605 and appointed Regius Professor of Greek in 1615, identified 'the special profit of history' as coming from the critical explanation of 'stratagems and plots', of men's character and conduct, of the reasons for success or failure in action and policy, and of 'all things that may serve for proof or disproof, illustration or amplification of any moral place'. When historians describe and explain actions in the remote past, 'they may do it with great wit and elegancy, express much politic wisdom, frame very beautiful pieces', but Hales doubted that they reached the true mainsprings of motivation. The first-hand knowledge of men writing from experience of their own times was likely to be wisest. Serious readers, seeking historical patterns to follow and emulate, should instead study the books 'of those who wrote the things of their own times, or in which themselves were agents'.[14]

Sir Walter Raleigh, who was a contemporary of Camden and Hales, thought similarly to them. He held that 'the end and scope of al Historie [is] to teach by example of times past, such wisdome as may guide our desires and actions'. Judgements of past rulers might be taken as implicit censure of living governors. 'But this I cannot helpe,' he wrote in his preface to his *Historie of the World*, which was planned for the counsel and under the auspices of Henry Stuart, Prince of Wales. 'If there be any, that finding themselves spotted like the Tigers of old time, shall find fault with me for painting them over anew; they shall therein accuse themselves justly, and me falsely.' Publication of the book was suspended on King James's orders for its 'saucy', that is impudent, criticism of princes. Later, in 1618, Raleigh was sent to the execution block by James to appease Spain in another matter. His *Historie* ran through ten editions in seventy years. Oliver Cromwell urged his son to read it for its comprehensive sweep: 'It's a Body of History; and will add much more to your understanding than fragments of Story.'[15]

To Thomas Fuller, author of the first history of the Crusades written in English (published in 1639), it was clear that the reading of history could teach prudence and discretion. 'What a pity it is to see a proper gentleman that hath such a crick in his neck that he cannot look backward!' Fuller exclaimed.

> History makes a young man to be old, without either wrinkles or grey hairs; privileging him with the experience of age, without either the infirmities or inconveniences thereof. Yea, it not only makes of things past, present; but enables one to make a rational conjecture of things to come. For this world affords no new accidents, but in the same sense wherein we call it a new moon, which is the old one in another shape, and yet no other than what hath been formerly. Old actions return again, furbished over with some new and different circumstances.

Civil history, though, had the potential to provoke, disturb, threaten, and to bring retribution on its authors. Its origins and stimuli were wars, bloodletting, political disintegration and social loss.[16]

In 1630 Enrico Davila's *Historia delle guerre civili di Francia*, his history of the French wars of religion of 1562–98, was published in Latin. It was a fine example of what Hales called the special profit of contemporary history, and won a striking success among the literate classes of Europe. Davila was a former page in the service of Catherine de Medici who had served both as a soldier in the later stages of those wars and as an official in the Venetian republic. His experiences as a participant in the wars, and as a minor courtier and administrator, enabled him to depict, with rare cogency, the misconduct and perfidy that led to civil wars, and the disorder and death that resulted from them. After the outbreak of the Great Rebellion in 1642, King Charles I besought William Aylesbury, who had been a gentleman-commoner of Christ Church in 1628–31, to render Davila's Latin text into English. The monarch subsequently read and approved the manuscript of his finished work. Aylesbury, whose sister married Edward Hyde, afterwards Earl of Clarendon, dedicated his translation to the monarch on its publication in 1647–8.

For part of the time when Aylesbury was at work on his Davila translation, his brother-in-law was secluded on the island of Jersey and meditating the masterpiece that became Clarendon's *History of the Rebellion*. Camden was an avowed influence on him, for he reread and annotated Camden's *Annals* while in Jersey. So, too, were the precepts of the Great Tew circle. Clarendon belonged, most of all, in the tradition of Guicciardini and de Thou: he was a strong and subtle politician who wrote a history of episodes in which he had been a participant or bystander. It was completed before his death in 1674, and became a sumptuous addition to historical literature after its publication in 1702.

Clarendon's historiographical views were precursors to those of Bradley, Woodward, Collingwood, Hancock, Bloch and Geyl, as summarized in chapter 1. He denied that specialist scholars, operating as delvers and recording angels in archives, made the best civil historians. 'It is not', he wrote,

a collection of records or an admission to the view and perusal of the most secret letters and acts of state that can enable a man to write a history, if there be an absence of that genius and spirit and soul of an historian which is contracted by the knowledge and course and method of business, and by conversation and familiarity in the inside of Courts, and with the most active and eminent persons in the government.

Clarendon acknowledged the influence of Tacitus on his work: he read Livy and Cicero, too, when writing the early sections. As Blair Worden has shown, Clarendon used quotations from and allusions to Roman writers in order to affirm the long historical resonances and intellectual discernment of his narrative. As one example, in assessing the character and achievements of Oliver Cromwell, he began by quoting a Roman senator saying of the Consul Cinna that he attempted things which no good man would have dared, and accomplished things which only a great and valiant man could have done. Then Clarendon gave his own balanced judgement on the Lord Protector: 'no man with more wickedness ever attempted anything, or brought to pass what he desired more wickedly . . . yet wickedness as great as his could never have accomplished those trophies, without the assistance of a great spirit, an admirable circumspection and sagacity, and a most magnanimous resolution'.[17]

Like Camden, Clarendon never painted scenes, or evoked displays, in the manner of *Hall's Chronicle*. Readers who seek dramatic accounts of executions or public spectacles are disappointed. Clarendon is set on explaining motives and the significance of actions. He describes, and prints long extracts from documents, and then he analyses the substance of what he has described. Clarendon, like Camden, de Thou, Davila and Sarpi, uses history as a means to give counsel to rulers. His intention, says Worden, is to inform Stuart monarchs, and their advisers, and the governors of the nation in future generations, of the errors of policy and conduct that brought the Crown to destruction. Like other *politiques* writing history, he gives trenchant judgements on his own generation. Readers are encouraged to emulate the virtues and to shun the vices that he recounts. The *History of the Rebellion* is a continuous exercise in the techniques of persuasion, and is a lesson to its readers in those techniques. More valuably still, it endows readers with the finest gift of the best historical writing – an acute sense of uncertainty. 'Clarendon', says Worden, 'is the great historian of the contingent, to whom everything in the civil wars might have happened differently.'[18]

Hopes invested in virtue politics are sure to be betrayed, Clarendon's *History of the Rebellion* teaches. Humanist ideals are based on bogus suppositions. Witness, he says, the case of George, Lord Digby, afterwards second Earl of Bristol, who matriculated at Magdalen in 1626, served as Secretary of State to Charles I in 1643–9 and was High Steward of the University of Oxford in 1643–6 and 1660–3. Ostensibly, Digby incarnated the ideal of virtue politics, but betrayed all his promise:

> The Lord Digby was a man of very extraordinary parts by nature and art, and had surely as good and excellent an education as any man of that age in any country: a graceful and beautiful person; of great eloquence and becomingness in his discourse: he was equal to a very good part in the greatest affairs, but the unfittest man alive to conduct them, having an ambition and vanity superior to all his other parts, and a confidence in himself, which sometimes intoxicated, transported, and exposed him . . . his fatal infirmity was, that he too often thought difficult things very easy; and considered not possible consequences, when the proposition

. . . was delightful to his fancy, by pursuing thereof he imagined that he should reap some glory to himself, of which he was immoderately ambitious.

Digby had, said Clarendon, 'a volatile and unquiet spirit' – which was, to a State Man, the most inauspicious of temperaments.[19]

Clarendon became Chancellor of the University of Oxford after the Restoration, and took Dean Fell as his coadjutor. He sent two of his sons to study at Christ Church in the 1660s, too. Leopold von Ranke reckoned him to be one of 'those who have essentially fixed the circle of ideas for the English nation'. Lord Macaulay thought that 'no man was better acquainted with general maxims of statecraft' or 'observed the varieties of character with a more discriminating eye'. The Christ Church-trained historian Henry Hallam said that Clarendon combined the bold sweep of ancient historians with the acute character portraits and intimate minutiae of the French memoirists Cardinal de Retz and the duc de Saint-Simon; and surpassed the Frenchmen by his sincerity and involvement with the significance of his narrative. John Morley admired Clarendon's intellectual power, his astute knowledge of human motives and his grasp of public business. 'Even where he does not carry us with him,' writes Morley, 'there is nobody of the time whose opinion is better worth knowing.'[20]

In the 1640s Henry Peacham's *Compleat Gentleman*, which had first been published twenty years earlier, was one of the favourite books of the Cavaliers with whom Clarendon associated. It returned to fashion, and circulated widely, after the Restoration in 1660. 'No subject', wrote Peacham, 'affects us with more delight than History, imprinting a thousand forms upon our imaginations, from the circumstances of Place, Person, Time, Matter, manner, and the like.' History, he continued, gave lessons in discretion, prudence and success: nothing could be more profitable than to learn from the experiences of those 'who hath trod the path of error and danger before us'. For instructive examples of strong or weak government, Peacham recommended Thomas More's life of Richard III, John Hayward's of Henry IV and Samuel Daniel's history of the English monarchy together with Philip Sidney's *Arcadia* and Bacon's essays.[21]

Contemporary history treated the enduring themes of national policy, personal allegiance, civil and continental war, turns of fortune, contingency, accidents and opportunities. More than ever, after the Restoration, its lessons were studied by the more thoughtful and responsibly minded national leaders and by some provincial dignitaries, too. Take Richard Myddelton, who matriculated at Brasenose College, Oxford in 1670. After leaving the university, he inherited a baronetcy and Chirk Castle in Denbighshire, and represented his county in thirteen parliaments. First elected after James II's accession in 1685, he remained continuously in the Commons until the reign of George I. In politics, he was a Tory who disliked extremities. In 1714 he accepted the Hanoverian succession without qualms. He bought biographies, travel books and contemporary histories as well as standard texts of classical literature and ancient history. His shelves bore Camden's *Remains Concerning Britain* and *Annales of the Reign of Elizabeth*, Raleigh's *Historie of the World*, Lord Monmouth's translation of Cardinal Bentivoglio's history of the revolt against Spanish rule in the Netherlands, Izaak Walton's *Lives of John Donne, Henry Wotton, Richard Hooker and George Herbert*, Peter Heylin's *Help to English History*, John Spottiswoode's *History of the Church and State of Scotland*, James Heath's *Chronicle of the Late Internecine War*, Lord Castlemaine's history of the Anglo-Dutch wars and John Milton's history of England. No doubt history was for him partly, in Thomas Fuller's phrase, 'a velvet study, and recreation work'; but it also taught civil responsibility, prudence, moderation and the weighing of consequences, and the techniques of successful persuasion. Honour and dishonour, of individuals, families, parties and nations, provided its great themes. The origins and results of mistaken policy, confused action, poor judgement of men, personal misconduct, negotiation and compromise were its staple subjects. No wonder, then, that readings of recent history helped to make Myddelton into a pattern, it was said, of 'the man of honour'.[22]

During the reigns of the four Georges, from 1714 until 1830, the Tories were held by the Whigs to be obscurantist and ill-read. Oxford, as the former royal capital of the Stuarts in England, was thought to be rotten with Jacobite prejudices. Daniel Defoe, for example, lamented the decay of learning, the corruption of education and the growing indolence in the arts of conversation that he saw in England of the 1720s. 'We have been a brave and learned people, and are insensibly dwindling into an effeminate, superficial race,' he lamented in 1728. 'Our young gentlemen are sent to the universities, it is true, but for . . . a feather for the cap, merely to say that they have been at Oxford or Cambridge, as if the air of those places inspired know-ledge without application.' Twenty years later Lord Chesterfield noted that the reputation of Cambridge University 'is sunk into the lowest obscurity; and the existence of Oxford would not be known, if were not for the treasonable spirit publicly avowed, and often exerted there.'[23]

Often the High Church clergy of the Augustan age were accused of lax and meagre scholarship; but there were, in truth, Tory dons with broad and informed views, who taught their pupils to draw inferences and make political sense for themselves by reading modern histories. In 1717, for example, a stalwart Tory Canon of Christ Church, William Stratford, advised a favourite pupil, Edward Harley, afterwards second Earl of Oxford and Mortimer, to read Famiano Strada's *History of the Low-Countrey Warres* (first published in English in 1650), Emanuel van Meteren's *Histoire des Pays-Bas ou Recueil des guerres* (set in the 1570s) and Cardinal Bentivoglio's history of the war of Flanders as a way of bettering his political acumen. When Harley had the leisure, 'the story of Philip the Second, and his son Don Carlos, may afford you amusement and reflections too', Stratford added. The High Tory leader Henry St John, Viscount Bolingbroke, who became a Jacobite exile in 1715, maintained that systematic historical training was requisite in the education of a young man of rank, ambition and ability. 'A constant improvement in public and private virtue' was, Bolingbroke believed, the true and proper object of historians. There was no place for aimless pottering or inquisitive antiquarianism in the subject. 'Any study, that tends neither directly nor indirectly to make us better men and better citizens, is at best but a specious sort of idleness . . . and the know-ledge that we acquire by it is a creditable kind of ignorance, nothing more.'[24]

The Whig belief that historical knowledge tended to moderate partisanship prompted the decision in 1724 to found a combined Regius professorship of modern history and modern languages in both of the English universities. These chairs were the brainchildren of Edmund Gibson, who had been appointed Bishop of London by Sir Robert Walpole a year earlier. Gibson was a methodical scholar, who had codified English canon law, and a deft politician, who guided Walpole's ecclesiastical appointments. The Whig frame of mind would be fostered by the lessons of history, he felt sure. Gibson intended that two 'prudent' men, who were adept in modern history and in modern languages, would enable the universities to provide 'constant supplies of learned and able men to serve the publick in both Church and State'. The Regius chairs were so named because George I endowed them from royal funds: Gibson and Walpole intended their foundation to denote the liberality and enlightenment of the Hanoverian dynasty, which had succeeded the Stuarts only ten years earlier. The new opportunities for remunerative employment and gratifying influence that were promised by the study of modern history and modern languages would benefit members of the university.[25]

The first holder of Oxford's Regius chair was a young and able Christ Church man, David Gregory. His travels in Europe, his fluency in foreign tongues and his reading had convinced him that prevalent notions of scholarship in Oxford were backward-looking, cramped and shallow – and therefore liable to foster Jacobite sympathies. Gregory saw the study of modern history, proficiency in modern languages and the conciliation of the landed classes to the universities as ends that were virtuous and akin. 'The methods of Education in our Universities have been in some measure defective, since we are obliged to adhere so much to the rules laid down by our forefathers,' he wrote in 1728. 'The old scholastic learning has been for some time despised, but not altogether exploded, because nothing else has been substituted in its place.' Gregory hoped to find intelligent undergraduates, and to instruct them in law, history and living European languages so that they formed an echelon which served the Hanoverian state in diplomacy and other official work.[26]

Despite Gregory's determined and systematic ideas, the governors in Whitehall soon lost interest in training modern historians as the high-flying sentinels of the Hanoverian monarchy. He relinquished his professorship to an anodyne President of St John's College in 1736. Twenty years later, though, he gained his second chance of mentoring young Oxford men when he was appointed Dean of

Christ Church by King George II. Gregory proved to be a strong, consolidating head of the House, who reinvigorated the traditions established a century earlier by John Fell. He found that the best young classicists in the college were not expected to read the historians, dramatists and orators of Greek antiquity. Cicero, Lucretius, Virgil's *Aeneid* and the Homeric *Iliad* provided their material. One highly regarded undergraduate of the 1750s, William Conybeare, was described approvingly as 'an elegant Latin scholar, struck with horror at any phrase or idiom which could not vouchsafe Ciceronian authority, and a great reader of Clarendon, [but] with little Greek, and no mathematical or physical science'.[27]

Gregory devised a new curriculum, which included algebra for the first time, and gave emphasis to the study of Greek and Roman history and to Greek literature. The new syllabus, according to Gregory's biographer, was 'the most regular . . . and the most extensive that was ever proposed to the youth of the university'. It was enhanced by his successor as Dean, William Markham, afterwards Archbishop of York. At Markham's instigation, Herodotus and Thucydides were brought to the fore in teaching during the 1770s, and works by Xenophon were set for the first time. Markham also introduced Greek drama to his college, notably Aeschylus, Euripides and Sophocles. This attention to ancient Greece reflected a renewed respect for Greek classical antiquity. When the great war minister William Pitt, Earl of Chatham sent his namesake son to Pembroke College, Cambridge in 1773, he enjoined that Thucydides, 'the eternal manual of statesmen', should be the first Greek that the boy should be set to study. Polybius was the second Greek text prescribed by Chatham. Other young men he advised to begin their historical reading with Gilbert Burnet's *History of the Reformation of the Church of England* (1679–1715), and to pay close attention to the seventeenth-century strife between Crown and parliament. Chatham held a functional view of history, as an oblique means of understanding contemporary affairs, and had no sense of it as a subject which should be studied for its own pure sake.[28]

The expanded reading lists, which were instigated by Gregory and Markham and met the ambitions of fathers like Chatham, had an implicit thought embedded in them: that the study and writing of history is ripest and most useful when handled by people who are

writing of recent events with present-day knowledge, insight, subjectivity and allegiances. It mattered little if the historians were working
in antiquity, such as Thucydides and Xenophon, or in Stuart England,
as Camden and Clarendon did. In all cases they relied on evidence
that was piecemeal and makeshift: the value and vitality of their
work came from their acumen, personal experiences and even bias.
In their hands, the subject became a set of parables about the reasons
for success or failure in action and policy: the explanations of failure
often proving more instructive than examples of success. History
writing of this class can provide maxims of statecraft and possibly,
too, rational conjecture of things to come. It is a study of the causes
and speed of change, the measuring of losses, the workings of contingencies, the pliancy of ideas, the instability of reputation and the
missing of chances. The speaker in Clough's 'Amours de Voyage'
must be a historian when he says,

> Fact shall be fact for me, and the Truth the Truth as ever,
> Flexible, changeable, vague, and multiform, and doubtful.

CHAPTER 4

The Great Charm of Lucid Order

Each college constitutes an independent realm of memory. Their buildings and possessions, their stateliness and intimacies, their statutes and oral traditions, their bias and prized distinctions, make them unique. The beauty and grandeur of their stones and quads excited imaginations, aroused lifelong loyalties, inspired the ambition to serve national rather than personal ends. 'My first entrance into Oxford I shall never forget,' Cardinal Manning recalled in old age. 'I arrived after dark. The streets and Colleges by lamplight seemed to me a fairyland.' He felt that he had reached 'a sort of intellectual Elysium', and he never lost, so he said in old age, his awe of Oxford. Henry Scott Holland, after his election as a Student of Christ Church in 1870, walked through the hallowed buildings, feeling almost physical union with his surroundings, hearing (he said) his voice mingling in the church bells, absorbing himself in the masonry and feeling integral to the loveliness of college and university. Falconer Madan, the Bodley's Librarian, wrote in 1885: 'The towers and spires, numerous and yet varied in character, the quadrangles old and new with their profusion of carved stonework, the absence of large factories and tall chimneys, the groves and avenues of trees, the quiet college gardens, the well-watered valleys and encircling hills – all these make Oxford the fairest city in England.' The short views and long perspectives from archways and windows, the shafts of light and falling shadows, the visual richness of rooms and quadrangles, had more formative and enduring influences on some young men than tutorials or lectures: for them the joy and triumph of Oxford was visual and environmental.[1]

By general consent, Christ Church was one of the fairest of the colleges by sunshine and lamplight alike. It was one of the richest of Oxford's individual realms of memory, and was distinctive in its constitution and endowments. In other Oxford colleges, the award of sundry fellowships and scholarships was restricted by the founders' statutes to young men who could prove their genealogical descent from the founder's family (known as 'founder's kin') or to persons born in particular localities or educated at particular schools. Christ Church, though, was not hampered by obsolete statutes, because the death of King Henry VIII during his process of founding the college had left it without any statutes at all. There were no obligations to founders' kin or to particular counties and towns in awarding junior or senior studentships. Thomas Gaisford, Samuel Smith's successor as Dean, declared in 1854 that the college never allotted studentships as the equivalent of academic prizes to mark 'mere intellectual merit'. Financial need was the prevailing criterion: the choices were mostly sound and never scandalous.[2]

Christ Church had more professors than any other college in Oxford: divinity, Hebrew and Greek; the readership – that is, senior lectureship – in anatomy, too, was tantamount to a chair. The college also endowed readerships in divinity, rhetoric, logic and Greek philology; later, too, a lecturer in mathematics. It also had five or six college tutors at a time when some other colleges struggled to find one or two men with the aptitude for tutorial work. This meant that the classes at Christ Church had fewer undergraduates than at other colleges, and more personalized teaching. Tutors could adjust the level of their lessons to the ability of their young men. For 'reading men', as brighter students were known, tutorial lectures were less helpful than good tutorial advice about the choice of books to read, methods of study, management of their time and avoidance of side issues. Its reading men achieved no fewer than thirty-one firsts in 1831–40.

Christ Church was akin to a miniature university within a bigger corporation. It might be likened, too, to an autonomous duchy within a larger federated kingdom. Its ruler was appointed by the Crown, following advice tendered by the Prime Minister. In 1809, when Jackson retired as Dean, Lord Liverpool jobbed his former tutor Charles Hall into the post. Hall knew that he could never match Jackson, but did his best to imitate his predecessor's manners, posture and ways: he cut a handsome, haughty figure marching up and down Christ Church hall, with his hand stuck in the belt of his cassock and his cap tilted towards the bridge of his nose. His attempts to impress drew him into living beyond his means, and to save himself from his debts he exchanged the deanery of Christ Church for the more remunerative one of Durham in 1824. Lord Montagu of Boughton thought Christ Church was 'abominably mismanaged' under Hall and fell from the standards and discipline of Jackson, so he consigned his ward, the fifth Duke of Buccleuch, to St John's, Cambridge rather than Christ Church. He thought that it would be slow work to restore the college. He feared, moreover, that the young duke would be allotted to the 'Old Growler', as Thomas Vowler Short was familiarly known: 'a downright college Tutor, without an idea that he has not gathered within the walls of his College'.[3]

Although Christ Church kept its good intellectual record under Hall and Smith, with fifty-one firsts in 1821–30, the fate of Lord Conyers Osborne, younger son of the sixth Duke of Leeds, shows the rowdy indiscipline of college life. Osborne matriculated in 1829 when Smith was Dean. Mark Pattison, afterwards Rector of Lincoln College, Oxford, remembered him as 'a lively, bright, well-mannered, and gracious young man', who could 'write Latin verses fast without a false quantity'. The duke sent his boy to the House attended by a private tutor, Thomas Paddon, formerly Fellow of Caius in Cambridge. Paddon's expectations of his pupil were cheated, though, by the derision of Osborne's social set in college. They thought it 'unworthy' for a tuft to work at his books. Osborne misspent his time in exuberant futility until, in 1831, he was killed in a late-night brawl in Peckwater Quad by Lord Hillsborough, afterwards fourth Marquis of Downshire.[4]

Many colleges were richer than the university. Their Fellows repulsed outside interference. There was no expectation that dons would make scientific discoveries or engage in original research. Although colleges had extruded the monks in the sixteenth century, they kept a repressive vestige of medieval monasticism by insisting that Fellows make a pretence of asexuality by remaining celibate, and resign their fellowships if they chose to marry. Accordingly, few Fellows laid plans to stay in the university: they waited for college livings to fall vacant, and then left to work in parishes where they would be free to marry. This proud, insular and sedate frame of mind was not fit to meet the exorbitant needs of the early nineteenth century.[5]

Industrialization during the reign of George III turned an agricultural and commercial people into a manufacturing and imperial state. The velocity of economic advance and the rate of population growth were unprecedented. Moreover, a powerful minority of strong minds and hardy characters was advocating a new system of thought called utilitarianism. Its founder, Jeremy Bentham, collected his adherents from a generation which was, in Keith Feiling's words, 'violently critical . . . of a tangle of ancient regulation and local ignorance'. They regarded the existent legislature, public institutions and social systems as inadequate to keep the nation steady in the factory age. In reaction, Church of England traditionalists, all of them educated at either Oxford or Cambridge, objected that 'the paltry morality' of utilitarianism was upsetting 'the existing order of things'. This new generation of complacent materialists denied the moral omnipotence of God by believing in human perfectibility. They reduced God to a figure of 'infinite benevolence', demoted evil to the status of 'a mere defect' and rejected 'the sinfulness of sin'.[6]

Adamant in purpose, and armed with a battery of statistics, the utilitarian movement began an inquisition into national institutions and methods. The universities, like parliament, the Poor Law, the prisons, the law courts and the municipalities, were found to be outworn and enervate. The threat delivered ever more loudly to inefficient or failing institutions was that they must voluntarily amend themselves from within, or face being formed anew by exterior forces. Moreover, after 1828, a new generation came forward in public business: younger men, as Walter Bagehot related, 'who did not remember the horrors of the French Revolution, and had been teased to death by hearing their parents talk about them'. As part of the reflexive rejection of parental certitudes, there developed in the 1830s an expansive desire to alleviate and improve old structures and hard customs.[7]

Campaigns to reform the two ancient English universities gathered pace and force after the publication in 1831 of two bruising articles in the *Edinburgh Review* by Sir William Hamilton, an Edinburgh

professor who had studied at Balliol and admired Humboldt's new
research university at Berlin. In 1834 resident members of Cambridge
University's Senate, including two heads of houses and nine professors, petitioned parliament for the abolition of all religious tests that
excluded young men from matriculation. The matter to which they
objected was the irrefragable obligation to subscribe to the Thirty-
Nine Articles. These Articles had been framed early in the reign of
Queen Elizabeth to define the tenets of the Church of England and
to further the cause of moderate Protestantism. Initially their
tendency was latitudinarian. The seventeenth-century divine Thomas
Fuller, for example, likened the Articles to children's clothes, made
large so that children might grow into them. But in the reign of
Charles II a new stipulation that everyone matriculating in the
universities must attest to his full agreement with the Articles served
to exclude dissenters – that is Christians who were not members of
the Church of England – from university education. By the 1830s
this seemed intolerable to Benthamite utilitarian feeling. 'We are
only asking for a restitution of our ancient academic laws and laud-
able customs,' the majority in the Cambridge Senate maintained.
These compulsory religious tests had been imposed upon a reluctant
university 'during times of bitter party animosity and during the
prevalence of dogmas, both in Church and State, which are at vari-
ance with the spirit of English Law, and with the true principles of
Christian toleration'.[8]

Some months later the Oxford heads of colleges voted by a
majority of one to replace the obligatory subscription to the Thirty-
Nine Articles by a general declaration of belief. Among the
supporters of this movement to admit non-Anglicans to the university was Renn Hampden, a tolerant, charitable man who was White's
Professor of Moral Philosophy. Together with Thomas Arnold, the
future Regius Professor of Modern History, Hampden was the most
academically distinguished Oxford Whig. Arnold's son Matthew
later wrote that his father was 'painfully awake to the truth that
to profess to see Christianity through the spectacles of a number
of second or third-rate men who lived in Queen Elizabeth's time
(and this is what office-holders under the thirty-nine articles do)
– men whose works one never dreams of reading for the purpose
of enlightening and edifying oneself – is an intolerable absurdity'.[9]

In 1835, after long debate, the Dissenters' Admission to Universities Bill, which granted a right to admission to English universities without religious tests, was passed by a large majority of MPs (185 to 44). But in the House of Lords it was defeated by 187 votes to 85. A royal duke who was Chancellor of the University of Cambridge decried the bill as a cruel measure which, by diminishing the Anglican character of the universities, would separate the national Church from the state and end in the toppling of the throne. The Duke of Wellington, as Chancellor of the University of Oxford, insisted that enactment of the bill would spread 'dissent and schisms' throughout both universities. Henry Phillpotts, Bishop of Exeter, warned that if the bill received Royal Assent most Oxford men would prefer to become 'penniless and homeless' rather than comply in destroying 'what they deem to be most valuable in this life, because it is connected with the interests of the life to come'.[10]

In 1836 an outcry was raised in Oxford against the appointment by the Whig government of Renn Hampden to the vacant Regius professorship of divinity. The ensuing boycotts, polemics and accusations of heresy were the opening salvos in the disruptive onslaught of the zealots who became known as the Oxford Movement or the Tractarians. They were a combination of romantic medievalists and spiritual revivalists who strove to confound the prosaic Protestant orthodoxy, the chill rationalism and the infidelity of the Georgian age. Their creed was avowedly retrograde: like divines in the reign of Charles I, they upheld the doctrine of the Divine Right of Kings. Their inquisitorial spirit, harsh peremptory arrogance and conspiratorial spite led Thomas Arnold to dub them the Oxford Malignants.

Pre-eminent among these zealots was Edward Bouverie Pusey, who lived for fifty-four years as a Canon of Christ Church. After studying at Christ Church and Göttingen, Pusey was appointed Regius Professor of Hebrew at the age of twenty-eight. 'In the presence of Dr Pusey,' wrote the Church historian Henry Offley Wakeman, 'men felt that they were dealing with one of the great ones of the earth.' Some deplored him as a miserable pietist and, in the words of Lyulph Stanley of Balliol, 'the head of the reaction in Oxford'. Pusey described himself as 'scarred all over and seamed with sin, so that I am a monster to myself'. His spiritual masochism took such forms as always walking with eyes cast down to the ground. He would never jest or look at anything out of mere curiosity. He resolved never to smile, 'if I can help it, except with children, or when it seems a matter of love'. He sought to scarify with his sermons, preached in the cathedral, on eternal punishment. He told his fellow Tractarian John Henry Newman that he had lost hope of attaining a godly Oxford when Oriel, against his protests, indulged itself by serving French wines with the turtle soup at a dinner celebrating its fifth centenary.[11]

Newman's secession from the Church of England to the Church of Rome in 1845 brought deliverance for the university from the throttlehold of Tractarianism, the bane of sectarianism and the misdirection of the energies and purpose of a nineteenth-century university. Andrew Lang, who was elected as a Fellow of Merton in 1868, looked back on the Tractarians with amazement. 'On what singular topics men's minds were bent!' he exclaimed. 'What queer survivals of the speculations of the [medieval] schools agitated them as they walked round Christ Church meadows!' His generation were determined never to let clerical zealotry or obscurantism achieve such dominion again. 'It is as if they spoke in tongues, which had a meaning then, and for them, but which to us, some forty years later, seem as meaningless as the inscriptions of Easter Island.' The rout of Tractarianism proved to be the essential enabler of university reform. As Benjamin Jowett of Balliol warned in 1847, it was unlikely that his university would be allowed to remain an exclusive, insular body, possessing 'enormous wealth without any manifest utilitarian purpose', and too narrow and remote in its studies to incorporate new branches of knowledge.[12]

In 1850 the House of Commons approved, by a majority of 140 to 45, the issue of Royal Commissions to inquire into the condition, discipline, studies and revenues of Trinity College, Dublin and the two English universities. The Oxford commissioners employed Arthur Stanley of University College as their Secretary, and Goldwin Smith as Assistant Secretary. Five years earlier Goldwin Smith, who had entered Christ Church at the age of fifteen, had come top of an examination to become a Fellow of the Queen's College only to be rejected because of his anti-clerical views. This affront confirmed him as a foe to clericalism, and a self-styled Red

among Oxford reformers. The ascendancy of Anglican clergy in
the university was harmful, he declared in 1850, 'especially now,
when the most intellectual and thoughtful of the men, and those
whom it is the most desirable to retain among us, are shrinking
from taking orders'.[13]

A notable member of the Royal Commission was Henry Liddell,
who missed only one out of eighty-seven meetings. Liddell had
matriculated at Christ Church in 1829, gained a double first in
classics and mathematics in 1833, worked as a college tutor from
1836 and became the college's Reader in Greek in 1838. After vacating
his studentship on his marriage in 1846, he became Headmaster of
Westminster School. Goldwin Smith was impressed by him: 'a man
of stately figure, character, and mind; an artist, drawing beautifully,
as well as a great classical scholar and a first-class in mathematics.
He sometimes made me think of the union of art and science in
Leonardo da Vinci.'[14]

Oxford's Hebdomadal Board (its ruling council of heads of houses,
professors and other high college and clerical dignitaries) insisted
to the commissioners that there was no need for reforms. It declared
instead that the Laudian statutes of 1636, which still governed the
university, were 'admirably arranged, at a time when not only the
nature and faculties of the human mind were exactly what they are
still, and must of course remain, but the principles also of sound
and enlarged culture were far from being imperfectly understood'.
The Council wished to preserve the university as an Anglican semin-
ary for the nation's Protestant clergy.[15]

The reports of Royal Commissions were a major force for developing public opinion in mid-nineteenth-century Britain. Those on
the universities, which were delivered after two years of deliberations,
had numerous conclusions and recommendations. Many of the
recommendations relating to Oxford were embodied, after another
two years of preparing public opinion, in the Oxford University Act
of 1854. This legislation extinguished the university devised by
Archbishop Laud and Bishops Sheldon and Fell. The obligation to
subscribe to the Thirty-Nine Articles was abolished. Fellowships
which had been founded for the avowed purpose of benefiting the
clergy were secularized. College endowments given for the support
of religion and education were reallocated to maintain laymen in

their careers. The obligation to take holy orders was lifted for most fellowships, and the number of fellowships tenable by laymen was increased.

Henry Parry Liddon, a Puseyite who had graduated from Christ Church in 1850, felt that once undergraduates were no longer bound to subscribe to the Thirty-Nine Articles, and when nearly all college offices were opened to laymen, the Church of England was finished in Oxford. Christians of 'intrepid faith' and 'stern self-discipline' were henceforth expected 'to tone down what they had to say, to the popular standard'. When younger Christian dons laid plans for reinvigorating Anglican leadership in the university, Liddon used to shake his head mournfully and say, 'Dear friend, you are doing nothing else but combing the hair of a corpse.' The university was beset by materialism, he warned in a sermon delivered at the university church of St Mary's: 'We may shortly live to see what has been a home of the Church for a thousand years become a place of purely secular instruction which might have been founded last week by a company of shareholders.' These were general sentiments in the House. 'Oxford', wrote Lord Redesdale, who was an undergraduate at Christ Church in 1855–8, 'ceased to be a place of learning for English gentlemen of the reformed Christian faith.' Edward Talbot, a devout Christian who entered the same college in 1862, felt distress as he watched the bright young men who attended sermons in St Mary's. The expressions on their faces, he remembered, 'were not docile; nor sympathetic; very critical; perhaps some of them not a little cynical or even contemptuous'. He himself was unsettled both by Darwin's teachings on evolution and by John Stuart Mill discounting any primary authority in conscience. He feared that 'when we find *how* God has done something, we give up the belief that He has done it'.[16]

Robert Browning, Honorary Fellow of Balliol, wrote his poem *The Ring and the Book* in the mid-1860s. 'There's a new tribunal now', one couplet announces:

Higher than God's, the educated man's!

After the passage of the University Act, the two ancient English universities adapted their ideas and efforts to meet a new primary purpose: the populating of a tribunal of educated men. Thinking dons set themselves the task of instilling a distinctly Protestant ideal of manhood, which would improve the characters of both individual undergraduates and the nation state. The components of this ideal of manhood were listed in 1875 by Edward Dowden, who later gave the first Taylorian lectures at Oxford. 'Energy, devotion to the fact, self-government, tolerance, a disbelief in minute apparatus for the improvement of human character, an indifference to externals in comparison with that which is of the invisible life, and a resolution to judge all things from a purely human standpoint.' This was the late nineteenth-century model for virtue and sense in the university: it was, too, what the coming generations of nineteenth-century modern historians set out to provide to both undergraduates and the nation.[17]

'The most important point about English history is that the English were the first people who formed for themselves a national character at all,' declared Mandell Creighton, a former Fellow of Merton and now Bishop of London, delivering the Romanes lecture in Oxford in 1896. 'The great product of England', he continued, 'is not so much its institutions, its empire, its commerce, or its literature, as it is the individual Englishman, who is moulded by all these influences, and is the ultimate test of their value.' Creighton was the greatest of the creators of the School of Modern History at Oxford. Lord Acton, who was installed as Cambridge's Regius Professor of Modern History in 1895, admired his Olympian dispassion: Creighton, he said, passed 'through scenes of raging controversy with a serene curiosity, a suspended judgment, a divided jury, and a pair of white gloves'. Always Creighton adjusted his views when they needed a finer balance. Accordingly, six months after praising national character in his Romanes lecture, he was moved to warn against the self-sufficient complacency of islanders and the vanity of confusing historical exceptions with national genius. 'The great fault of the English is their insularity, and insistence on the English ideal as the only one possible.'[18]

Henry Scott Holland recalled that by 1870, when he was elected as a Student at Christ Church and Creighton was ordained a deacon in the Church of England, it seemed 'almost incredible that a young don of any intellectual reputation for modernity should be on the Christian side'. Creighton's intellectual creed, though, was unshakeable. 'God has decreed that history should take the place of miracles, that the Church should be a standing proof of God's presence within her,' he said in 1885. If the study of modern history in late nineteenth-century Oxford was primarily an exploration of the origins and adaptations of national character, it also gave (in the minds of some of its best practitioners) proof of the truth of Christianity, and lessons in adaptive or evolutionary resilience to the Church of England in an age of religious doubts.[19]

The rest of this chapter portrays the efforts and erudition, the temper and bias, of four Christ Church men, Edward Nares, John Cramer, Halford Vaughan and William Stubbs, who held the Regius chair of modern history (not in direct succession) between 1813 and 1884. It shows their roles in making Oxford's modern history curriculum into a study of nationality, national character and national ideals at a time when the primacy of the Church of England was receding. They saw their discipline as giving lessons in shrewdness. History endowed its students with the means to appraise evidence and to criticize opinion: it honed their capacity to make fine distinctions, to draw inferences and to take sound decisions; with historical knowledge people might foretell mistakes and perhaps avert some of them.

After the retirement in 1736 of Gregory, the first holder of the Regius chair in modern history and modern languages, the involvement of Christ Church with his professorship fell away. His successors as Regius professors were listless, undistinguished men: two of them members of unreformed Oriel, and another from the similarly impaired Balliol. No pupils were rallied by them to their subject. William Mitford was an Oxford undergraduate in the 1760s and began publishing a multi-volume history of Greece in 1785: Lord Byron admired Mitford most among modern historians for his 'learning, research, wrath, and partiality'. It was not from the tepid Regius Professor of his day that Mitford acquired his historical inquisitiveness and systematic purpose in collecting and interpreting facts. The paramount lessons in scholarly methods he took from the lectures and commentaries on the history of English law given by the Professor of Jurisprudence, Sir William Blackstone.

A. V. Dicey praised Blackstone for remembering always that 'the primary object of a teacher is to excite the intelligent interest of his readers or his hearers'. In presenting evidence or pressing arguments, Blackstone 'knew when to curtail and when to abound'. He was 'neither a legislative reformer, nor a logical dogmatist, nor a legal antiquarian'. He selected only important themes of constitutional law, shunning 'the vice of logical formalism', avoiding 'the maze of pedantic antiquarianism', interpreting the past from the present standpoint and recent experience of a professor of law who had been a judge of the King's Bench. No one had researched and pondered the historical records more carefully than Blackstone, but he did not sedate or sterilize his work by pretending to impartiality or impersonality. Blackstone's procedure charmed Mitford's generation, and set an example for some of the best historical teaching in nineteenth-century Oxford. Certainly, his shapely narrative, with its examples of English exceptionalism and of continuous adaptation, provided the battlements of national identity.[20]

For a century and a quarter after the inauguration of the Crown appointment of a Regius professor of modern history, there was no school in Oxford teaching contemporary history to undergraduates. 'The thought of Europe had been from its very beginning profoundly historical, in that the whole body of knowledge was the result of accumulation through the centuries; but this accumulation owed nothing to historical investigation,' as Richard Southern put it. The substance of history was thought to derive from divine revelation rather than from fresh investigation and new criticism. 'History could accumulate and refine, but God and reason alone could guarantee the truth of the whole system.' By 1800, though, the system of biblical chronology had been discredited among many thinking people, and its rejection was complete by 1850. 'The discovery that the fundamental chronology, on which the whole system of a divinely ordered and rationally comprehensible universe had rested, was profoundly untrue, not just in detail, but in its essential framework', struck mortal blows to the Christian order of life. The result, says Southern, was a 'dreadful fall . . . into a vast pit of doubt'. Gladstone, who sat as MP for Oxford University in 1847–65, was one of those who saw the School of Modern History as a means to clamber from that pit. 'The thorough, as opposed to the merely picturesque study of history is a noble, invigorating manly study, especially political and judicial, fitted for, and indispensable to, a free country,' he told Stubbs in 1875. 'It is the truly historical treatment of Christianity, and of all the religious experience of mankind, which . . . will supply under God effectual bulwarks against the rash and violent unbelief, under the honourable titles of physical and metaphysical science, rushing in upon us.'[21]

It was 'Jenky', the Christ Church-trained Prime Minister Lord Liverpool, who appointed Nares to the Regius chair at the prompting of Cyril Jackson in 1813. Nares had entered Christ Church as a commoner a quarter-century earlier, when Lewis Bagot was Dean. His tutors there had, he felt, neglected him. Nevertheless, he was amiable and sedulous enough for the senior members of Merton to elect him to their fellowship in 1788. His pleasantries gained him an entrée at Blenheim Palace, where he excelled in amateur theat-ricals (in which Liverpool had also joined as an undergraduate). In time Nares eloped with a daughter of the Duke of Marlborough. He entered holy orders, and was made incumbent of a parish in Kent where his preaching, as shown by his *Sermons Composed for Country Congregations* (1803), was lively and accessible.[22]

In his Bampton sermons at Oxford in 1805, published as *Views of the Evidences of Christianity at the End of the Pretended Age of Reason*, Nares presented orthodoxy as static and immutable. 'Christianity, issuing perfect and entire from the hands of its Author, will admit of no mutilations, nor any improvement. It is dogmatic; not capable of being advanced with the progress of science, but fixed and immutable.' The Bampton sermons estab-lished Nares's reputation as a clear-headed conservative who thought that, in England at least, events and ideas were tending to the good. He added to his renown by writing two best-selling novels about smart society in Regency England, *Thinks I to Myself* (1811) and *I Says, Says I* (1812).[23]

Nares saw historical books as a branch of 'polite literature'. He denied 'that much in the line of *History* remains to be discovered'. The atrocities of the French revolution assured him that the English were front-runners who did things best. 'England had long ago done for herself what France was now attempting,' Nares wrote of the crisis after 1789, 'and accomplished her point a whole century before France began to assert her liberties.' But, in his reading, the potential benefits of French institutional reform were lost because the cause was urged onwards not by a disciplined party spirit but by the fitful swings of public moods. 'The French revolution . . . had no distinct leader, no Cromwell or Fairfax.' Revolutionary figureheads were actually followers, not institutors, of mass opinion. When demagogues set up the cry of 'the sovereignty of the people' or of 'liberty and equality', wrote Nares, 'nothing could ensue . . . but continual struggles to be uttermost'. As a clergyman of the Church of England, he saw deism and atheism being stoked by revolutionary libertinism: 'the immortality of the soul and the resurrection of the body [were] scouted at, and death pronounced to be an eternal sleep . . . the tree of liberty substituted for the cross, and the goddess of reason elevated above the God of Christians'.[24]

As Regius Professor, Nares's inaugural lecture series in 1816 attracted 124 listeners, which was thought a good number. He then made a bold decision, that his lectures of 1817 would address, in his words, a subject which 'the University had been censur'd for neglecting, and which was particularly mention'd in the warrant of my appointment', namely political economy. This was a reversion to the original objects of the chair, when it had been established ninety years earlier, of providing a well-informed, pragmatic set of graduates who would be useful to the state as officials and legislators. There was scant interest in the 'curious science', as Nares called it, in any Oxford college. The Church of England had no truck with the claims of political economists that self-interest was the propellant and the uniting bond of modern societies. Self-centred people, having no love for anything on earth except themselves, no fear of eternity and no reverence for God, 'set up their own understanding on the throne of a degraded, godless, chance-ridden universe', as the clergy brothers Augustus and Julius Hare wrote in 1827 in opposition to utilitarianism.[25]

None of the treatises and texts of political economy, which had stirred the world outside the university, were available in Oxford bookshops. Nares, though, was determined to master all that was meant by *The Wealth of Nations*, trade, commerce, foreign exchange, taxation, the Sinking Fund, the Poor Laws and the Malthusian *Principle of Population*. He bought the books elsewhere, and pitched himself into the study of them:

> Like all other literary novelties it soon became extremely inter-esting to me. I devour'd book upon book, indoors and out of doors, notwithstanding the damage I might be doing to my eyes. But it was a hard task to make others sensible of what I was about, and the immense amount of knowledge I had to acquire in but a few months. A thousand engagements would interfere. A casual visitor would sometimes rob me of a whole morning; and, being a family man, I could not extricate myself from some annual parties without making a parade of study, which I had ever care-fully avoided.

Yet when, after months of concentrated work, Nares delivered the first of the lectures in his innovative course, there were only eight or nine men in his audience. After this mortification, he secured a commitment to attend his lectures from thirty-seven men, including some eminent tutors and a few noblemen. But undergraduates – even those who complained to him that college teaching was too much like the rote lessons of school and excluded the latitudes of broad knowledge – were so occupied with meeting the requirements of the reformed examination system that they did not have the time or mental energy to attend professorial lectures. College teaching was considered to serve academic purposes better than university occasions. For his last course in 1835, Nares had two listeners. Little wonder that he wished that university regulations empowered profes-sors to compel undergraduate attendance.[26]

Nares relinquished the Regius chair in 1841: his successor Thomas Arnold, Headmaster of Rugby, gave his inaugural lecture in December of that year. The primary concerns of modern history, said Arnold, were 'national identity' and 'national existence'. No useful lessons for the English could be drawn from the period of their subjection to Roman legions. 'Nationally speaking, the history of Caesar's invasion has no more to do with us, than the natural history of the animals which then inhabited our forests. We, this great English nation, whose race and language are now over-running the earth from one end of it to the other . . . were born [in the ninth century] when the white horse of the Saxons had established his dominion from the Tweed to the Tamar.' Arnold maintained that modern history was a progressive and conclusive subject bearing 'marks of the fullness of time, as if there would be no future history beyond it'. It was also a goad to virtue, and the foe of open falsehood. 'History forbids despair,' Arnold said. 'It explains why more has not been done by our forefathers: it shows the difficulties which beset them, rendering success impossible; while it records the greatness of their efforts which we cannot hope to surpass.' The story of the Resurrection of Jesus was, he maintained, the best-attested fact in history.[27]

After Arnold's premature death in 1842, John Cramer was appointed as the ninth holder of the Regius chair. Cramer had been an undergraduate, Student and tutor in Christ Church. One of his tutorial pupils in the 1820s remembered him as 'an elegant-minded man', and twinned him with another Student, Charles Longley, whose ascent from Christ Church ended with his enthronement as Archbishop of Canterbury in 1862: Longley was welcome everywhere as a gentlemanly scholar, and Cramer fell little short of him in amiability. He was Swiss-born, and showed his love of mountains in a study of Hannibal's journey over the Alps. Accounts of ancient Italy, ancient Greece and ancient Asia Minor followed, in which he treated history, geography and cartography as inter-reliant disciplines. In 1831 Cramer became Principal of New Inn Hall. This was a hostel for undergraduates situated between Worcester and Balliol colleges which had no students because Cramer's predecessor, in addition to being Vinerian Professor of Law and a Fellow of All Souls, was the estates manager of the Duke of Marlborough, lived in Woodstock and seldom set foot in New Inn.[28]

Gaisford was appointed Dean of Christ Church in the same year of 1831. He and Cramer soon reached an understanding whereby New Inn received the overflow from Christ Church. Fast-living reprobates from the House and slow-thinking drones, who wanted either more liberty or more patient help than was available from the tutors, and unsuccessful examinees from other colleges, were sent to Cramer at New Inn Hall, which became known as Dull-boys'

College or Try-again Hall. The cooperation between Gaisford and Cramer culminated in the former using the influence of Christ Church to press Robert Peel to appoint Cramer as Regius Professor of Modern History in 1842.[29]

The new professor admitted in his inaugural lecture that he thought of himself as a theologian and as a student of ancient literature rather than any form of modern historian. He also had to contend with the entrenched opinion that modern history was inferior to ancient: John Stuart Mill, for example, maintained that 'the battle of Marathon, even as an event in English history, is more important than the battle of Hastings'. Cramer, realizing that he must make bold claims for his subject, determined to follow Arnold in treating modern history as the study of nationalities. 'It is, above all, the mind, the genius, and character of a people, that we seek to be acquainted with,' he declared. History without a sense of nationhood is 'but an empty shell, a valueless narrative of dry and formal events'. Ancient history was pre-eminently the study of Mediterranean people. The study of northern nationalities and mentalities, together with scrutiny of the traits that put England and Scotland foremost in European industrialization, was proper work for scholars in an age that believed so confidently in progress. 'Ancient History is the wreck of an old world,' declared Cramer in his inaugural lecture. 'Modern History is the world in which we live, the state of things in which we exist, the society in which we move and stir.' The Renaissance, but not medievalism, mattered to him. 'After centuries of barbarism, ignorance, and darkness, a brighter light diffuses itself over the horizon – human reason gradually emancipates itself from the trammels of error and superstition – society wears a new aspect – civilisation, intelligence, and knowledge advance with rapid steps, till we finally arrive at the meridian lustre of the present age, when the arts and sciences have reached their climax.'[30]

Historical studies had the potential to regulate and improve the present and the future. They were 'indispensable', Cramer said, 'to everyone who is desirous of taking his place in society, as a well-informed and educated person'. The Regius chair to which he had been appointed had been founded by the state, in the reign of George I, and not by the university. 'And the reason for this would seem to be, that the State appears to be more directly concerned in the encouragement and promotion of this branch of learning. There is certainly no species of information which is more essentially needed in all the higher departments and functions of government.' For anyone involved in public business or parliamentary debate, 'a ready acquaintance with the transactions of past ages will furnish him with examples and illustrations, which will add strength to his words and authority to his arguments. For these are not to be considered as mere rhetorical embellishments, but as really appealing to sober sense and sound reason.' Particular circumstances may determine the course of particular events, but generally, 'human nature being the same in all ages and countries, the same results may be expected to follow from the same analogous causes'.[31]

After Cramer's death in 1848, the Prime Minister Lord John Russell, who had attended Edinburgh University, appointed Henry Halford Vaughan as his successor. Russell was an anti-clerical, and sought to help a man whose early career had been blighted by his conscientious refusal to seek ordination. Vaughan, indeed, was the first non-clergyman to occupy the Regius chair. He had matriculated at Christ Church in 1829, and was one of five men from the House who obtained first-class honours in Greats in 1833.[32]

Halford Vaughan saw his subject as a coalition of two distinct themes: the formation and disintegration of nation states; and the evolution and durability of communities. 'The whole character of Modern History is due to the fact, that while nations perish, society lives on,' he proposed in his inaugural Regius lecture in 1849. Its practitioners therefore have to comprehend, combine and interpret all the diverse elements that form a society: 'public and household life, religion, moral principles, passions, sentiments, tastes intellectual and physical, social maxims', as well as 'all the modes of suffering, enjoyment, action, capability, sensibility, and power'. History shows national unity 'sometimes as suddenly and violently severed; while, in many of these instances, the social unity survives the shocks, or the principle of natural decay, by which the national unity has been broken up'.[33]

Often the undergraduates who attended Vaughan's Regius lectures were reading Greats rather than engaged in the new School of Law and Modern History. They were, said Charles Conybeare, member

of a dynasty of Christ Church divines, struck by the beauty of
Vaughan's language, 'with the imagination and wide illustration as
well as the philosophical power of mind'. Yet at college level it was
the competent but not outstanding youths, who were incapable of
achieving classical honours, who were drawn by modern history. As
Jowett and Arthur Stanley averred in 1848, 'the stupidest undergraduate in a Livy lecture will brighten . . . if you speak to him of
the revolution in France'.[34]

As one example of Jowett and Stanley's point, Lord Fordwich,
afterwards Earl Cowper, who entered Christ Church in 1851,
admitted that after 'plodding away' at six or seven pages of Plato,
he always grew helplessly bored. 'Not that the old philosopher does
not interest me, for I think some of his ideas rather fine, but the
fact is that I cannot read anything that takes much trouble,' was his
frank if condescending explanation. In college he was reputed to
have 'got through moderations without opening a book', he told his
mother. 'This is, of course, not true, but it proves at least that there
is an advantage in being idle, for people always give one credit for
being idler than one is.' His set of friends admired him for achieving
second-class honours without any apparent working pains. Cowper's
appetite for books of modern history was avid: 'everything connected
with the lives of nations; everything which had reference to human
life and character in every form and shape; the results of success or
failure of the various methods of government'. Revolutionary France
interested him, as it did Jowett's undergraduates bored by Livy, and
he espied 'true Jacobin doctrine' appearing in the 'transient and
factitious majority in the House of Commons'.[35]

It was to accommodate young men like Cowper, and to ward off
outside political interference in the university by those who wanted
a wider curriculum, that a new school was inaugurated in the university in 1853. Goldwin Smith, following his appointment to the Regius
chair of modern history in 1859, described the new faculty as 'a
School of Social Science' which was intended to provide a proper
education for those members of the nobility and gentry who intended
to assume political, official, regional and colonial leadership. It was
to be a version of Starkey's abbey academies or Dean Fell's Christ
Church fit for nineteenth-century needs. Legal studies were included
in the new school at a late stage of its planning for inchoate and

imperfect reasons: law was the weaker partner, and came first in the school's title only because L precedes M in the alphabet. The jurist and historian Frederic Maitland, the Downing Professor of Laws at Cambridge who declined the Regius chair there, was best placed to explain the irreconcilability of his two disciplines. 'What the lawyer wants is authority, the newer the better,' he declared in a lecture of 1888: 'what the historian wants is evidence, the older the better.' The medievalist Horace Round renewed the charge in 1910: 'The lawyer's vision is bounded by his books; the historian goes behind his books, and studies the facts for himself. What is "authority" for the one is absolutely none for the other.'[36]

The historical component of this new school was the beginning of a far-reaching change in the university. It seemed to provide an exit route from the cruel and destructive wrangling which had marred the university in the 1840s. The charges and counter-charges raised by the Tractarians, the deprivations and degradation, the vindictive rancour turned mild and apathetic men into liberal reformers set on emancipating the university from the thrall of regressive, disputatious zealots. The rise of the School of Law and Modern History was a concomitant of the determination of a new generation in the university, in the words of Jowett, 'to reform and emancipate the University, to strike off the fetters of medieval statutes, to set it free from the predominance of ecclesiasticism, recall it to its proper work, and restore it to the nation.'[37]

There were eight entrants for the first examinations in the joint school, and twenty-seven in 1860. Until 1864, the option of transferring to the new school was open only to undergraduates who had already achieved a preliminary pass in classics. Edward Freeman denied that law and modern history were enough alike to hold joint examinations in them: one might as well set an examination in law and hydrostatics, he thought, or in phlebotomy and modern history. Indeed, the distinctions drawn by lawyers between private and public morality were rebarbative to those historians who saw their subject as disclosing moral lessons or inculcating the importance of fulfilling personal and public obligations.

After 1866, undergraduates were permitted to specialize either in law or in modern history. Modern history (defined as beginning with the Fall of Rome and ending in the eighteenth century) became an independent honours degree in 1872. There were thirty-one candidates for law in 1873, and fifty-nine for modern history. By 1900 the School of Modern History was the largest of the Oxford schools. Among Edwardian undergraduates, it was twice as popular as jurisprudence, and ten times more so than mathematics. By its acme in the 1920s over a third of all Oxford undergraduates were reading modern history. This proportion began to fall in the 1930s: about a quarter of undergraduates were modern historians in the final academic year of peacetime; in the post-war university the proportion continued to diminish; by the start of the 1960s the figure was little more than 15 per cent.

Nares and his successors as Regius Professor had been put under new obligations to pay for subordinates to teach modern languages in the university. This stipulation was resented by Vaughan, who decried the study of foreign languages. 'There is no study', he declared, 'which could prove more successful in producing thorough idleness and vacancy of mind, parrot repetition, and sing-song knowledge – to the abeyance and destruction of the intellectual powers, as well as to the loss and paralysis of the outward senses – than our traditional study and idolatry of language.' In truth, Vaughan thought insularity was salubrious in undergraduate life. A few years after the European revolutions of 1848, he expressed relief at how few foreigners, 'not subjects of the English Crown', there were in Oxford. 'National clubs, secret societies, and tumults are little to be feared in a city, whose police is managed by the University, whose students are all the Queen's subjects, who live in the very midst of free and popular institutions, – in a land never visited by war, and a society not pestered by brawls.' Nineteenth-century Oxford contained few foreign undergraduates. 'My generation of students had little chance, and we had certainly no desire, to come into contact with any except of their own nationality,' recalled Lewis Farnell, who matriculated at Exeter College in 1874. It was not until the institution of Rhodes scholarships in 1902 that there was any organized effort to recruit young Germans to the university.[38]

When Vaughan retired from the Regius chair in 1858, Goldwin Smith accepted nomination as his successor despite doubting that modern history was a substantial or systematic subject. He was a bore. His private lectures to the Prince of Wales, who studied for some months at Christ Church in 1859, comprised no more than a terse commentary as he leafed through the pages of William Flaherty's historical epitome *The Annals of England*. His professorial lectures were nicknamed the Catechetical Class, because he did little more than read aloud from Flaherty's *Annals*. Like Vaughan, he mistrusted the teaching of modern languages at university: they were best learnt abroad; 'they do not form a high mental training; they are often possessed in perfection by persons of very low intellectual attainments'. French in particular must be excluded from the curriculum. 'It is not like medieval Latin, a neutral language; its prevalence would render dominant the political and moral ideas of the French nation.' Doubtless its use in the education of women is 'a cause of the inferiority of the female mind'. His sympathies were Teutonic. He saw Germany as the best hope of European civilization because, more than any other nation, it lay under the dominion of the knowledge and ideas on which future progress would be built. Lord Acton, who had mastery of the chief European languages, recognized Goldwin Smith's sincerity, but deplored 'his lax criticism, his superficial acquaintance with foreign countries, his occasional proneness to sacrifice accuracy for the sake of rhetorical effect, his aversion for spiritual things'.[39]

Goldwin Smith presented the veneration of his university as an 'ineradicable and invincible' national sentiment. 'It is the ideal England we have in our heart of hearts; the England of the imagination, the England great in history, the England that might be,' so he felt. 'And of this England, the Ideal Oxford is the crown.' The university did not reciprocate his enthusiasm. Goldwin Smith resigned his Regius chair after eight years and moved to America.[40]

His successor, William Stubbs, was the fifth of the six Christ Church men to hold that office in the nineteenth century. Stubbs had arrived at the House from Ripon Grammar School in 1844, as a disdained servitor (poor scholars who were exempt from accommodation charges and given free meals). Although he took a first in classics, college custom disallowed a former servitor from becoming a senior Student of the House. He was instead elected as a Fellow of Trinity in 1848. 'Handsome, healthy, kindly, courteous, shrewd, frugal, witty, industrious, and business-like, he had all the qualities that help a man to rise in life': so said Frederick York Powell, the final nineteenth-century Christ Church man to be Regius Professor of Modern History. Stubbs took holy orders, and for sixteen years as a country parson he conducted two services a day and delivered 100 sermons a year. He said that he knew every toe of every baby in his Essex parish. Parochial responsibilities shouldered by such men, at a time when they were also committed to scholarly work, gave them sympathetic insights into human character and conduct that were inaccessible to bachelor Fellows who were immured in college rooms. Stubbs's prose was elegant, lithe and exact, without any verbiage, fallacy, platitude or affectation. He had a horror of wasting time, and of people who tried to clutter his retentive memory with banalities and side issues. His greatest work was his *Constitutional History*, published in several volumes in the 1870s: nothing on such a scale had been attempted in England since Gibbon's *Decline and Fall*. 'It is a model of its kind,' York Powell judged. 'Darwin has had no finer monument raised to him than this astonishing record of the natural growth and development of some of the most complicated and important social organisms that have ever arisen among men.'[41]

The essence of modern history, as well as the 'living unity' of the world, derives from Christianity, Stubbs declared in his inaugural lecture as Regius Professor in 1867.

The Church in its spiritual work, the Church in its intellectual work, the Church in its work with the sword, or with the plough, or with the axe; the soul and spirit of all true civilisation, of all true liberty, of all true knowledge; the Church in its work of evil, in the abasement of its divine energies, in the vile fetters of priestcraft, in the blind paroxysms of popular fanaticism, in the strange varying fortunes that allies Ireland with Rome, Scotland with Geneva, setting father against son, and husband against wife.

These were the ruling themes of modern history. Christianity, as represented by the Church of England, was, he said in 1873, 'the tamer of cruel natures, the civilizer of the rude, the cultivator of the waste places, the educator, the guide, and the protector, whose guardianship is the only safeguard of the woman, the child, and the slave against the tyranny of their lord and master'.[42]

Stubbs was gratified when, during his tenure of the Regius chair, the subjects of modern history and law, which he thought were fundamentally different, were separated into two distinct schools. Historians collect new testimony, revise their judgements, take slow decisions and pardon as well as condemn. 'History', he said, 'knows that it can wait for more evidence, and review its older verdicts; it offers an endless series of courts of appeal, and is ever ready to reopen closed cases.' By contrast, lawyers apply case law so as to be swift, determined and irrevocable in their verdicts: in England there was no Court of Appeal until 1875, and no Court of Criminal Appeal until 1907. 'History, unlike law, does not assert its infallibility simply because it must have perfection in decisive action.'[43]

The discipline of modern history had 'the great charm of lucid order', Stubbs said. It imbued a love of truth and justice, and a skill in drawing inferences and fine distinctions. Accordingly, it would tend to produce honest, intelligent politicians, and could provide, he thought, a training in citizenship for an electorate which had been enlarged by the Reform Acts of 1867 and 1884. Historically minded citizens would be better able to spot the impostures of bad leaders and their adulteration of good ideas. Historical knowledge enabled electors to take shrewd views of public events, public duties, politicians and parties 'by accustoming us to trace events to their causes, to trace opinions to their roots, to trace narratives to their authorities, institutions to their germs; it trains us to the pursuit of origins.'[44]

'He was a Tory of the Tories', Henry Scott Holland wrote of Stubbs, 'partly out of a pessimistic despair at the ignorance, the shallowness, the vanity, the folly of all us average men; partly out of his vivid realization of the power of that amazing constitution, the growth and life of which he had been the first to unravel and interpret.' Stubbs divided humankind between the advocates of order and the advocates of change: he thought both groups contain about an equal number of the wise, the stupid and the indifferent, all of whom could learn from the study of modern history to improve the honesty of their thinking. 'The stock of information acquired is only secondary in importance to the habits of judgment formed by the study of it', he insisted. The purpose was to make 'citizens of the great communities', members of 'the civilized world', fit for action. This was to be done not by cramming them with information, but by imparting the right ways of collecting and using factual truth. 'Our students ought not to go into the world a prey to newspaper correspondents: they ought not to go into public life ready to be moulded to the political views of the first clique that may catch hold of them.' He recommended the teaching of history in schools so as to 'raise up a generation who will not only know how to vote, but will bring a judgment, prepared, trained, and in its own sphere exercised and developed, to help them in all the great affairs of life'.[45]

In Stubbs's presentment, medieval history lasted half a millennium until 1500. Thereafter, for some three centuries, so he said in 1880, the ruling idea was the balance of power in Europe. The partition of Poland in 1772 was a world-changing event, which forced the idea of nationality upon Europe. 'The destruction of that kingdom was a precedent for the destruction of any kingdom; the extinction of that nationality . . . awakened an idea of the importance of nationality as a reconstituting idea in reformed society.' The formation of the Hellenic republic in 1822 and the foundation of the Belgian monarchy in 1830 gave material strength to the notion of national self-determination, Stubbs asserted. The reconstruction of Italy on the principles of nationality (1861), of Austria (1867) and of Germany (1871) brought its nineteenth-century apogee.[46]

Stubbs gloried in his own nationality. 'England has always been on the right side in all her foreign wars,' he suggested in one lecture. 'In every European perturbation our country has been on the side of order and freedom.' The English, he added, should be proud that their nation had always kept their treaties 'with a manly fear of all that is dishonest and untrue, and in spite of every reproach that envy and hatred have dictated'. There was in the medieval growth of the English constitution 'little to be ashamed of; little of conspiracy, little of fanaticism, little – as little as there can be in the essential character of a politician – of self-seeking'.[47]

English exceptionalism was an evident truth to Stubbs. 'The cause of freedom in England has been a consistently triumphant and progressive cause, and so has been checked by fewer mistakes and disgraced by fewer crimes than are to be found in the struggles of other nations for freedom,' he explained. 'There were no unlawful means used in the real winning of our liberty: we have no causeless rebellions, no secret assassinations, no going to war for ideas, no sentimental conspiracies, no justifications of means by ends.' The success of English public life in achieving, by the nineteenth century, 'a greater and more widespread purity of political character' was because, said Stubbs, the nation had preferred gradual to sudden, disruptive change. Scholarship had a leading part in achieving this happy state. England was 'the nation of Modern Europe in which the study of History has long most conspicuously flourished'. In consequence it was 'the most successful' nation of the nineteenth century, 'notwithstanding its character for sentiment and its addiction to the Gospel of Force'.[48]

Stubbs's *Historical Introductions to the Rolls Series*, essays collected and arranged after his death by Arthur Hassall of Christ Church, remain a joy to read for their passion, eloquence and maxims. They give both pleasure and a general education. 'All the Plantagenet kings were high-hearted men, rather rebellious against circumstances than subservient to them,' he wrote in an essay on the reign of Henry II.

> But the long pageant shows us uniformly, under so great a variety of individual character, such signs of great gifts and opportunities thrown away, such unscrupulousness in action, such uncontrolled passion, such vast energy and strength wasted on unworthy aims, such constant failure and final disappointment, in spite of constant successes and brilliant achievements, as remind us of the conduct and luck of those unhappy spirits who, through the middle ages, were continually spending superhuman strength in building in a night inaccessible bridges and uninhabitable castles, or purchasing with untold treasures souls that might have been had for nothing, and invariably cheated of their reward.

Three centuries of Angevin kings did not impress him: 'it is with the extinction of the male line of Plantagenet that the social happiness of the English people begins'.[49]

Southern Europe, and its people, had scant appeal for Stubbs. The Mediterranean interested him neither as a sea nor as a cultural influence. His reflexes, allegiances, tastes and pride were those of a northerner. 'Southern Europe owes everything that is vital, sound and good to the influence of the North one way or another exerted upon it,' he averred. Perhaps the homoeroticism underlying the idealizations of such enthusiasts as Walter Pater or John Addington Symonds convinced him that classical antiquity was essentially insalubrious. 'Roman civilisation', he said, 'had except for selfish purposes no power whatever or inclination to extend itself; it was not incompatible with the most debased life, the most tyrannical policy, the most monstrous vices, the most oppressive slavery and servility. It had no root of good in it, it had no religious element.'[50]

Stubbs, like Goldwin Smith, preferred Germanic culture to French. 'The Teutonic is the paternal element in the English race, as shown in physique, in language, in law, and custom,' he maintained. There had been 'a community of interest, sympathy and race, a friendship between England and Germany throughout the middle ages which contrasts very strongly with the inbred hostility between England and France'. Both the German and English races were 'non-aggressive' by nature: 'order and peace are and always have been in their eyes far before conquest: both are successful in colonisation, both are strongly patriotic, both full of independent zeal for freedom'.[51]

By contrast, the spirit of French rulers, and probably of their people, was 'aggressive, unscrupulous, false', Stubbs declared. 'The French kings were probably the very worst set of kings that ever disgraced the name.' Francis I was the pre-eminent in badness among them. All the shreds of nobility and tatters of virtue about him were 'a very sorry sham, a very ragged covering to the mismanagement, misrule, and tyranny that make him the fit representative . . . of the worst dynasty that ever reigned in Europe since the rotten empire of Rome fell to pieces'. The French revolutionary crises of 1830, 1848 and 1870-1 aroused in Stubbs an inextirpable distrust of contemporary France. 'It should be an article of faith for the English to hate the French,' he said. 'You will remember Lord Nelson's three rules of faith and duty: 1. To obey commands without asking the reason why; 2. To look on everyone who spoke ill of the king as an enemy; and 3. To hate every Frenchman as the devil.'[52]

In 1871, when Stubbs had held his Regius chair for half a decade, parliament abolished all religious tests for professorships, fellowships, lay degrees, academic offices and emoluments. By then, the phrase 'accepted religion' was increasingly hollow. Jowett noted in 1874 that before Darwin, Mill, Huxley and Spencer began to dispel notions of a transcendent governing providence, 'people, or at least some people, cared about their souls; now they hardly know if they have souls or not'. In the same year John Morley gave a similar description of the new mental environment. 'In the last century men asked of a belief or of a story, Is it true? We now ask, How did men come to take it for true?' At the undergraduate level, Lewis Farnell suspected that few of his contemporaries at Exeter College held orthodox Christian beliefs. They came from homes where the words of the Holy Writ were accepted without question, but never forgave the hortatory dreariness of chapel services at their boarding schools. At most the majority of them approved the Church of England's performance of good works in an increasingly materialist society. They adopted an outward conformity which Farnell characterized as 'a cautious insincerity and conventionality serving as a camou-flage'.[53]

Many felt that the temper of the university was growing mercenary, secular and ungracious. John Morley, who had been an undergrad-uate at Lincoln College, wrote in 1874 that his *alma mater* presented a rare paradox: 'so much detachment from the world, alongside of the coarsest and fiercest hunt after the grosser prizes of the world'. Henry Parry Liddon, Canon of Christ Church, deplored from the pulpit his university's tendency to become 'more and more a great shop, trading on the tastes of the great British public, abandoning to public prejudices its own best traditions [and] feeling that it cannot trifle with the general tastes of its customer'. By 1889 it seemed to Thorold Rogers, Drummond Professor of Political Economy at All Souls, that colleges had been turned into hotels, 'in which the greatest pains are taken with those guests who are likely to get the college talked about'.[54]

The anxiety that the university was turning into an admixture of hostelry and shop was certainly felt in the leading discussion group of Oxford historians in the 1880s, which named itself the Stubbs Society. Most of the society's members felt that the corrupting power of materialism was making their world gimcrack, mindless, garish, cocksure and defective. Yet Stubbs himself remained an exemplary and grateful Oxonian. 'Please to think of me as of one who . . . tried to do his duty,' he said in his valedictory lecture as Regius Professor. 'Tried to maintain for History its proper place among the studies of Oxford, and to maintain the reputation of Oxford as a nursery of historical study among the academies of Europe; tried and worked hard to do honour to the University, to Christ Church, and to the Colleges, to which he owes, humanly speaking, all that he has and is, and his capacity for doing better.'[55]

PART TWO

CHAPTER 5

Frederick York Powell: Heathen, Anarchist and Jingo

If Jude the Obscure had applied to Christ Church instead of Christminster, and if Frederick York Powell had charge of college admissions, a place would have been found for him. One can imagine Powell, as he was depicted by H. A. L. Fisher of New College, 'joyous, profound, large-hearted, curious of everything, spurning the vulgar things which stand in the path of knowledge', interviewing the stonemason from Wessex, calling him Fawley and finally welcoming him with a hearty laugh and a firm handclasp.[1]

York Powell was never a typical or outright Oxford product. London had stronger claims on him. He was born there in 1850, at 14 Woburn Place, Bloomsbury. His father was a provisions merchant with an office in Mincing Lane. He spent two years boarding at Rugby School, by which time his parents had moved to 8 Lansdowne Terrace, on the brow of Ladbroke Grove in Kensington. When later he went to study in Oxford his family home was 6 Devonshire Place, near the Regent's Park in Marylebone. For two years from 1872, when he was a law student, he lived in his father's next house, 69 Lancaster Gate, north of Hyde Park. This was a notably opulent address: the neighbours included the industrialist Samuel Courtauld, the banker Samuel Montagu, the merchant-shipper Eustratius Ralli, the armaments manufacturer Stuart Rendel and the trader Reuben Sassoon. 'The world of cheerful commonplace and conscious gentility and prosperous density, a full-fed, material, insular world, a world of hideous florid plate and ponderous order and thin conversation': so Henry James characterized the households of Bayswater.[2]

After marrying, York Powell took a house at Stamford Grove West in Upper Clapton. Later, both as a senior Student of Christ Church and as a Regius professor, he lived in the newly built Bedford Park district between Hammersmith and Chiswick, with his wife (until her death in 1888), their daughter and his stepchildren. Only some years after his appointment as Regius Professor of Modern History in 1894 did he finally settle in Oxford. For much of his life the *estaminets* of Soho were his homes-from-home.

Rugby School did not suit York Powell's exuberance. At the age of sixteen he left the control of schoolmasters for a self-educative expedition lasting eighteen months. He toured Europe from Scandinavia to Spain, living in capital cities but also exploring remote provinces. He learnt Swedish, became an expressive speaker of Spanish and acquired a reading knowledge of Catalan and Portuguese. Dialects delighted him. After returning to England in 1868, he studied old French, German and Icelandic while living with an educational coach on the Isle of Wight.

At first York Powell was unwanted in Oxford. In 1868 he sat an entrance examination to enter University College, but the religious doubts which he showed in the divinity paper scared its Master, who forbad his admission. Rejected by Univ., Powell approached George Kitchin, who had charge of the first set of 'unattached' students availing themselves of Oxford's newly inaugurated non-collegiate system. Kitchin replied that he would hold no inquisition on a man's religious beliefs and took him as a non-collegiate student in the new combined School of Law and Modern History. After a year, Kitchin discerned that Powell had 'fine gold in him', and begged Dean Liddell to take him at Christ Church, 'because I knew he would do well by the "House". Liddell liked him and took him, with capital results.' In 1869 Powell began to study law and modern history at Christ Church under the tutorship of Sidney Owen senior, the University Reader in Indian History.[3]

The appointment of a dean of Christ Church was a national event. The choice of Liddell was announced in the House of Commons in 1855, and was greeted by cheers from Liberal MPs. It was a signal of his radical sympathies that he demoted undergraduate noblemen from the high table at dinner in Christ Church hall in 1862 and replaced them with senior Students. The botanist Sir William

Thiselton-Dyer, who had matriculated at Christ Church a year later, recalled 'dull apathy amongst the men and a good deal of sullen discontent'. Peck Quad was in his time, said Thiselton-Dyer, 'a barbarous community dominated by the Duke of Hamilton'. Hamilton had also matriculated in 1863, soon after inheriting his titles at the age of eighteen when his father was killed by a drunken fall in a Paris café. At Christ Church the young duke seemed strong enough to fell an ox with a fist: on Guy Fawkes night of 1865, he and a friend held an archway of the Mitre Hotel against a fighting mob during a town-and-gown riot. His red hair, ruddy complexion, bull neck, brutal speech and free spending intimidated the weak. Cronies admired him for entering an Oxford shop, buying a pound of treacle, instructing the shop assistant to pour the treacle into his hat instead of a jar, clapping the hat on to the head of his victim and then rushing into the street.[4]

As in other large and rich colleges, undergraduates divided themselves into social 'sets' which did not intermingle. Each year's matriculations brought a crop of studious and earnest idealists. These included Edward Talbot (1862), who became a senior Student and the college's tutor in modern history in 1866, Walter Phillimore (1863), who took a double first in classics and in the combined School of Law and Modern History and was then elected to All Souls, and Lord Percy (1865), afterwards seventh Duke of Northumberland, who was happiest when engaged in historical research and archaeology but enough of a scientist to be elected Fellow of the Royal Society and President of the Royal Institution. Talbot, whose subsequent career included the first wardenship of the new Keble College, Oxford in 1869 and enthronement as Bishop of Winchester in 1911, thought that too much of the government of the House had been in Liddell's hands. 'A high-bred gentleman of lofty character,' wrote Talbot, 'a man of unusual artistic sympathy and cultivation, certified to all of us as a great scholar by his work on the Lexicon; but too much aloof and temperamentally too reserved and distant to have much influence with the undergraduates, and not a man to put energy into the religious life of the place.'[5]

In the governing body Liddell was able to quell prolonged discussion by a minatory cough which signalled his impatience. His personal authority enabled him to negotiate an agreement between the senior Students and the Canons whereby the latter agreed to relinquish powers which they had held since the sixteenth-century foundation. The Christ Church, Oxford, Act of 1867 created a unique educational institution in which the Dean presided over a mixed governing body of Canons, most of whom held professorial chairs, and Students, who were less and less likely to have been ordained in the Church of England.

As a churchman Liddell was bland and mistrustful of religious enthusiasm. 'There was a tendency to preach Christ as the perfect English gentleman with a firm loyalty to the Liberal party,' according to Harold Anson, who matriculated at Christ Church in 1886. Broad churchmen of Liddell's type almost appeared to regard the Church of England as a branch of the civil service, said Anson. Their inclination was 'to soft-pedal, if . . . not deny, all those parts of the Gospel which were distasteful to the modern cultured Englishman. Human nature was regarded as a noble and amiable creation of God, and British human nature as being the best of all God's products.' If miracles were not disclaimed, they were often explained in the materialist terms of modern science. Original sin was not emphasized. By the last quarter of the nineteenth century, wrote Anson, 'the ruling tendency in Oxford religion was to reduce the supernatural element in Christianity to its lowest possible terms, and it was with great difficulty that a more solemn and serious view of man's disastrous state could be preached'.[6]

Little of this touched York Powell. By the time he reached Christ Church he professed socialism and agnosticism as his creeds. He was assertive, mutinous and uncompromising in argument, and inclined to a playful perversity of opinions. Kant and Schopenhauer were the only philosophers to interest him. 'I mean', he declared, 'to be as decent a heathen Aryan as I can.' As an avowed Darwinian and anti-clerical, he abhorred waffle about the perfectibility of human nature as much as he did the bleating of philanthropic Christianity. Utilitarian thinkers, sanctimonious meddlers and unsolicited advice irritated him.[7]

Christ Church in the 1870s was 'no doubt the first College in the University', according to Algernon Methuen (né Stedman) of Wadham: indeed, he added, 'the most splendid educational institution in the world'. It was certainly the best possible college for York Powell, as his biographer Oliver Elton explained in 1906:

> Christ Church, the most aristocratic and wealthy, as well as the most orthodox of the colleges, identified more with well-born, well-bred, well-to-do English society than any other foundation. But such a place, curiously, is in some ways as tolerant as any in the world. For one thing, it is itself impregnable in its social and doctrinal ideas, and far beyond compromise; it has none of the uneasiness of the half-believer. Also it looks first of all at personal qualities, not at opinions. It meets tact with tact, and assumes that gentlemen do not say anything to jar on one another's convictions. It was easy to see tact in Powell, to see that he was a gentleman. He himself loved those qualities; had, indeed, the practical weakness of never being able to act long with anyone whom he did not think a gentleman, in the better English or French sense of the term. He felt that a college, in self-preservation, must admit only such persons, and no mere brains or power could compensate in his opinion for want of breeding.

The latitudinarianism of the House was such that it sheltered York Powell for thirty years without him ever attending a service in the cathedral.[8]

Many Christ Church undergraduates, outside of the 'fast set', had pleasantly enquiring minds, and applied themselves to their studies without any ambitions to achieve glory in their examinations. York Powell, though, gained first-class honours in the School of Law and Modern History in 1872. He rejoiced at this award without overvaluing the distinction. 'Fifty short and hasty essays, done under cruel pressure of time, by a young man just of age, as the fruit of a few years' training', were not, he later said, 'a training for any occupation except journalism, where the conditions of the Schools are nightly more or less reproduced'. After his finals, York Powell returned to London, where he studied law and was called to the bar in 1874.[9]

At about the same time it was decided that the recent division into two of Oxford's School of Law and Modern History required the teaching work in Christ Church to be allotted anew. Powell's old tutor, Sidney Owen, recommended him to Liddell for the vacant lectureship in law. Herbert Blunt, Student and philosophy tutor at Christ Church, judged that Powell's law pupils 'were poor material, usually regarding the school as a soft option for the Pass Schools; and I fancy they got something more than they bargained for from Powell – sometimes inspiration, not necessarily on law lines, and reluctantly enough received'. As well as law, Powell prepared candidates for the Indian Civil Service, and lectured on political economy. Liddell and Jowett assured the India Office that residence in university would likely rectify the shortcomings of ICS candidates, who (they said) were often 'men with no or little knowledge of the world, with no knowledge of their fellow-civilians, and (from want of experience) with hardly that courtesy of manner which is . . . necessary in dealing with natives of India'. Although suavity in command was hardly Powell's forte, he provided some remedies sought by Liddell and Jowett. His former pupils sometimes visited him at Christ Church during their ICS furloughs, which suggests affectionate gratitude on their part.[10]

Stephen Paget, who was a Christ Church undergraduate in 1875–8, recalled the college then as 'a very beautiful and magnificent place for a young man to be living in; it was indeed a more pleasant life than words can say; but it was rather too full of good things'. The university's reposeful air of permanence, which came from its hallowed buildings, its fixed customs and its social ease, was nevertheless jarred by the continuous clash of ideas. 'In Oxford, as in the world at large', wrote Andrew Lang (who was a Fellow of Merton in the 1870s), this was 'the age of collapsed opinions'. There had been cleavages of judgement and intentions in the university during the sixteenth and seventeenth centuries, but never before divisions that were so incommensurate and unbridgeable. The welter of riders, gainsays, stipulated reservations, qualifying amendments, conditional endorsements made in college and university meetings created an appearance of constant disaccord. The cavilling produced, as Thomas Fowler lamented at the time of his election as President of Corpus Christi College in 1881, 'the curious, unnatural, spasmodic kind of life we lead in Oxford'.[11]

Mandell Creighton had been one of the examiners when York Powell gained his first in finals, and had found Powell's papers memorable. He renewed contact when Owen brought the young man back to Oxford, and became his mentor there. Creighton's educational maxims doubtless influenced Powell.

The sole use of knowledge is to enable you to distinguish between what is true and what is plausible.

An untrained mind does not see the nature or the limits of the problem.

All the best work has been done by those who with difficulty found time for it in crowded lives.

Only when we are perpetually asking ourselves questions, only when we are struggling to get further and further on, are we really beginning to learn.

All true knowledge contradicts common sense.

The two chief means of teaching are exaggeration and paradox.

It does not so much matter what you do as where you are tending.

The surer I am that I am right, the less I care about getting my own way.

Education consists simply in developing a perpetual curiosity, and education has been a failure when it has led a man to think that he really knows anything at all.

Despite Powell's fervid anti-clericalism, his affection for Creighton never relented.[12]

It was, however, the indefatigable Scandinavian scholar Guðbrandr Vígfússon who proved to be Powell's closest associate. After settling in Oxford, Vígfússon had been helped in the compilation of his great Icelandic dictionary by Dean Liddell, who praised him as a 'capital fellow'. After the dictionary's publication by Oxford University Press in 1874, Powell collaborated with Vígfússon in translating and publishing Icelandic historical sagas and mythic Norse poetry.[13]

York Powell's proficiency in teaching law and political economy at the House was born of his indifference to the subjects. His feelings were too much engaged in history to teach it with lucid calm. When Creighton recommended him for extra work in Trinity College as tutor supervising the teaching of English history and as a lecturer on the War of the Roses, he disappointed expectations. This was despite him considering the fifteenth century to be an 'enchanting' epoch of English and European history. 'Cruelty, dirt, ignorance, and misery, of course, there were in plenty, and no lack of greed and selfishness; but even such hypocrites as Cosimo and Richard of Gloucester were not so vile . . . as the hypocrites of later ages.' Rodrigo Borgia was preferable to Tartufe or Pecksniff, in Powell's view.[14]

The President of Trinity at this time divided his undergraduates into two opposing camps. '(1) the Whites, hard-reading scholars, steady, conscientious men (preferably teetotallers and non-smokers) destined to be clergymen, schoolmasters, writers on Social Reform, philanthropic manufacturers of great municipal activity, or Radical Members of Parliament; (2) the Blacks, hunting men, betting men, frequenters of billiard-rooms, taverns, and houses of ill-fame – the sporting, the low-toned, the lewd, the cynical'. Some Trinity under-graduates, White (we may imagine) more than Black, complained that York Powell's teaching wandered from the syllabus and seemed too haphazard to promise success in examinations. Although three of his Trinity pupils won first-classes, his appointment was not renewed at the end of the year.[15]

York Powell's incapacity in teaching the syllabus was partly the outcome of his contempt for Oxford's examination system. Examination marks were made necessary, he thought, 'like railway tickets and other nuisances, by the dishonesty and stupidity of the minority' who tried to travel free through the university. He despaired of 'the mass of useless "memorizing" and the deliberate "cramming" that chokes and overgrows the time and powers of those who have to teach History in our Universities'. Pass students were unfit for the modern history course, he maintained.

> We have no right to cumber the history schools of any University with a number of worthy persons who have to be pap-taught because they will not or cannot learn properly, and must be forced through their degree without their being able to gain any accession of real knowledge or training of their reasoning powers whatever, or even being able to acquire the sure conviction they should have of their complete ignorance.

Only honours students could meet the challenge of learning 'how to collect and classify facts, how to put down the results of his work in a concise and orderly way with scrupulous exactness, how to judge of the accuracy and judgment of other men's statements . . . how to read a map, how to make a simple diagram, how to draw up a pedigree'. The other requirements of a successful undergraduate in modern history, such as proficiency in palaeography and statistics, were not tasks for the lethargic or the incurious, and still less for rich dunces.[16]

'More than half of our educational troubles are due to *humbug* and *make-believe*,' York Powell declared in 1902.

> We go on doing things we know to be almost useless, we go on teaching persons who do not want to learn, and who sit under us simply because degrees are supposed to mean money, and parents want degrees. We grant degrees to people who are intellectual incapables and turn them loose to humbug others with their supposed attainments. We scrape together large roomfuls of unfit and inapt persons whom we dub 'students'. We refrain from weeding out what sportsmen call the 'crocks' under our training, the worst of the worst, because we are afraid of losing fees . . . We are terribly afraid of making people pay properly for education, so we tax imbeciles and cumber ourselves with the elaborate, cumbrous, and pretentious *teaching of unteachables*, in order to retain a few rays of honesty to cloak our naked and shivering consciences.

Young men and women should not be allowed to matriculate at any university unless they could read fluently in at least two languages other than their native speech, and could write to dictation in those languages, and speak them with decent pronunciation. He wanted undergraduates in the School of Modern History to know elementary facts of geology and geography, and to have visited famous sights in the British Isles. 'A noble building, a mountain range, a great seaport are within the reach of almost every boy or girl.'[17]

The ecclesiastical historian and political biographer William Stephens deplored the quality of mid-nineteenth-century histories written for the young: 'These wretched little compilations, dry lifeless epitomes, excluding everything which could excite enthusiasm for what was grand, or noble, or poetical'. One of the few exceptions was York Powell's *History of England from the Earliest Times to the Death of Henry VIII* (1885), which was commissioned by Creighton in his role as general editor of a series of history books for schools. It was, together with Powell's *Early England up to the Norman Conquest* (1876), his only substantial piece of historical writing. Neither of them entailed any archival research or delving in primary documentation. Both of them provided an eager, vivid narrative modelled on those of the Viking sagas and studded with arresting character sketches. Henry I, so York Powell told his readers,

> had a comely face, dark curly hair, a high brow, and large eyes; he was not tall but strongly built. His voice, like his father's, wonderfully deep and strong. A good man of business, wise in planning, and cautious and patient in carrying out his designs, fond of learning (whence his nickname Beauclerc) and with a taste for art, but selfish, hard-hearted, and grasping; Henry's greatest title to our praise lies in the stern strength of his rule.

There is gusto in *Early England* when Powell describes diet and customs, and makes excursions into the styles of language, architecture and clothes. The book's vivacity 'raises it far above the crowd of bread-winning and often mind-destroying manuals that flood the class-room', wrote Oliver Elton. When offering moral judgements, 'he does not mince matters, or spare epithets, but he inclines to find counterpoising virtues, to see value in the net historic effects of a character that has many admitted blemishes, and in general to trace a total drift towards progress and goodness in phenomena that at first might seem merely evil'.[18]

It was Liddell who ensured Powell's election as a Student of Christ Church in 1884. 'One is well paid to teach people who don't want to learn,' Powell told W. P. Ker of All Souls in 1889. For Liddell, as 'a just man and kindly, and a good scholar, and a handsome gentleman', he felt admiration and gratitude. But in Ker he found a kindred spirit. Both of them delighted in the sagas of Iceland, in the earthiness of manual workers and in rough seas. 'Sociability and *hilaratis* – a virtue he held in supreme esteem – were the dominant notes,' friends said of Ker, as they might equally have written of Powell. Ker's departure from Oxford to become Professor of English Literature and History at Cardiff in 1883 was marked by a farewell dinner which resulted in the launch of a new Oxford institution: the dining club known as The Club. York Powell was one of its founding members, along with such modern historians as H. A. L. Fisher, C. R. L. Fletcher of Magdalen, Arthur Hassall of Christ Church, Richard ('Dickie') Lodge of Brasenose and A. L. Smith of Balliol. Another founding member, Lancelot Phelps of Oriel, remembered Powell's paradoxes, Ker's banter and Smith's epigrams enhancing the gaiety of their dinners. In the 1880s they were young, vigorous and eager, said Phelps, 'untainted by research, devoted to our colleges'.[19]

In the House common room after dinner, York Powell yielded the primary place to Henry Parry Liddon. Liddon, as Powell remembered, 'was a fine talker, full of humour and observation, an excellent mimic, a maker of beautiful and fine-coloured phrases, a delightful debater'. Charles Dodgson ('Lewis Carroll') never let the talk flag in the common room: he wove fantastic paradoxes, sparred on theological or philosophical questions and set puzzles; but his manners were abrupt and disconcerting, and he could be unlikeable in his behaviour. Often, after the common room, Powell worked in his rooms until after midnight, then prowled the college to find someone else awake. Claude Blagden, who was elected as a Student in 1895, recalled him yarning until three in the morning, smoking his pipe, laughing and coughing, and discussing every subject in heaven and earth, from the prophets to county cricketers.[20]

York Powell was unpunctual, dilatory and shambolic, and loved novelty. When in London, he loitered in Soho, where he talked, gesticulated, drank and smoked with political refugees drawn from everywhere between France and Armenia. 'Isn't this ripping!' he exclaimed on entering a Soho café full of foreign exiles hailing him, in a babel of accents, as their friend. He knew Kropotkin and sundry nihilists. The men with the look of cut-throats, whom he brought to dine at high table on Sunday nights were known to Dodgson as 'Powell's assassins'.[21]

York Powell preferred gipsies, prize fighters and old salts to pen-pushers. In the Kentish fishing village of Sandgate, near

Folkestone, he delighted in the company of two old men whom he had known since he was two years old: an octogenarian fisherman and a septuagenarian blind fiddler. 'They tell me tales of the old world, before the flood of railway, steam, electrics, nerves, &c; such wise old views of life, such patience and content and cheery constancy.' Another boon companion was William Hines, an Oxford chimney sweep and herbalist, who was known as a radical orator on the village greens of Oxfordshire and who compiled a penny garland of poetry entitled *Labour Songs for the Use of Working Men and Women*. York Powell thought it was far better to be a good fisherman or a good chimney sweep than to be an intellectual. He opened wide his arms, said his Irish artist friend John Butler Yeats, and hugged great armfuls of happiness. William Butler Yeats included two jaunty poems by his father's friend in *The Oxford Book of Modern Verse* of 1936.[22]

Books were assimilated by York Powell at astounding speed. He read them a page at a time, not by the line or by the word, and could find the heart of a book walking between the college library and the Meadow Building. Venetian treatises on statecraft were read alongside lurid weekly magazines for juveniles. His interests were too promiscuous to have any coherent outcome, and his vast accumulated knowledge was shown only fitfully. Lewis Farnell of Exeter revelled in his company: 'The whole world of great literature was a treasure-house for him to ransack; and he flung his nets too widely to become a severe specialist: and as all such literature from Homer downwards was warm and alive and modern for him, there could be no arid or pedantic touch in his work.'[23]

York Powell took special pupils, such as William Lock Mellersh, who went to Oxford in 1891 on the family understanding that he was destined for the law, but read Mods and Greats. Powell's advice, as recorded by Lock Mellersh, gives the flavour of the tutorials:

> Ask questions everywhere, and put the results down as notes at once: no knowledge is useless.
> Do not flatter poor people: point out to them the fact.
> In the present age, what Gladstone calls the 'dreadful military spirit' is not nearly so harmful as the 'love of Mammon'.
> Keep out of theological disputes: all *decent* people have practically the same religion.

As regards life, there are two things that history shows: eventually the most complex forms in nature die out; and, the more civilized nations become, the greater is their tendency to lessen the number of children.

Every man ought to marry, because he is not properly educated until he is married.

Keep up your interest in natural history, antiquities, and music; and mix with other people who take an interest in such things: they are always the nicest class of persons.

(advice as a solicitor) A closed mouth, but an open mind and face; make others talk.

Help poor clients by persuading them not to go to law.[24]

In 1894 the Regius Professor of Modern History, Froude, died. The Prime Minister, Lord Rosebery, had matriculated at Christ Church in 1866, but had left before taking a degree. Someone told him of York Powell, to whom he wrote with an offer of the Regius chair. The envelope had an official frank, was mistaken by Powell as an income-tax demand and put behind a clock or in a boot, along with tradesmen's bills, and not opened for a fortnight. 'Everyone knew and liked York Powell, but the conception of him as even the theoretical head of the History School was difficult,' Charles Oman recalled. 'A burly, bearded, athletic man, always in a blue serge jacket, a low collar with a wisp of black tie, and with a briar pipe, he looked like the captain of a coasting steamer. No one would have taken him for a don.' Yet, by the caprice of Lord Rosebery, a Regius professor of modern history was what York Powell incongruously became.[25]

His comments on his predecessors in the Regius chair show both his aspirations and his aversions. In the afterlife, in which he disbelieved, he imagined Freeman with Stubbs in a quiet arbour on a delectable mountainside; but Froude would be confined with journalist scribblers in 'a kind of Eternal Hellfire Club, where the men drink and sneer at each other and tell old stories and quarrel'. Froude's 'demon of inaccuracy' shocked Powell, whose reverence for truthfulness was shown in his tribute to Freeman on the latter's death in 1892. 'His sharp, Dantesque scorn of shams, of lying, of sophistry and humbug, was instant and outspoken, and naturally bitterly resented by those he detected and gibbeted. But there was no bitterness in his real nature' – this was true of Powell too – 'and his humour, which was as spontaneous and as naïve as that of a child, often gave point and edge to a remark which from other lips would have fallen harmless, unsteeled, and ineffective.'[26]

Holders of the Regius and Chichele chairs in modern history strive to impress in their inaugural lectures. Never again, or not until their valedictory lectures, will they be able to command such a large and influential audience. Not so York Powell, whose incoherent blurts in his inaugural Regius lecture petered out after thirty minutes. Undergraduates found him the most ramshackle lecturer in Oxford. He drew untidily from his stores of knowledge, dived into intricate and unimportant details, rattled onwards at speed, but occasionally faltered with nervous hesitancy. Nevertheless, the onrush of facts, hypotheses and quotations with which he showered his audiences was mostly in support of a definite line of argument. 'His lectures on English place-names, on the history contained in Anglo-Saxon law terms, on Danish military terms, were full of freshness,' recalled Sir Owen Edwards, who was an undergraduate in the mid-1880s and afterwards tutor in history at Lincoln College. 'He not only made history intensely interesting, but he made the search for truth more interesting still. He very rarely criticized any other historian, but he opened our eyes to material which was very destructive to nearly everything we had read before.' Historical figures were judged by the standards of their own time, and not according to modern ideas. 'His blazing indignation against oppression, political or intellectual or social or religious, and his manly defence of the despised, brought occasional bursts of eloquence into his lectures,' Edwards recalled.[27]

H. A. L. Fisher, newly elected to a classical fellowship at New College and inclined to take up modern history on the side, befriended Powell in 1889. 'I used to pay regular weekly visits to those wonderful rooms in the Meadow Building at Christ Church, with their stacks of folios and quartos and octavos and duodecimos, and their delightful litter of miscellaneous curiosities: and here Powell would . . . rarely let me escape without an armful of volumes (generally French or Italian medieval literature) taken down from the shelves.' Fisher, like Owen Edwards, found York Powell's lectures replete with information but formless and desultory.

I heard him lecture in one term on the opening of Japan, on the French Commune, and on the Seven Weeks' War. He talked from a few notes, abundantly enough, but with a hurried, nervous movement, and without any clear plan. His material was splendid; his views fresh and unconventional; there were fine, picturesque touches, and gleams of humour, and many keen sayings; but it was all very tantalizing. With a little more arrangement, a little more concession to the common art of exposition, with a little thinning out of the small facts, and a little more insistence on the large ones, what lectures these might have been! As it was, they just failed to be effective, unlike his talk, which never failed.

Undergraduate audiences wanted lecturers to expound first principles, to offer plausible generalizations, to fix adhesive labels and to settle questions: York Powell would give none of this. Indeed, during the nine years that he held his chair, until his death in 1904, he neither published a major book nor mustered young researchers in his train.[28]

Every Thursday evening, as Regius Professor, York Powell was at home to any undergraduate who chose to visit his college rooms. He talked in his rich, deep voice with a hummingbird rapidity on a multitude of subjects: the prize ring, Rabelais, fencing, Dante, soldiering, Greek tragedies, Elizabethan verse, methods of enamelling, brigandage, folklore, Thomas Cromwell, the genius of music-hall artists, Japanese prints, Indian warfare, Persian literature or the latest Portuguese novel of José Maria Eça de Queirós. Other people's talk was emboldened by his oaths and exclamations and sonorous, volleying laughter.[29]

Undergraduates who were in scrapes with women or creditors went clamouring to York Powell for advice. Poets seeking publishers, portrait artists seeking sitters, beggars wanting money and shy scholars needing jobs all consulted him. Such visitors distracted him from scholarly work. 'I can't help thinking of Powell as a kind of floating sympathy,' wrote Sir Walter Raleigh. 'Writing was not his game. He lived too much in the impressions of the passing hour to be able to concentrate his imagination.'[30]

Powell preferred anonymity to fame. 'He had the passion for obscurity, as others have that for advertisement,' Oliver Elton found.

'He printed his best things in penny papers, without his name, often not even seeing what was printed, or in limited issues of private editions or rare magazines that soon perished.' Sometimes he did not bother to send his manuscripts to a printer, but abandoned them in a cupboard or drawer. 'One of his deeper instincts was certainly to distrust the life that is staked upon reading or writing books or winning glory for them. He thought he knew too much about books to suppose that they were worth all that.'[31]

York Powell was on good terms with all of the three Deans of his time, Liddell, Paget and Strong. Paget's estimate of him is worth extensive quotation – not least for his depiction of his college as a sanctuary for precious freedoms. 'There are', Paget wrote, 'large tracts of society, old and middle-aged and young, earnestly bent on becoming as conventional as possible. But still there are some sheltered spots, unswept by the dry winds of publicity and success, in which a real human being can live his life and be himself.' Oxford college traditions, with Christ Church foremost among those colleges, said Dean Paget, arouse 'even in the most progressive heart . . . a subliminal conservatism' because they provide 'the liberty in which the rich and deep and manifold diversity of character comes out'. In these havens from a brash and busy world, 'it is still quite possible to be unlike other people; to cherish one's own tastes, to serve one's friends in every rank of life, to look at all things with a frank, fresh eye, to think out one's own thoughts, to make up one's own mind'. This was what the word 'liberty' meant to Dean Paget. 'In such liberty,' he wrote, 'York Powell lived and worked, and was as unlike most men as any man whom I have known.'[32]

The timidity of university appointments and college elections was blamed by York Powell on clerical influence. The clergy love mediocrity, he said, 'electroplated mediocrity, so safe, so easy to work with, so respectable, till the gilt wears off'. They were at one with the rest of the English, he said, 'a stupid people', and too easily satisfied by the 'middling well'. Stubbs had advised him that serving on committees taught the dynamic of institutions better than any book. But he was too uncooperative for group deliberations, too anarchic to organize people and too unorderly to frame regulations. He thought the committee intrigues that absorbed so many university colleagues were monastic in their triviality.[33]

York Powell put less care into his university lectures than into his addresses to working-class provincial audiences. In 1902–3, when he knew his health was failing, he took uncharacteristic care in preparing two long discourses which give, in rich amplitude, his historical credo. Modern historical method, when well conducted, 'collects and sifts facts, gets them down as correctly as it can, classifies them, and then, making hypotheses, tests and tries these till it arrives at conclusions that stand every test and trial it can apply'. Fine writing, higher gossip, amusing narratives and ingenious parables have no part in the subject. Modern history never searches for ethical pointers or moral uplift: it is a ruthless pursuit of truth, which never heeds irrelevance. 'Remember that bad history, prejudice, false witness as to past and present facts, delusions of the most mischievous and far-reaching kind, can only be properly met and destroyed by the historian.' He deplored historians like Treitschke or Thiers who misused their material as a source for partisan or sectarian briefings on contemporary issues. 'For the historian there is but one goal, one test, one point of honour – the truth, the whole truth, and nothing but the truth – the truth, if need be . . . against the world.'[34]

History is not a science, for it does not rely upon the test results of controlled experiments. But many late nineteenth-century scholars aspired to what they called 'scientific history', and York Powell ranked Charles Darwin as the greatest scientific English historian. Darwin's magnitude lay, he said, in enabling historians to realize that healthy institutions and nationalities are capable of evolving in order to survive, and that weak, sickening powers are not. The savant Charles Bonnier, who often visited York Powell in Christ Church, honoured him as a vestige of the era of Darwin and Huxley. Huxley had urged that history 'ought to be taught in a new fashion, so as to make the meaning of it as a process of evolution – intelligible to the young'. York Powell agreed with this, and likewise with Huxley's injunction that the very air breathed in universities 'should be charged with that enthusiasm for truth, that fanaticism of veracity, which is a greater possession than much learning; a nobler gift than the power of increasing knowledge'.[35]

Second to Darwin stood Stubbs, whose *Constitutional History* was not only an admirable textbook, but (in Powell's view) one of the best examples of the process of evolution ever worked out. He agreed with Stubbs's opinion, as expressed in 1889, that if people studied modern history and reflected more carefully about its lessons 'we should not care so much for the voice of the press, or the voice of the people'. The subject teaches 'temperance in estimating character, and even in estimating the curve of developing progress'. It impresses on its pupils that 'the evil is always mixed with the good in human affairs; that no school or party or leader was ever so entirely in the right that to oppose him was an infallible proof of falsehood or insanity or idiocy'. Stubbs had convinced him of the necessity of suspending judgement on many matters, 'not to make us sceptical, but first to make us tolerant, and then to make us hopeful'.[36]

Adam Smith was ranked by Powell alongside Stubbs. Henry Mayhew's *London Labour and the London Poor* (1851), Charles Booth's *Life and Labour of the People in London* (1889–91) and Seebohm Rowntree's study of poverty in York (1901) were admired for amassing and interpreting a plethora of facts. The epidemiologist, statistician and pioneer social scientist William Farr taught English historians and anthropologists how to use statistics, said Powell, and thus did 'more to advance History than all the descriptive and brilliant describers who have been content with aiming at rhetorical distinction and the popular applause of the general public'. He ranked Balzac among the finest nineteenth-century French historians. 'He alone perceived the dangers which commercial greed and shameless speculation and selfish dynastic dreams were to bring upon the most artistic and most conservative nation in Europe – a nation which most needs, if it can, to respect its own high ideals, and which is ever more ready to forgive a magnificent failure than a sordid success.'[37]

Commercialism, speculation and ostentation were loathsome to York Powell. He thought that rich people were 'disgusting fools' because few of them knew how to amuse themselves or take pleasure in life. 'Race-hate is largely a creation of cherished historic sentiments maintained by ignorance long after the conditions on which it is supposed to rest have departed,' he said in 1903. Nevertheless, he had a savage prejudice against Jews, plutocrats and especially the Jewish plutocrats who were his father's neighbours in Lancaster Gate. Anti-Semitism pervades his writings.[38]

His antipathy to capitalism is evident in his praise of the Christ Church man whom he valued above all others, John Ruskin. 'He was never tired of proclaiming that the grime and pretence and squalor, all the dull, stupid, vulgar horror of the modern city, were the results above all of ignorance and greed and lack of truth,' Powell wrote. 'He was not willing to tell working-men that they are wise in matters of which they are ignorant, honest when he knew that they are too often lazy and stupid, fine fellows when they are obviously, too many of them, more drunken, brutal, and dirty than they need be.' Ruskin's war against the philistines, his protests against the mindless compulsion to production and profit, his indictment of the destructive effects of materialism won Powell's fealty. 'He was not content to live meanly or think meanly or act meanly,' Powell said. Instead, he was implacable in his insistence that 'the headlong national pursuit of riches' could only lead 'to the reckless damage of body and soul, and to the callous and wanton injury of every beautiful place and beautiful thing in these islands'.[39]

York Powell supported Irish Home Rule in accordance with his general belief in the liberalizing and liberating effects of nationalism. 'I would willingly see much forgotten in Ireland that Irishmen choose to remember: old feuds, old prejudices, old lies,' he wrote in 1899. It dismayed him that the Irish so easily forgot what was most valuable for them to remember: 'the cradle song of their mothers, the hymns their grandmothers sang, the wise, quaint talk of their elders, the joyous verse and the sad mourning verse of their own poets, and the whole fabric of their folk-lore, their own names, and the names of the hills and rivers and rocks and woods that are so dear to them'.[40]

Bourgeois politicians, utilitarian radicals and factory-owning MPs were anathema to York Powell. He preferred noblemen and workers to people who sat at desks. Yet mid-century prime ministers drawn from the nobility often disappointed him. He found Lord John Russell, for example,

a nimble-witted man of little real knowledge or ability, full of restless, meddlesome activity, untrustworthy and fond of intrigue, inflated with self-confidence, and unabashed by repeated failure; ineradicably convinced of his own wisdom and tact; [he] was a mere politician, with the ordinary views of the Whigs, with whom he had a hereditary connexion. He maintained his position by his cunning and self-assertion, and, like other mediocrities, profited by the failings of better, wiser, and stronger men. His impudent courage from time to time gained him the half-amused encouragement of the public, but no one save himself ever seriously believed in him. He is by far the meanest figure among English Ministers of this century.

York Powell was less damning of Lord Aberdeen than of Russell, but hardly flattering: 'one of those well-meaning, highly moral, indecisive, gullible, and unobservant gentlemen who may manage to pass through life respectably without great catastrophe, but are positively dangerous in any position of trust or command, for they may awake to their own imbecility at the wrong moment and drift rudderless to ruin.'[41]

York Powell had low expectations of the extensions of parliamentary suffrage. 'Democracy is no heaven-born institution. There is no right divine about it.' The remedies promised by universal suffrage were likely to disappoint. 'If this country is not healthier, stronger, wiser, happier, and better off in the highest sense under a democracy than it was under an oligarchy, democracy will have failed, and some other plan of government will be tried.' He knew where the greatest perils lay. 'The greatest enemy of the democracy is the lie-maker, the flatterer, and the person who tries to persuade the voter that dishonesty is not always the worst policy, and that a bit of boodle for himself cannot hurt him or anyone else.' Populism, he understood, was more erratic, and therefore potentially more destructive and inhumane, than oligarchy. 'It is worse and more unpleasant and more dangerous to be ruled by many fools than by one fool or a few fools. The tyranny of an ignorant and cowardly mob is a worse tyranny than the tyranny of an ignorant and cowardly clique.'[42]

Yet, despite his contempt for surly, uninformed, obtuse opinions, York Powell became a jingo after the outbreak of the war in South Africa in 1899. The aggression of populist patriotism pleased him by its antagonism to settled and complacent authority. It is as if he saw jingoism as an English brand of nihilism that might shake apart the stable order. As a supporter of social and economic disruption

York Powell became, after Joseph Chamberlain launched his protectionist campaign in 1903, President of the Oxford branch of the Tariff Reform League, although a few years earlier he would have been disgusted by its business jargon. The irresponsibility of York Powell's espousal of disruptive populism is almost unforgivable, given his insistence that 'if there is one thing the study of history shows to be certain, it is *that an ignorant democracy cannot last long*'.[43]

CHAPTER 6

Arthur Hassall: The History Ring

'We pursue culture in a manly spirit,' was the motto for the University of Oxford that was suggested by William Courthope, who was elected Professor of Poetry weeks after Oscar Wilde's trial in 1895. Godfrey Benson (later Lord Charnwood), who had got a first in Greats at Balliol in 1887 and lectured there for a few years before his election to parliament in 1892, wrote approvingly of the two ancient English universities as having 'the supreme aim, consciously pursued by the governing powers, of helping nice boys to grow into good and useful men'. George Gordon, the President of Magdalen, who was one of Courthope's successors in the chair of poetry, said of Charles Fisher, Censor of Christ Church, after he was killed at the battle of Jutland: 'We lighted our little rushlights at his torch, and when we felt womanish and academic, we went to him for a great breath of manliness.'[1]

Arthur Hassall, who was appointed to succeed Sidney Owen senior as tutor in modern history at Christ Church in 1883, and elected as a Senior Student in 1884, ran on the same lines as Courthope, Benson and Fisher. He taught modern history at the House for forty years; he helped nice boys to turn into useful men; he gave friendly and interesting tutorials to women undergraduates; he shrank from anything academic; his life's work was the promotion of cultured gentlemanliness.

Hassall, like York Powell and in the next generation Keith Feiling, came from the class that prospered from buying and selling. He was born in 1853, just across the River Mersey from Liverpool, at Bebington in Cheshire. His father Henry Burton Hassall was a Liverpool share-broker who died in 1883 leaving an estate valued at the considerable sum of £35,685. The family were settled during

Hassall's boyhood on the Wirral peninsula: first in a spacious villa named Mount Pleasant, on Sea View Road in Liscard; later in a similar house called 'Powyke', in the village of Spital.

In 1868 Hassall followed his elder brother to board at Uppingham in Rutland, where an earnest, energetic headmaster, Edward Thring, had remade a fusty provincial grammar school into a thriving public school. Thring believed that a teacher should give equal attention in class to pupils, regardless of whether they were clever, ordinary or dull; ability was latent in every child. He deplored social Darwinism, or undue rewarding of winners. 'The appeal to success, Prizes, and Prize-winning, bids fair to be the watchword of the day,' he wrote in 1883. 'But what does this do for the majority, for the non-competing crowd; who nevertheless do not politely die off, and make room; and cannot, through modern squeamishness, be killed off, and buried?' The Uppingham model of education served Hassall well, and was adapted by him for use in Oxford.[2]

'The Public School system is the greatest thing in England, not even excepting the House of Commons,' Gladstone told the break-fasting Fellows of All Souls in 1890 – giving three slaps of his hand on the table for emphasis. He was saying something tremendous. The public schools and by extension the colleges of Oxford and Cambridge had overthrown the old hierarchical scaffolding by which men climbed and held on to power. The world of family connections and local allegiances, which had determined political prospects, ministerial and official appointments and social groupings, the intricately ramified set of genealogical, social and geographic associations which Sir Lewis Namier and his acolytes later traced for the eighteenth century, was being dismantled by the 1870s. The new fealty of male friendships was substituted for it. Cooperation in public work, recruitment for positions of responsibility, political alliances, social aspirations: all these derived from networks of affection and affinity, sometimes developed in boarding schools, and often in the collegiate households of Oxford and Cambridge. Dons refashioned their colleges into communities in which the junior members were instilled with an ethos which was every bit as enveloping as in boarding schools. 'The virtue of a college education consists not so much in what the college has to teach,' wrote Edward Dicey in 1872, as in 'that peculiar *esprit de corps* which membership of a college engenders.'[3]

Neither home influences nor Church teaching could vie with the impact of peer pressure from fellow pupils and the public spirited-ness of a new generation of dons. Schools and colleges sought to give meaning and purpose to the lives of their undergraduates. In the process they enlisted and trained a new governing cadre that made England the most rationally administered European state, with the most stable and incorruptible bureaucracy, until the twenty-first century.

It was Thring who made a modern historian of Hassall during his five years at Uppingham. He saw that many boys, who had no aptitude for studying ancient Greek and Latin literature, enjoyed learning history. He fed their imaginations, broadened their minds and enriched their articulacy by setting them to read Mommsen's *History of Rome* or Motley's *Rise of the Dutch Republic*, Macaulay's essays on Clive of India and Warren Hastings, and Charlotte Yonge's *Cameos of English History*. Primed by the lessons of his Uppingham years, Hassall matriculated at Trinity College, Oxford in 1873, and was later elected as a history exhibitioner there.

The President of Trinity in Hassall's time was 'Sammy' Wayte, who presided over a contented, united college which was agreeably free of a strenuous competitive spirit. Randall Davidson, future Archbishop of Canterbury, who had been a Trinity undergraduate a few years before Hassall, described Wayte as short, plump, ugly and stuttering, with a head like a tadpole's and the gait of a crab. Trinity's reputation rose during Wayte's presidency, for he managed college business with harmonious efficiency. It was a sociable college, standing at the upper end of both examination lists and boat races on the river.[4]

Trinity did not have a tutor or lecturer capable of teaching more than a smattering of the modern history course. Probably, like Davidson, Hassall was sent for teaching to Mandell Creighton of Merton, and to Hereford George of New College. The two men were apt and shrewd in their lessons, but took different directions in their careers. Creighton accepted a church living in Northumberland so as to obtain the liberating isolation, free from exigent college duties, which enabled him to begin the research, thought and writing that resulted in his great *History of the Papacy in the Period of the Reformation*. George, though, held to his college responsibilities, and never aspired to originality. He produced synopses of other scholars' work, such as *Battles of English History*, and handbooks for examinees, such as *Genealogical Tables Illustrative of Modern History*. He neither immersed himself in archival research nor regarded his fellowship, as previous generations had done, as a time-filler before preferment to a parish. Hassall followed the example of George.

In 1877 Hassall won first-class honours in modern history. He was, too, in that same year, one of the Oxford runners in the three-mile race against Cambridge. This early athletic prowess and his lifelong love of sports brought him, according to his obituary in *The Times*, into 'easy touch with all manner of men of all ages in the University and in the county'. Thring had extolled the high value of individual influence, exerted by mind touching mind, and this became the basis of Hassall's tutorial life too. He talked of outdoors life, as well as of books and current affairs, to reach his pupils.[5]

Hassall's permanent Oxford life began in 1880 when he was appointed historical lecturer at Keble College, where the Christ Church man Edward Talbot had been Warden since 1870. He was promoted to the post of tutor in history at Keble in 1881, but was not elected to fellowship. Perhaps it was evident that he was not a natural fit for this new foundation. Its raw red bricks, wrote Stephen Paget, who matriculated at Christ Church in 1874, 'had a strange, uncomfortable air; they hardly seemed to belong to Oxford'. When Raymond Asquith returned from a visit to Cambridge in the 1890s, he was asked by a Balliol college servant, 'What sort of a place is it? Something in the Keble line?'[6]

The college had been founded to house undergraduates who needed to live economically. Its combination of sober, frugal living with strict Church of England principles meant that it received more applicants than it could admit. Yet, despite its undergraduate numbers, few first-class honours went to Keble men. The college did not produce national leaders until the Labour parliamentarians Andrew Adonis and Ed Balls in the 1980s. In Hassall's time, its undergraduates were shackled by multiple rules. Their rooms, as at the women's college of Girton in Cambridge, were arranged on corridors rather than staircases, so that the college's domestic staff could monitor all visitors, and preserve virginities. Undergraduates were required to eat all their meals together in hall, and were forbidden to bring groceries and alcohol into college from outside. Such regulations hindered them from making friends in other colleges, and prevented them from holding the pleasant breakfast or lunch parties known elsewhere. Keble was therefore insular: its junior members were forced to see more of their corridor neighbours than they might wish. Members of other colleges regarded Keble at best 'with quiet condescension', at worst 'with dislike and even contempt'. Its code of manners was ungentlemanly.[7]

Although grateful for his employment at Keble, its high-minded stinting was not to Hassall's taste. Moreover, coming from a moneyed Liverpool family and from a modern Midlands school, he appreciated the resolve of the universities to instil the values, manners and bearing of gentlemen in their undergraduates. 'It is well to be a gentleman, it is well to have a cultivated intellect, a delicate taste, a candid, equitable, dispassionate mind, a noble and courteous bearing,' Newman had written in the year before Hassall's birth. The inculcation of these gentlemanly traits was the object and the ideal of a university. Competitive examinations, the abolition of religious tests and other changes did not alter the truth of Newman's declaration for most Oxford men. 'The quality of a gentleman is so very fine a thing,' Gerard Manley Hopkins told Robert Bridges in 1883. 'If the English race had done nothing else, yet if they left the world the notion of a gentleman, they would have done a great service to mankind.'[8]

There were not enough of such notions at Keble to please Hassall. In 1883 he left the modern history tutorship there for that at Christ Church, where he was elected as a Student in the following year. It is unclear why the House plumped for an outsider rather than a gremial (someone who had been an undergraduate there); but Liddell's policy was perpetuated by the subsequent Deans, Strong and White, in their recruitment of Feiling, Masterman and Harrod in 1911–22.

Although Hassall came to Christ Church in Liddell's time, he reached his ascendancy in the college after Francis Paget succeeded Liddell as Dean in 1892. 'There was no limit to Frank Paget's capacity of keeping up the game,' Henry Scott Holland recalled. 'He had the wit that revels in surprises. He could let himself go.' To a junior member of the college, Henry Nevinson, Paget seemed 'refined, humorous, capable of elegant epigram, a faultless verbal scholar . . . exquisite in dress and bearing, polite to embarrassing excess, and almost feminine in playful charm'.[9]

Hassall became the trusted coadjutor of Paget's successor as Dean, Thomas Banks Strong. 'Tommy' Strong had entered Christ Church as an undergraduate in 1879, became a college lecturer in 1884, took holy orders in 1886, was elected as a Student in 1888 and was appointed Dean by the Crown in 1901. The responsibilities of the post of Censor had been enlarged since the 1870s: it was no longer the buffer between the cathedral chapter and other dons; it became instead an intermediary, administrative and disciplinary office coping with the college's junior members, Students and governing body. Strong was Censor of the college, with Hassall as Junior Censor, at the time of two disciplinary crises, the Blenheim Ball of 1893 and the Bullingdon Club dinner in 1894, which culminated in drunken undergraduates smashing most of the windows in Peckwater Quad. At these low points in college history, as at other times, Strong and Hassall were in accord. The Blenheim row had a lasting consequence. Several young noblemen were sent down for ignoring the prohibition by the Censors of their attendance at the Duke of Marlborough's shindig. Their expulsion was resented by their families, who severed their connection with Christ Church and henceforth sent their sons to Magdalen, to Balliol and elsewhere.

In the epoch of Liddell and Paget, the deanery at Christ Church had been, with the Warden's Lodgings at All Souls, the two most dignified and ceremonious centres of hospitality in Oxford. But Strong was not one of the bachelors who have a flair for entertaining. In his time, the tradition that royal personages visiting Oxford stayed at the deanery fell into disuse. 'The Dean himself, shy and fidgety and ill-dressed, with the nervous habit of cracking his knuckles, and of eating and drinking so fast that he had always finished his meals before anyone else at table, might be looked upon as a strange successor to the great men of the past.'[10]

In any case, the social cachet of the House was falling by the time that Strong and Hassall began to hold college offices. Lord Salisbury, who had succeeded Lord Derby as Chancellor of the university in

1869 (they were the eighth and tenth Christ Church prime ministers), had preferred to send his sons to University College. So, too, did the ninth such Prime Minister, Gladstone. 'Strong', said Anson, 'was not greatly interested in keeping up the connexion between the House and the landed classes.' Although he felt no resentment against the privileges of hereditary landed proprietors, and got on easy terms with the nobility, Strong wanted to raise the college's academic reputation. He relished the sight and sound of undergraduates whose ancestors had been at the House for generations, and appreciated those scholars, like himself, who had had difficulty in raising enough money to attend university at all. Hassall, who preferred pupils with whom he could discuss country sports, adapted to Strong's shift in admissions policy. Both men thought there was value in the House providing 'an education and a social tradition for men of quite average ability, who were likely to occupy important positions in the country in after life'. They thought a mixture of intellectuals, athletes and 'average Englishmen' would make a salubrious college, and that a collection of intellectual prodigies would not.[11]

The widening of the House's intake led to opprobrious comments. 'It is still true to say that Christ Church is the chief resort of the aristocracy', wrote an anonymous contributor to Leo Maxse's National Review in 1906. 'This is, in many ways, good for Christ Church, and not bad for the aristocracy, but a less pleasant feature is that the presence of this same aristocracy attracts to the House an entirely undesirable element of Greeks and Hebrews.' This was a noxious exaggeration: Leonidas Argenti in 1901, and John Economou in 1902, hardly constitute a Greek wave; nor Cecil Blumenthal (afterwards known as Count Pecci-Blunt), Frederick Stern and Sassoon Sassoon in 1903–4 a Jewish influx. 'The sons of cosmopolitan financiers who patronise Oxford's most celebrated foundation for the sole purpose of rubbing shoulders with the aristocracy' were an alien influence, commented the National Review, but the House was so populous and spacious that no undergraduate need have 'intimate contact with "the Ghetto" unless he wishes'.[12]

Infractions of etiquette among undergraduates were repressed by scary self-regulation. An Edwardian freshman at Christ Church could never bow, or say 'good-morning', to a senior undergraduate living on the same staircase unless they had been introduced. 'The senior would, perhaps, leave a card on the freshman, choosing a moment when he was not at home,' recalled Stephen McKenna, who entered the college from Westminster in 1906.

> The freshman must return his call, but it was not enough to leave a card: he must go on calling until he ran him to earth. In all things a freshman must consort himself humbly, taking a distant seat in the junior common room, and leaving the arm-chairs in front of the fire to those who better deserved them. There were rules of dress, and rules of conduct; there were clubs which a man would feel honoured to join and clubs which he would avoid: there were games worth playing, and games that were waste of time.

Each year's Michaelmas term intake was, though, thrown hugger-mugger together. 'At the freshmen's table in hall, the freshmen's pews in the cathedral, on the football-ground, in the common room and clubs, and at a score of breakfast parties given for their benefit, the men in their first year came to know one another. There followed testing, sifting, and an occasional change of value.' Few undergraduates had the hardihood to venture beyond their college bounds to make their reputation. 'Oxford is a loose confederation of jealous independent states,' said McKenna, 'and a man must have considerable personality or prowess to be known outside his college.' His novel *Sonia: Between Two Worlds* (1917) has scenes set in Christ Church before 1914.[13]

The early 1880s were a good moment for Hassall to start a college career in modern history. It was better, 'as things stand now', said the All Souls constitutional historian A. V. Dicey in 1885, 'to be charged with heresy, or even to be found guilty of petty larceny, than to fall under the suspicion of lacking historical-mindedness, or of questioning the universal validity of the historical method'. The Faculty of Modern History, rather than divines and theologians, provided the university with its core orthodoxy. More than that, it was hoped that historical methods – the combination of accumulation of knowledge and critical interpretation – would provide new values for humanity with general if not universal appeal.[14]

Hassall reached the House during a phase of statutory change. The Oxford and Cambridge Universities Act of 1877 had necessitated the introduction of new statutes for Christ Church in 1882. Whereas the strongest mid-century pressure for university reform had come from the House of Commons, it was the body of resident teachers who demanded in the 1870s that college emoluments be opened to all without restrictions, and that Fellows holding college offices be permitted to marry. After the legislation of 1877, fewer than one-third of dons were clergy or proceeded to ordination. The celibacy rule, that vestige of monasticism which required men to resign their college fellowships if they chose to marry, ended in 1882. Thereafter, the bulk of men elected to fellowships remained in university teaching for the rest of their working lives, and were not obliged to become clergy in college livings if they wished to marry. Until this change, it was 'horrible', said Goldwin Smith (who married at the age of fifty-two), to expect to have one's dead eyes closed by a scout (that is, a college servant who ministered as valet and waiter to individual dons). Yet, when Goldwin Smith revisited Oxford during 1886, the change that he most regretted was that 'the old Common Room life, which was very pleasant in its way, has been extinguished by the irruption of marriage'.[15]

In August 1883, midway between leaving Keble and starting at Christ Church, Hassall married Mary Anne Ferguson Clarke-Preston. She had been born at Rice Lake, Ontario, third daughter of a Church of Scotland clergyman who later inherited and settled on the small estate of Valleyfield in Perthshire. Her brother, on inheriting the nearby Ardchattan estate in 1878, had taken the new surname of Campbell-Preston: his descendants inherited Blair Atholl Castle from the tenth Duke of Atholl in 1996. Cecil King, who matriculated at Christ Church as a modern history undergraduate in 1919, thought that Mrs Hassall was an attractive woman to whom her husband owed his position in the college. The Hassalls lived for over forty years in a fine ashlar stone college house, at 8 St Aldate's, until his death in 1930.[16]

The temper of the Christ Church common room had been spoilt in 1883 when the clerical party vetoed the election as a Student of Reginald Macan, who taught ancient Greek history and had the strong backing of the tutors. Pusey and Parry Liddon condemned

Macan's book on the Resurrection as heretical, and predicted that he would contaminate the Christianity of his pupils. Macan's proscription impaired the teaching of Greek history at Christ Church, led to poor results in Greats and aroused persistent ill-feeling until Hassall was chosen to be Curator (that is, acting host and overseer) of the common room nearly ten years later. Hassall's temper was never ruffled, nor his courtesy ever impaired. He held no grudges, and his example of goodwill restored free and easy talk to the common room. There were several fine exponents of the art of conversation there, including Dodgson, Parry Liddon, York Powell and Lord St Cyres, a Student who wrote studies of Pascal and François de Fénelon. These men generally dined together in hall, and then adjourned to the dimly lit common room, with its panelled walls hung with paintings by Cuyp, Frans Hals and Gainsborough. There, if there were not too many of them, they sat at a single table, often with Hassall presiding, and put on displays of wit, ceremonial erudition and playful ripostes.[17]

Hassall was less patient at meetings of the governing body. Masterman recalled him leaving his seat to stand in front of the fire, and sometimes raising a cry of 'Divide! Divide!' if he thought the discussion was overly prolonged. He was contemptuous of university business, which he advised Masterman to shun whenever possible. 'Pair with two people, and then vote twice,' he adjured.[18]

Hassall's métier was tutorial work: choosing subjects, setting essay titles, supplying reading lists, listening and talking. Sometimes, as a prelude to the formal teaching, he talked of current political issues as a way of understanding his pupils and of suggesting comparisons between past and present. After hearing his pupils read their essays, he noted omissions, corrected weak arguments and false inferences, elucidated doubtful points of fact, posed questions and weighed conflicting possibilities. His fault as a teacher was that he was over-ready with encouragement: he assured pupils that they were going to get first-class honours when in the event they scraped thirds.

His tact with weak pupils was shown in his handling of the Crown Prince of Siam, afterwards King Rama VI, who arrived at Christ Church to read modern history in 1899. The Siamese authorities expected him to be awarded first-class honours, but it was plainly impossible for him to obtain even a pass. Hassall's solution was to set him to write, week after week, essays on the war of the Polish succession waged in the 1730s. Hassall then reported that the Crown Prince had so excelled at historical research that he could dispense with taking a degree. Instead, in 1901, his eighteenth-century studies were printed in Oxford as a small book: most copies were exported to Bangkok, where they were admired if not read; the thanks given to Hassall in the preface were acknowledged to be princely.

Tutors like Hassall were administrators and classifiers of information – not scholars. They organized the existing fund of knowledge in reading lists, tutorials, lectures, handouts, textbooks and examinations. Incessant reading was required of them even during vacations: standard texts, new commentaries, freshly minted monographs, the recent ideas of French, German and Italian scholars, all had to be consulted and their contents integrated into the weekly round of tutorials and college lectures. As preparation for the endless cycle of examinations, tutors distributed handouts to their pupils, which summarized possible examination answers under heads. These handouts taught undergraduates the great lesson that the surest way to examination success was to learn the answers. Familiar, well-tried answers they must be; new answers might be wrong, or seem conceited. Everybody who heard Hassall speak of, say, Tudor England or Louis XIV felt their efforts were amply repaid when they found questions in their examination papers which had been set by Hassall along the lines of his lectures.

Hassall's kind had no time for original work or for developing specialist expertise, and were reduced instead to writing manuals and primers. 'Oxford college tutors are very far from possessing the leisure of a German or American professor,' Hastings Rashdall of New College rued in 1907. 'They have to choose between publishing imperfect work and not publishing at all.' Their consolation, said Rashdall, who had previously been a tutorial Fellow at Hertford and Balliol, was that their tutorial hours discussing pupils' essays face to face enabled them better to appreciate the needs of students than professors who only saw the young over the podium of a lecture room. The preferred teaching method, noted a visiting Canadian academic Stephen Leacock, was for a college tutor to light a pipe, talk to his pupils and smoke at them. Pipes and cigarettes engaged the teacher and the taught; fug brought a manly fellowship to the room. The theory was, Leacock supposed, that 'men who have been systematically smoked at for four years turn into ripe scholars'.[19]

Professors, though, found fault with tutors. Thorold Rogers, who held the Drummond chair of political economy at All Souls, was a tireless critic of college tutors. No one knew them outside their own colleges, he wrote in 1889. 'They live in an atmosphere of mutual admiration, and it is no wonder, considering that they are allowed to ticket their pupils for life, that some of them are under the impression that they train and guide the rising intellect of the country.' Charles Firth, who succeeded York Powell in the Regius chair in 1904, complained in his inaugural lecture that undergraduates studying modern history were taught by rote to memorize successful answers, were the passive recipients of their tutors' knowledge and learnt 'results instead of methods; not how to find out, but what to remember'. Hassall and his fellow tutors in modern history – Edward Armstrong of the Queen's College, C. R. L. Fletcher of Magdalen, Arthur Johnson of All Souls and A. L. Smith of Balliol – treated Firth's remarks as an affront to their authority in their colleges and as a challenge to collegiate autonomy.[20]

In Christ Church there was no entrance examination to identify and exclude weak or unsuitable candidates. Any young man could qualify for the House by passing the only moderately challenging oral test called Responsions. This would assure him of uninterrupted residence for five terms, even if he made no effort to pass any further examination. In the 1880s such ducal sprigs as Lord Henry Bentinck and Lord Henry Grosvenor decided that they wished to attend on that basis. Other Christ Church noblemen in the same period began to aspire to take degrees. John Marriott spent the summer vacation of 1882 at a shooting box in Dumfriesshire belonging to the Duke of Buccleuch. There he coached the Duke's grandson, Lord Eskdaill, whose subsequent appearance in the list of fourth-class honours in the School of Modern History made Marriott's reputation. Worcester College, where the undergraduates reading modern history were of poor calibre, saw the chance of improving their record in the Schools, and elected Marriott to a fellowship.

Around the turn of the century three of Hassall's pupils were awarded first-class honours in modern history, gained fellowships in other colleges and taught the subject: Geoffrey Baskerville, heir to Crowsley Park near Henley-on-Thames, who went to Keble in 1899; Walter Buchanan-Riddell, heir to a Northumbrian baronetcy, who went to Hertford in 1901; and Edward Wood, heir to a Yorkshire peerage, to All Souls in 1903. Buchanan-Riddell and Wood had well-trained intelligence, but were not scholars. The only truly learned pupil was Baskerville, whose book *English Monks and the Suppression of the Monasteries* combines first-rate scholarship with ironical wit. But Baskerville was forced to leave Keble in 1914 after being detected in sexual indiscretions with undergraduates. 'I wish I knew what to do for Baskerville,' Dean Strong wrote. 'These offences are usually if not always the emergence into act of much mental self-indulgence: but I never think that any crime even if proved should extinguish all hope in life.'[21]

It was impossible for any single college tutor or lecturer to cover the entirety of the modern history syllabus. No college could afford to appoint more than one man in the subject, and some colleges not even one. In 1868 Mandell Creighton at Merton, Robert Laing of Corpus (who renamed himself Cuthbert Shields after a nervous breakdown), Charles Lancelot Shadwell at Oriel and Edward Talbot at Christ Church opened their lectures free of charge to each other's students, and apportioned the subjects between them according to their expertise. This was the beginning of Oxford's Modern History Association. After Talbot left Christ Church in 1869 to become first Warden of Keble, his Christ Church colleagues Sidney Owen senior and George Kitchin joined the scheme, as did Charles Boase of Exeter and Hereford George of New College. By 1880 intensive and numerous lectures were accessible to undergraduates of almost every college. Those that stood outside the arrangement were either geographically on the edge of the university (Pembroke and Worcester) or newly founded and jealous of their autonomy (Hertford).

These lecturers were known as the History Ring, as if they were investors who had cornered a market. In time the Ring was enlarged to include J. F. Bright of University College, Fletcher of Magdalen, Johnson of All Souls, Lodge of Brasenose, Marriott of Worcester and Hassall's former Keble pupil Dudley Medley. The quality of lectures naturally varied: in Gertrude Bell's undergraduate ranking of 1886–7 Fletcher's were the worst ('Everything he says comes straight out of Stubbs'); Bright excelled ('has such a personal feeling for all the great actors in the European drama, and is so witty'); but 'quite the best lectures' were Johnson's. They were delivered with zest, and evoked cheers when he trenched on contemporary politics. Marriott agreed that Johnson took over Creighton's mantle as the finest lecturer in the School of Modern History, and the best private coach of his day.[22]

The lecturers of the Modern History Association were keen to protect their subject from disparagement as a mere listing of dates and facts. They emphasized, as a device of reputational preservation, the staunch continuities in their themes. Constitutional history, as developed by Stubbs, was the core of the course. The set reading for undergraduates challenged them with the intricate technicalities in Stubbs's *Charters* and his *Constitutional History*, in Henry Hallam's *Constitutional History of England* (1827), Erskine May's *Treatise upon the Law, Privileges, Proceedings and Usage of Parliament* (1844) and Walter Bagehot's *English Constitution* (1867). Constitutional history was seen in semi-Darwinian terms as an evolutionary process that found the fittest institutions and practices and strengthened national character and corporate identity. The delineation of national traits and improvement of individual character were indeed the chief aims of Hassall's generation of Oxford modern historians.

English political history was subordinate to constitutional history. Monarchs, dynasties, the relations of Church and state, diplomacy and wars were its remit. E. A. Freeman's *Norman Conquest* (1870–6), J. R. Green's *Short History of the English People* (1874), Ranke's multi-volume history of England in the sixteenth and seventeenth centuries and Macaulay's *History of England from the Accession of James II* (1848–55) comprised the staple reading here. The third ingredient of the course was the modern history of Europe, beginning with the fall of Rome in 476. The conflicts and accommodation between foreign states, and the development of 'national character', were its chief subject material. After 1885 the course prescribed the study of a few set texts in political science and political economy: Aristotle's *Politics*, Hobbes's *Leviathan*, Mill's *Principles of Political Economy* (1848), Henry Maine's *Ancient Law . . . and its Relation to Modern Ideas* (1861) and Bluntschli's *The Theory of the State* (1875–6), which was translated into English by several members of the History Ring and published by Oxford University Press in 1885.

Hassall's most trusted colleague was Henry Offley Wakeman, a former scholar at Christ Church, who had gained a fellowship at All Souls and followed him to Keble as tutor in modern history. They had no need of a vast array of facts and ideas given in orderly sequence in order to meet their aim of instilling the techniques of statesmanship in their pupils, but every need of enlivening insights set in an invigorating narrative of events. Wakeman's approach was described as popular rather than scientific: Hassall's as 'direct and simple', with 'plain' and 'lucid' expositions. Their chief divergence was in their attitude to women: Wakeman deplored their attendance at university; Hassall enjoyed teaching women undergraduates, as shown by the affectionate accounts of him by his pupil Gertrude Bell, of Lady Margaret Hall, who was awarded a first in 1888.[23]

Thring set the primary example for Hassall's working life, but Stubbs had the strongest influence on him as an historian. He vouchsafed this by editing three posthumous volumes of Stubbs's essays and papers in 1903–6: *Introduction to the Rolls Series*, *Lectures on Early English History* and *Lectures on European History*. Each volume is exemplary in its selection and presentation, and shows the grace, agility and playfulness of Stubbs's erudition. Hassall knew the work of Stubbs so well that when, as Censor, he was presenting candidates for degrees and forgot the correct Latin formula, he would recite a couple of sentences plucked from Stubbs's *Charters* and was never challenged on their legitimacy.

Together with Wakeman, Hassall co-edited a volume in the Stubbs tradition entitled *Essays on English Constitutional History by Resident Members of the University of Oxford* (1891). Hassall's essay covered the period from the deposition of King Richard II in 1399 to that of Henry VI in 1461. The latter monarch, Hassall concluded, 'was unfortunate enough to live in a period which saw the end of a system of government unfitted for the age, and the absence of any new system in its place'. The War of the Roses, in other words, was a disjuncture in the evolutionary process of English constitutionalism which was central to the School of Modern History at Oxford.[24]

Anglican churchmanship stamped an indelible impression upon the historical ideas and methods of Hassall, Wakeman and their like-thinking contemporaries in the School of Modern History. Hassall's alarm at the prospects for Anglicanism was noted in 1882:

'He thought that the most strenuous efforts were needed to strengthen the Church's position and to make her truly the Church of the poor.' Otherwise, religious dissent would continue to increase yearly in strength. Two critical mistakes had weakened the Church of England, he believed. The Act of Uniformity of 1662 had driven some 2,000 Church of England ministers to resign their benefices, and to build the earliest Protestant nonconformist chapels. This had given bricks, mortar and roofs as well as spiritual impetus to dissent. The Church of England's subsequent neglect of the cure of souls of the poor had left a wide opening for John Wesley and the Methodists. Hassall followed Wakeman in considering Wesley the greatest English religious leader of the eighteenth century. 'Men cannot for long nourish their spiritual life on negations,' Wakeman wrote. 'They will not long adhere to a religion which recommends itself on the ground that it is less unreasonable and less inexpedient than any other known system of faith or unbelief.'[25]

The attempt to win back the ill-educated and outcast resulted in the publication in the 1890s of three successive volumes entitled *Oxford House Papers*. These were essays on religious and theological subjects written by Oxford dons for the intended readership of working men. Christ Church was the animating force in the thirteen papers collected in the first volume. Seven of the contributors were from the House, including two future deans, Paget and Strong. 'What Has Christianity Done for England?' by Wakeman and 'Magna Carta – the Church and English Freedom' by Hassall were put in sequence together. 'The history of the Christian world', wrote Wakeman, 'is a history of . . . progress which, though gradual, is continuous and permanent.' Christianity, he argued, made England into a nation, created English liberty, moulded national character, civilized both the people and their manners, consecrated national purpose and provided education. Hassall's aim was to rebut the notion that churchmen were enemies of liberty and progress. King John had been forced to sign the Great Charter of 1215 largely at the behest of Stephen Langton, Archbishop of Canterbury, he wrote. 'It is forgotten how ignorant, selfish, and factious a large majority of the barons were. It is forgotten how helpless, how dependent on leaders, the people were. It is forgotten how the Church was the only body capable of taking the lead in a great national crisis.'[26]

Modern history, as taught in Oxford colleges, had a wider end than gaining honours degrees. 'A better school of statesmanship it would be difficult to devise,' John Marriott wrote. 'It afforded an admirable training for public service, for politics in the widest sense.' Lord Curzon of Kedleston, who was installed as Chancellor of the University of Oxford in 1907, affirmed that the two ancient English universities, Cambridge and his, provided 'a mechanism for training the well-to-do to a sense of responsibility, and a capacity for public affairs which it would be the height of folly to throw away'. The Modern History School at Christ Church had no intellectual reputation before 1919. 'It was regarded', Masterman judged, 'as a sound education for the average man and a good training ground for men in public life.'[27]

As Reba Soffer has shown, tutors taught and pupils learnt the models to emulate, the procedures to avoid, the evaluation of alternatives and the assessment of motives that contributed to individual distinction and to national greatness. Undergraduates were encouraged to admire the virtues of those men who used their powers for good and to despise the vices of lesser men who played life's games for personal advantage. Modern history narrated the emergence of nineteenth-century England as the best of the world powers, and as the model of other nation states' aspirations. Hassall and the History Ring saw their work as fulfilling a national service: their aim was, in Soffer's phrase, 'to empower a generous conception of intelligent citizenship rather than to further a professional discipline'.[28]

The promulgation of intelligent citizenship was the purpose underlying Hassall's best historical work, such as his *Life of Viscount Bolingbroke* (1889), his *Louis XIV and the Zenith of the French Monarchy* (1895) and his *Viscount Castlereagh* (1908). These books stood apart from the manuals and textbooks – feats of compression and order – that Hassall compiled to get youngsters through examinations. *The Expansion of Great Britain, 1715–1789* (1907) and *The History of British Foreign Policy* (1912), for example, were his workmanlike summaries of Sir John Seeley's *The Expansion of England* (1883) and *The Growth of British Policy* (1895).

Henry St John, Viscount Bolingbroke was the best orator of the Augustan age, in Hassall's telling, and a paragon of his period. 'His intellectual qualities were of a high order, he had an intimate knowledge of the great authors of antiquity, he had a perfect mastery of French and Italian, and a fair acquaintance with Spanish.' He loved knowledge, learning and literature for their own sakes and had an enviably retentive memory. Best of all, said Hassall, he excelled in history. Bolingbroke's greatest achievement, in Hassall's telling, was the Treaty of Utrecht in 1713. It dished the Whig foreign policy which aimed at establishing great continental alliances and installed the Tory policy of freeing England from continental connections. The Utrecht peace enabled the creation of the British Empire, Hassall argued. 'For the marvellous expansion that was in store for her, England required a long period of peace.' By extricating the nation from the Whig project of war with France, Bolingbroke readied the English for the conquest of Canada and India. He deserved recognition, said Hassall, 'as one of the founders of England's imperial greatness'.[29]

Hassall's biography of Louis XIV was a pair with that of Bolingbroke. He quotes Bolingbroke saying of the *roi soleil* that 'if he was not the greatest king, he was the best actor of majesty, at least, that ever filled a throne'. His own judgement is that Louis was 'a second-rate man', 'showy but essentially heavy, commonplace, and vulgar', and ill-educated:

> Though the Jesuits had superintended his religious training he was in reality ignorant of the rudiments of Christianity, and his general education had been scandalously neglected . . . He remained ignorant all his life . . . He always disliked brilliance of intellect, and distrusted men of distinguished abilities. Like Walpole, he preferred to see around him mediocrity of talent . . . What aggravated the faults engendered by Louis' bad education was his pride.

Excessive pride led to the haughtiness, delusions of omnipotence and self-glorification of the Sun King. In the course of a long reign, 'his ignorance grew into something like stupidity, his firmness developed into obstinacy, his pride became mere arrogance and selfishness. Hence he considered himself above sworn contracts, hence he showed no regard for human life'.[30]

Hassall's views were long and broad if not deep. He saw the division of the Low Countries in 1830, with an independent kingdom of the Belgians carved out of the kingdom of the Netherlands, as a misfortune, which made it easier for Germany to invade one or both. For him, the Prussian war against Denmark of 1864, fought for possession of Schleswig-Holstein, was a watershed in European history. Some Germans, he reported, saw 1864 as the year in which England was conquered unawares. Prussia's defeat of France in 1870, and the subsequent preponderance of the military empires of Germany, Russia and Austria, followed from the failure of England and France to concert their intervention in the Danish war. Four years later, in 1870, the renewed inability of England and France to act together, in the crisis of the Franco-Prussian war, led (argued Hassall) 'to the temporary relegation of England into a secondary place in Europe, the fall of the French Empire, the supremacy of military monarchies, and the formation of the German Empire'. The war of 1870, which overthrew the existing balance of power, 'could have been prevented if, for twenty-four hours, the British people could have been furnished with a backbone'. Thereafter the future of the continent depended on the outcome of the contest between the Bismarck-made empire and its English rival. 'The future of European civilization', Hassall judged in 1912 in a thumping High Tory non sequitur, 'depends upon the ability of Great Britain to unite closely with her colonies, to develop the backward races in her scattered dominions, and to give them self-government as soon as they are ready to govern themselves.'[31]

High Tory traditions in Oxford were well described by the literary historian George Saintsbury, who had been an undergraduate at Merton in the 1860s. 'Toryism', he wrote, 'rests, in the first place, on the recognition of the facts that all men and women are born unequal; that no men or women are born free . . . and that if you leave two healthy brothers or sisters alone together they will frequently, if not continually, fight.' Toryism took from history the lesson that 'all attempts to establish Liberty, Equality and Fraternity have failed more or less disastrously and disgustingly, whatever camouflage of success they may have kept up'. Tory principles upheld, so Saintsbury maintained, inequality, heredity and property.[32]

Such views, particularly after the electoral defeat of the Conservative government in 1880, no longer seemed viable to Hassall. Calling himself 'a Democratic Tory', he urged his party to adjust to the changes brought by the extensions of the franchise in 1867 and again in 1884. Late Victorian party leaders needed to accept that democracy was imminent, and the next generation needed to be equipped to manage it. In this respect, as in others, he was a votary of Stubbs. 'Those who read History intelligently', the former Regius Professor said in 1889,

> do not speak of the present condition of England as being under a democracy, although they do not shut their eyes to the fact that many public men are to all intents and purposes democrats, or that democratic principles are largely leavening legislation. Some of us may think that the sooner the state of things thus indicated comes about the better; others may think, so much the worse; others will be satisfied if, when the time comes, we or our children shall be duly prepared to take our part in it; but whichever view we hold, if we try to read the state of the world honestly, we shall hate claptrap, and assumption of infallibility, and decline to listen to the dictation of party war-cries.

Similar ideas were mooted by Hassall with his brighter pupils.[33]

He also pressed his opinions in meetings of the Canning Club. This had been founded as a discussion group and rallying point for Oxford Conservatism in 1861. It was reinvigorated after Disraeli's defeat in 1880 by the leadership of George Curzon, a Balliol undergraduate who was elected a few years later to a fellowship at All Souls. Hassall joined the Canning while he was attached to Keble and is first mentioned in its minutes discussing a paper on the Church of England and its critics delivered in Michaelmas term of 1882. Curzon's renewal of the Canning owed much to the participation of the clever, provocative Cecil brothers whose father Lord Salisbury had succeeded Disraeli as Conservative leader. It owed much, also, to the sense of urgency imparted by the third Reform Act of 1884 and the Redistribution Act of 1885, and the consequent enfranchisement by Gladstone's Liberal government of male agricultural workers.

In Hilary term of 1885 Lord Robert Cecil read a thoughtful paper on necessary adjustments to the new electoral conditions. In the subsequent discussion, C. R. L. Fletcher, then a Fellow of All Souls and tutor in modern history at Magdalen, intervened: English democratic traditions were both matchless and sacrosanct, he maintained; 'Conservatives should make up their minds on what points to resist, and then to resist to the end'. Hassall was roused by Fletcher's view, which he called 'suicidal'. The history of the French revolution had shown the dangers of social classes becoming isolated from one another. In England, he said, 'the dangerous class is the town population; but personal intercourse . . . between the middle class and the proletariat may save the democracy'. The task for the Conservative party was the conciliation of class mentalities, 'not indulgence in fruitless pessimism'.[34]

Hassall spoke on modern education at a meeting in 1891 marking the thirtieth anniversary of the Canning's foundation. 'In Oxford,' he said, 'there was an extraordinary desire on the part of certain men to disregard all past traditions . . . for the sake of so-called progress'. Reformers were a dictatorial breed, who preferred disruptive innovation to the gradual evolution of institutions that had been charted and celebrated by Stubbs. The universities, Hassall told the Canning, 'must repel the insidious proposals of the friends of progress'. He also decried the influence of corrupting novels and voluptuous poetry among young men: 'literary charlatanism had taken the place of literary merit'. Possibly he was thinking of *The Picture of Dorian Gray*, which had been published a few months earlier. In the subsequent Canning discussion, a young Christ Church man spoke up. 'Lord Beauchamp welcomed Mr Hassall as a rare specimen of the nearly obsolete high and dry Tory,' the club minutes record.[35]

Hassall's generation pursued culture in a manly spirit, to reuse Courthope's phrase. He and Charles Fisher wanted nothing feminine in their college. Indeed, they had a hankering for the ideal of celibacy: Fisher's fiancée broke their engagement because he insisted on postponing their marriage until he had completed his turn as Censor. Hassall, though, was not a total prude. In 1915 he joined the law tutor Albert Carter and the lecturer in Roman epigraphy John Anderson in carrying the nomination of their fellow Student,

John Beazley, the university lecturer on Greek vases, to be Junior Proctor of the university. This was despite Dean Strong, the prurient R. V. 'Robin' Dundas and a tetchily repressed Student named John Murray suspecting Beazley of immorality. 'Once in conversation he differed definitely about the duty of [masturbatory] self-control,' Murray told Dundas. 'On another occasion he betrayed a knowledge of what other people look like in copulation.' The Murray–Dundas brand of primness affected impressionable undergraduates. K. P. S. Menon, India's first Foreign Secretary after independence in 1948, who adored his years at the House, learnt misogyny there as well as slang. A 'healthy contempt for women', he said, 'enabled me to remain a virgin as long as I was at Oxford.'[36]

It was Menon who was reading aloud an essay to Hassall on the morning of 11 November 1918 when Christ Church's Great Tom bell began to peal. Hassall ran from the room calling out that peace had come. Within a year or two of the Armistice, he had become a remote and obsolete figure in the college. He could not comprehend and was irrelevant to the shibboleths and vogues adopted by undergraduates, and throughout the university, during the early 1920s. The leading aesthetes at Christ Church, Harold Acton (who matriculated in 1922 and read PPE) and Brian Howard (who matriculated in modern history in 1923 but transferred to law), were sexually adamant. They despised their *fin de siècle* predecessors as eunuchs. Languorous attitudes held no appeal to them. Nor did the earnest anxiety of swots. The volume of undergraduate *Oxford Poetry*, which Acton and Peter Quennell assembled with advice from Howard in 1924, was 'meant to be scandalous but is just silly', Hassall's generation thought. The *Oxford Magazine* condemned it 'as vulgar as an overdressed woman', 'showy and unprincipled', 'slovenly and unintelligent'.[37]

Leslie Rowse, who arrived at the House to read English literature in 1921 but transferred to modern history, recorded continual discussions of psychoanalysis in the college accompanied by lashings of guilt. 'Only the other day,' so he recorded in Michaelmas term of 1922,

> there was a meeting at the J.C.R. addressed by Dr Wm Brown who is Wilde Reader in Philosophy, and was a Harley Street specialist

in mental & nervous diseases. My greatest friend here, [Julian] Wadleigh, goes to Dr Brown for treatment in order to get rid of the habit of self-abuse which is very strong with him. Throughout the time that I have been in Oxford I have been purer than ever in my life before, though I cannot say that the thing is securely driven out of me. Many others are in just the same position: I had never realised before that that disease had such a hold upon young men. I had always looked upon myself as being abnormal; and I thought that with me the thing was an obsession such as no other people could possibly have experienced. Now I realise to what the melancholy in my life has been due.

In Hilary of the next year Rowse returned to the theme: 'everybody talks of sex, everybody thinks of sex, the accursed thing enters into every moment of our lives'.[38]

John Betjeman, over at Magdalen, found that there was more talk of homosexuality than action. There were always a few love affairs among the less open-air undergraduates, he said, and 'the athletic and tougher sets may let themselves go after a long period of training'. Their mutual provision of sexual relief arose from 'nothing more complicated than the absence of women'. He did not think such antics counted as homosexuality.[39]

Hassall took few pupils after 1920, mainly those with whom he could discuss manly sports. He pronounced his own *Nunc dimittis* as a tutor in 1924. High camp in Peck, flirtation across the table in hall, setpiece performances of ambivalence, licentious candour, JCR discussions of masturbation, athletes pleasuring one another were alien to an old man whose generation had asserted that college culture must be virile without any vitiating influence that was womanish or academic.

CHAPTER 7

Keith Feiling: Never Hurry, Never Pause

For modern historians at Christ Church the twentieth century began in 1911. That was the year when Strong and Hassall recruited Keith Feiling to the House as a tutor in modern history. Initially working as Hassall's coadjutor, then replacing him, and engaging the support of J. C. Masterman, Roy Harrod and others, Feiling brought the modern history side to top form. It trained future prime ministers of Britain and Ceylon, foreign secretaries of Britain and India, permanent secretaries of the Foreign Office and the Treasury, a head of the Security Service and of the Secret Intelligence Service, a director of the Bank of England, a lord mayor of London, a chairman of the Atomic Energy Authority, a Regius professor of modern history, a publisher of the *Daily Mirror*. Men who had read modern history at Christ Church were strewn through the stout red reference books that were the quality assayers of twentieth-century England: the *Directory of Directors*, *Dod's Parliamentary Companionage*, the *Foreign Office List*, *Kelly's Handbook to the Titled Classes*, *Who's Who* and the rest. Feiling attained indirect influence, through his former pupils, in the leadership and direction of Conservative politics before 1979. He and the scientist Frederick Lindemann, afterwards Lord Cherwell, were crucial to Christ Church's claims to be, in the twenty years after 1919, foremost among Oxford colleges and to have, in some departments of life, 'out-Jowetted Jowett'. He was 'legendary' among Oxford modern historians by 1939: this is the testimony of John McManners, whose postgraduate research was supervised by him, and whose career culminated in the Regius chair of ecclesiastical history with a canonry of Christ Church.[1]

Keith Grahame Feiling was born in 1884 at Leatherhead. His paternal grandfather had been a native of the kingdom of Saxony, became the German master at City of London School, translated a collection of German tales into English, edited an Anglo-German dictionary and compiled a students' guide to German grammar. His maternal grandfather was concurrently Headmaster of St John's School, Leatherhead and Vicar of St Bride's Church in Fleet Street. Ernest Feiling, father of the future historian, liked to present himself in official documents as a 'gentleman', without any need of work. In fact, he was a stockbroker who died on the day after his son Keith's eleventh birthday in 1895. He left the substantial sum of £38,000. The family were settled in Surrey: first in a stockbroker's villa at Leatherhead, and later at The Grange, Horley. In 1897 his widowed mother married her cousin Roland Grahame, a clerk in the Bank of England. This marriage had a tragic outcome, for their son was born in 1900 with mental deficiencies that confined him as an adult to a sanatorium. His mother's death in 1911, aged forty-eight, was hastened by her domestic difficulties: the Grahame household at Church Lane, Billericay was less prosperous than The Grange at Horley.

The stability of his grandparents' time was idealized by Feiling. He extolled the mid-Victorians for holding faith in both God and progress, for seeking knowledge without being overexcited by it, and for the steadiness of their temper. The late Victorians showed a declension, he thought. His schoolmasters, after he went to board at Marlborough College, neither stimulated him nor noticed his potential. He came to feel that the lowering uniformity in boarding-school education, and the preference for mannerly forms over sincerity, dulled personal initiative and spread national complacency. His generation were weakened characters living under a nimbus formation of vaguely philanthropic, vaguely Christian, vaguely moral usages.[2]

In 1903 Feiling followed his uncle Anthony Hope Hawkins (author of *The Prisoner of Zenda*) to Balliol. The tutorials, lectures and collegiate life enlivened him, and he was soon promoted to the rank of exhibitioner in modern history. As a fatherless boy, who had felt neglected by indifferent schoolmasters, he was responsive to his Balliol tutors, A. L. Smith (who was elected Master in 1916), Francis ('Sligger') Urquhart and Henry Carless Davis (who succeeded Firth in the Regius professorship of modern history). Tutorials outside

Balliol, notably with Ernest Barker of Merton, also remade his views. His mentors in Oxford, by their tutorials and lectures, tried to show human individuality, which might better be called personal character, prevailing over economic forces and religious indoctrination. They were concerned, too, to enhance understanding of national identity. Often Feiling spoke of the study of modern history in cloudy language: as 'humane reconciling work', 'full of restorations and recoveries'; but as a historian of the Tory party and theoretician of Conservatism he was clear that 'the final criterion of political activity was always its effect on individual character'. Inattention to this historical truth could have lamentable consequences. 'Mankind has often enough ignored history, poisoned, exploited, or defied it, and others have paid for that.'[3]

Smith, Urquhart, Carless Davis and Barker became Feiling's intellectual sponsors. A fine estimate of Smith was given by Kenneth Bell, who matriculated at Balliol in the same year as Feiling. 'There have been greater historians, deeper thinkers, abler organizers, but there was never a better tutor. He had all the requisites of that exhausting *métier*, the technique of which he learnt from his own tutor, Jowett. Of these perhaps the greatest is vitality.' Smith's influence continued, after his death in 1924, in such pupils as Feiling and Bell. They recalled him leaning against the mantelpiece of his college room and raking a pupil's weekly essay with 'a fusillade of close-knit, witty comments which tore away like flashes of lightning the black pall of darkness that had enveloped the subject'. It was hard to resist the erudition, aptness, quirky facts and spry ideas with which he enlarged the imagination of his pupils. 'Like all good tutors, he suggested far more than he told you: you were given not a meal, but an *apéritif*,' wrote Bell. 'He did not want everyone to be alike; he was intensely interested in their differences; he held no hard and fast theories of character, was wedded to no coherent philosophy of life.'[4]

It is a mark of Urquhart's favour that between 1904 and 1912 Feiling was included in four of the summer reading parties that he organized in his chalet in the Swiss Alps. Urquhart was an avid reader of memoirs and a keen student of human types. Talk by Stubbs's followers of institutional evolution bored him, because it seemed to obviate individuality. Economic history, as practised by his chalet visitor Harry Tawney, was to him a symptom of the sickening commercialism of the twentieth century. 'Democracy', he told another chalet habitué, Harold Macmillan, 'seems to me to take such low forms, to encourage this horrid, degrading, cheap press, to grow in vulgarity and bad manners, to misuse so woefully the greater leisure it has.' His appointment as a tutorial Fellow at Balliol in 1894 had been the first of a member of the Church of Rome in the university since the sixteenth century. As a recusant he felt that the curriculum of the School of Modern History was 'blatantly nationalistic and protestant . . . full of progress-trumpeting and megalomania'. He did not train his pupils for examinations, and little minded what class they got. 'You are, I am sure, quite indifferent to your little First by now', he told one of his successes.[5]

Carless Davis shared Urquhart's indifference to the history of the populace. In his inaugural Regius lecture of 1925, he decried historians who delve into the experiences of the common man in expectation of finding the quintessence of humanity.

> They tell us that what we need most to know about any civilisation of the past is what its poorer and more illiterate members thought and did. How the social order affected the welfare of these people is indeed a momentous question. But the historians of the commonplace have in their minds a confused doctrine of the wisdom of the humble . . . I can find no justification in history for the belief that what the masses think to-day society as a whole will infallibly believe to-morrow; that religions, philosophies, political ideas rise like exhalations from the cottage, the workshop, and the market-place. On the contrary . . . new ideas . . . make their first appearance somewhere near the summit of the social fabric and percolate downwards, not infrequently suffering adulteration or corruption in the process. Our common humanity is best studied in the most eminent examples that it has produced of every type of human excellence.

If Carless Davis was not enamoured of John and Barbara Hammond, the indefatigable historians of the English labouring class, Hegel's dialectic of history left him unconvinced too. Hegel seemed to believe, he said in this same lecture, in a gradual ascent towards omniscience, and therefore towards the perfect social state. He thought of history as an intellectual process in which there was no room for accident, or the victory of the lower over the higher reason. A comfortable doctrine if it could be corroborated from the facts, if waste and destruction were not so obvious and so frequent, if the fitness of the survivor could be more regularly established, if it were clear that each great civilisation of the world had always handed on the best of what it discovered or imagined.

Carless Davis recoiled from progressive hopes of a coming sublimity: 'Is it not to be expected of imperfect and fallible men that in their highest thoughts, their wisest policies, their most scientific institutions, there should always lurk the hidden flaw, the something rotten, which in the end breeds inconsistency, hesitation, mistrust, the sure symptoms of a moral paralysis, a social decadence?'[6]

Balliol sent Feiling for private hours with tutors in other colleges: Edward Armstrong at the Queen's College, Herbert Fisher of New College and (at Urquhart's instigation) Ernest Barker. Of this trio, Barker had the deepest influence on his ideas. After reaching Oxford as an undergraduate, Barker – the son of a Cheshire coalminer – had resolved that he must never leave the intellectual treasury of university life. He won first-class honours in Greats in 1897, but as the School of Modern History seemed to offer better employment prospects, he read that subject under Smith's guidance, and obtained a first in 1898. Barker was an optimist and patriot, author of a thoughtful if sometimes exasperating book *National Character*, who taught that 'our island' had a uniquely successful political system: 'the English constitution might be worse, and England, after all, is not a bad country'. Feiling called him 'one of the great teachers of history and politics in his generation', whose 'work has always been a projection of the best Victorian scholarship, of memorable days when liberal teaching governed the English-speaking world'. He quoted Barker as saying, 'The duty of goodness abides whatever the conditions of our life may be.' For Barker, Feiling continued, 'politics are not the dynamics of power, numbers, and will, but a moral art'.[7]

The lessons instilled during tutorials by Barker, Carless Davis, Smith and Urquhart remained a vital force in Feiling's work for nearly sixty years. In the short term, he graduated with first-class honours in 1906. A few months later he won an examination fellowship at All Souls. After fulfilling his obligatory first year living in college, he spent two years as a lecturer in modern history at the University of Toronto. At about the time of the expiry of his All Souls fellowship in 1911, he was recruited by Strong and Hassall to strengthen the modern history side at Christ Church.

This was a striking appointment. Few colleges were willing to elect men as Fellows teaching modern history unless they had gained first-class honours in Greats. Balliol would elect neither Feiling nor Namier to a fellowship on the modern history side because they had not read even Mods as undergraduates: the Balliol historians Arnold Toynbee, Tawney and Galbraith, elected to fellowships of the college in 1912, 1918 and 1928, had all worked at Greats. Bell's election as a Fellow and tutor in modern history in 1919 was permissible only because of the exceptional needs of Balliol's first year of peace. Thomas Case, who lectured in Greek history at Christ Church until 1889, when he was elected Waynflete Professor of Moral and Metaphysical Philosophy, represented a body of Oxford opinion when he apostrophized readers of *The Times* in 1911: 'in language and literature, in poetry and prose, in art and science, in philosophy, speculative and practical, and especially in that comprehensive view of the relations of nature, God, and man within the universal system of things which is common to Greece, Rome, and Christianity, the achievements of the Greeks are the main causes of modern civilization'. It was in accord with Case's temper that George Binney Dibblee, who had read Greats at Balliol before his election to All Souls, described the study of modern history in 1924 as 'selective, pernickety, interpretative, and prepared for endless repetitions'.[8]

Feiling's standing in Oxford was given an early fillip, before his candidature at Christ Church, by his installation as Chairman of the Oxford University Appointments Committee. He probably owed this post to the support of James Strachan-Davidson, a senior Fellow of Balliol, Vice-gerent and eventual Master of the college. Strachan-Davidson had been the informal liaison between government departments and the university in matters of official recruitment and training since the 1890s, when his friend William Courthope had combined the posts of First Civil Service Commissioner and Professor of Poetry. And although the remit of the Appointments Committee, on its formation in 1892, had been limited to finding jobs for schoolmasters, Feiling soon enlarged its ambit to civil and colonial service appointments. He doubtless did this in consultation with Strachan-Davidson and Hugh Egerton, holder of the Beit professorship in colonial history at Oxford. 'Ultimately, the goodness or badness of an Empire depends upon the character of the men who administer it,' Egerton believed. Because of the exemplary character of British colonial officials, 'we can honestly say that the permanence of British expansion' – the words come from an Oxford lecture of Egerton's – is 'in the interests of the world at large' as well as to the benefit of all British colonial subjects.[9]

No one was satisfied with the methods of selecting civil servants for home departments, colonial and Indian service or diplomacy. 'For many years England has rivalled China in the waste and multiplicity of examination,' the Edwardian Tory Charles Whibley complained. 'There is one avenue, and one avenue alone, to preferment. A long room, lightly furnished with tables and benches, with red blotting-paper, foolscap, and quill pens, represents to many a loyal servant the hard-travelled road to Empire.' These were useless tests, Whibley thought, for colonial or other official responsibilities. 'To seek the governing spirit in an examination room is,' he protested, 'like looking for a Derby winner in a circus.' As to the Foreign Office, Strachan-Davidson warned Courthope that none of the Balliol firsts in Greats had enough family money to afford embassy life. 'What you want is the type of man who is born to a competence and has been to a public school. This sort of man could not live in an examination like Class 1 except by being crammed to the throat.' Courthope, if he wanted 'decently educated' young men for the Foreign Office, must recruit from the School of Modern History, where undergraduates were likelier to have private incomes.[10]

Under Feiling's leadership, the University Appointments Committee selected the young men who, without the paper examinations that their counterparts in the Indian Civil Service underwent, were sent to rule the outposts of the British Empire as district commissioners. 'A mystique surrounded them,' as Peter Brown recalled of the DCs whom he knew in Sudan in the 1930s. Most of them were college men from Oxford or Cambridge, where they had excelled at sports rather than brainwork. 'They were an odd lot,' Brown added: 'tough, sociable, and resourceful'; courageous, too, and socially exclusive – traits that Feiling, like Hassall, commended.[11]

Feiling took charge of the Appointments Committee soon after the university's Chancellor, Lord Curzon of Kedleston, had raised a pennant for progressive change in his book *Principles and Methods of University Reform* (1909). 'We desire that Oxford should supply a focus of culture, a school of character, and a nursery of thought,' Curzon declared. To meet this desire, the university must provide the best teaching, over the entire range of knowledge, to the broadest sample of pupils. This was more than ever necessary, Curzon continued, given that 'whole classes of the nation hitherto excluded or dormant are now themselves knocking for admission'. Voluntary self-reformation would be best. 'Institutions which last the longest and work the best are those which have been erected on older foundations, and, under skilful treatment, have assumed fresh or more harmonious shapes.' Curzon noted with satisfaction that a larger annual sum was disbursed on the teaching of modern history at Oxford than in any other university in the world.[12]

Throughout Feiling's early manhood England was battered and destabilized by industrial unrest, by conflict over the nature of parliamentary rule, by discontent in Ireland and by the burgeoning threat of European wars caused by 'that narrow modern patriotism of the cock-on-the-dunghill type', to use Norman Douglas's phrase of 1917. The late Victorian and Edwardian governments had forsaken Splendid Isolation and made alliances which repudiated the foreign policy that had been settled since the Treaty of Utrecht in 1713. Treaties were signed with England's old enemies France and Russia, and aimed against Germany, which Stubbs, Goldwin Smith and old Oxford had regarded as a friendly power. At the same time the mighty forces of equalitarianism, technology and business imperialism were remaking the international order. 'The revolutionary principles of 1789 had worked out their logic in spreading the notion of liberty to one people after another, and binding this freedom to the idea of racial nationality,' as Feiling explained.

This national passion, denouncing minorities and all else that stood in its way, was spread by the instruments of democracy, the press, and organized opinion, even in the most undemocratic States; massing the pan-Slavism of Holy Russia or the feuds of every Balkan people until it entered Africa through Egypt, and Asia through India and Japan. Simultaneously, the free-trading epoch ended in the spilling of European capital over every un-developed continent, in a scramble for colonies, raw materials, and markets. The very progress of humanity redoubled its danger. For the concentrated power of each State had multiplied many times since the wars of the past, being now built on principles which called forth national unanimity and universal military service.

Beginning in 1888 there was a European armaments race, first in battleships but soon including land artillery, naval guns, submarines, airships and explosives. 'And all this', wrote Feiling, 'in an age when the restraints of religion were disappearing from the human soul.'[13]

When war was declared in 1914, Feiling wanted to enlist in the army. This was forbidden by Dean Strong, who was at first inclined to pooh-pooh the martial spirit. 'We are all very full of patriotism and ardour just now,' the Dean wrote on 18 August. 'Our tails are cocked . . . and our bristles are erect. But in a month or six weeks we shall be liable to all kinds of hysteria and panics, and one great protection against these will be that the ordinary business should go on much as usual.' Feiling, who disliked to oppose the Dean's wishes, distracted himself by writing *Italian Policy since 1870* for the series of explicatory Oxford war pamphlets published that autumn. After Strong lifted his veto on enlistment, Feiling was commissioned into a Scottish regiment, the Black Watch, in December 1914. He was posted to India eighteen months later, and became Secretary of the Central Recruiting Board of India. He did not return to Christ Church until Trinity term of 1919.[14]

Soon after his election as a Student Feiling married Caroline Janson, the daughter of a Lloyd's insurance broker. They had a daughter, who disappointed her class-conscious parents by marrying an unpolished South African, and a son, who worked in the War Office until he failed a security vetting during the Whitehall purge of male homosexuality in the 1950s.

In 1917 Dundas caused trouble by insinuating to Dean Strong

that Feiling was yielding to the extramarital temptations of wartime. Feiling took his revenge a dozen years later. He made an issue of an undergraduate's complaints about Dundas's salacious quizzing of his sexual habits and experience (the philosopher A. J. Ayer believed that the undergraduate was Auden, who was irritated by Dundas's sanctimonious self-deception; but alas for a good story, the dates do not match). In Trevor-Roper's account, Dundas, 'in umbrage, took leave of absence for a year and sailed round the world, viewing naked boys, brown, black and yellow, diving for sponges etc.; which pleased him mightily'.[15]

There were bigger squalls in the governing body than malicious tale telling over Feiling's suspected girlfriend. The cathedral's Chapter Fund, which was the first charge on college revenues, was not abated during the war, although the earnings of the tutorial side suffered a precipitate drop. When Herbert Blunt, a Student who had taught Greats since 1887, remarked in the governing body that the Canons held, in effect, preference shares in the House, and called them 'the debenture-holders', his metaphors outraged Arthur Headlam, who had been appointed Regius Professor of Divinity with a Christ Church canonry in 1918. In addition to Blunt, Frederick Soddy, the Professor of Chemistry, was an obstreperous man who quarrelled with Headlam inveterately, and the senior tutor Sidney Owen junior, too, was aggressive and voluble. Headlam detected anti-clericalism in the Christ Church governing body, which he decried as 'the most disagreeable body of which I have been a member'. It seems, he said in 1920, 'to nurse old grievances and quarrels, and . . . tries to keep all authority in the hands of a clique of College tutors'.[16]

The Harvard historian Samuel Eliot Morison savoured 'the soft and sheltered days' when he was a Student of Christ Church in 1922–5. Despite Soddy and Headlam, he prized the privilege, as a member of the senior common room, of partaking in 'the conversation and the company of the most humane and intelligent group of people I have ever known'. The bureaucratization of both the university and the House had proceeded apace in recent years: Morison was interested to see that almost all university and college business, of the sort that is settled by the president or the dean in American universities, was remitted in Oxford to boards and committees of tutors and professors. 'The time consumed is well worth the loss in efficiency,' Morison judged in 1925, 'for the system gives everyone an official finger in many pies, and an opportunity to air his views. The universal craving to mind other people's business is thus satisfied.'[17]

The 1920s were a momentous epoch in the history of Christ Church. Some months after the Armistice three professorships, of anatomy, chemistry and experimental philosophy (physics), were endowed from the funds bequeathed to the House by Matthew Lee in 1755. The chemist Soddy was awarded the Nobel Prize for Chemistry in 1921 for his work on radioactivity and isotopes. The anatomist Arthur Thomson and the physicist Lindemann attained high eminence in their subjects. In addition, the biochemist Sir Archibald Garrod succeeded Sir William Osler as Regius Professor of Medicine, and was in turn succeeded by the neurologist Sir Farquhar Buzzard in 1927. The election of the economist Roy Harrod as a Student in 1924, of the philosopher Gilbert Ryle in 1925, and of the ecologist Cecil Morison in 1928 showed the rising curve that peaked with the election of Albert Einstein in 1931 and hardly declined with the classicist Denys Page in 1932 and Ayer in 1935.

The 1920s were also the high point of the undergraduate study of modern history in Christ Church, in the University of Oxford, throughout the British university systems and indeed in the higher education of the English-speaking world. The proportion of Oxford undergraduates reading modern history began to decline in the 1930s, perhaps because the teaching was too orientated towards the Victorian preoccupations with constitutional and parliamentary history, perhaps because the Edwardian interest in colonial and military history lost its appeal, certainly because both tutors and curriculum were slow to respond to the burgeoning interest in socio-economic history and anthropology. The new School of Politics, Philosophy and Economics (PPE), which took its first undergraduates in 1921, increased its appeal after the economic crisis of 1931. Sir G. N. Clark was the first holder of the Chichele chair in economic history, which was inaugurated in 1931 and attached to a college, All Souls, with no undergraduates. Alfred Radcliffe-Brown was appointed the first Professor of Social Anthropology, again at All Souls, in 1937.

Feiling felt sure that strong personalities and sound instincts amply compensated for the lack of adequate system in England. Feiling distrusted scholars with a tidy and deliberated methodology. Instead, he romanticized lone scholars whose impulses and intuitions might be more fruitful than the meticulous precision of systema- tizers. George Gordon of Magdalen, in his inaugural lecture as Merton Professor of English Literature in 1923, extolled Oxford scholars, such as Feiling, who 'had their own way of working, and were willing to suppose that other men had theirs'. Whimsy had its place in scholarship, Gordon continued. 'No progress in the organ- ization and machinery of research can ever supersede the single enquirer and the lonely work of the mind.'[18]

The eminence of the Students who taught the modern history side at Christ Church in the 1920s is indicated by the knighthoods accorded to three of them (Feiling, Masterman and Harrod). The working peerages granted in the 1940s to two Students, Lindemann and Pakenham, were precursors to the more senatorial peerages that Blake, Gordon Walker and Trevor-Roper received in the 1970s. During the inter-war years the modern history side at Christ Church produced fifteen men who were subsequently elected to Oxford college fellowships: Cuthbert Simpson, Gordon Walker, Trevor- Roper and Charles Stuart to Christ Church; Roger Makins, Leslie Rowse and Ian Bowen to All Souls; David Cecil, F. W. D. ('Bill') Deakin and Lawrence Stone to Wadham; Raymond Carr to New College; Eric Collieu to Brasenose; Michael Maclagan to Trinity; William Pantin to Oriel; and John Stoye to Magdalen. These young men stood ahead of the standard noted in 1925 by Samuel Eliot Morison after nine terms as a Student of Christ Church: 'The Oxford "first" has an admirable command of language, and a brilliant style that comes of writing to impress clever people. He can make less knowledge go further, and write what he has to say far better, than the *summa cum laude* men of the American universities. But he has seldom gone to the bottom of anything.' Full of self-confidence, ready to mug up any subject in a fortnight, the Oxford first is, Morison found, 'inordinately proud of the things he does not know'.[19]

Sir Charles Firth, in his inaugural lecture as Regius Professor of Modern History in 1904, had annoyed college tutors by disparaging

Thomas Wolsey, founder of Cardinal's College. 'His energy stretched over all worlds,' said Keith Feiling, 'but his soul, not without grandeur, had a gross and fleshly side'.

Henry VIII, founder of Christ Church, was 'a masterful animal,' said Feiling. 'If greatness can be held irrespective of virtue, [he] must be held a great man.'

Francesco Guiccardini was the finest historian between Tacitus and Gibbon. English historians, notably Camden and Clarendon, emulated his methods of 'civil history'.

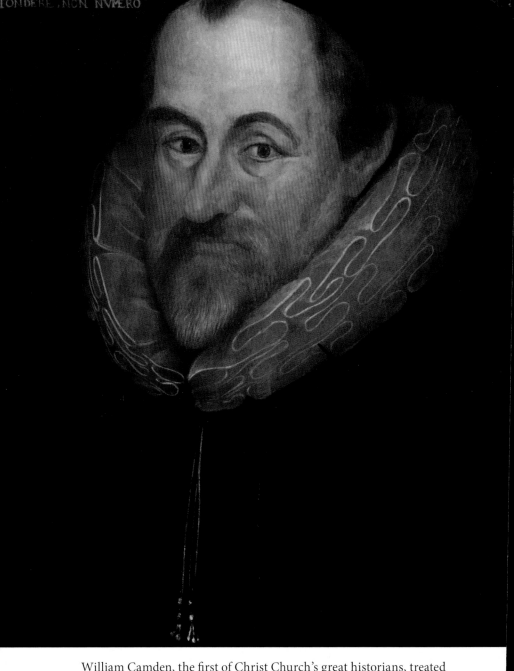

PONDERE NON NVMERO

William Camden, the first of Christ Church's great historians, treated
contemporary events with the best techniques of Renaissance historicism.

Edward Hyde, Earl of Clarendon, hated violence, revered the law and recommended leniency. His *History* gave exemplary lessons in statecraft to English conservatives.

John Fell was the leader of Restoration Oxford. With Richard Allestree and John Dolben as his allies, he made Christ Church into a training college for power politics.

John Locke, before and after his expulsion from Christ Church, was 'the philosopher of government by the gentry,' said Lord Acton, and thus 'the originator of the long reign of English institutions in foreign lands'.

Cyril Jackson, who became Dean in 1783, heightened Christ Church's standing as a nursery of statecraft. His prized pupils were taught state policy, the management of people and the causes of national grandeur and decay.

Christ Church cathedral in Dean Jackson's time.

The choir of Christ Church cathedral.

their teaching and syllabus. Oxford's School of Modern History only existed in order 'to give men who do not wish to study classics, or mathematics, or science a sort of general education through history'. It taught the devices whereby students achieved first-class honours, or respectable seconds, but had scant interest in training scholars who added to the sum of knowledge. The best that might be said of the school was that 'it produces well-informed politicians and journalists, good civil servants, and many useful persons in less conspicuous spheres'. Firth wanted more original research in primary sources to underpin historical scholarship, and fewer synoptic books. Although Feiling made no show of support for Firth, he broke with the habits of York Powell and the traditions of Hassall's History Ring by undertaking primary archival research, and by writing revisionist histories rather than derivative surveys to help examinees. G. M. Trevelyan and Namier, rather than Firth, are the historians with whom Feiling is best matched.[20]

Feiling's first book was a neatly argued volume of political dialogues entitled *Toryism* (1913), which was partly a response to Lord Hugh Cecil's tract *Conservatism* published a year earlier. Samuel Taylor Coleridge was the governing influence on its ideas, followed by John Ruskin and William Morris. It had a sequel in his essay 'What is Conservatism?', which was commissioned by T. S. Eliot and published in his magazine *Criterion* in 1930. The piece disappointed Eliot: it is pedagogic, overwritten and abstruse. Finally, the co-editors of the *Political Quarterly* felt that they should run a special issue on Conservatism in the coronation year of 1953. They turned to Feiling for the introductory essay entitled 'Principles of Conservatism': it is more readable than the *Criterion* essay, but flat. Of these three tracts, I have written elsewhere.[21]

The American scholar Wallace Notestein paid Feiling the ambiguous compliment of saying that his pages abound in metaphors that were as tortuous as those in George Meredith's novels. He found himself asking, as he read Feiling's work, 'This is excellent, I must remember this; but where are we?' Some Christ Church men, including Blake, Rowse and Trevor-Roper, mocked the allusiveness and thick opacity of Feiling's prose. His sentences were better crafted than his paragraphs, which sometimes did not slot together in a smooth sequence.[22]

This obscurity perhaps served some psychological need. Feiling's handwriting was a frantically hurried, scratchy scrawl. Even expert decipherers of manuscripts found it illegible. He had, too, a disruptive stutter, which was much imitated in Christ Church in the 1920s. It vied in fame with the urgent stammer of the undergraduate Harold Acton, who copied his mannerism from an actor with the stage name of Robert Farquharson. A momentary hesitation before uttering his phrases, piercing syllabic emphasis and a voice shooting up and down the scales: these were Acton's tricks of diction which some of his contemporaries emulated. Feiling's impediment and Acton's theatricality took the twentieth-century 'Oxford accent' to extremes. Dacre Balsdon, who arrived as an undergraduate at Exeter College in 1920 and remained as a Fellow there until 1969, denied that it was an accent at all. Rather, it was the trick of pausing for breath in mid-sentence as a way of holding the attention of one's listeners. After using the artful pause to decide how to arrange the words of their next sentence, Oxford speakers would spring forward without a quarter-second's pause for the full stop. 'Jumping your full-stops – that is the Oxford accent,' Balsdon advised undergraduates. 'Do it well, and you will be able to talk forever. Nobody will have the chance of breaking in and stealing the conversation from you.' Although speakers might be interrupted without rudeness at the end of sentences, it was presumed that few people would be so rude as to interrupt unfinished remarks in mid-sentence.[23]

The crisp style with which Trevelyan wrote his Whiggish history and the tone of hortatory Toryism that Feiling sometimes struck were intended to impress and convince their readers, but suggested deeper divisions between the two men than actually existed. They saw the truth in each other's descriptions of events and assessment of individuals, and complimented one another in print with ceremonious sincerity. Trevelyan wrote that Feiling's work gave 'fine intellectual entertainment from beginning to end', was 'fascinating', 'important', 'occasionally brilliant in epigram' and always vivid in its characterization. Feiling, in turn, preferred Whiggish morality to modern mischief: 'book for book, I still prefer Acton or Hallam to *Dorian Gray*'. He followed Trevelyan in producing a one-volume *History of England* with which to engender both patriotic pride and a moderating tolerance.[24]

Edward Armstrong had taught his undergraduate pupil Feiling that, in books, 'trifling incidents, the straws and feathers of history, are often more illustrative than a monolithic commentary or a lumpy lecture'. Feiling's pupil Jack McManners, whose book *Death and the Enlightenment* won the Wolfson Prize for History, admired Feiling's historical technique, with its use of trifles. 'How well in his books the picturesque details were piled up: he was the brilliant exponent of the ironies of contemporaneity, presenting the diverse details of incidents that happened simultaneously as each individual followed his interest, lust, or personal design against the backdrop of national events.'[25]

Feiling respected provincialism. Regional history, he thought, is vital to a proper understanding of national history and to keeping alive a general interest in history. He mastered the constituency squabbles, trade interests and religious affiliations in the counties. 'His England is', as Notestein saw, 'made up of West Ridings, Worcestershires and Cornwalls.' He knew England's county families as well as a genealogist. 'We miss', he said, 'a means of understanding the coherence of long-lived causes, the descent or extinction of loyalties, if we do not look, as those ages themselves would have looked, to de Vere, Sidney, or Wharton, or names that shone less brilliantly, but often lived the longer, Fettiplace or Pakington or Isham.'[26]

Only Namier could match him in this respect. His relations with Namier, though, were unamicable. Where Feiling savoured sentiments and traditions, Namier discounted the strength of ideas and emotions in historical movements and was happiest when compacting material facts into biographical capsules. Feiling celebrated partiality as bringing vigour to scholarship: Namier aspired to neutrality, which he thought was attainable. Namier's jealousy was such that, after his election as a Fellow of the British Academy in 1944, he prevented Feiling's similar election. In the history departments of Manchester and London there were younger scholars whom Namier had trained as postgraduates in his techniques of parliamentary history: in Oxford, by contrast, historians had less inclination to collect disciples. The young Namierites used an excellent tactic to lift their mentor's reputation by lowering Feiling's: they all but ignored Feiling's works, which was more lethal to his standing than attacking them.[27]

Feiling dismissed the Namierite pretence that immaculate objectivity might be reached by writing histories reliant upon unprinted manuscripts: 'the vicious selection of documents is as easy as a partial presentation from printed books'; 'bias is not so much made by the source you use as the spirit in which you use it'. In other ways he tried to make the Namierites flinch. 'Only those', he wrote, 'who have delved in hundreds of unprinted documents dealing with a small subject, or a limited era of time, can know the creeping insensibility to real values, the growth of incredulity, and the pumice-stoning of vitality which begin to afflict one . . . a jargoning of "monographs" and "authorities" fills the air which should be vibrating with life and light'. This fear that specialization would prove a deadly constriction on the discipline of modern history was shared with Trevor-Roper.[28]

At his core Feiling was a late case, and a peculiarly Tory example, of the nineteenth-century public moralist. He intended in his writings to stir the emotions, to enlarge the ideas, to sharpen the thinking, to enliven the intelligence and to vitalize the actions of England's university-educated reading public. There was a sentence in G. M. Young's *Victorian England* that he held in his heart:

> In the far distance I can well conceive the world turning wistfully in imagination, as to the culminating achievement of European culture, to the life of the University-bred classes in England of the mid-nineteenth century, set against the English landscape as it was, as it can be no more, but of which, nevertheless, some memorials remain with us to-day, in the garden at Kelmscott, in the hidden valleys of the Cotswolds, in that walled close where all the pride and piety, the peace and beauty of a vanquished world seem to have made their last home under the spire of St Mary of Salisbury.[29]

A History of the Tory Party, 1640–1714 (1924) made Feiling's reputation. It opens with an eloquent section in which Feiling emphasizes the provincialism of seventeenth-century England: 'the localism of the Middle Ages had not yet disappeared,' he wrote; 'society ran in genial channels of local allegiance'. The even application of English monarchical authority prevented the territorial hatreds that were the bane of other kingdoms: 'Cornwall was not a La Vendée . . . Buckinghamshire neither a Catalonia nor a Galloway.' Overall, as the *Oxford Magazine* concluded, the book is not so much a history of the Tory party 'as a brilliant picture gallery of individual Tories, accompanied by an elaborate discussion of the endless parliamentary groupings and combinations.'[30]

The Restoration statesman Edward Hyde, Earl of Clarendon was presented by Feiling as the most important single figure in the history of the Tory party. Clarendon told parliament in 1660 that its task was to restore the nation 'to its old good manners, its old good humour, and its old good nature – good nature, a virtue so peculiar to you, that it can be translated into no other language, and hardly practised by any other people'. Feiling revered – the word is not too strong – the Clarendon-made Tory party of late Stuart England for upholding what he valued most: 'the divinity of the state, the natural sanctity of order, the organic unity of sovereign and people, and the indisputable authority attaching to the work of time – without which a nation would lapse to a drab barbarism.'[31]

A History of the Tory Party showed, as did Feiling's *British Foreign Policy, 1660–1672* (1930), how far history writing had advanced since the heyday of the History Ring. Both books were grounded in archival research: they were no mere synopses of other scholars' writings; the volume of 1930 covered a dozen years in slightly more pages than Hassall's *History of British Foreign Policy* covered the years 449 to 1914. It drew on manuscript sources found in the Public Record Office in London, the Rijksarchief at The Hague, and the Spanish archives at Simancas. Feiling consulted Oxford collections, including Sir Leoline Jenkins's papers and Lord Clarendon's. He also gained access to private collections, notably the Bath papers at Longleat, the Clifford papers at Ugbrooke and the Cottrell-Dormer papers at Rousham. 'Mr Feiling has gone to original sources,' wrote the historian of the Whig supremacy Basil Williams, 'but, like a true historian, has not made himself their slave. Though there is much apt quotation in the narrative, the reader is not distracted by gobbets of irrelevant material simply because it happens to be new, while he feels that there is much reserve power of information by which Mr Feiling could, if need be, justify almost every word of his narrative.'[32]

Feiling strove to instil his pupils with a sense of the mystique of conservatism. Surveying the history of England since 1815, he found it hard to discern an intelligent or consistent Tory policy. 'I can see some – Liverpools or Eldons – dying in the last ditch, some like Peel selling the breach, and others like Disraeli cutting the dikes to bury friend and foe alike under a flood of innovation.' In his tutorials, and in his talk with politically minded undergraduates, he showed his pupils, by historical examples and precepts, how to manage political change with more imagination than Liverpool, more ductility than Eldon and more principle than Disraeli. This was tricky in a newly enfranchised, aspirational and dissatisfied democracy: almost impossible in a period of volatile, gullible, rash but increasingly aggressive public opinion.[33]

The Lloyd George government created a Ministry of Reconstruction in 1917, which continued fitful economic and institutional operations until 1923, but to Feiling there seemed greater need of a Ministry of Restoration working in the realm of ideas. After the overthrow of Lloyd George's protectorate in 1922, he set to work at Christ Church as a Balliol missionary intent on converting the minds of the future ruling caste. He reverted to the old ways and means that had been practised by Dean Fell after the Restoration in 1660, by Dean Gregory in the reign of George II and by Dean Jackson in the decades of the French wars. The nineteenth century had been a general triumph for Liberal ideas: the rights of man, submission to majority opinion, Free Trade. Feiling hoped to restore what had been best in the nation by making Christ Church into the most influential Conservative college in Oxford (as Herbert Butterfield did to Peterhouse in Cambridge after 1945).

Feiling once told David Cecil, after he became a Fellow of Wadham, that a don must not be on too friendly terms with undergraduates. He allowed himself a favourite student, though, in Alan Lennox-Boyd, who was awarded a Christ Church scholarship in 1923. As Secretary of the Canning Club, and President of both the Union and the University Conservative Association, Lennox-Boyd proved conspicuously able, wrote Frank Pakenham, 'to strike a happy mean between impudence and obsequiousness in his dealings with great visitors'. He became a welcome visitor to John Buchan at Elsfield, and had the High Tory, imperialist, anti-Bolshevik, anti-trade unionist, anti-Prussian views of Buchan's most famous fictional creation, Richard Hannay. He advocated a Romanov restoration in Russia, and the adoption of the theory of the Divine Right of Kings by the Conservative party. That party, he told the Canning Club in the year of the General Strike, must reanimate the 'splendid' spirit of the Cavaliers of the 1640s 'if the old order in Great Britain was to survive'. Conservatism, he declared in the *Oxford Magazine*, is an attitude of mind held by people who feel 'veneration for the social and political system which the genius of the British race has evolved, [and] respect for those traditions that find more fitting expression in Oxford than anywhere else in the world'.[34]

In 1926 Lennox-Boyd won an essay prize endowed by a South African mining magnate named Beit on the subject of British colonialism. It was written in a mood of reaction to the granting of independence to Ireland four years earlier. In Lennox-Boyd's view, the Irish Free State had come into being as a result of the bad character of a Welsh prime minister and the weak natures of his English ministers. With assertive confidence and oppressive vocabulary, he argued that if the British people were led by strong men, there would be no faltering in the nation's march at the forefront of progressive imperial destiny. 'The greatest test of any government in its dealings with backward races', Lennox-Boyd averred, 'is to be found in the character of the men whom it appoints to positions of authority.' This was the orthodoxy of Hugh Egerton, the former Beit professor, and the viewpoint from which Feiling's Oxford University Appointments Committee had been working with the Colonial Office since 1919. Lennox-Boyd also quoted with approval Lord Milner's tribute to 'the practical instinct which enables men of British birth . . . to make the best of limited opportunities without troubling their heads about theoretical interpretations of system'.[35]

Feiling expected Lennox-Boyd to get first-class honours in his finals, and thought he had a good chance of following the recent Christ Church scholars Roger Makins and Leslie Rowse to an examination fellowship at All Souls. Lennox-Boyd, though, dispersed his energies too widely in political activities and failed on both points. Outside the university Lennox-Boyd impressed people as 'an 18-carat man', and in 1931 he was jobbed into a safe parliamentary seat. '6' 7" of fun conceal the learning of a don and the heart of a schoolgirl', a fellow backbencher wrote of him in 1938. He rose in the party to serve as Secretary of State for the Colonies in 1954–9, and was then created Viscount Boyd of Merton.[36]

Another of Feiling's Christ Church pupils was Derek Walker-Smith, Minister of Health in 1957–9, afterwards Lord Broxbourne. Walker-Smith began his career with the panache of Lennox-Boyd. He won an open scholarship to Christ Church at the age of seventeen. Victor Gollancz published his novel *Out of Step* while he was still an under-graduate. Tom Harrisson, in *Letter to Oxford*, described him as trying at the age of twenty-one to be mistaken for thirty-five. First-class honours in history, the Middle Temple and the Conservative back benches came in smooth succession. Feiling's imprint on Walker-Smith's ideas is evident in the essay that the younger man contributed to *Red Rags: Essays of Hate from Oxford* (1933). Chamfort's saying that while 'the French revere authority and despise law, the English despise authority and revere the law' no longer held true, Walker-Smith wrote. England had once been 'a country where every stick and every stone spoke of liberty and respect for law; but to-day there is a growing respect for authority, whatever its sanction, while the law, as such, is a target for mockery, ill-informed criticism, grumbling and contempt'. This mentality was, he said (sounding in every sentence like Feiling's pupil), polluting the fresh stream of national life. 'No culture can subsist without faith, and faith has gone from England to-day.'[37]

Later, Walker-Smith wrote a volume of Conservative advocacy, subtitled *The Politics of Plenty*, published when the going was far from plentiful in 1948. In it he warned that the mid-twentieth century was being swamped by a new materialism which was as 'gross' as the unrestricted capitalism of its nineteenth-century precursor. 'A view of politics exclusively conditioned by the possibilities of personal advantage and perquisites is a double betrayal. It is a betrayal not only of personal dignity and manhood, but of the whole cause of free politics.' Nations fail in times of bread and circuses, said Walker-Smith: 'If you ask for tit-bits, you get tyranny.' The accent and sentiments of Feiling can again be heard in Walker-Smith's opinions.[38]

Outside the college, among the stock of undergraduates in the university, Feiling organized the men who were to be eminent in Conservative leadership until the 1970s. In 1924 (at the request of ministers in the Baldwin government) he took the labouring oar in founding the Oxford University Conservative Association, where undergraduates with political aspirations could practise their crafts and forge contacts with visiting parliamentarians. He pushed promising or ambitious youngsters to think about the patterns and episodes of the past. 'If', he counselled in 1930, 'we go to history in order to learn, and not to inflict upon her our own petty prejudices, the last thing that we shall find is a fixed programme and the first thing is a continuing spirit.'[39]

Rowse, who was a prize pupil of Feiling's in the 1920s, felt sure that he wanted at that time to be one of the MPs for the two-member constituency of the university. But neither Lord Hugh Cecil, who had been elected as a Conservative burgess in 1910, nor Sir Charles Oman, who had joined Cecil in a by-election of 1919, wished to retire from parliamentary life. It must have exasperated Feiling that Oxford Conservatism was represented by such stubborn diehards. 'Oman was the greatest reactionary I have ever known,' Rowse later wrote. 'He was really an utter innocent about politics . . . yet the University Conservatives . . . sent him to the Commons election after election . . . where he was known as Stone Age Man.' In the troubled 1930s the Neolithic attitudes of these old men weakened Conservatism in the university. A non-partisan maverick Alan Herbert was elected when Oman stood down in 1935. Two years later Cecil was succeeded by the Popular Front internationalist Sir Arthur Salter.[40]

Not surprisingly Feiling complained that the inter-war Conservative party was 'too deferential to wealth, too patient of old men, too closed to the young, and too unwelcoming of brain'. It had three types of leader: 'stalwarts of sheer prejudice and fixed tradition, whose altogether admirable but unchanging code does not easily adjust itself to the fluid policies of world peace, social democracy, and economic experiment'; tacticians, who only think of manoeuvres that will win votes from parliamentary factions or from constituents at election time; and lastly, 'men of good-will, who . . . hold that character in itself constitutes a programme'. None of these types were suited to determining policy.[41]

In the hope of remedying this defective leadership, Feiling gave lectures to the Conservative Central Education Committee in the

1930s, and joined the party's Post-War Problems Committee in 1941. Always, in his books and speeches, he distinguished between the Conservative and the Tory traditions. For him, Clarendon, Blackstone, Eldon and Peel were true Conservatives defending the existing order to the last ditch. Burke was their Messiah. Such men held fast to the political saws of their fathers, had a horror of abstractions, were indiscriminate in their resistance to change and obstinate in their loyalty to superannuated leaders and faded chivalries. They were not only backward-looking but irascible. They rallied in support of the firebrand preacher Henry Sacheverell and the ultra-prejudiced backbencher Charles Sibthorp. They defended excessive violence, as in the cases of Edward Eyre, the Governor of Jamaica who suppressed the Morant Bay rebellion in 1865, and General Reginald Dyer, author of the Amritsar massacre of 1919. They liked Dr Jameson for his anti-Afrikaner raid on the Transvaal in 1895, and the blimpish Home Secretary Sir William Joynson-Hicks for ordering a police spy-hunting raid on the offices of Soviet Russia's trade organization in 1927.

Feiling, though, counted himself among the Tories, whose best leaders he listed as Harley, Bolingbroke, Pitt, Canning and Disraeli. 'They viewed their party less as representing the dominant classes of the present than as standing for the most permanent, and hence the most vital and entirely natural, interests of the people as a whole,' he wrote in 1925. 'They recognized, it would seem, that this national heritage must necessarily find very different interpretations in different ages, and therefore that conservatism consisted less in maintaining fixed institutions than in acting in tune with the conservative spirit.' They all met Samuel Taylor Coleridge's definition of the purest patriot: 'accustomed to regard all the affairs of man as a process, they never hurry, and they never pause'.[42]

Feiling took his convictions from Coleridge. Radicalism in Coleridge's time, socialism in Feiling's, was 'the inevitable revenge of the neglected poor'. If governments or aristocracies treat people like commodities, denying their human value and assessing them as objects, then (Feiling followed Coleridge in thinking) the poor, with reason, and almost in self-defence, would seethe. Coleridge and Feiling loathed the harshening priorities given to production and profits. 'You talk about making this article cheaper by reducing its price in the market from eight pence to six pence,' wrote Coleridge. 'But suppose, in so doing, you have . . . demoralized thousands of your fellow-countrymen, and have sown discontent between one class of society and another, your article is tolerably dear, I take it, after all.'[43]

If Coleridge was Feiling's literary model, the younger Pitt was his hero as a statesman, and Canning was his exemplary parliamentary leader. Pitt's personality was winning: 'He enjoyed a ride to hounds, shot partridges in the year 1799, took his duty as Warden of the Cinque Ports like a Tudor Warden of the Marches, built and planted, talked bad French, kept up his classics, overspent, and drank quite enough.' He faced challenges much like those confronting England in the 1920s. 'He found an Empire lately in disruption and in course of change, old markets lost and established industries dying, an outworn commercial system, new and aggressive classes of society, party ties in dire confusion.' Pitt was 'a ceaseless, radical reformer' who exemplified 'reform in action'. He introduced eighteen Budgets, most of which made sweeping innovations. The Sinking Fund to administer the national debt, the Consolidated Fund, a national audit system, income tax and legacy duty were instituted by Pitt. He reduced and simplified a tariff system which rested on stifling monopolies and wasteful prohibitions. He began departmental reforms in the Excise, the War Office and the Civil List. The Royal Navy and the government of India were remodelled. Advantageous treaties were made with the United States and Spain. In Ireland he enfranchised members of the Church of Rome. In England he legalized Catholic schools. He conceded the principle of outdoor relief to the poor. He gave legal recognition to friendly societies. He advocated compulsory arbitration in industrial disputes. He appointed stipendiary magistrates in London. Above all, the Regency Bill of 1789, which he introduced during George III's first bout of mental derangement, put the authority of parliament above that of the Crown. Pitt wrote Feiling, 'left this project of modern England safely in the way to something new and better'.[44]

After Feiling's belated election as Chichele Professor of Modern History in 1946 (following Oman's long-awaited death), his lectures impressed undergraduates. Ian Gilmour, who began to read modern history at Balliol in 1947 and was afterwards a Conservative minister

and thinker, ranked Feiling with A. J. P. Taylor as the most interesting lecturer in the Oxford history faculty of the post-war period.
Edward Boyle, another thoughtful Conservative minister of
Gilmour's generation, was similarly influenced by Feiling's mistrust
of anyone claiming to have an exclusive hold on truth.[45]

Samuel Finer, in his study of *Backbench Opinion in the House of
Commons, 1955–59*, published in 1961, showed that in every parliamentary controversy of that period the MPs who had attended
university in Oxford were divided in their views from their colleagues
from Cambridge and other universities. Oxford men were more
hostile to birching and hanging criminals than Cambridge men,
disfavoured long prison sentences and were sometimes willing to
advocate or vote for a reduction in the criminal penalties on male
homosexuality. They were less supportive than Cambridge men of
increasing expenditure on hospitals, clinics, housing, education and
pensions. They hankered, but in vain until the 1980s, for economic
deregulation and lower taxation. In the conflict among Conservative
MPs between pro-Europeans and the partisans of Commonwealth
trade, those holding constituencies with impregnable majorities were
predominantly pro-Commonwealth while those from marginal seats
inclined towards Europe. Distinct from this, most Oxford graduate
MPs sought closer European exchanges, while their Cambridge
counterparts, as well as MPs who had graduated from Sandhurst,
felt nostalgic affection for the Empire, admired the Commonwealth
and prized national sovereignty.

In 1956 the Eden government had its mini-Gallipoli in the form
of the Suez crisis, in which the governments in London and Paris
colluded with the Israelis in an ill-judged invasion of Egypt. Finer
found no distinction in the behaviour of graduate MPs and non-
graduates during the Suez episode. There were few critics of government policy from Cambridge (Anthony Nutting was the leading
exception), but Oxford MPs were polarized. A high proportion of
unforgiving critics came from its ranks, but so did some of its ardent
supporters. Feiling sided with 'the weak sisters', as Anthony Eden
called the dissidents, and resigned his membership of the Conservative
party in protest at the invasion of Egypt. 'Ministers have acted as if
the Commonwealth were negligible,' he complained in *The Times*.
'They have brushed aside its doubts, and taken life and death

decisions without consultation.' Since the 1920s Oxford undergraduates taking certain options in modern history had studied the
process by which self-governing dominions had come to be consulted
on Westminster's imperial policy. The Eden government nullified all
that had been taught. Canada, the oldest of the dominions, 'whose
measureless sacrifices for us in two world wars earned our lasting
gratitude, has been excluded from vital consultations'. The snubbing
of India, 'still potentially of such mighty value to us, our bridge to
the millions of Asia', whose soldiers had fought and died for Britain,
was, like the rest of the Eden government's policy, said Feiling,
'short-sighted, ungrateful, and politically imbecile'.[46]

Why were Oxonians more European, more internationalist, more
libertarian in their economics, and less punitive than their opposite
numbers from Cambridge? Was it, Finer wondered, because
Cambridge was noted for mathematics and science, Oxford for
Greats and PPE, and that these disciplines required different standards of evidence and verification? Or that Cambridge had
evangelical traditions whereas Oxford produced High Churchmen?
Noting that Oxford drew many more of its members than Cambridge
from major public schools, Finer surmised that families with a
tradition of political initiative and leadership preferred to send their
sons to Oxford rather than Cambridge. His general picture of 'an
aristocratic, detached, sophisticated and internationally minded
Conservatism associated with Oxford, compared with a more
popular, more nationalist and blunter Conservatism from Cambridge'
was fair. Finer suspected that political clubs like the Canning were
partly responsible for Oxford's distinctive political traditions. But
surely the influence of individual dons mattered most. Rather as
young Labour dons, including Patrick Gordon Walker and Frank
Pakenham, kept the cause of social democracy alive in Oxford during
the inter-war period and discouraged university opinion from
turning communist, so Feiling helped to defend Oxford conservatism
from militarism, xenophobia, authoritarianism and outright class
antagonism. His pupils made no excuses for Governor Eyre, General
Dyer or Dr Jameson.[47]

Yet England's old institutions were not in good fettle. The understanding at the time of the passing of the Parliament Act of 1911
that the Lords would be remade so as to provide oversight of the

decisions of the Commons majority was abrogated and forgotten. In consequence, the bicameralism of the Westminster parliament became a thin, frail, enervate shadow play rather than a healthy reality. Moreover, the electoral system that sent MPs to Westminster was inequitable. At the general election of 1929, as Feiling noted, 287 Labour members were returned by 8,360,000 votes, 261 Conservatives with 8,664,000, and 59 Liberals with 5,300,000. There was a breakdown between 1916 and 1945 of the adversarial two-party system which Feiling had made his historical study. England, Ireland, Scotland and Wales were ruled by a coalition government under Liberal leadership, with Conservative support, from 1916 until 1922. After the secession of all but six counties of Ireland in 1922, there was another coalition government from 1931 until 1940, which was led first by a Labour prime minister and then by two Conservatives. During 1940–5 there was a wartime coalition of three parties led by a Conservative who had once been a Liberal.

British Documents on the Origins of the War, 1898–1914, published in a dozen volumes after 1926 under the editorship of Harold Temperley and G. P. Gooch, contributed to the bleak general views of modern historians in the 1920s. Four years of continental war and the broken hopes of national self-determination brought a dour tone to their discussions of relations between nation states. Nationality was no longer conceived as a matter of rights, liberties and virtuous responsibilities. Idealism was devalued, even treated as cant. Expressions of pride in national character were seen as an embarrassment. Foreign policy, as depicted in E. L. Woodward's *Great Britain and the German Navy* (1935) or A. J. P. Taylor's study of Bismarck's colonial policy published three years later, was represented in terms of force, national might, conspiratorial planning and outright duplicity.

Feiling found this way of thinking to be demoralizing of young minds and overly cynical about national leaders and national institutions. As an antidote he bade farewell to Tory history in 1938 and embarked upon his most ambitious and demanding work. *A History of England* took ten years of his life and ran to 600,000 words. He set himself the task of unifying a divided nation, of providing the basis for a quiet patriotism and of accounting, with a blend of romanticism and pragmatism, for the development of national character and national institutions. Although completed at Christmas of 1948, it was published by Macmillan a full two years later so as to signalize the coming end of Feiling's tenure of the Chichele professorship (for he, unlike Oman, was subject to an obligatory retirement age). Its governing theme was England's lead in 'great power' politics.

A History of England was a riper version of J. R. Green's *Short History of the English People* published in 1874. There was no simplistic patriotism in it, but whenever possible Feiling used the possessive determiner 'our' to describe the nation. As a sound pupil of Carless Davis, he was interested in the management and direction of the nation, which at its best might be called statesmanship, rather than (like Green) the populace. He examined the ideas, tempers, fears and hopes of educated rather than unlettered people. The book is too vast and varied to summarize in brief. Only one pivotal chapter can be noticed here: that describing the seven years, culminating in the Reform Act of 1832, which determined the domestic character and global reach of nineteenth-century Britain.

Feiling entitled this chapter 'The Age of Canning', because those seven years, he believed, were dominated by the personality and oratory of Cyril Jackson's protégé. Canning was 'an intellectual, hypersensitive, contemptuous of second-class brains, and not disposed to sacrifice to party his own future', in Feiling's account. Thomas Love Peacock caricatured him as Anyside Antijack in a novel admired by Trevor-Roper, *Headlong Hall* (1815). Canning, wrote Feiling, 'disbelieved in parliamentary reform, adhering always to Burke's teaching that democracy was one form of tyranny and liberty implies variety, an inherited society, and private property as the instrument of talent'. The commercial and financial schemes of his allies William Huskisson and Robert Peel held no interest for Canning. 'He was, rather, an opportunist, intensely insular in the higher sense that he felt the England of his master, Pitt, had saved Europe, and was worthy to be preserved in her historic character.' He was a nationalist who wanted the British Isles to obtain a stable neutrality between what he called those 'two conflicting bigotries', despotism and democracy.[48]

The bigotries of despotism and democracy remained a menace in the 1930s, Feiling believed. On one side were the autocracies of Stalin and Hitler, and the fascist states in Italy, Spain and elsewhere.

On the other were nations in which the majority opinion of the electorate was a malleable, fallible compound moulded by cheap newspapers. Politicians in parliamentary democracies increasingly shirked their responsibilities by following rather than leading public opinion, or rather by listening to those people who shouted loudest that they represented the majority opinion. For most of the 1930s Feiling favoured the conciliation of Germany. But his confidence in the League of Nations policy receded as the Scandinavian states and the Low Countries, Spain and Switzerland showed that they expected France and Britain to shoulder all the burden of the League's work without aid from the smaller European powers. King Leopold III's declaration in 1936 of Belgium's neutrality in a future war seemed to him a grave reverse. He supported the National government's policy until, but not beyond, the Munich settlement of 1938. The vacillations of armaments policy stuck in his gizzard, he later said, and he thought the Anglo-French guarantee of Poland's territorial integrity in 1939 was an imprudent commitment.[49]

Feiling's Christ Church colleague Lindemann introduced him to Winston Churchill in the 1920s. Churchill's delinquent son Randolph went to the House to read modern history in 1928, enjoyed college life there and wrote to his father of Feiling's verve. But the boy would not settle to college life: Feiling was tasked with explaining to Churchill why Randolph was refused leave of absence to campaign in the general election of 1929, and why he was terminated as an undergraduate after decamping in term time to the United States in 1930. Winston Churchill described Feiling in 1931 as 'the greatest of our modern Oxford historians', and employed him as a research adviser on his biography of the Duke of Marlborough and his *History of the English-Speaking Peoples*. Feiling in return regarded Churchill as 'the best stored and most fertile mind in British politics' – 'supreme', too, 'in all the gifts of what our fathers called a great parliament man'.[50]

After Neville Chamberlain's death in 1940, Feiling was commissioned by the former Prime Minister's widow to write his authorized biography. The result, published by Macmillan in 1946, has the fewest moral tutorials of any of Feiling's books. It celebrates the private man, 'simple, sensitive, and selfless, arduous, just, and merciful', growing delphiniums, fishing in the Piddle, reading Logan Pearsall

Smith, keeping *Middlemarch* by his bedside as he lay dying of cancer. It is to Chamberlain's credit, says Feiling, that he was a weak electioneer, ill-equipped to be a hail-fellow-well-met and unsettled by hecklers. Internecine political warfare, the collapse of coalitions and the near dissolution of parties buffet Chamberlain, and Hitler's aggression finally kills him; but, says Feiling, none of these episodes fell the Conservatives, because the party spirit – 'transmitted to, or shared among, spiritual legatees' – is imperishable.[51]

With his histories of the Tory party, his respect for parliament men, his official biography of Chamberlain, his collaboration with Churchill, his cherishing of the shire counties, his trust in the benefits of imprecision in the expression of political feelings and ideas, Feiling of Christ Church seemed to be, in mid-century England, the chief trustee of Conservatism's spiritual legacy. His last book, *In Christ Church Hall*, was published in 1960 when he was in his late seventies. It contains twenty or so essays appreciating men who had sat in that hall, as junior students, from the reign of Elizabeth to that of Victoria. On the title page there is an epigraph from *The Winter's Tale*: 'I have served Prince Florizel, and in my time wore three-pile; but now I am out of service. But shall I go mourn for that, my dear?' Reading *In Christ Church Hall* gave me the first prompting to write *History in the House*. 'Clever men, chattering doctrinaires, abound in all ages,' Feiling wrote in his opening essay on the Tudor geographer Richard Hakluyt. 'To look for truth wherever it may be found, to learn from our enemies, to neglect no instrument however rude, to disregard the mob and work for things that should last, such were his precepts.'[52]

CHAPTER 8

J. C. Masterman: Doyen of the Modern History Corps

Masterman began his memoirs with a rueful admission. 'All my life,' he wrote, 'I have followed the conventional course. To do the right thing – or rather what public opinion regarded as the right thing – was a stronger influence with me than the dictates of reason or even of morality.' He found safety in conventions. People lived and worked better together if they had common understandings, shared inhibitions, similar appearances and group affinities. In his ideal world, the right men were in the right places, proceeding by right ways, at right times and in the right clothes. When he was Provost of Worcester College in the 1950s, Harry Pitt, the Fellow who taught modern history there, heard him telephone a man whom he had invited to a lunch party on the coming Saturday. Masterman confirmed the arrangements, and then, just before replacing the receiver, added crisply, 'Brown suits, of course.' A conventional man, then; contented and grateful, too, to judge from the readiness with which in old age he recalled the closing lines of John Masefield's poem 'Biography':

> Best trust the happy moments. What they gave
> Makes man less fearful of the certain grave,
> And gives his work compassion and new eyes.
> The days that make us happy make us wise.[1]

The tokens of a liberal education, as listed by J. I. M. Stewart, a Reader in English literature at Christ Church, were 'a contemplative habit and a tentative mind, poise as well as force, reserve rather than wariness'. Masterman had all these traits long before he became, in his early fifties, an officer in the wartime Security Service (MI5). He knew when to look immovable, and how to stay silent. He watched, listened, deliberated, kept his counsel and concealed. Yet his straitened manner was deceptive. W. H. Auden, who was elected an Honorary Student of Christ Church in 1962, might have been thinking of Masterman when in 1933 he began a review of a potboiler written by Winston Churchill: 'The English are a feminine race, the perfect spies and intriguers, with an illimitable capacity for not letting the right hand know what the left hand is doing, and believing so genuinely in their self-created legend of themselves as the straightforward, no-nonsense, stupid male that at first others arc takcn in.'[2]

John Cecil Masterman was born in 1891 at Crescent Lodge, his maternal grandparents' house on Kingston Hill in Surrey. He was addressed as 'J.C.' by almost everyone who knew him except his mother and elder brother. The disadvantage of the knighthood that he received from the Macmillan government in 1959, after his retirement as Vice-Chancellor of the University of Oxford, was that it brought the unwonted intimacy of being called Sir John Masterman. The Kingston grandfather was a retired clergyman who had been, long before, a Fellow of New College. His paternal grandfather had been a City solicitor. After his father's retirement as a naval officer, the family settled in a villa called Heathcroft, at a place called Cricket Hill, on the southern edge of the Aldershot plain. The background was static.

At the age of twelve Masterman was sent as a cadet to the Royal Naval Colleges at Osborne and Dartmouth. Conditions there made him feel miserable and degraded. Accordingly, in 1909, he escaped from naval training, and applied to read history at a small, placid and beautiful college, Worcester. As he sat his examinations in Worcester's panelled hall, beneath a ceiling designed by James Wyatt, in a building of which Nicholas Hawksmoor had been architect, and gazed at the chimneypiece by William Burges, his craving to become a member of the college felt almost overwhelming. In the evening, following the final examination, the bursar, Francis Lys, took him ambling in the college gardens and asked about his finances. Masterman admitted that he could not enter the university without a scholarship (even an exhibition would be insufficient) and that if admitted as a scholar he would need to live in cheap rooms. Lys reported this to Worcester's governing body, which duly offered a scholarship.

Lys, whom Masterman was to succeed as Provost of Worcester in 1946, became an exemplary figure for him. He learnt the craft of impassivity from Lys. Deep feelings should be shown not in silence but with restraint. Praise should be sparing. A reserved, judicious manner would prevail over demonstrativeness. In private discussions and governing body meetings alike, Lys and Masterman were deliberative, unhurried and tenacious. They attained the leadership of their communities by making a performance of being self-reliant, sincere and resolute. They told the truth, but with prudence rather than forthright indiscretion. Masterman's air of confidentiality imbued him with authority. There was a touch of emotional covertness about him. He lived by the principle that a man should discuss his difficulties only when they are over.[3]

Masterman liked and admired J. A. R. Marriott, who had charge of the modern historians at Worcester. Marriott was a Conservative party activist in Oxford, who was elected MP for the City in 1918, but that was not what he meant when he insisted that he should be described as a 'politician'. For him the word meant someone who espoused the state and promoted statecraft. The teaching of history, and the writing of history books, was as much an act of political responsibility as sitting in parliament. Marriott was a booming, hustling man: Dean Strong said that when he swore the oath necessary to taking his seat in the House of Commons, he made more stir than anyone since Charles Bradlaugh, at a similar ceremony in 1880, tried to affirm as an atheist. It was in Marriott's sense that Masterman can be called a lifelong politician. He espoused the state, taught its craft and during the 1940s gave singular service as its servant. Although he concentrated his focus on his college and pupils before 1940, his politicking in both Whitehall and his university thereafter became inveterate.[4]

Masterman's opinions were formed in the confident, progressive age of liberalism and science before 1914. In his youth he believed, like a good Whig, that the revolution of 1688–9 had endowed England and Scotland with a commitment to civil and religious liberty which might remain the distinctive and unifying theme of public life for perpetuity. It was a tenable proposition that a moderating, enlightened liberty had been attained by the Westminster parliamentary system, and that a passable rate of progress was being maintained by the same system. Asquith and Grey commanded Masterman's allegiance as party leaders. These comforting ideas were dispelled by the formation of the wartime coalition government in 1915 and Asquith's downfall in 1916. Thereafter Masterman was taciturn about his political opinions; but the crudeness of the Lloyd George and Bonar Law governments of 1916–23 and their contempt for hallowed notions of liberty were surely offensive to him.

Of all Liberal statesmen the most impressive to Masterman was John Morley. Morley had no truck with the stolid positivism which thinks all problems are soluble. For him the world was full of wickedness and obscurity: it might be improved, but it could never be made good. He advocated Free Trade and national self-determination, opposed colonialism and militarism, in order to ameliorate evils that could not be abolished. Morley preferred a minimum of governmental regulation, resisted socialism and had scant interest in workers' conditions. He was a rationalist and agnostic who respected clergy of all denominations so long as they had intelligent dignity. One can see why Morley's enlightened aplomb and philosophic radicalism became a model for Masterman. 'He had the calm of complete self-confidence,' J. C. Squire wrote after Morley's death. 'He was more than ordinarily certain about wisdom and unwisdom, never in danger of conversion, schooled against the escape of feverish emotion, though never without heart.' Morley had been one of the first nominations to the newly created Order of Merit in 1902, and Masterman was an acolyte of the OM culture: he revered the values and sentiments of such members of the Order as James Bryce, H. A. L. Fisher, G. P. Gooch, R. B. Haldane, Gilbert Murray, Sir George Otto Trevelyan and George Macaulay Trevelyan. Like Morley they were busy and constructive men who provided literary and academic culture with a Liberal slant. Masterman outlived Morley by more than half a century, but never shed, although circumstances made him adapt, his grounding in Morley's mentality, with its love of truth and aversion to display.[5]

People seeking to reduce social injustice and political instability must, Morley reiterated, accept the value of compromise. His treatise *On Compromise* (1874) begins with an epigraph from Richard Whately, a past Drummond Professor of Political Economy at Oxford: 'It makes all the difference in the world whether we put Truth in the first place or in the second.' England has its full share of truth seekers, Morley declares. He identifies as 'inveterate' national characteristics 'a profound distrust . . . of all general principles; a profound dislike both of much reference to them, and of any disposition to invest them with practical authority; and a silent but most pertinacious measurement of philosophic truths by political tests'. As much as the highest Oxford Tory, Morley believed in studying and improving national character. 'The *character* of the country', he insisted as late as 1900, 'is the most important thing now in issue.' Masterman followed Morley in never doubting that the elevating of national character, by the moulding of young minds, was as important as any task. But he held that no definition of a nation's character stays accurate for longer than twenty years.[6]

If Morley was the chief influence on Masterman's early thinking, Winwood Reade's history of humankind, *The Martyrdom of Man* (1872), counted too. Reade – physician at a cholera hospital, war correspondent for *The Times* in the Ashanti campaign of 1873–4, author of a novel entitled *Liberty Hall, Oxon.*, expert on the habits of the gorilla and explorer of the source of the Niger – was suffused, said Masterman, with 'the Renaissance spirit – the desire, that is, to arrive at the truth, cost what it might, and the determination to accept nothing merely because it carried the seal of authority, but to admit only what could be tried and tested by experiment and by the intellect'. Reade thought of humanity as a petty life form in an immense and varied universe. He treated Christianity as a consoling set of myths which provided a pat explanation of the unknown and unknowable. Masterman summarized his message in these terms: 'Supernatural Christianity is false. God worship is idolatry. Prayer is useless. The soul is not immortal. There are no rewards and no punishments in a future state.'[7]

Mandell Creighton, when he was tutor in modern history at Merton, had chastised Christian preaching for inculcating 'an absence of abandon, an incapacity for living for the moment, a perpetual presence of law in daily life, an attitude of fixity and self-negation'. Masterman's generation at Oxford had similar misgivings about Anglicanism. They lived, so he said, in the present and for the present. They were energetic, competitive and striving; far from self-negating; and seeking explanations that fitted the newest states of knowledge rather than wrenching facts and ideas towards supporting old dogma. When, in about 1912, Gilbert Murray's daughter, Rosalind Toynbee, complained of all the dead bones rattling in Oxford, Arthur Heath, a young Fellow of New College, demurred. The university should be seen from the viewpoint of undergraduates: 'to them', he told Rosalind Toynbee, 'the place is anything but dead'. Masterman was one such undergraduate. To him, high spirits were always preferable to dourness: they were the signs of a sane, tolerant and balanced mind.[8]

Like many of his class and generation in Oxford, Masterman would not make himself conspicuous by any strong interest in Christianity. He described himself as 'normal', 'centre-of-the-road', 'conventional', and was too cautious to join in other people's enthusiasms. His attendance at acts of worship in the college chapel at Worcester and in the cathedral at Christ Church was not an avowal of religious faith. As Provost of Worcester in 1947–61, he enforced chapel attendance on all baptized and confirmed members of the Church of England, because he was convinced of the social and historical value of common observance and outward conformity. It brought orderliness and mutual sympathy to a college if its members worshipped together, or (as some might say) listened with respect to stories of ancient myths. Attendance was a form of 'commonsensality', a word which means fellowship at table, and in the context of Christ Church and Worcester meant eating together in the college hall. The sermons that Masterman preached in chapel struck the congregation by their pragmatism and equipoise.[9]

In 1913 he was encouraged to apply for a lectureship in modern history at Christ Church, with the likelihood of a full studentship after a probationary year. His interview by the selection committee at the House was perfunctory. Robin Dundas, who took peculiar pleasure in reminding Masterman over the years that he had opposed his candidature because he had not read Greats, was excluded from the interviewing panel. Dean Strong asked only one question: 'Mr Masterman, are you a candidate for this lectureship?' Masterman replied, 'Yes'. Then Herbert Blunt, who taught Greats, asked, 'Mr Masterman, are you married?' Masterman replied, 'No'. John Anderson, the lecturer in Roman epigraphy, interpolated in broad Aberdonian, 'Aye, but hae ye perhaps any entanglement?' Masterman again replied, 'No'. Then Charles Fisher, the Senior Censor, enquired: 'Mr Masterman, what do you do in the afternoons?' This question felt tricky to Masterman, who replied cautiously: 'It depends on the weather'. The post was his.[10]

Christ Church encouraged him to go to Germany to learn the language, to meet scholars and to attend lectures. Imperial Germany, with its scrape-and-bow customs, was congenial to Masterman. The officer class of the Hohenzollerns, and the learning and reasoning of German university men, generally impressed him. He felt that European civilization was too advanced for a continental war. At Kassel in Hilary term of 1914 he befriended a carpet designer. 'An agreeable, unworldly, cultured yet simple man,' he wrote forty years later, 'lacking ambition and wholly without the talent of success – but none the worse for that, for only those who have a touch of weakness in their character are, as it seems to me, fit for friendship.' He went to spend the summer term at Freiburg armed with an introduction to the carpet designer's brother Anton, who was a junior lecturer at the university. The two young men met occasionally, and always with pleasure, for they recognized in each other the desire to impart knowledge and to correct error. Early in July Masterman was joined in Freiburg by Timothy Eden, a baronet's heir who had been sent to him for supervised preparatory reading in modern history before matriculating at Christ Church in the autumn. '*Very* pleasant – knows nothing . . . & would pay pretty well,' Hassall wrote in recommendation. On 29 July Eden was joined by Jock Balfour, who had come to Germany to prepare for a diplomatic career.[11]

The likelihood of Anglo-German conflict became real to Masterman when, a day or so after the German declaration of war on Russia on 1 August, his Freiburg landlady came to him shedding tears. Because her brother was an army officer, she explained, the Englishman could not spend another night under her roof. He was the target of fierce glares when some hours later he went for lunch in a hotel restaurant. He was beginning to suspect that he would be refused his soup when a uniformed figure came across the room to him. He recognized Anton, whose voice and eyes were full of sympathy. 'Herr Masterman,' he said, 'I shall be glad if you will come and sit at my table; it is not good for foreigners to eat alone in Germany to-day.' Anton said that he was leaving in a few hours with his battalion for the front, but otherwise they did not mention the looming war. They spoke together, said Masterman, as educated gentlemen who were closing a period of their lives. Anton's last words as they parted had the power of reticence that Masterman always appreciated. He said, undemonstratively but decidedly, 'I am glad that we got to know one another.'[12]

On 5 August Balfour, Eden, Masterman and the other Englishmen in Freiburg were detained. In November they were sent to an internment camp which had been improvised on the imperial trotting course at Spandau known as Ruhleben. Early conditions there were punitive. Improvements were achieved as much of the camp's administration was delegated, during 1915, to its inmates. They ran a parcel service and post office, a kitchen and canteen, fatigue parties, a convalescent wing, sporting tournaments. A golf professional was put in command of the prisoners' own police force. A group of Cambridge scientists gave open-air lectures on their subjects: Masterman recalled the future Nobel laureate James Chadwick lecturing on radioactivity. There were over a hundred different theatrical productions over the course of four years as well as concerts and art exhibitions. A school was started, with seventeen departments and several hundred teachers. Masterman ran the history circle, and gave ambitious lectures. He learnt Italian.

Jock Balfour, his companion at Ruhleben, admitted in old age that many of the young prisoners in the camp, deprived of women for four years, gave one another sexual relief. There is no hint of Masterman's sexual experiences at any stage of his life. Doubtless he regarded exchanges with someone else of bodily fluids as a threat to his self-possession and to his sense of purpose, which were more prized by him than pleasure. Probably, for him, sexual desire was unwelcome because it was involuntary and awkward to control: the product of chance occasions and sensations; an extrinsic force, which needed to be quelled if the integrity of the being called J. C. Masterman was to be protected. In all likelihood he was akin to his Christ Church colleague, the philosopher Gilbert Ryle. Ryle was once asked by another former philosopher at the House, Ayer, who was seeking to break the monotony of a long car journey, if he was still, in his late fifties, a virgin. Ryle admitted that he was. Ayer posed a second question: if Ryle had been sexually involved with someone, was it likelier to have been a boy or a girl? 'Boy, I suppose,' Ryle replied.[13]

In the first of Masterman's lectures in Ruhleben he tried to rally the community spirit. He began with an appeal for all the inmates to live and work together for the common good: a prison camp was not a place for individualism. Then he turned to the lessons of history. 'For myself,' he said, 'I do feel that the deeper one delves into the history of the diplomacy & the policy of any one state, the more one is struck by the tortuous & callous ambition of the majority of rulers, diplomatists & statesmen.' Campaigns of conquest, involving 'crimes of aggrandisement', had been waged in all ages in the name of religion or to serve a nation's expansive pride. As prisoners in Ruhleben, 'Germany is very real to us': 'then for God's sake let us learn what we can about them. If there is any unforgivable fault it is surely the fault of remaining in ignorance when opportunities are offered of acquiring knowledge. It is the most insidious form of mental cowardice.' In the past the English had disdained the views and affairs of other nations. The current world conflict showed that 'an attitude of ignorant insularity . . . will be impossible in the future as it was ridiculous in the past'.[14]

At Ruhleben Masterman's nickname was 'To me! To me!' This was his cry on the hockey field: he wanted his team mates to pass the ball to him because his desire to score was overwhelming. Athletics had been his preferred undergraduate exercise: he won a half-blue at high jump in 1912. During the 1920s he represented England at both lawn tennis and hockey. He was a scratch player of golf and squash. In 1937 he was a member of the MCC cricket team which toured Canada. Although he was graceful to members of a team that had beaten his side, he could be testy with his losing team mates. Certainly his post-mortems on lost bridge hands could discomfit his partner. In life as well as in sports, he thought that he was a better tactician, and therefore better placed to score, than most people. In Oxford it was said that he was the inspiration for

Stephen Potter's best-selling book of 1947 on gamesmanship, which was subtitled *The Art of Winning Games without Actually Cheating*. 'J.C.', said A. T. ('Bill') Williams, Warden of Rhodes House and a fellow member of The Club, 'always cheats, but he always cheats by the rules.'[15]

Following his release from Ruhleben, Masterman returned to Christ Church, where he was promoted from his lectureship to a studentship in 1919. After four years of captivity, he thought of writing a book on famous political imprisonments of the past, but did not persist with the project. His mood was anxious and depressed. His friends and contemporaries had fought in the war. Many had died. He felt ashamed of his four years as a non-combatant. Dean Strong told Masterman that his self-preoccupation was a morbid indulgence. Instead of brooding, he should drive at full throttle at his college work.

Masterman liked Strong, and admired his ability to bring meetings to a decision. The Dean's considerate nature was exemplified when he left the House to become Bishop of Ripon in 1920: he sent hand-written farewell letters, all of them different in their wording, to every member, both senior and junior, of the college. Masterman resolved to emulate Strong's phenomenal memory for persons and faces as best he could. For years, as an examiner in the modern history school, he compiled private notes of the names and visages of undergraduates from other colleges. Those for Trinity term of 1934 were typical. John Plamenatz of Oriel, a Montenegrin who later succeeded Isaiah Berlin as Chichele Professor of Social and Political Theory, was misdescribed as 'big, black, spectacled Jew'. Other unfortunate young men had faces that were 'foolish', 'Fascist', 'common', 'blokey', 'hook-nosed' and 'honest'.[16]

Although there was much dispute about which was the best college in the university, it was generally agreed, reported the *Oxford Magazine* in 1920, 'that the Deanery of Christ Church is the greatest permanent post here'. Lloyd George was bent on nominating William Temple as Strong's successor as Dean. Temple had taken a first in Greats at Balliol, had become a philosophy don at the Queen's College, but had been refused ordination by Paget, Bishop of Oxford and former Dean of Christ Church, because of his dubiety about the Virgin Birth. Temple became an active president of the Workers'

Educational Association in 1908, was finally ordained in 1909 and received swift preferment in the Church. He was a man of glorious intellectual imagination who would have made a great dean; but the Professor Canons and older Students mistrusted him as a radical and resisted his nomination. They enlisted the help of Lloyd George's reprobate Lord Chancellor, Birkenhead, who was a Fellow of Merton and a boon companion of Masterman's. Birkenhead came to the rescue, as he saw it, of his friends at the House and urged the claims of another Merton don, Henry Julian White, to be Dean. After a skirmish with Lloyd George, Birkenhead prevailed.[17]

White was, said Roy Harrod, 'loyal in all his dealings, as straight as a die, not a very intelligent or cultured man, but an assiduous scholar and utterly devoted to Christ Church'. He had been born in Islington, where his father was a bank clerk; and by the 1920s his voice trembled with pleasure at the mention of a duke. For White the two dozen dukes, in precedence from Norfolk to Westminster, were a sacrosanct part of the establishment of Church and state. It was a grief to him that the shy but sturdy Duke of Norfolk failed his Responsions three years running, despite coaching by Father Ronald Knox, and therefore could not be admitted to the House. As a consolation for White, the future Duke of Richmond and the future Duke of Argyll both matriculated at Christ Church in the 1920s. So, too, did the Duke of Portland's younger son Lord Morven Cavendish-Bentinck, described as 'the stupidest boy alive' by an Eton housemaster who believed that the House, 'while resolutely refusing the stupid and idle boy', should 'still find room for the stupid but hard-working one'.[18]

As a Worcester undergraduate Masterman had decided that undergraduates in an arts subject could not work at their books with any benefit for more than six hours a day. He held to this view more strongly than ever at Christ Church, where it was good form for conformists to pretend that they slacked in their work. Kenneth Kirk, Regius Professor of Moral and Pastoral Theology there, after-wards Bishop of Oxford, told Masterman that the first of the two principles which should be observed at Oxford was that 'no gentleman works after dinner'. And the second? Masterman asked. That 'no gentleman works after lunch', said Kirk, who had himself achieved two first-classes and must therefore have flouted his principles. Anyone who studied eight hours or more daily had wasted their time, Masterman maintained. He felt that the difference between a top second and a first was made by traits, such as intelligence and powers of concentration, which were innate rather than acquired in tutorials or by intensive study. The 'private hour' spent together by tutor and pupil was for Masterman the joy of his university. 'It's the weekly talk and discussion between pupil and tutor which is the essence of Oxford life,' he wrote. He deprecated Hassall's generation, which had often misused the private hour to 'pump information' into pupils. 'Ought not', he once asked, 'the tutor to pride himself more on the honest and industrious men of virtue whom he has guided safely into the second class, or even more, perhaps, on the low and dubious third whom he has saved from disaster?'[19]

'In the 1920s, what a place Christ Church was!' Masterman enthused; 'magnificent yet friendly, regal yet tolerant.' In its common room he learnt the pace and skills of a winning raconteur: his after-dinner speeches, too, were masterpieces of timing and occasion. He loved Worcester, but never doubted after 1920 that Christ Church was the greatest of all Oxford colleges. *Freedom and Continuity* was his motto for it. For him there was no typical member of the House: 'The glory of Christ Church lies in its diversity.' There was no need of a coercive college spirit. Junior members of the House were not expected to toe any lines. 'Christ Church was large enough and great enough to let each go his own way and develop his own interests. There was room for artists and athletes and aesthetes . . . as well as for scholars and scientists and future statesmen.'[20]

The twentieth-century understanding of 'diversity' was not the twenty-first's. Women were not admitted to Christ Church until 1980. The fires of English nativism made Oxford crackle with sparks of racial superiority. When Solomon Bandaranaike arrived at Christ Church in Michaelmas term of 1919, Sidney Owen, who was then Senior Censor, told him that only English public schoolboys were suited to read *Literae Humaniores*. The future Ceylonese Prime Minister nevertheless insisted on doing so. He felt that thereafter he was known as 'the "darkie" who had the temerity to read for the Honour School of Classics'. He was put in lodgings with a family called Best. 'Oh! the horror of that sitting-room,' he recalled. 'Drab, dreary, smug – two smug porcelain figures on the mantelpiece with a square box in the centre, pretending to be a clock, although it had long ceased to function as such, the smug upright chairs with their dreary reddish upholstery, the dingy curtain – it nearly drove me mad. Why do people imagine that what is ordinary and drab must essentially be sane and safe?' Life was no more agreeable in college than *chez* Best. 'In all directions I found myself opposed by barriers, which, though invisible and impalpable, were none the less very real.' A story that he submitted for the college magazine, the *Cardinal's Hat*, was returned. He failed even to get a trial for one of the Christ Church tennis teams. He never caught the President's eye at Union debates. There were other humiliating signs that he was unwanted. 'It is terribly wounding, after laboriously patching up an acquaintance with one's neighbour at dinner in Hall or at lectures, to be passed by him in the street as though he had never seen one, or, still worse, to see him hurry off with a hasty nod through fear that he might have to walk with one along the street.'[21]

The New College historian Hastings Rashdall said that a dinner invitation from an undergraduate is the greatest social triumph available to a don. By this gauge, every term was filled with triumphs for Masterman. His favourite pupil, who gave him most dinners, is telling about his preferences. Victor ('Teenie') Cazalet arrived at Christ Church in 1919 after military service on the Western Front and in Siberia. His family assumed that he would leave Christ Church after two years, with an enhanced social sheen, and seek adoption as Conservative candidate in a safe parliamentary constituency. He was a conventionally minded youth whose questions were no more searching than his reactions were original. English public schools, he declared after playing racquets at Wellington, are 'immeasurably superior to anything [else] in the world. They make England.' His diary jottings have an identical tune about his tutor: 'Masterman is so reasonable, so balanced,' and 'such a nice man & so competent'. It was doubtless with Masterman's help that Cazalet read a paper to the Canning Club (15 March 1922) on a favourite interest of his tutor, Bismarck. It was certainly Masterman's persuasion that ensured that Cazalet completed his three years and sat his finals despite his parents' indifference to examination results.[22]

Everything that Masterman liked in Cazalet left Bandaranaike unimpressed: to the Ceylonese he bore 'the stamped-upon look' of 'the average English gentleman'; seemed 'entirely colourless and lacking in personality (a display of personality would be "bad form" to one of his class), possessed of a superiority complex which sat on him so naturally that it transcended mere snobbishness'. Probably the celibacy of Cazalet attracted Masterman, too. 'The nearest Teenie ever got to sex', Harold Nicolson said, 'was once when he got an erection thinking about a young duke at Eton.' He made several proposals to Curzon's daughter Irene Ravensdale, but as he was a teetotaller who insisted on an unconsummated marriage, and she was a highly sexed drunkard, she refused him. He was nicknamed the Pompadour of the Foreign Office and slept (probably chastely) with Henry 'Chips' Channon, the louche Belgravia playboy who attended Christ Church in the early 1920s. 'A loyal and loving lad', Channon called him, whose 'horror of alcohol or of anything to do with sexual acts was certainly abnormal'. This was the man whom Masterman called 'the perfect friend', and 'the most gifted and the most to be admired of all the many men who passed through Christ Church in my time'.[23]

Masterman's vocation was to be a don. He studied Newman's *Idea of a University* and decided that its central sentence was the declaration that a university is 'not a factory, nor a mint, nor a treadmill'. He agreed with his Worcester friend C. H. Wilkinson that Oxford colleges were consecrated to two overlapping purposes. 'There is the encouragement of learning, but learned men, like saints, are uncommon', Wilkinson said. 'A college will also – and especially – cherish the important majority . . . who will do the work of the country in Church and State, in the Services, the Professions, and Business – men who all make their bow to knowledge and pick up their pebbles on the edge of its ocean.' Masterman feared that if colleges competed to obtain the best degree results rather than steadied themselves by cultivating all-round abilities, the universities, and then government service and business, would decline into 'orthodox mediocrity'. The expansion of undergraduate numbers in the 1950s, and the publicity given to the examination grades achieved by undergraduates of different colleges, turned universities into mass-production degree factories. University education was no longer, he said in 1958, 'a ladder to be climbed, but an escalator on which the student stands and on which he is conveyed from one stage to another without individual effort or initiative'.[24]

Until the 1940s, and with the exception of competitive sports, Masterman avoided distractions outside Christ Church. Feiling, he thought, lost some of his authority as a teacher of history by his activity as a Conservative partisan in the university. As a member of the Liberal intelligentsia he had no truck with the squalid opportunism of Lloyd George. Moreover, after 1922, Liberal MPs were elected by remote rural constituencies, Anglesey, Barnstaple and Caithness for example, where the philosophic radicalism of Morley had no pull. Masterman's estrangement from partisan Liberalism increased after 1930, when he and his former protégé Roy Harrod, who was a leading Liberal in university politics, became adversaries in college business. At the core of Masterman's being was a wish to conserve whatever was of existing value. He wished to hold, protect and enhance present benefits. The chance of some marginal addition of profits by changing or jettisoning institutions, buildings, landscapes and mentalities was not enough to justify the spoliation of a familiar amenity or current advantage. He disliked abrupt change or disruptive innovations and valued orderliness. In a lecture on the French revolution he quoted Burke: 'A spirit of innovation is generally the result of a selfish temper & confined views.'[25]

The ways in which Morley's Liberalism tinged his teaching are clear from the course of ten lectures which Masterman gave in the early 1930s on Italy from the Congress of Vienna in 1815 to the incorporation of Rome into the recently unified state of Italy in 1870. For Morley the history of the political, secular and ecclesiastical problems involved in the Risorgimento, or movement for Italian unification, 'was in many ways the evolution of European Liberalism in its widest and grandest sense'. For G. M. Trevelyan, in his trilogy on Garibaldi, the history of Italy's resurrection became 'part of the imperishable and international poetry of the European races', a line quoted by Masterman. And the Italian nationalists who attained unification thought they were building 'a monument of civilization' such as the world had never dreamt of. 'Once humanity is organized on this basis [of nationalities], there will be no more war in the world,' promised Bettino Ricasoli, the Tuscan nobleman who was Prime Minister of Italy during the 1860s. Italian unification was, he maintained, necessary for Europe, necessary for humanity, necessary for Christianity, necessary for morality.[26]

Such talk appealed to Masterman. The struggle to unify the Italian people, and to free them from Austrian or French occupiers, was (he believed) both a national epic and a morality tale in which virtue vanquished vice. 'It illustrates the victory of the great principles of the 19th century. The will of the people prevailed. The people succeeded in overthrowing the arrangements of the Congresses [of Vienna, Troppau and Laibach, 1815, 1820–1]. More important still, it is the most triumphant assertion of that other great principle of the century, the principle of Nationality.' Masterman stressed the 'nobility & singleness of purpose' of the architects of Italian unification. Theirs was not initially a populist movement, but 'the work of a true aristocracy, and all the best elements of Italian life took part in it. For this reason the study of the Risorgimento is the best antidote to the study of the Realpolitik of the 19th century.' Prussian military aggression against Austria, Denmark and France made a unified Germany, said Masterman, but Italy came into being without foreign wars. 'It represents not the triumph of power but the triumph of an ideal, and it is the most encouraging proof of the truth that the power of an ideal is in the long run the greatest force of all, even in politics.'[27]

Prussian policy from the reign of Frederick the Great to the apogee of Bismarck was the subject of many Masterman lectures. He took his view of eighteenth-century politics from Albert Sorel's L'Europe et la révolution française (1885). As he summarized Sorel's arguments to his lecture audiences, 'Policy was based upon "reason of state". The doctrine that in politics everything for the advantage of the state was justified was taught to the world by Rome & revived at the Renaissance. Machiavelli describes it. Richelieu, Mazarin & Louis XIV applied it.' Such notions were anathema to those, including Morley and Masterman, who believed in justice, equity and truth. European conditions deteriorated after Frederick's accession to the Prussian throne in 1740. 'The key to the Frederician tradition was *a belief in material success*, the most damning, the most fatal of all

creeds,' said Masterman. 'Frederick originated nothing; he simply
. . . pushed the theories of his predecessors to their logical conclusion, and his resources to the uttermost. Men worship success, &
therefore they accepted his policy.' Frederick began 'a vast series of
political immoralities. He is the true revolutionary, the real mischief-
maker in Europe.' His march into Silesia in 1741 was a pivotal
moment in history: a show of 'the naked policy of might'; a declaration for all Europe that 'politics are outside morality'. It began a
spiral of aggression in which a state like Prussia seized a province
like Silesia because it had the strength to do so.[28]

Hassall, as a Tory democrat, had extolled Bolingbroke in a biography of 1915. The Tory publicist Charles Whibley celebrated him
in a paper read to the Canning Club in 1919. Masterman was of a
different mind. In his lectures on eighteenth-century England he
paraphrased Morley's judgement on Bolingbroke: 'Of all the characters in our history, he was most of a charlatan.' More than any
other man, Masterman told his pupils, Bolingbroke envenomed the
politics of Georgian England. 'He was a consummate posture-maker,
hollow, flashy, & insincere. He was a bad, clever man.' At every
occasion he fomented quarrels, showed himself as vain, presumptuous and corrupt. He quoted to Bolingbroke's discredit a phrase
which had amused Hassall: this was the Tory patriot's boast of how
to manage the House of Commons: 'they grow, like hounds, fond
of the man who shows them game, and by whose halloo they are
used to be encouraged'.[29]

For Masterman the lessons of failure were rich and abundant.
The eighteenth-century statesman John, Lord Carteret, later second
Earl Granville, interested him greatly. It was not just that Carteret
had been educated at Christ Church, whence, as Swift said, he 'carried
away more Greek, Latin, & philosophy, than properly became a
person of his rank'. Masterman was adept in German, French and
Italian and understood Spanish: linguistic skills were valued by him.
'Amazingly able,' he called Carteret: 'one of the best classical scholars
of his time, and at the same time a master of modern languages, &
the only minister who could converse with the king [George I] in
German. His knowledge of the politics of Europe was unrivalled.'
He praised Carteret in lectures to Christ Church audiences:

Courageous beyond any doubt; a really great orator, as all his contemporaries agreed. In private life full of charm. 'That shrewd, jolly man', says Horace Walpole. You are to think of him as a great aristocrat and as a great gentleman. Proud, open-handed, rather contemptuous of small men & small things. With all these qualities he had the corresponding failings. In the political pamphlets of the day he is 'Jack Headlong'. He was without doubt prone to rash & hasty measures (so for that matter was Chatham) . . . Carteret's brilliant intellect was clouded by drink. He was incapable of that which a statesman most needs, 'self-contained patience'. He was a great patriot, but he was unsuited to parliamentary government. He was fitted for the part of a Strafford or a Richelieu; that part he could have played to perfection. He was autocratic in the extreme. It seems indeed strange that such a man should have left so little impression on us. Yet what a career!

In foreign policy Carteret wanted to return to the old Whig formula and to unite as much of Europe against France as possible. The pacification of Germany was the first essential condition to success, as he always urged on English ambassadors.[30]

A pithy sentence of Lord Rosebery's encapsulated the flawed gamesmanship of Carteret: 'He played his political chess with the big pieces alone, and neglected the pawns.' Masterman taught that Carteret failed because he would not stoop to party management. 'The small people and the small things destroyed him, though he despised them.' He concluded, 'The final lesson of his career is: Don't despise machinery. You have got to get things done, and you can't get them done if you affect to consider yourself above the consideration of ways and means. Carteret never learned this lesson. Pitt had to.'[31]

The drawing of fine and if necessarily wavering lines was 'the most essential thing which we learn at the University', Masterman said. The best that could be learnt in arts subjects was 'how to discriminate between the important and the unimportant'. Modern history, if well taught, must give lessons in judicious discernment. 'Of course,' he conceded, 'it's desirable that men should study for the love of learning, but if you press your argument too far you are . . . in danger of changing, and spoiling, the University.' It would be a dull place if it only contained people fixed on academic research, or those whom the Victorians had called 'reading men'. As Masterman wrote in 1953, 'We want, we must want, to bring here not only the scholars and the men of learning, but also those who will govern our country and control our Empire and fill our professions and spread our business (and with it our good name for honesty and integrity) over the world.'[32]

'Some students may study history', Masterman suggested, 'for sheer love of truth and with no other aim, but the majority should study it for the great mass of vicarious experience that they gain from it.' The subject taught shrewdness, prudence and tact. Alec Douglas-Home, who became Prime Minister in 1963 and served for almost seven years as Foreign Secretary, had many 'private hours' with Masterman in the 1920s. Tutorials in seventeenth- and eighteenth-century European history, and especially the special subject of William and Mary (1688–1702), taught him to appraise evidence before taking a decision, to recognize the need for ruthlessness in a crisis and to grasp the rudiments of managing colleagues and subordinates. Probably Masterman repeated to Douglas-Home, as he did to other pupils, Morley's advice to a young man starting in politics: 'If you do two good things, and prevent six bad ones, and compromise on everything else, you will have had a successful and useful career.' Douglas-Home was gravely ill during the winter and spring of 1924–5. He preferred to sit his finals in 1925 rather than claim an *ægrotat* (medical exemption), and got a third-class degree. He worked better and harder than this suggests.[33]

Lectures on the growth of the Westminster parliamentary democracy were a boon for undergraduates with political hopes. In Masterman's telling, the Reform Bill of 1832 inaugurated government by 'shopocracy': his coinage for commercial interests making laws and taking decisions for their own sectional benefit. His treatment of the Reform Act of 1867 was bracingly revisionist. Lord Derby and Disraeli, leading the Conservatives in the two chambers of parliament, decided on a pre-emptive parliamentary reform bill, which was intended to 'dish the Whigs' by enlarging the suffrage. Their bill was so thoroughly rewritten by the Commons that by the end of the debates only four of the sixty-one sections of the bill had not been amended. The tactics of the Derby–Disraeli government

were 'immoral', Masterman told his pupils. The act of 1867 'introduced an era of opportunism'. It endowed with burgeoning political
power 'men who had not been educated up to an understanding of
civic duty and responsibility'.[34]

He circulated advice to his pupils before they sat their finals. 'The
Schools are a test of character just as much as a test of intelligence,
or a test of knowledge. Therefore you've got to fight for yourselves
– and to do that you've got to be fit – *and fresh!*' He gave his ruling
precepts:

1. Everyone is a law to himself, but there are certain general
   principles, confirmed by experience.
2. *The all-important principle.* You must go into the Schools with
   a *fresh* mind. You are being examined on the results of three
   years' work; everything you have learned at one time or another
   is buried somewhere; you can dig it up if your mind is fresh,
   & you can't if your mind is tired. A tired mind means tired &
   dull work. Remember that this is a six-day examination – and
   that you want to be writing good stuff on the sixth day as well
   as on the first. It's quite easy to train a man, or cram a man,
   for a one day's examination – he can burst on the next day.
   But this is a long-distance affair.
3. So arrange your revision that you have finished it by the Sunday
   before the Schools, and have a rest for the three days. June 1,
   2, 3. If you've *not* finished what you meant to do by then, no
   matter. Leave the rest undone. You *must* have a fresh mind on
   June 4. Whether you go away for June 1, 2, 3 or stay in Oxford
   depends on individual tastes. But whichever it is: no work.
4. You have to arrange your days (& nights) properly while you
   are actually in the Schools . . . You will be doing 6 hours a day
   intensive work in the Schools – therefore arrange for the period
   5–8 [pm] out-of-doors if possible.[35]

Masterman's situation at Christ Church brought him total satisfaction. Rather than leave the beauty and fulfilment of the House, he
declined overtures to become Second Master of Winchester in 1925,
and Headmaster of Eton in 1933. Geoffrey Dawson, Editor of *The
Times*, recommended him to Sir John Reith, Director-General of

the BBC, who was looking for a deputy to reorganize the Corporation. Reith interviewed him, heard him claim that he lacked the crusading zeal necessary for the job and took his recommendation of Colonel Alan Dawnay for the post. When Dawnay collapsed in 1935, Reith reapproached Masterman, who again declined to leave the House.

Year after year at Christ Church Masterman contended with other Students, such as the classical archaeologist John Beazley, who thought pure research was more important than the influences of the private hour. The appointment of a subcommittee of the governing body to consider the claims of research, and the possibility of accommodating more researchers, led to a flurry of manifestos from Students in 1931. Ryle, the classicist J. G. Barrington-Ward and Harrod circulated papers supporting Beazley's line. Masterman responded with a counterblast which was, by his standards, outstandingly sarcastic.

Masterman urged that control of Christ Church be confined to those whose working lives were spent teaching the junior members of the college rather than shared with 'half-trained youths', as he called researchers holding short-term appointments, who were unversed 'in the intricacies and vexations of college politics'. The existing membership of the governing body was 'far more likely to serve the interests of Christ Church than a heterogeneous mob of persons – many of whom can, in the nature of things, be with us only for a short period, and who can be but very imperfectly acquainted with our problems, our policy and our traditions'. The scheme of Barrington-Ward and Ryle might, after compromises by both sides, have ended in agreement. But this prospect had been shattered by the disruptive proposals tendered by Harrod. An influx of research Students – 'the incursion of the Harrodian hordes', in Masterman's phrase – would overcrowd the common room and high table, and force undergraduates to lodge in rented rooms outside the college. 'But perhaps this last point is irrelevant', he said in a further barb. 'The undergraduates, neglected, contemned and untaught, would no doubt soon disappear from Christ Church.' Usually Masterman concealed his feelings, but in 1931 he let himself utter a cry from the heart. 'For years Christ Church has trained and turned into the world a very worthy and often distinguished body of men, a vast majority of whom has done, or is doing, useful and even notable work.' It was the weekly 'private hour' of tutorial instruction that had been the making of these men. 'It is inconceivable to me that the present college teaching can be adequately replaced by the casual conversation of Mr Harrod's dilettante researchers, using their spare hours to scatter a few crumbs of culture among undergraduates of whom they will know almost nothing, and for whom they will care less.'[36]

Once Masterman had expected to write history books. His incarceration, his busy years as Junior Censor under Dundas and his busier years as Senior Censor above Frank Taylor, however, gave scant time for research or composition. After relinquishing the censorship in 1931, he planned a study of French leadership during the first Bourbon restoration of 1814–15. Then, while he was working in Paris on sources in the Archives Nationales and the Bibliothèque Nationale, he realized that he could never meet his historical aspirations. He shared all the rash vehemence of one set of partisans and could not respect their opponents. He decided that Feiling was right to say that imaginative partisans came nearer to the truth than professedly objective scholars. But all his life he had tried to efface his feelings: he could not bring himself to show his historical passions in the chapters of a book. Dons, he wrote, 'spend so much of our lives criticising the work of others that we can't bring ourselves to be creative. We're continually polishing and refining and altering what we've done, and the world gets nothing.'[37]

After his renunciation of historical writing in Paris, Masterman wrote two novels, *An Oxford Tragedy* (1933) and *Fate Cannot Harm Me* (1935). Fifteen years later, he composed a book of dialogues entitled *To Teach the Senators Wisdom* (1952). In it an ex-soldier bursar, a chaplain, a scientist, a young ex-diplomat and an old-fashioned don extol the spacious, urbane, tolerant and civilizing influence of the Oxford college system. A novel of crime prevention, *The Case of the Four Friends* (1956), into which he squirrelled some revealing comments on the espionage of Burgess and Maclean, and a collection of occasional writings, *Bits and Pieces* (1961), followed. His memoirs *On the Chariot Wheel* (1975) were produced by Oxford University Press.[38]

The declaration of war in 1939 was redemptive, in some respects, for Masterman. 'For twenty years I had lived under the weight of an inferiority complex, never frankly admitted and never openly expressed, but none the less burdensome to me. I could never rid myself of the hateful feeling that I had played no part in the first war and that I had in some way let my country down.' His temperament was suited to high-level wartime planning and administration. 'I don't think', said Harry Pitt, 'that he ever moved or spoke without considering the consequences of what he was doing or saying, and following the possible repercussions through in his mind to see what the long-term outcome might be. I never saw him flustered or unprepared; he was not easily surprised and not, I think, shockable, though he could be disappointed if one did not behave as he thought an educated man should behave.' People became cautious in his company: some in emulation of him; others because they sensed his talent for drawing opponents into irreversible missteps or dead ends.[39]

Everyone, said Masterman in his Christ Church lectures, should despise secret societies: they promise much and deliver little. But secret services were different. In 1940 he was admitted to the Intelligence Corps, and was then seconded to the Security Service (MI5). There he became Chairman of the Twenty (XX) Committee, which was formed in 1941 as a revival of the old practice of *ruse de guerre* and set out to misinform and misdirect the enemy by means of turning captured agents into double agents. Harry Pitt once asked him if there had been any German agents who refused to be turned. 'No,' he replied, 'after a little reflection they all considered what the alternative was.' XX's greatest coup was in misleading the German High Command about the Allied landings in France in June 1944. Large defensive forces were retained in the Pas de Calais region rather than in Normandy, where the Anglo-American forces always planned to land. In 1945 Masterman wrote a history of XX which, after much opposition from the keepers of official secrets, was finally published in 1972 under the title *The Double-Cross System*.[40]

'This has been very much a dons' war,' Isaiah Berlin wrote from his post in the British embassy in Washington in 1944 to his former tutor at Corpus, G. B. Grundy, author of *Thucydides and the History of his Age*. 'On the whole it does not seem to be too badly run by our profession, which seems to have destroyed its reputation for starry-eyed incompetence once and for all. Nobody is so fiercely bureaucratic, or so stern with soldiers and regular civil servants, as the don disguised as temporary government official armed with an indestructible superiority complex.' The philosopher Oliver Franks and the political economist John Maud were 'practically controlling the home departments in London', Berlin told Grundy; but he did not mention those dons, such as Masterman, whose wartime work was covert. Franks was elected Master of the Queen's College, Oxford in 1946, Masterman succeeded his mentor Francis Lys as Provost of Worcester in the same year, and Maud became Master of University College some years later. Maud found that the great difference between heading a Whitehall department and leading an Oxford college was that as Master he had the influence to cajole the governing body, but not the power to coerce it.[41]

The oration at the Censor's dinner of 1947 was given by Masterman. 'No one could leave Christ Church without regrets,' he began. 'So much, so very much of all that is best in Oxford is concentrated here.' The peculiar excellence of the college did not lie in its piety and learning, or in its training of men for the higher reaches of Church and state, for other colleges had managed that. The superiority of the House arose from the fact 'that in all ages we have had of all people the best opportunities of living a full and spacious life'. The college constituted its own realm of precious memories, precious sights and precious objects:

> Think of our Library & our pictures, our Cathedral music & our playing fields & our garden, our dinners in Hall & our common rooms, & you see a picture of a good & full & spacious life. Barrington-Ward who understood & loved the House used always to speak of our noble relics. We are indeed the most favoured people in the world, or, if you like, the most highly privileged. Then let us not be afraid to say that the maintenance of these privileges is beneficial to the community in general & let us work rather to increase than to diminish them. And it does seem to me that in this respect Christ Church has a great opportunity now. It was a gracious way of life that we followed in days gone by; we have to recover all that was best in it now – and if any

institution can do that, it is Christ Church. We want the culture, the spaciousness, the good taste and the enjoyment of good things. Whatever we do we must not allow ourselves to become cramped or standardised or deferential. Some extravagance, some panache is surely better for us than a sort of nationalised mediocrity.

One of the secrets of Christ Church, Masterman said, was its felicity. He ended his speech by quoting Robert Louis Stevenson saying that no duty is as constantly neglected as the duty of being happy.[42]

In 1948 the Attlee government decided that it must appoint a committee of inquiry into the political activities of civil servants. This was the year in which the Cold War started, and also, as shown by the launch of the annual BBC Reith lectures with a series given by Bertrand Russell, the dawn of the age of the English public intellectual. Ministers wanted a don, preferably a political scientist, to chair the committee. The Cabinet Secretary, Sir Edward Bridges, who doubled as a Fellow of All Souls, suggested A. D. Lindsay of Balliol, Sir Frederick Ogilvie of Jesus or Oliver Franks. The Chancellor of the Exchequer, Stafford Cripps, supported Lindsay for the chair, and counselled: 'Don't put Franks onto this second-class job. He is wanted . . . for higher things.' (Soon afterwards Franks was sent as Ambassador to the USA.) John Maud recommended Warden Sumner of All Souls. Ernest Barker was judged to be too old; G. D. H. Cole to be too partisan; Kenneth Wheare, Michael Oakeshott and Denis Brogan too academic. Support for R. B. McCallum of Pembroke College, 'a sensible and level-headed man who would not be carried away by any fanciful ideas', was dispersed after Maud warned that he 'would not add brightness or distinction'. In the end, the chairmanship went to Masterman. He wrote the report himself after gaining unanimity from his committee. As a liberal, he wanted to allow political activity to as many civil servants as possible, but he knew that few freedoms can be illimitable. Accordingly, he demarcated lower-grade civil servants, who were free to participate in party politics, from upper grades who must not imperil their neutrality.[43]

'J.C. had little time for politicians,' recalled Harry Pitt. 'He thought of them as operating in a risky, rickety, transient world which could collapse overnight.' He mistrusted the areas of government that were susceptible to stormy groundswells of public opinion. He put his trust in the higher ranks of officialdom, Lords of Appeal in Ordinary, ambassadors, bishops, chairmen of Royal Commissions, public school headmasters. 'If they were sound, all would be well with England,' Masterman declared. They owed their positions to private tests of merit or private processes of selection. They were seldom crabbed by the crudity, volatility and potential injustice of democratic control. Better still, they were not subject to dismissal by democratic process. Their independence enabled them to protect the national interest, which was best served, Masterman thought, by moderation and continuity, from the headstrong and disjunctive popular will. He was a consummate fixer who achieved his ends by going to the top man with the power of ultimate decision (in his epoch it was invariably a man). He had almost clairvoyant gifts in perceiving who would be the best man (again it was always a man) for positions of responsibility. He was consulted by university colleagues, Downing Street officials, government ministers, school governors, and often had the satisfaction of seeing his candidate chosen to be a headmaster, Regius professor, company director, school governor or intelligence chief.[44]

During the 1950s Masterman was the acknowledged doyen of the Modern History Faculty in Oxford. He never hustled for change, but adjusted to it swiftly. The scrappy mess that came from lingering in last ditches had no appeal to him. 'He never regretted the past and never recriminated,' wrote a colleague. 'He seldom gave a confidence and never asked for one: his loyalty was absolute and he expected it to be returned.' Irrelevance was for him a prime intellectual fault, and a grievous error in all forms of governance. Time-wasting attention to inessentials and side issues was intolerable, too. 'Skilful, sometimes ruthless in business and always watchful . . . he was, in his worlds, as much an accomplished statesman as those eighteenth-century Whigs whom he understood and admired.'[45]

CHAPTER 9

Roy Harrod: Keynesian on a Slum Island

Roy Harrod was one of the staunchest of Christ Church men. Only a full biography, rather than this thematic essay, can meet his merits. He qualifies for a chapter in *History in the House* because he was, during the 1920s, the junior colleague of Hassall, Feiling and Masterman. Hassall, by then, was approaching seventy years of age and took only a few pupils for private hours in which he discussed the hunting field rather than their essays. Feiling and Masterman had no interest in teaching the early centuries of the curriculum. Harrod agreed to tighten the consequent teaching slack. He counts, too, as a historian because in the 1950s he wrote two works of contemporary history, showing the dominance and value of intellectuals in government, books that impressed reviewers and were memorable to their readers. Yet it was not love of history that made him accept the post of a Christ Church lecturer in 1922. He could find no better way of getting ready money, which he needed to pay the expenses of his widowed mother, who was then living in a residential hotel in South Kensington. It does not seem to have struck him how much the life of a bachelor don living in college resembled that of that of a lady living in a small private hotel.[1]

In addition to the history side, Harrod was also required to give tutorials to any Christ Church undergraduate who chose to read the newly inaugurated school of PPE. So far as the governing body of Christ Church was concerned, the economics part of the syllabus lagged hindmost behind the philosophy and politics. It was, nevertheless, the discipline in which Harrod made his mark. He co-edited the *Economic Journal* from 1945 until 1961, served as an economic adviser to the International Monetary Fund and was President of the Royal Economic Society. By his official biography of Keynes (published in 1951) he became the evangelist of Keynesianism whose voice reached furthest. Yet he never intended to be an economist. Philosophy was his first preference. Of all his books, he invested most in *Foundations of Inductive Logic* (published in 1956). He consoled himself in the 1950s with the thought that economists had achieved their main successes when they emulated philosophers by devising concepts and classifications. Economics could not be accepted as a science so long as its laws could not be expressed quantitatively or tested by experiment.[2]

Harrod was born in Chelsea in 1900. His father had matriculated at New College in 1877, converted to the Church of Rome a year or two later and was induced by his priests to avoid the contaminating ideas of an Anglican university by leaving early without a degree. He moved to Clapham, took articles with a solicitor and practised law with enough success to live during the 1890s in bachelor chambers in Down Street, off Piccadilly. In two unlucky decisions, he became a member of the London Metals Exchange, and then Secretary of a copper mine on the north coast of Anglesey. He sank his capital in the mine, went bankrupt in 1907 and lost his marital home in Chelsea's Oakley Street. Thereafter he worked as a City clerk at a salary of £3 a week, received a weekly allowance of £2 from a brother-in-law and numbed his feelings with alcohol. It took ten years to discharge his bankruptcy. A year later, he died. He had such meagre assets that there was no need for probate on his estate.

Frances ('Frankie') Forbes-Robertson, his wife, was a hardier character. She was daughter of the art critic of the *Sunday Times*, sister of the actor Sir Johnston Forbes-Robertson who was considered the finest Hamlet of his generation, and sister too of Eric Forbes-Robertson, a member of Gauguin's Pont-Aven school and one of England's few Post-Impressionist figure and landscape painters. She herself was a portrait painter and novelist whose fictions were praised by readers as varied as Walter Pater and Rebecca West. In 1930 a reviewer described her work as 'witty, reflective, and extremely observant'. If her marriage had prospered, she would have shone as the vivacious doyenne of a salon in which editors, authors, artists, fashionable dons, pulpit celebrities, intrepid travellers and gifted amateurs met in genial admiration of one another. As it was, Harrod sat, as a small child, on Henry James's knee and played tennis with Ford Madox Ford.[3]

The Forbes-Robertson family remained staunch friends of Oscar Wilde after his downfall in 1895. He found Frankie especially 'sweet', empathetic, and trustworthy. Knowing that she would keep it 'a strict secret from the general world', he wanted one of the two typed extracts of De Profundis to be sent to her. He also allotted one of the first printed copies of The Ballad of Reading Gaol to her. Frankie often talked with animation and emphasis of Wilde to her son, who provided an interesting summary of her views after the publication of Wilde's letters in 1962. 'My mother held that of all the people she had known', he wrote in the Times Literary Supplement, 'Oscar Wilde gave her the greatest feeling of certainty that everything he said came straight from the heart. His integrity was absolute. That was her most insistent testimony.'[4]

After the financial crash of 1907, the Harrods occupied a small flat on the fourth floor of Abingdon Mansions off Kensington High Street. In 1911 their only child gained a scholarship to St Paul's School, the civic day school which lay at the western extremity of the High Street in a locality that called itself West Kensington to avoid the smear of Hammersmith. It was a competitive forcing house, which drilled its pupils in the ways to win college awards, first-class honours and university prizes. They were resolute under examination conditions, where they provided fluent, well-practised, standard opinions, but they left the school often unresolved and uninteresting in character. Fortunately, at a school sports day, Frankie Harrod heard cockney accents, and transferred her son to a better London public school, Westminster, in 1913. Its setting, next to Westminster Abbey and hard by the Palace of Westminster, gave urbanity to its pupils. Eccentricity was tolerated there so long as it was amusing. Small boys were able to tease bigger boys as a puppy might play with an Alsatian, without rough retaliation. Bullying and initiation rites were worse in most other schools of this type. Compulsory morning prayers in the abbey made a militant agnostic of the young Harrod, who remained irreligious for perpetuity.

Although he was a King's Scholar at Westminster, his parents could not afford to pay for him to board with other scholars. He therefore attended as a day boy, as he had at St Paul's. Instead of a daily soaking in the assumptions and habits of a boarding house he ate his breakfasts and spent his evenings in a little flat with his anxious and depressed parents. His unhappy home life gave him mettle. From it he learnt to be an acute psychologist of types. His mother's thwarted hope to keep a salon in which she could assemble and display the cognoscenti implanted in her only child a presumption of affinity with illustrious people. He became confident and inquisitive in the company of both the truly great and the materially imposing. It was by living with his mother that Harrod came to know all about the human intensities. The sorry results of her impractical emotionalism made him resolve to be not only passionate but realistic in his doings. More than that, his father's null and tipsy defeatism roused him to admire men of bounding self-assertion such as Maynard Keynes and Frederick Lindemann, Lord Cherwell – the subjects of his major books of 1951 and 1959.

Latterly, at Westminster, Harrod renounced classics for modern history. He studied the subject well enough to win a history scholarship at New College in 1918. After leaving school that summer, he enlisted in the Royal Field Artillery as a cadet, and vowed to himself that he would never return to the clutches of his parents and their emotionally depleting atmosphere. While he was training on Salisbury Plain, his father died suddenly, a few days after the Armistice, on 16 November.

At New College in 1919, despite Harrod's history scholarship, Warden Spooner cajoled Harrod into reading Greats. The fourth Reform Act of 1918 had turned England, Scotland and Wales decisively towards a mass-suffrage parliamentary democracy; but it was understood that efficient government must remain oligarchic. Greats at this time continued to be upheld as the highest intellectual experience to be found in England, or perhaps in the world. It remained, so its tutors thought, indispensable training for young men destined to hold official or political power. In Harrod's words, 'even a democracy must have an élite, and Greats was deemed to provide an élite of the élite'.[5]

During the academic year of 1920–1 Harrod attended the thrice-weekly lectures given at Balliol by A. D. Lindsay on theories of the modern state. They enlarged his ideas, and the two men continued to have friendly dealings for thirty years; but he came to feel that

Lindsay's thinking was 'woolly' and his criticisms 'shallow'. Worst of all, Lindsay was stubborn in his belief that a well-managed economy could be attained by bringing people of goodwill together at conferences rather than by systematic academic preparations. Harrod, like G. N. Clark, felt that Lindsay was too informal and self-confident in his approach to challenging issues.[6]

Lindsay was a prime mover in inaugurating the School of Politics, Philosophy and Economics in 1921 after the foundering of a pre-war proposal for a new School of Science and Modern Philosophy. The new school met the demands of younger dons, such as Arthur Heath of New College, who hankered for a reformed university in which undergraduates of every type could assimilate the ideas, arts and ethical values of European culture. 'Why cannot modern, even perhaps contemporary, civilization be studied all round – its literature, its social structure, its thoughts and beliefs – in the same sort of way we try to study Greece?' Heath demanded shortly before his death in the trench warfare of Flanders. Post-war discussions of PPE were dominated by philosophers, who assumed omniscient jurisdiction over everyone else. Lionel Robbins, who began teaching economics at New College in 1923, said that to listen to J. A. Smith, Waynflete Professor of Moral Philosophy, 'pontificating on the methodology of economics, with which his acquaintance was zero, was to gain new conceptions of the possibility of human absurdity'.[7]

As an undergraduate, attending a meeting of the Jowett Society, Harrod heard Smith deliver a mellifluous, lofty and condescending speech on another subject of which he knew little. Smith had once strolled in Christ Church Meadow with Einstein, and on the basis of this experience refuted the Theory of Relativity. The annihilating corrections of his mistakes, which were flung at him by better-informed attendees at the Jowett Society, did not shake his composure. The presumption that a non-scientific, non-mathematical Greats man could invalidate Einstein's theories infuriated Harrod, whose disgust is clear in his account of Smith's speech written forty years later:

Did he not know that science was being carried forward by men of great intellectual acumen, that it was international, that each published finding was subject to the most severe checks? And if he did not know that, if he was living remote in some fastness of Greats, was he, or others like him, really capable of giving a first-rate intellectual education to those destined to be responsible for the intelligent management of the affairs of the great British Empire? What was this Greats? If, in this arsenal of British thought, there could be such inspissated parochialism and complacency, were we not in a parlous position?

The technological advances of the early twentieth century, and the broadening of technical knowledge and expertise, as much as the violence and grief of the European war, created a gulf between Smith's generation and Harrod's. The former's smugness and provincialism were not the specialized vices of the ancient universities, Harrod believed, but nationwide. He thought that the condition of England deteriorated after 1918, as again after 1945, precisely because of the national combination of low expectations with high self-satisfaction.[8]

Harrod found his New College philosophy tutor, H. W. B. Joseph, to be deflationary in his teaching, pettifogging and dogged. The biographer of Joseph's pupil J. L. Austin describes the old man as 'dry, captious, and negative', indeed 'a professional refuter, falling tirelessly, elaborately, and ferociously on whatever triggered his highly developed sense of affront'. It was essential, though, for Harrod to get a first as a precursor to a fellowship. Accordingly, he conformed to Joseph's thinking, and answered the philosophy questions in his finals, for which he knew Joseph to be an examiner, with resolute insincerity. At the Jowett Society discussion of physics, after Smith's ebullitions, Joseph balanced a pair of pince-nez near the tip of his nose and began to read aloud from a thick wad of manuscript. He had mastered the Oxford don's trick of speeding from one sentence into another, as Harrod recorded. 'He rushed on and on; one could not complain that any single word was of obscure meaning, or even that any single clause was. None the less the whole was difficult to follow.' Joseph instructed the Jowett Society that the Theory of Relativity must be wrong because it was an unchallengeable truth that space was Euclidean. Lindemann, newly appointed to the chair of physics, who heard Joseph's disquisition, felt no surprise at such condescension. He had recently complained to Margaret Pember, wife of the Warden of All Souls, about the low status of science at

Oxford. 'You need not worry, Professor Lindemann,' she had replied, 'my husband says that a man who has got a First in Greats could get up science in a fortnight.'[9]

Harrod felt that he had imbibed the best part of his undergraduate education from his peers, as had Keynes at Cambridge. Introducing his Chichele lectures, given in Trinity term of 1970 at All Souls, he took time to name the formative friendships that he had made half a century earlier at New College. His set's gossip about one other, their jokes and their appraisals of college life, current events, books, plays, public figures and historic episodes made, he thought, indelible marks in his development. Lectures or laboratory work gave pupils the rudiments of their chosen subject, but undergraduates of any intellectual distinction learnt more of permanent value from the talk of their contemporaries. Conversation is 'the most satisfying pleasure known to man', he wrote. 'By its give and take, by the interplay of minds, one may go deeper and further and come nearer to wisdom than by reading the best book in the world. After all, a book cannot be cross-examined; it cannot answer back.' Confidence in explaining one's ideas, in defending them from criticism and in admitting when they are shown to be false was learnt in the 'subtle blend of flippancy and intimacy' which refined the undergraduate experience. Whereas Victorian and Edwardian family life and schooling were founded on the belittlement, subordination and control of other people and on the snubbing of originality, undergraduates learnt mutual respect from the clash of their opinions. 'It is de rigueur in the university', said Harrod, 'to pretend to understand the merits of the opposite point of view; one ends by really doing so, and thereby becomes an educated man.'[10]

For a time Harrod shared undergraduate rooms in Broad Street with Beverley Nichols of Balliol, whose precocious novel *Patchwork* was published in 1921. Harrod appears in *Patchwork* as a character called Whitely (the Bayswater equivalent of the Knightsbridge department store Harrods was called Whiteley's). Young members of the House also appeared under aliases: Cazalet is Victor Cartaret, 'Chips' Channon is Henry Channing, Edward Marjoribanks is called Marchmont, Lord David Cecil is Lord Henry Vane and 'Sligger' Urquhart is 'Tugly' Fortescue. Nichols presented Whitely/Harrod as 'a scholar of New College, with pronounced views on God and marriage, against both of which institutions he cherished a fierce resentment'. Whitely's set decry 'the sham and rottenness which lay behind the faded pomp and circumstance of war' rather as young Harrod insisted that the recent war had been avoidable, unnecessary and futile. Harrod, though, was no pacifist: he and Maurice Bowra defended their friend Idris Deane Jones with their fists when, in 1920, some thugs tried to ransack his rooms and began smashing his belongings as punishment for supporting strikers.[11]

Bowra and Deane Jones were among the closest of Harrod's New College friends. No one could rival Bowra's axioms, quips, wordplay, retorts, absurdity, exaggerations and ferocity, Harrod said in his obituary of his friend which was published anonymously in *The Times* in 1971. Bowra started the Immoral Front in inter-war Oxford, a group which was anti-puritanical, irreverent, pleasure-loving, rule-breaking and ostensibly guilt-free. Front members modelled themselves on the ancient Greeks of the aristocratic age. They upheld their position and their privileges, which they made the basis of 'a gallant and generous existence'.[12]

As an undergraduate Harrod had a sexual affair with at least one young man. He told the therapist or analyst whom he consulted during 1928–9 that he agreed to the youth's overtures because he could find no reason to decline them: their sexual activity was not particularly satisfying, he claimed, although they continued for about a year. Thirty years later he confided to John Sparrow, the Warden of All Souls, who had recently published a study of anal sex in *Lady Chatterley's Lover*, that an unnamed friend had once tried to 'bugger' him, 'but I don't think that he got any satisfaction out of it, as he did not seem to succeed; I certainly got none.' Possibly this was 'Tommy' Tomlin whom Harrod recalled half a century later:

Stephen Tomlin was my greatest friend; and, looking over my life, I think that perhaps he was the greatest friend I ever had. He was a person of artistic temperament, but also a very exact scholar whose Greek and Latin verses usually got top marks. He was also a very charming and affectionate friend, who entered sympathetically into the emotional stresses that young men up at university are apt to have . . . It was very sad, the most lovable and interesting undergraduate in New College, being so distraught and forlorn.

In his biographies of both Keynes and Cherwell he presented Tomlin as an entrancing talker who replenished life. He considered, after Tomlin was killed by alcoholism at the age of thirty-five, proposing marriage to his widow Julia Strachey. Instead, after taking advice from the unlikely figure of John Sparrow, he married Wilhelmine 'Billa' Cresswell in 1937. Bowra's poem 'The Dying Duke' (1941) suggests that Harrod's lover was not Tomlin of New College but Edward Sackville-West of Christ Church. Sackville-West, who was a year younger than Harrod, had, Virginia Woolf noted, 'a voice like a girl's and a face like a Persian cat's, all white and serious, with large violet eyes and fluffy cheeks'. Tomlin or Sackville-West? It scarcely matters.[13]

After winning his first in Greats, Harrod, by fast and concentrated work, took three terms to gain his first in modern history. The brevity and compression of his answers worried his examiners, who agreed after discussion that while he had omitted superfluities, he had missed nothing relevant. Recently he had given formal tutoring to a Christ Church undergraduate, 'Jim' Wedderburn, afterwards Earl of Dundee. Feiling and Masterman liked the Scotsman, who had a fresh, open mind but was not bookish, and were pleased that he was marked *alpha* by both examiners in his special subject and therefore avoided a third-class degree. Wedderburn's results weighed in the Christ Church decision, in July 1922, to elect Harrod to a lectureship in modern history and economics, with the promise of a studentship at the end of his probationary period.[14]

Although the modern historians had ready work for Harrod, Christ Church's overriding need for a new man arose because the new honours school of philosophy, politics and economics was to be examined for the first time in the summer of 1923. For the next half-century, Harrod insisted on using the phrase Modern Greats, as indicating that the spirit of the ancient Greeks was to be applied to twentieth-century conditions, and as a protest against the ugliness of the acronym PPE. Samuel Eliot Morison, after retiring as a Student of Christ Church and holder of the Harmsworth chair in American history in 1925, questioned the role of college tutors like Harrod. 'Tutoring', he declared, 'is admirably fitted for teaching *Literae Humaniores*, for which it was devised; but more modern subjects, such as the promising new school of philosophy, politics and economics, are somewhat refractory to one-man teaching. Tutoring tends to become mere cramming, both with facts and with clever answers to "spotted" questions.' The college tutor was falling to the level of a paid coach, such as Harrod had been with Wedderburn.[15]

Harrod gave tutorials for up to twenty hours a week: half of his time was allotted to understudying Masterman and Feiling in modern history and the rest to teaching economics to undergraduates reading PPE. He began with the grounding of someone who had achieved first-class honours in modern history. The basic disposition of the modern historian was fundamental to his development as a teacher of economics and a writer on the subject. In weekly tutorial hours with his pupils Harrod corrected stylistic and structural weaknesses in their essays, noted weak arguments or logical faults and discouraged bumptious criticisms of established authorities. He indicated how pupils might better arrange their data or press their arguments. After 1945 he interjected into tutorials reminiscences of people and episodes drawn from his wartime experiences as a Whitehall official and his post-war efforts as an adviser to ministers. Brighter pupils left his rooms in Killcannon feeling that they had been vouchsafed a glimpse into the backrooms of power. But he never sought to muster disciples.

Senior figures at Christ Church were happy for the new school to be taught, if the emphasis was on philosophy and politics; but they dismissed economics as a menial subject which, it was surmised, could be easily mastered by studying just one good textbook. Their sense was that classicists and modern historians look at the long run and draw inferences from centuries of evidence, whereas economists (for all their talk of quasi-scientific rules and time cycles) were quick-sell, short-run merchants. When Tawney dined in Christ Church hall in the 1920s and admitted that he lectured at the London School of Economics, he was told that was like working at Selfridge's. Similarly, in 1925, Joseph Wells, who was then Vice-Chancellor of the university as well as Warden of Wadham, composed a Latin oration in the Sheldonian Theatre to denounce the electors responsible for the appointment of G. D. H. Cole to a newly created readership in economics, with a fellowship of University College attached. Certain men, Wells lamented, learned but not wise, had scurried after unproven novelty rather than follow tried and sensible ways. Cole's instatement disgraced the entire university, Wells averred.[16]

Such uncomprehending hostility in the 1920s made it important, Harrod felt, 'that economics should not be overlaid with technical jargon'. The subject should be dressed so that politicians, officials and journalists would be able to retain its essential principles within their comprehension. He began by admiring, and hoped never to forget, the 'linguistic conservatism' that made the writings of Alfred Marshall in Cambridge so lucid and serviceable. Marshall's sense of responsibility without the itch for power, his strict and proud self-respect and his judicious restraint helped to make his ideas durable and commanding, Harrod believed. So, too, did Marshall's instincts as a performer, his 'sense of how, when one is a great master, one should act the role of great master'.[17]

Christ Church released Harrod for Michaelmas term of 1922 and Hilary term of 1923 in the expectation that he would go abroad (as Masterman had done in 1914) to get a tighter hold on the subject that he was expected to teach. With a letter of introduction from the Liberal politician Walter Runciman, he visited Maynard Keynes at his house in Bloomsbury to seek his advice on what to do. Keynes was giving lunch to a young economist from Paris. 'There was quick, exciting talk,' Harrod recalled during a BBC Home Service broadcast of 1948, 'about immediate actualities; what was happening, what was going to happen.' The paintings on the walls of Keynes's rooms belied the inhumanity of talk about supply and demand. They hinted at his host's intimacy with the arts and its practitioners, Vanessa Bell, Duncan Grant, Roger Fry; and with writers, too, notably Virginia Woolf and Lytton Strachey. 'It was a circle of great charm, witty and brilliant talk, and intellectual vitality,' he recalled: the ideal that his mother had set before him.[18]

It was settled that Harrod should spend Michaelmas term in Cambridge, where Keynes arranged for his admission as a member of high table at King's. He wrote weekly essays for Keynes, attended his lectures and participated in meetings of his Political Economy Club. Returning to Christ Church, after three months of intensive Keynesian tuition, he was upbraided for devoting too much effort to the sideline of economics, and urged to go overseas. In December 1922, he left for Berlin, where his experiences did not match those of Cambridge. On his return to Oxford in April 1923, he took regular lessons at All Souls from F. Y. Edgeworth, the illustrious Drummond Professor of Political Economy. The difference between them, he later said, was this: Keynes was one of the rudest men he had ever met; Edgeworth one of the most gracious.

Some months after Harrod's term at King's Dundas, the Christ Church busybody, met Keynes at the dinner of Eton Collegers held annually on the eve of the Eton–Harrow cricket match. 'His only criticism of you as a pupil was that it was a little difficult to make you talk,' Dundas reported to Harrod. Keynes had evidently teased Dundas, whose virginity, voyeurism and intrusive sexual questioning of undergraduates were notorious, with tales of Harrod having had 'mild affairs of the heart at Cambridge'. This Dundas had expected, 'but whether Maynard's own heart was involved (as I prophesised to you) or not, neither he nor I discussed; nor well could, as the occasion was a big dinner'. Certainly, George ('Dadie') Rylands made an impression, as shown by Harrod's account, written thirty years after the event, of his first dinner in hall at King's. 'A young man, his hair very fair, exquisitely dressed in a double-breasted blue suit and red tie, stepped forward to read grace. He paused a moment, and his poise seemed perfect.' Three other young Cambridge men took Harrod's fancy besides Rylands: Adrian Bishop was 'the wittiest and most amusing, a little too flippant, perhaps, for the severe Cambridge tradition, a little Oxford in fact'; Keynes's debonair lover 'Sebastian' Sprott, afterwards a sociologist and penal reformer; and Steven Runciman, the elfin son of the Liberal minister who had recommended him to Keynes.[19]

Two other young Cambridge men excited Harrod's intellectual admiration: Richard Braithwaite, a logician and philosopher of religion, and Frank Ramsey, a prodigy in philosophy, mathematics and economics who had translated Wittgenstein's *Tractatus* from German into English at the age of eighteen. 'He had a beautiful laugh, not loud or hearty, but sudden, genuine, and convulsive,' Harrod recalled of Ramsey:

He discussed philosophy in an extraordinarily easy style. Subtle thoughts were distilled into simple, straightforward sentences. In an entirely effortless and almost gossipy way, he set out the quintessentials of a problem. To me he was a tremendous stimulus, for, having studied philosophy as a schoolboy, I had met with much frustration and bitterness at Oxford, where, to my judgment, the true was often reckoned false and conversely.

It relieved Harrod to hear Ramsey's contempt for the orthodoxies with which Joseph had plagued him at Oxford.[20]

'Harrod begins to tell already,' Feiling said when the examination results in modern history were published in the summer of 1923. But Harrod's seniors were taciturn, undemonstrative men. 'Call me Robin, if you like,' Dundas would say to younger Students, 'but I don't see what's gained by it.' They seemed to disregard Harrod, rather than encourage him, and he consequently felt unable to speak at large, or to ask for what he wanted. His inhibitions caused a contretemps in 1924. Herbert Blunt, who had been a Student of Christ Church since 1887, was nearly blind. He could neither read lecture notes nor consult written authorities during his private hours. He took pride, moreover, in formulating long, intricate and perplexing sentences. 'No one who has attended my lectures for Greats and lasted to the end of them, has ever failed to get a first-class,' he said, 'unless, of course, he ended in a madhouse.' In his blindness Blunt depended heavily on Claud Sutton, a gremial two years older than Harrod, who held a college lectureship in philosophy. Perhaps Sutton chafed at being a blind man's carer; perhaps he was vexed that he had not been elected to a studentship; perhaps he feared that, as Blunt joked, he would end in an asylum if he remained at the House. For whatever reason, Sutton decided in 1928 to leave Christ Church. He joined the exiguous staff of a newly formed hostel for students of limited means who aspired to be candidates for holy orders or foreign missionaries. Sutton became its tutor in philosophy, and published *Farewell to Rousseau: A Critique of Liberal Democracy* in 1936.[21]

Feiling and Masterman realized that Harrod was only secondarily interested in history, but mistook his primary interest as economics. Neither they nor Blunt appreciated his preference for philosophy: nor, when Sutton's departure was announced, did Harrod show detectable signs of wanting to succeed him. He was nevertheless upset when Sutton's post was allotted to Ernest Jacob, a medievalist, then a prize fellow at All Souls, later to beat Trevor-Roper in the contest for the Chichele chair of modern history in succession to Feiling. He sent a pained protest to Dundas, who was Masterman's chief confidant. Long letters, both explanatory and placatory, were sent winging to Harrod. 'You know how greatly Keith & myself value your co-operation,' Masterman wrote.

Perhaps because of our belief in your powers we have given you more varied tasks than we should have. But Jacob's advent ought to make it easier to confine your history to those periods & subjects most useful to your economics. I think everyone in our School feels that he knows a little about a great many things, & nothing much about anything – & I think, too, that at least ½ one's teaching must be in almost all cases against the grain. This is heresy, but I can't help it! So let us go on & see how things turn out. If philosophy will not be denied, then in time to philosophy you must go. But it may be that economics will have the stronger claim. I don't know.

After Jacob's election, Harrod was relieved of all but a remnant of his history teaching.[22]

'Your mind is quite Abstract enough, and if you want to teach successfully, you cannot be Abstract always,' Feiling told Harrod. Some of the elder Students in the House found him, as Dundas warned, too 'intellectualist & doctrinaire'. In turn, he considered them too staid. Common-room talk lacked that 'probing, ardent, even feverish quest for solutions to fundamental problems' in which he had revelled as an undergraduate. For years the most interesting remark that he heard in the common room was uttered on his first evening. Arthur Slessor, the Steward, or equivalent of domestic bursar in other colleges, a retired major in the Sherwood Foresters, was warming himself in front of the fire when he suddenly uttered, apropos of nothing, 'A pity about that feller Oscar Wilde. A great pity. He was clever as paint, you know, clever as paint.' Harrod always wished that he had asked Slessor to say more; but knew that probes were discouraged, even snubbed. Dons preferred to dispute innocuous facts, such as etymologies or geographical distances, or to assess the characters and abilities of their contemporaries. University gossip, and especially predictions about elections to the headship of colleges, to professorial chairs or to fellowships, was particularly relished. For Harrod in his early manhood, though, such chatter was too placid.[23]

He was lonely. Conventional undergraduates, of the Jim Wedderburn sort, were shy and deferential with him. Remembering his enjoyment of the company of lively Cambridge male beauties, he tried for two or three years, beginning in 1924, to revive those pleasures by cautious flirtation with the rich aesthetes in Christ Church. They had commodious rooms in Peck, swift wits, shameless candour, epicene valour and artistic sensibility. For a few years he enjoyed carefree intimacy with the hectic hedonists who became known as 'bright young things'. Looking as thin, translucent and fragile as porcelain he was called 'the Chinese' by Evelyn Waugh and 'Ming' by 'Chips' Channon. In autobiographical notes written for the analyst or therapist whom he consulted in 1928–9 he denied that he had experienced any sexual action with them.[24]

Beverley Nichols said that the smart talk of Harrod's Oxford contemporaries was a *réchauffé* of the dialogue in *The Importance of Being Earnest*. There was provocative posing by young men who were attracted to women but chafed at the narrowing signifiers of masculinity. It was in order to twit his conventional-minded elders and contemporaries that Evelyn Strachey, undergraduate editor of the *Oxford Fortnightly Review*, which was subsidized by Conservative party headquarters, wore a straw hat hung with pink ribbons while batting for the Magdalen cricket XI in 1922, and breakfasted at noon on chocolate cake and crème de menthe. When a Christ Church undergraduate, Richard Rumbold, revived the defunct English Club with a meeting at the Randolph Hotel, people attended in their hundreds because the guest speaker was Wilde's lover Lord Alfred Douglas. Harrod was among the guests at the dinner given for Douglas by Rumbold beforehand.[25]

Yet despite the reverence for Wilde he was not the primary cult writer of the 1920s. 'Between the two world wars,' a former Univ undergraduate Tangye Lean recalled in 1953, 'Proust's *À la recherche du temps perdu* was a kind of optional university which we attended or dodged but, because of its great and dazzling stature, were unable simply to ignore.' The novel's lessons in genius and memory, and studies in the captive powers of love and jealousy, seemed more valuable to Lean's generation than the teaching in college tutorials. Thus, in the Oxford novel *Sixth Heaven*, which L. P. Hartley set in 1920–1, a socially alert but mentally idling undergraduate begins to feel that he has to pose as a reader of Proust although a page of *Temps perdu* overtaxes him. The novelist Henry Green recalled that he heard the name 'Charlus' (Proust's haughty invert nobleman) uttered every evening that he spent in the Oxford of 1924–6. Harrod started at Christ Church in the year of Proust's death. He entrenched himself in the college as the last volumes of the French masterpiece appeared on people's shelves. As a young Student at the House he had the sensibility of an outright *Proustien*. The description and dissection of Paris salons in *Temps perdu* was a life-enhancing version of his mother's perennial brooding over the salons she had lost. At a meeting of the Canning Club in 1928, he attributed his enjoyment of life and even his health to reading Proust. He used Proustian inflexions, such as 'inversion' as a synonym for homosexuality.[26]

On becoming Junior Censor in 1927, Harrod distanced himself from the invert or pretend-invert set with their pink 'Oxford bags' trousers and purple dress suits. Later he maintained to his therapist that he became bored by his younger friends' emotional parasitism and hardened inner core of selfishness. The truth is that he feared being compromised by their peccadillos. In any case, the aesthete phase of Oxford life petered out after 1929. Following the financial crash in October of that year, and particularly after the economic slump of 1931, fewer parents were willing to stump up at least £400 a year, which was the minimum cost of the clothes, accoutrements, scents and liqueurs required for the peacocking of an aesthete. Young men who thrived on performance and display found a much cheaper outlet, after 1929, in college theatricals and Oxford University Dramatic Society productions. Oxford stagecraft was invigorated by the demise of aestheticism after 1929, although the university prohibition of female undergraduates from acting alongside their male contemporaries was not lifted until 1940.

On Christmas Day of 1929, Harrod become Senior Censor, and felt himself to be second only to the Dean in college life. 'The Senior Censor knows everything that is going on in the College; the life of the College pulses in him; he knows all the undergraduates personally and all about their affairs; he mingles much more with them than do the other dons.' He also took the leading part in choosing each year's new admissions. For someone who loved what Henry James called 'the hungry futurity of youth', the senior censorship was a happy time. When disheartened by his colleagues, he turned to cheery undergraduates with whom he quaffed champagne. These were no longer vivid and epicene tearaways, but purposeful, easy-going members of the House. His choicest younger friends in 1931 were Ran Dunluce, afterwards Earl of Antrim and Chairman of the National Trust, and Francis Lennox-Boyd, who died in 1944 when he fell prematurely from an aircraft carrying parachutists to France.[27]

Harrod loved Christ Church. His pre-war experiences in the college, the opinions and sentiments that he formed by talking there with men who excelled, formed a personal philosophy which, as we shall see, provided the thrust of his socio-economic prescriptions in the 1940s and 1950s.

The pursuit of truth was, for Harrod, the finest of all human activities. The purpose of colleges was to provide a setting of 'quiet culture': that of dons was to supply 'standards of precision and self-discipline in research, so that the young men can get a glimpse, an inkling, of the exacting nature of the pursuit of truth'. To fulfil the quest for truth, one needed 'zeal, patience, imagination, accept-ance of repeated disappointments and frustrations, continued perseverance and the ruthless stripping away of the distracting influ-ences of the ego'. Mental clutter, acquired from family, school, neighbours, newspapers and one's own indiscriminate thinking, had to be discarded to acquire the substantive knowledge that would help undergraduates to find worthwhile work or responsibilities after they left university. This was Harrod's ideal for Christ Church: never attained in full; perhaps within grasp during some of the inter-war period; receding fast from the 1950s as the demands of the curric-ulum seemed to him to become exorbitant. 'I dissent violently from the view that the main service of the University is in the provision of courses and examinations, and in the insistence on the desirability of obtaining high classes,' he wrote in 1959. He deplored the collect-ive tendency of dons 'to encroach upon the life and time and energy of undergraduates' by setting further tests and targets. Dons who spoon-fed facts or ideas during tutorials appalled him. In his view,

Hassall's provision of pat answers to the broad questions that were likely to be posed to a pupil sitting in the Examination Schools was wrong.[28]

Harrod adored his mother: his letters over the course of three decades can leave no doubt of this. Yet, until his marriage, he also felt at times stifled by a sort of overwrought co-dependence. By his own admission in 1928, he had nurtured for two years, in 1919–21, the idea that it was his duty to end her anxious and discontented widowhood by killing her. He had a grandiose fantasy of standing trial for matricide and of avowing his act, or else of committing suicide after killing her. Bowra, who met her in New College days, recalled her as a 'majestic ruin' who talked with intensity. 'Roy was angelic to her, but she was a fearful drain on his vitality, and made awkward scenes with him in front of others. She hated poverty and old age, and longed for the glorious past, and Roy was expected to revive it.'[29]

There was much to admire in Frankie Harrod. She was a resilient worker who tried to make money in the 1920s by writing novels that addressed – sometimes with picturesquely Edwardian brio and dialogue – the tensions of contemporary England. *The Triumphant Rider* describes the experiences of Marcia Wells, the by-blow daughter of a burnt-out Oxford college star and a streetwalker, after she joins a gilded, blasé, immoral smart set in London. *Temperament* is the tale of a workhouse bastard and labourer who becomes a fashionable artist and faces a false charge of murder. *Stained Wings*, set in a private residential hotel, describes the involvement of a sensitive, self-loathing woman with a black singer called Drake Grosvenor. The precariousness of social status and personal reputation, and the difficulties of adjusting to psychological realities, are Frankie Harrod's steady themes.

She needed her only child to spend his vacations from Oxford with her: these were the only occasions when she could pour out her bottled wretchedness. In the ten years after the Armistice, he did not manage to have more than ten weekends of holiday away from her. Although their mutual devotion was unfeigned, Harrod felt depleted by the intensity of her feelings. It was on this ground that he identified himself with that eminent Victorian Walter Bagehot, 'the devoted son of a brilliant and too excitable mother', whose sense of filial duty, as he said, brought 'the lifelong strain of agonizing anxieties'. One heartbreaking letter from Roy to Frankie, dated 1929, shows the crushing strain that he felt:

> when you are a little tearful one feels all one's instincts rush towards consolation. But when you are very miserable, when a horrific unassuageable sorrow comes upon you, I am so terrified, so horror stricken, so paralysed, even now after all these years, that the words of kindliness are frozen on the tongue, all one's instincts are held in suspense; I feel powerless and abject in the face of this great force of melancholy which I feel to be stronger than myself. Instead of reaching towards saying something comforting, I feel all my reactions held up; I feel literally paralysed and completely, of course, miserable. This is not the state of someone who does not love you, as you often say. The trouble is that I love you too deeply.[30]

Their holidays together, which resembled scenes from a novel of Ivy Compton-Burnett, hindered Harrod's early development as an economist. As he was busy with college and university business during the three terms of the academic year, vacations were his only free time to study economics: yet he reported that sometimes his nerves were so upset during vacations that he just sat gazing, as if he was blind or illiterate, at the unread page of a book.

It was not until 1927 that Harrod began to publish: a sound article by him appeared in *Economica* that year. But a crisis engulfed him when, in 1928, he submitted to Keynes an ambitious paper introducing the concept of the marginal revenue curve for publication in the *Economic Journal*. That summer he went with his mother to the Mullion Cove Hotel on the Lizard peninsula in Cornwall. She had been living pent-up as a resident in a small room in the Sesame Club, a base for professional men and women in Grosvenor Street, Mayfair: Edith Sitwell was its most famous long-term resident. Freed from the restraining protocol of the Sesame, Frankie gave vent to her accumulated exasperations, bickered with other guests at Mullion Cove and needed to be appeased by constant filial attentiveness.

Harrod's friend Frank Ramsey, who often vetted submissions to the *Economic Journal*, reported to Keynes that most of it was 'neat and nice', but recommended that Harrod should be asked to revise his treatment of cartels. A request for some reworking of details was hardly a crushing rejection, but the comments of Ramsey and Keynes, which reached Harrod while he was confined with his mother in Cornwall, induced a nervous breakdown. It felt, as he told John Betjeman, as if someone was continually tugging a long hair that was entangled in his brain. He reeled so wildly from this small blow that he spoke of leaving Christ Church for a career at the bar: he ate dinners at the Inner Temple and conned textbooks of law.[31]

Harrod was by now on confidential terms with Lindemann, whom he had first seen at the Jowett Society meeting at which Smith and Joseph had spoken with such hapless self-confidence. He told his troubles to Lindemann, who arranged for him to consult a Harley Street physician, who was described as a neurologist at a time when that noun was loosely used. Nothing is known of Harrod's treatment except for the confessional account that he wrote about his conflicts with his mother, his sexual ambivalence, his isolation, his devotion to Christ Church and his joy in his studentship there. This account is the source for the more intimate parts of this chapter: it is preserved in the British Library, where it is miscatalogued as notes for an autobiography.

Lindemann had first been known to Christ Church undergraduates as 'the Witch-doctor' and (according to Cecil King) disliked for his arrogance and shameless tuft hunting. As his position settled, the more respectful soubriquet of 'the Prof' superseded the hoodoo nickname. Later his surname of Lindemann yielded to his peerage title of Cherwell. The intimacy between Cherwell and Harrod flourished despite the older man being callous, ultra-reactionary, pessimistic, harsh and cynical in his politics while the junior man was a Liberal meliorist. Cherwell thought Harrod 'perhaps the most acute & active intellect in the House' during the 1920s, and deplored the way his creativity was 'sterilised' by the routine of teaching. As Cherwell's staunch ally – some said tool – in various schemes and feuds, Harrod developed a taste for political manoeuvring. Masterman particularly distrusted him as the Prof's listening device and excluded him from consultations. Cherwell and Harrod, when acting and speaking in combination, were a rankling influence in the governing body of the 1930s: they audibly dismissed some of their fellow Students as 'riff-raff'. Their example encouraged public gestures of resentment. E. R. Dodds remembered A. J. Ayer appearing in the Christ Church common room in 1940, wearing the uniform of the Welsh Guards and declaring that he would return after the war with his army revolver. Ayer pointed at three senior Students in turn: 'I am going to shoot first him, and then him, and then him.'[32]

Harrod's memoir of Cherwell, entitled *The Prof*, was published in 1959. It is an Establishment testament: after reading it the mathematician and humanist Jacob Bronowski called Cherwell 'overbearing and self-effacing at the same time, and passionate yet contained: the very type of the Grey Eminence'; the Cabinet Secretary, Sir Norman Brook, took the galley proofs to read in the Soviet Union as respite from fraught negotiations and oppressive banquets with Khrushchev. *The Prof* has the characterization, scene painting, archness and autobiographical subtext found in novels, and was accordingly appreciated by practising novelists as *un roman manqué*. Angus Wilson found *The Prof* 'brilliant and fascinating' in its piety towards Cherwell. 'At its deepest level it is a purposeful act of homage to greatness of mind and to "character", addressed to an age that Sir Roy clearly thinks is dangerously lacking in a sense of veneration.' Another novelist, C. P. Snow, enjoyed *The Prof*, called Harrod 'a funny duck' and Cherwell 'the most unpopular man in Oxford'.[33]

Harrod's Liberal activism in Oxford never jarred with Cherwell's despotic, illiberal temperament. This activism began when he lodged with Beverley Nichols in Broad Street and helped him to revive the Oxford Liberal Club in 1919. Throughout the 1920s he was Liberal party agent for Gilbert Murray's candidature for the University of Oxford constituency. Walter Runciman and Lord Buckmaster were two Liberal leaders whom he particularly admired. The paper on trade cycles that he read to the British Association for the Advancement of Science in 1925 was, he admitted, 'utter bosh' because, instead of concentrating on its preparation, he had given his surplus time and energy to campaigning for the former Liberal Prime Minister, Asquith, in the contest to elect a successor to Lord

Curzon of Kedleston as Chancellor of the university. Like Keynes, he attended Liberal Summer Schools and felt sure that he was giving his support to 'the intelligent party'. 'Liberals believe', he wrote, 'that, given an adequate framework of free institutions, there is a sufficient element of goodwill and reasonableness in the greater number of men to work those institutions effectively, and therefore join issue with the cynics who see in human imperfections a fatal barrier to progress.'[34]

Harrod's repute as a young Liberal intellectual was such that C. P. Scott offered him a senior editorial job on the *Manchester Guardian* in 1926. Five years later, he rejected Runciman's suggestion that he become economic adviser to the National coalition government. He had no truck with the National leaders' shearing of government expenditure. At the general elections of 1931 and 1935 he made platform speeches in support of Labour candidates in constituencies where no Liberal was standing. He was one of nine Oxford economists who contributed to a book planned and edited by G. D. H. Cole, which was published by Gollancz under the title *What Everybody Wants to Know about Money* (1933).

For a time Harrod attended the Pink Lunch Club, a symposium of Labour activists which met fortnightly in an Oxford restaurant under the auspices of Cole. The intelligentsia at the Pink Lunches envisaged an all-inclusive, unbreachable scheme of national economic planning implemented by central government. Socialism required, they agreed, working-class empowerment, public ownership of productive industries and services, public control of the distribution of income, public control over prices as well as over purchasing power. By contrast, Harrod favoured the rule of an enlightened oligarchy fostering individual initiative, competitive enterprise, unequal remuneration, inherited wealth and the minimum of state regulations. He explained his creed of 'collectivist Liberalism' to Rowse in 1932:

Though a liberal by heredity and probably because liberalism was the important force practically in my boyhood, I have always been deeply steeped in views of economic egalitarianism. That has been my background of feeling – the tradition of the later Mill and then socialism. Yet now, oddly enough, when I begin to feel that

Labour is the practical force which should be supported rather than Liberalism, the old egalitarian feeling is waning rapidly. I am ceasing to think that equal distribution has the importance [that] it looked as if it was going to have for humanity some time ago.

It was no longer the case that the riches of a minority must entail the misery of an impoverished majority. 'My impression is that now, given the proper organization, we can *all* be extremely rich.' He insisted to Rowse, who was later to write *Mr Keynes and the Labour Movement*, that the priority should be the attainment of 'general affluence' rather than talk of 'levelling down' by taxation or appropriation: 'above all there must be no talk of class struggle'. Harrod loathed 'stupidity, obscurantism & die-hardism . . . narrow self-interest and stupid conservatism'. But he felt that 'on the side of pure justice, there is much to be said in favour of letting those who are used to more to have more. There is a strong and good instinct in man to fight against being degraded.' By both temperament and reasoning he thought that Keynes had 'probably more wisdom and truth in him than in any living Englishman'.[35]

Like Keynes, Harrod believed the materialist religion of Marxism to be tedious obscurantism. He had, too, some of the showmanship of his mother's family. Hence Pakenham's account of Harrod lecturing in Christ Church hall on 'Marx in the Keynesian Analysis' in 1937 or 1938:

Roy is not a Forbes Robertson for nothing, and when in form is the most histrionic and arresting lecturer in my experience. Speaking in Christ Church Hall he suddenly swings round and addresses the portrait of Cardinal Wolsey behind him, whom for the moment he sees and makes us all see as Marx. 'What have you got to say for yourself, you old rascal?', he cries shaking his fist at the picture. 'How do you answer that, Marx? You do well to be silent! I will leave you skulking in your corner.' He swings round again to his audience. 'Thirty years in the British Museum had addled a once fine intelligence. What was left at the bottom of it? Mud, mud, mud!'

Harrod's rejection of Marxism resembled his lifelong repudiation of Christianity: he thought submission to any doctrinal orthodoxy was cloddish.[36]

Harrod's father had been received into the Church of Rome while an Oxford undergraduate. Roy and Frankie (who underwent conversion, at the time of their marriage, in order to please him) agreed after his death in 1918 that they would have nothing more to do with Catholicism, and as little as possible with Christianity. From Westminster School days onward, Roy thought it was wholesome and constructive to deny the power of prayer. 'Revealed religion, even if one could accept it, leaves most of the great problems unsolved,' he told Betjeman. Those who believed in a God, as creator and supreme ruler of the universe, were 'bores' to him, telling 'nothing of interest' and skulking in 'unreality'. Religiosity in the young shocked Harrod. He was infuriated by the way that weaklings and cowards, as he thought, sought safety from the instability and menace of the 1930s by hiding in the dim-lit defensive caverns of Christianity and Marxism. In England during the 1930s there were 12,000 conversions to the Church of Rome each year: when Philip Toynbee, recruiting officer of the Oxford University communists, visited the rooms of likely undergraduate recruits, he often found the Jesuit proselytizer Father Martin D'Arcy, of Campion Hall, already ensconced in them. Frank Pakenham was even set by D'Arcy to make converts of such unlikely figures as Ayer and Trevor-Roper.[37]

More objectionable to Harrod than Catholic proselytizing was the aggressive evangelism of Frank Buchman's Oxford Group (renamed Moral Rearmament in 1938). 'Oxford is going Communist and Buchmanist,' he lamented to Virginia Woolf in 1933. Perhaps he had been reading *The Group Movement*, recently published by Oxford University Press, in which Herbert Hensley Henson, Bishop of Durham likened the collectivism of the Soviet Union to the temper of Buchman's sect. 'The individual', wrote Henson, 'is merged in the Group, the "Cell", the State, and as such is bound into a system more analogous to a polity of bees or ants than anything properly human.' Buchman's followers spoke of him as 'God's right-hand man', 'out to make Christianity into an honest-to-God business proposition'. Their absolute certainty, invincible smugness, public confessions of sin and blokeish vocabulary were odious to Harrod.[38]

Absolutism of any kind was disagreeable to Harrod, who coupled a reluctant and unsure temperament to a training that made him accommodating and minutely careful. He was a full-throttle Liberal who believed that inter-war European diplomacy had failed because it was still animated by 'the quasi-instinctive and traditional ingredients in man's nature' and therefore conducted along 'cunning' and 'retrograde' lines. In his judgement, the economic depression of 1929–33 was more to blame for the resurgence of German militarism than the onerous terms of the Treaty of Versailles. He had enough progressive hope to imagine a future in which expert anthropologists had superseded British colonial administrators in Africa and Asia. In his words, 'the faded Union Jack, the rusty gun and the dilapidated governor-general might come to be regarded as the quaint relics of a decaying superstition, once an all-powerful religion'.[39]

For several years, when Harrod was donning the colours of a Keynesian economist, he was too busy to give his full mind to a reckoning with totalitarianism. Then, probably soon after the German repudiation of the military clauses of the Versailles Treaty in March 1935, but possibly following the earlier German withdrawal from the League of Nations, he spent an evening with Ayer and Lindemann in the common room. Ayer and Harrod bruited the Liberal arguments in favour of basing British foreign policy on the League: an international disarmament agreement, the removal of German grievances and the restoration of former German colonies were advocated by the younger men. The Prof met them with blistering rebuttals at every point. The Berlin government intended war: the London government must take every measure to trounce Germany's armed forces in battle on land and sea and in the air. Harrod said gloomily to Ayer, as they walked through a dark and sombre Tom Quad, 'I do not see the answer to all that.' Ayer shuddered, like a dog shaking off water, and replied in a downcast tone: 'No, it is difficult to see the answer.'[40]

For a time Harrod continued to urge that British foreign policy should rest on that of the League. In October 1935, three weeks after the fascist troops of Mussolini's Italy had invaded Abyssinia, he sent a long, careful letter to Winston Churchill, whom he knew slightly. His sympathy for the young, as he approached middle age, shines from it. Churchill, he said, had 'not . . . got the hang of the feelings of your younger countrymen'. Harrod, by contrast, thought he understood the 'ardour and enthusiasm for great causes' of men who had passed through Oxford, and other universities, since 1918.

I am not referring to a few rich young men, naturally anxious to consolidate their influence and position. I mean the ordinary young men, the men who have carried 'won't fight' resolutions at various Unions, the great mass who relapse for the time being into humdrum occupations, who are in fact England. They see this as a great opportunity for her to adopt a world role as a just arbiter and peacemaker and defender of treaties, with reasonable revision where necessary. Old Victorian Imperialism with contempt for the foreigner no longer appeals to them.

Harrod reminded Churchill that the Oxford Union, which had voted in 1933 not to fight for King and Country, had subsequently agreed by a large majority that the League of Nations should enforce its decisions with military measures involving British troops. Harrod wanted punitive sanctions to be imposed against Italy with speed, and to be applied with military and naval force. 'There could be no greater mistake possible than to regard the "won't fight" brigade as mugwumps,' he told Churchill. 'They are precisely all that is best in the country. They are willing to fight and die – more willing, I fancy, than any generation has been – but not for outworn causes.' If university men believed that armaments would be used under League of Nations auspices, 'they would be willing to arm like the devil . . . but if they think the arms will be applied for a Victorian policy, for selfish ends or vested interests, they will oppose Armament and they won't fight.' Churchill's response to Harrod was unconstructive and indeed Victorian. He was too nationalist to have truck with the League of Nations, and spluttered like Colonel Blimp. 'The harm done by the Oxford Resolution spread far through the world,' he replied. 'It played a traceable part in those feelings of contempt for Britain which led Mussolini into adventures so perilous to him and to us all.'[41]

During the general election of November 1935, Harrod spoke on the hustings in favour of using military force to deter Mussolini. He was dismayed when the speaker after him, Elizabeth Pakenham, the Labour candidate and wife of his Christ Church colleague, followed him with an ardent speech advocating that Britain should set an example for other nations by unilateral disarmament. 'You think our example will cause Hitler and Mussolini to disarm?' he challenged her afterwards. 'O Roy,' she replied, 'have you lost all your idealism?' He had. Others, too, reconsidered their positions. In Cambridge, G. M. Trevelyan resigned from the League of Nations Union after its local branch, at the same meeting, passed two resolutions: the first urged resistance to Mussolini in Abyssinia; the second opposed any British rearmament whatsoever.[42]

Harrod's depression about current events ballooned into predictions of global catastrophe and cataclysmic extinction. Falling birth rates in Europe became a premonitory fixation of his. In 1936 he invoked the 'determination, perseverance, ardours and endurance' of the human species over aeons of time. The individual consciousness of human beings, their sense of purpose, their heroism in surviving a hostile environment, their capacity to harness natural powers and to bring order to living conditions: all this had always set humanity apart from 'the blind, meaningless processes of nature, the gyrations of electrons, nebulae undergoing their pointless transformations in the great emptiness of space'. But now he wondered: perhaps humanity is not so special; perhaps it will soon 'fizzle out, just as we have reached the threshold of comforts, refinements, and knowledge undreamt of'. Humankind resembled a planetary titan who, after centuries of achievement, 'becomes wearied and turns over to his long sleep. It is too much bother. These squalling bats make too much noise. Then the ants may have a brief sway. Afterwards the glaciers will grind on their courses'. Harrod in the late 1930s was a man with the glooms.[43]

In September 1938, after the Munich agreement ceded the Sudeten lands of Czechoslovakia to Nazi Germany, Harrod collapsed in bed for a day or two. 'The most shattering political event of my lifetime,' he later called the Anglo-French betrayal. In the weeks that followed, as described in the next chapter, he joined with Pakenham and Richard Crossman in promoting the Popular Front candidature of 'Sandie' Lindsay in the City of Oxford by-election. Afterwards, he chaired a committee drawn from all the parliamentary constituencies near Oxford, which met at Lindsay's house. It sought to concert a non-partisan anti-appeasement front in preparation for the general election due in 1940.[44]

At Christ Church, in 1939, a Canadian named John Lowe was chosen as Dean because the Canons and Students were chary of being fictionalized. The leading runner for the post had fallen at a late jump when Dundas observed that his wife wrote novels in which the characters were based on people whom she had met. Several of the younger Students, notably Ryle, Ayer, Page, Harrod, Dodds, Gordon Walker and Colin Dillwyn, wished to laicize the college by appointing as head of the House someone who was not in holy orders. Feiling, who was known to wish that the cold draughts of Killcannon would fulfil their name, sympathized with the insurgents. One problem in separating the college from the cathedral was the legal opinion that the endowment seemed to belong to the churchmen and not the Students.[45]

On New Year's Day of 1940 Harrod joined S Branch, a group of irregulars assembled from outside the civil service by Cherwell. Its task was to feed bold ideas, sound data and freshly interpreted intelligence to Churchill at the wartime Admiralty. Churchill became Prime Minister in May, and a few weeks later Hugh Dalton, the newly appointed Minister of Economic Warfare, lamented that Winston's 'Brains Trust', meaning Lindemann and Harrod, were overstimulating him: 'What he really needs . . . are sedatives.' Harrod hoped that S Branch would be transmuted into an Economic General Council attached to the wartime Downing Street apparatus with himself in a post equivalent to permanent secretary. However, his imaginative rather than pragmatic plans, his tendentious handling of quantitative evidence, his florid techniques of persuasion fitted the needs of neither Cherwell nor Churchill. He recognized in retrospect that his attempt to assert his standing in a time of national crisis had been 'egoistic'; but, disappointed by his opportunities in S Branch, he resigned therefrom in 1942 and returned to Oxford. He continued to rank Churchill as 'one of the greatest Englishmen of all time' and felt lasting regret at his extrusion from the Churchill circle.[46]

After 1942 Harrod turned his thoughts to the peacetime settlement.

He wrote a party manifesto, *A Liberal Plan for Peace*, published anonymously by Gollancz in 1944. 'Everybody must feel that we have reached a turning-point in the history of mankind,' Harrod declared. Apprehension of war had been no hindrance to human progress before 1914: by 1939 the fear of war was oppressing the human spirit and threatening European civilization. 'With an ever-shortening interlude between the sufferings of war and the fear of another, no time will be left for the arts and graces of life, for the refining of human relations, for progress,' he predicted. 'In the haste of preparation and counter-preparation, our traditions will be lost. Progress and tradition are inextricably interlocked; without progress, traditions atrophy, and it is only tradition . . . that distinguishes man from the animal. Homer and Shakespeare and even the Gospels may fade from memory.' Little wonder that Harold Macmillan thought of Harrod as 'a prophet of woe.'[47]

More apprehensions were manifest in a pamphlet published by Macmillan in 1946. In it Harrod asked if Britain would remain a leader in the new world order, 'or is she to sink to being a nation whose querulous and disgruntled self-pity, whose myopic and obstinate egotism makes her a perennial source of trouble? . . . Is she permanently sick, damaged beyond repair, racked with hidden anxieties, her nervous system shattered?' There must be an effort of 'manly resolution' if Britain was to avoid becoming a global nuisance, Harrod wrote. 'Manliness means a firm resolve . . . not to join in the helter-skelter of every man for himself.' He believed in economic deregulation and individual liberty, but never confused these virtuous influences with the viciousness of unrestricted competitive individualism.[48]

In a lecture written in 1946, a few months after the death of Keynes, he quoted a passage from *The General Theory of Employment, Interest and Money* (1936) in which Keynes imagined the creation of an interest-free economy: 'it would mean the euthanasia of the rentier, and, consequently, the euthanasia of the cumulative oppressive power of the capitalist to exploit the scarcity-value of capital'. Harrod countered that the English rentier class had refined and embodied the best of 'civilization'. Rentiers provided leadership across the sciences, arts, industry, administration and political management and were responsible for bringing the nation's institutions nearer to the ideal.

Rentiers, indeed, Harrod argued, were analogous to 'the concept that we all have of Royalty, which stands before the public as an abstract ideal of perfection'. The preservation of the class system was necessary for national hardihood. It strengthened the country 'to give advantages to those whose forebears have proved themselves'. Campaigns for equal distribution of income:

> represent a naïve, almost schoolboy, level of thinking, or alterna-
> tively, since they have been advanced by learned professors, they
> smell very strongly of the lamp. Precise allocation by need is a
> recipe of the prison or of the nation at siege. The very stuff of life
> itself, the interest, the basis of all the charm in life, of romance,
> of drama, depends on variety. Precise allocation by the value of
> services rendered is little better. The society in which each person
> drew an income precisely related to his station in the hierarchy
> would be intolerably vulgar.[49]

Until the late 1940s he was an outright Liberal: so much so that, although he did not hold a parliamentary seat, he was elected by the Liberal Party Council to the party's Shadow Cabinet in 1946. His contemporaries regretted that he was never offered a peerage, for he was of senatorial type and would have made an authoritative legislator in the House of Lords. His nomination was probably blocked by Treasury and Bank of England officials whose policies and competence he had criticized. It cannot have helped that after 1956 he exchanged letters with his friend Guy Burgess, the Soviet spy who was living in Moscow exile. Both sides of the correspond-ence were intercepted by the Security Service.[50]

Harrod's predictions became gloomier with each phase of the overregulated, restrictive and austere Attlee state. 'Unless this country ceases to be mendicant and pauper and hopeless', he said in Cambridge in 1948, it would become within a few years 'a poor little derelict slum island'. In order to recover solvency and self-respect, Britain must follow the example of Belgium, which had undergone a swift post-war reconstruction by allowing individual profit-seeking initiative to operate without centralized government regulations, rationing of resources, direction of labour, controls of capital expenditure. Harrod's recipe for post-war reconstruction was based on an export drive, free convertibility of sterling against the dollar and other currencies, and cognate deregulatory measures. His later thinking on the best technical means to stimulate economic growth is recounted in Warren Young's *Harrod and his Trade Cycle Group* (1989).[51]

Harrod provided some of the lustre when the sunburst of the English public intellectual dawned in 1948. The BBC radio Third Programme launched its annual Reith lectures in that year, and showed the post-war nation's trust in academic distinction by the *ex officio* quartet which it recruited to its panel advising on the choice of the lecturer: the Master of Trinity College, Cambridge (Trevelyan), the Warden of All Souls College, Oxford (Sumner), the President of the British Academy and the President of the Royal Society. Bertrand Russell, a former Fellow of Trinity, gave the inaugural Reith lectures on 'Authority and the Individual'. Other names mooted as Reith lecturers in this phase included the Nobel laureate E. D. Adrian, Noël Annan, Auden, J. L. Austin, Alan Bullock, Lord David Cecil, Bill Deakin, Marcus Dick, H. J. Habbakuk, Julian Huxley, Michael Oakeshott, Veronica Wedgwood and Bill Williams.

The BBC talks department wanted trained thinkers, scientists, philosophers, historians and churchmen. Quality was paramount, its producer Grace Wyndham Goldie decided: stringent ideas rather than emotional slop. '"Good broadcasting should, if necessary, be sacrificed to "good thinking"', she explained. Radio talks were 'not to be an occasion for the views of the common man'. Aside from the Reith series, G. D. H. Cole, the Christ Church theologian Vigo Demant and the historians Geoffrey Barraclough, John Plamenatz, A. J. P. Taylor and Arnold Toynbee broadcast on the subject of the 'Western Tradition' during 1948. That same year Ayer, Cole and Russell, Annan, Cecil and Huxley, Trevelyan, Bronowski, Harold Laski, Lindsay and Woodward contributed to a series of radio talks on the Victorian mentality. Woodward, Demant, Lindsay, E. M. Forster and Arthur Koestler spoke in a series of Sunday-evening talks entitled 'The Challenge of Our Time'.[52]

Wyndham Goldie encouraged dons to drop the academic habit of impersonality and to speak of their personal convictions. Harrod was alarmed when E. H. Carr did this in six BBC radio talks of 1951. Carr pleaded that politics should be treated as a science, that free competition should yield to a planned economy and that mass democracy, by which he meant a collectivist society, was preferable to the cherishing of individualism. Harrod found Carr's arguments too authoritarian and set out to controvert them. Equality, he said, was a specious cause compared with liberty. The French revolutionaries who raised an outcry about *égalité* were not seeking equality of incomes, but equality under the law, which they supposed to exist in the United States and England. The design of starting all children with equal opportunities in life would destroy a precious freedom: 'the right of a man to use the fruits of his success or of his self-sacrifice to advance his children in life. This liberty is associated with the noblest motive and the highest virtue'. Social improvements and educational advance required rising national productivity to pay for it, and productivity depended in turn on the enterprise of a privileged minority. It was the expertise and resourcefulness of the few that would enable the rank-and-file population to be, in his words, 'enriched by the greatest possible degree of material well-being: good pay, short hours, good holidays, access to travel and to all known forms of culture and of sport'.[53]

Harrod thought that Labour policies, especially 'the degradation of the rentier', would lower the quality of life. 'Levelling down', he said, would replace everything 'that is graceful and charming and delightful' with 'something drab and dreary, and without charm or excitement'. The experience of post-war controls and crises convinced him that 'Leftist and stupid have become almost synonymous in politics'. When Quintin Hogg, the MP for Oxford City, inherited a peerage in 1950, thus forcing a by-election, he urged Harrod to seek the Conservative candidature. Two years later Harrod was shortlisted for a Bournemouth constituency when its sitting MP was promoted to the House of Lords.[54]

Harrod's epoch-making book, *The Life of John Maynard Keynes*, was 'an epic study of heroic deeds', G. D. H. Cole wrote after its publication in 1951. Cole, who felt that Keynes 'would have been a Tory paternalist, if he had not found most of the Tories such stupid people', lauded Maynard Keynes's denunciation of the Treaty of Versailles, *The Economic Consequences of the Peace*, as 'an essay, not in optimism, but in plain human decency in a mad world'. Harrod's adulation of the Bloomsbury–Cambridge axis in Keynes's life was nevertheless to

Cole 'a little sick-making'. The suppression in the book of the fact that
Keynes had been a conscientious objector during the war of 1914–18,
and Harrod's later denial of the true facts of the case, shocked many
people. He had, nevertheless, produced not merely a masterly biography, Noël Annan judged, but 'a great document in the history of
twentieth-century Britain; at once a study in the history of ideas, a
survey of the development of economics, and a portrait of the
outstanding intellectual of the age'. Harrod intended to show Keynes's
life work as an expression of the 'stability', 'self-confidence' and
'progressiveness' of 'Cambridge civilization'. Annan relished Harrod's
celebration of the prescience, altruism, care, dispassionate clarity and
public spirit of academics when they are given official authority. The
attractions and successes of academic privilege are perhaps upheld so
high in Harrod's *Keynes* because in 1948, while he was writing it, the
university constituencies were abolished by the Labour majority in
the House of Commons. Harrod certainly deplored this disenfran-
chisement of a select elite. Several Keynesian disciples, thinking that
they knew their protean master best, begrudged Harrod's book.
'Everything in it', complained Sir Hubert Henderson, 'was two or three
degrees out, just wrong by a thin margin, and . . . this produced a
continuous feeling of irritation.' The book nevertheless made a blaze
that lasted for thirty years: its flame only began to dim, although it
was never quenched, after Robert Skidelsky began to publish his
biographical studies of Keynes in 1983.[55]

Harrod did the utmost service to the House by mustering opposition
to the barbarian scheme to build a relief road through Christ Church
Meadow. Undeniably, the traffic in central Oxford had become brutal-
izing during the 1920s. Broad Street was turned into a glorified
car-park in 1928. Both J. I. M. Stewart and Cecil Day Lewis, in novels
published in 1936–7, described the roar and stench of combustion
engines, by day and night, in venerable streets along which past
generations of scholars and poets had sauntered in meditative calm.
During the day lumbering buses rattled windows in the High Street,
while dons' wives in four-seaters, undergraduates in open two-seaters
and tradesmen's vans jammed the city's narrow medieval streets. At
night Oxford fell under the dominion of haulage traffic: trundling
lorries and rumbling pantechnicons, with drivers pale from lack of

sleep, shook the town with their heavy loads. 'Past the portals of Christ Church,' the *Oxford Magazine* reported of St Aldate's, thunder lorries loaded with valuables 'which all the wealth of Wolsey could never have procured'. By 1941 members of some colleges abutting the High Street were hailing a plan to build a relief road, provisionally named Christ Church Mall, which would divert traffic from the High and send it through the Meadow. By 1954 traffic on the High seemed to a visiting New Yorker, Edmund Wilson, worse than anywhere in America. George Kennan, over from Princeton, was appalled by the congestion in the streets, the shoddiness of the shop-ware and the bleakness of the parks.[56]

In 1956 the Ministry of Transport unveiled a road-building scheme to scar the Meadow. The fumes from exhaust pipes, rumble from engines, squeals from tyres and hoots from road hogs were dismissed as nugatory. People with anti-Establishment prejudices welcomed plans that would mar the amenities of a privileged college. The city council endorsed the vandal project. Harrod, chief among the Students of the House but ably supported by Robert Blake and others, mounted a resourceful, ardent, ingenious defence of the Meadow from the despoilers. His efforts were incited by his wife Billa, who was a founder member of the Georgian Group. The final defeat of the road-building scheme in 1972 infuriated the Ministry: its vengeful officials had a retort in reserve, and proposed two years later to desecrate the Meadow by excavating for gravel needed for other road schemes.[57]

Westminster politics impinged on life at Christ Church in other ways during 1956. The Eden government's military incursion into Egypt in secret collusion with the French and Israelis caused a wide and deep rift in Oxford's intelligentsia. Harrod wrote to *The Times* and spoke at large in support of the Suez aggression. The reproach that he sent to Sir Edward Boyle, a Christ Church man who had resigned from the Eden government in protest at its Suez policies, was supercilious and disagreeable. The commissioning of Graham Sutherland to paint Anthony Eden's portrait, for display in Christ Church hall, was deferred because of the Suez imbroglio, and abandoned in 1959. Harrod subsequently exerted himself to arrange for a substitute portrait: Eden wanted to sit to Oskar Kokoschka; the work was finally executed by William Coldstream.[58]

'You can't tell what may come unstuck,' J. I. M. Stewart reflected
after the unravelling of Eden's Suez policy: 'only a Third Programme
economist could fancy he had a clue.' Despite such scoffing at the
certitude of the BBC's academic pundits, public intellectualism
remained a well-entrenched platoon fighting for national good.
During the general election campaign of 1959, David Astor, editor
of the *Observer*, commissioned three dons to write personal party
manifestos. The financial columnist Nicholas Davenport had recently
written, 'Sir Roy's heart is in the right place, even if he has a few
bees buzzing in his bonnet'; and it was to Harrod that Astor turned
for advocacy of the Conservative case. Ayer represented Labour, and
the political historian R. B. McCallum, Master of Pembroke College,
gave the Liberal position. Sixty-five years later all three credos remain
striking for their clarity, principles and ideas.[59]

Harrod began by declaring that the nationalization of industries
and services had discouraged personal initiative, group efficiency and
general welfare. State controls over investment, imports and other
economic activities were unproductive, frustrating and inefficient. 'I
am a stalwart democrat, in the sense of believing that constitutional
government with a democratic franchise is the only known shield
against the great evils of autocracy.' But the crude formula of majority
rule, which Harrod called 'arithmetical democracy', did not solve the
problem – so old that it had worried Plato – 'of how to get the wisest
and best thought to bear upon government'. The problem had wors-
ened since, in 'a ridiculously slavish subscription' to a foolish formula,
the universities' representation in parliament had been abolished. He
deplored the failure of Conservative governments to fulfil their manifesto pledges of 1950 and 1951 to restore the university franchise. 'I
am a firm believer', declared Harrod, 'in the transmission of valuable
social qualities through heredity, and favour maintaining special
opportunities for the descendants of those whose work has been of
special value to the community.' High on his wish list, too, was for
his country to be strong in armaments. 'She should allow herself as
many nuclear test explosions as the other fellows have had.'[60]

Harrod's strength never rallied after a portion of his stomach was
removed in an operation for a duodenal ulcer in the late 1940s, and
he took on a spectral thinness. Some of his fellow Students, who

were often snide about his wife Billa, suggested that his recovery was hindered by her unhappiness while her affair with the All Souls lawyer Sir John Foster was petering out. The misogynists in the House could not cope with a dauntless, forthright woman with a quick temper. She hid her irritation neither at the ill-savoured crabs in the college nor at the pettiness of university life. Her parties at the Harrods' home, 91 St Aldate's, brought a signal liveliness to Oxford in the early 1950s. Clever and original-minded undergraduates, including Mark Girouard and Thomas Pakenham, fell under her sparkling influence. She entertained theatre people from London and netted stylish young Christ Church noblemen such as Lord Weymouth. Tuft-hunting dons envied these social successes and spoke of them with malice.

In 1956 Harrod's mother died in her ninetieth year. Two years later Harrod's elder son Henry came up to Christ Church (his younger brother Dominick followed a year later). Billa Harrod determined to give her son privacy and freedom during his undergraduate years and moved to the house in Campden Hill Square which Harrod had bought his mother years before. She seldom appeared in Oxford thereafter, although she was a formidably supportive companion during Harrod's exacting tours of economics faculties in the United States and Japan. He joined her during vacations at their house in Norfolk, where she created a renowned garden.

Living alone in college in term time, Harrod developed, so Trevor-Roper and Blake thought, a neglected and unhealthy air. His manners declined, too. In 1958–9 the young literary critic John Carey spent three terms of residence at Christ Church giving tutorials while J. I. M. Stewart took a sabbatical year in America. Harrod pointedly did not say a word to him during their many evenings together at high table or in the common room. One night at dinner Carey, who was sitting opposite Harrod, heard him pointing out to a guest all the eminent men sitting at the table. When the guest asked who Carey was, Harrod replied, all too audibly, 'Oh, that's nobody.'[61]

No good was done to Harrod by taking the post of Curator of the Christ Church common room in 1962. He relied on 'alcoholic elevation', in Trevor-Roper's phrase, in order to be a gregarious host in the common room. His friends were soon distressed by the condition in which he nightly showed himself. There were worse scenes at the Cranium dining club in London (Berlin was initially blackballed for membership because he was not thought bright enough). During the 1950s the Cranium met at the Reform Club, under the aegis of its Secretary, Richard Garnett. His successor Stephen Keynes, who was parsimonious, moved its meetings to trattorias in Fitzrovia. The only member whose expulsion was ever discussed by fellow members was Harrod, as his behaviour became noisy and objectionable. This was tragic in a man whom the New College economist Henry Phelps Brown compared, in his intellect, literary craftsmanship and theoretical power, with Adam Smith and Hume. Harrod's decline was remarked and regretted across Oxford. Thomas Balogh, the Balliol economist, who regarded him as combining brilliance with engaging self-effacement in the 1930s, complained in 1961 of his 'ponderous pomposity', his 'shop-worn claim to superiority', 'his astonishing record of Malapropisms'.[62]

Harold Macmillan, who had reckoned Harrod among his 'dear, trusted, loyal friends', was saddened that he became a *'violent'* opponent of the British application to join the European Economic Community, founded by the Treaty of Rome in 1957. Harrod objected in 1962–3 that the Common Market was a protectionist group of rich nations setting limits on poor economies in Africa and Asia. Britain's moral responsibility and future prosperity depended upon a global attitude centred on the Commonwealth rather than a continental policy based in Europe. He insisted that Britain would be entering 'political bondage' if it was admitted into membership of the European market. 'It will be the end of a country which has played its part in the world since 1066, bad as well as good, but we like to believe the good has predominated,' he told Macmillan. The United States, he suggested, was encouraging the British application because of its vengeful wish, dating from the War of Independence, to eliminate its 'former masters' as a world power. This was intensified by President Kennedy's desire, as a man of Irish heritage, to weaken and humiliate the English. 'I regard him very highly as a man of considerable genius,' Macmillan wrote after Harrod's ebullitions had circulated in Whitehall: 'He is often wrong, but then he is often right.'[63]

In 1967, a month after Harrod had retired as a Student of Christ Church on reaching the age limit, a younger economist John Vaizey appraised him. Keynes was, Vaizey wrote, Britain's pre-eminent twentieth-century British economist, with Marshall, Arthur Pigou and Joan Robinson clustered behind him. 'For some reason,' he continued,

> Sir Roy Harrod, though without doubt the most distinguished economist writing at Oxford since Edgeworth, has never seemed to be as famous as the other four. He has written much, done a great deal, but his reputation has never quite matched his achievement. This is desperately unfair, because his work has been of a kind that entitles him to a major status as an originator of ideas and an acute analyst of the economic scene. Never, for him, the conventional wisdom – which is why more conventional minds have been listened to when they were patently moaning rubbish over the ether, as the iceberg loomed up ahead of them.[64]

CHAPTER 10

Patrick Gordon Walker: Writing for the Workers

Patrick Gordon Walker's supreme orientation as a Christ Church historian was that of an anti-Nazi. After his election as a Student, at the same time as Einstein in 1931, he was encouraged by the college to broaden his studies in German universities. He was consequently in Germany during the campaigns that brought Hitler to power. The violence of the far right and the ready corruption of capitalist leaders shocked him. In reaction he pledged himself to the empowerment of the working class because he felt sure they would contribute the most stalwart fight against National Socialism. He joined the Labour party, became a parliamentary candidate, was converted to the Marxist interpretation of history and presented the subject to his Oxford pupils and to the readers of his books from the standpoint of a recent eyewitness of Nazism in action. Gordon Walker felt sure, like many others in the Oxford of his time, that the proletariat were the only progressive class in society: they were invincible in their truth telling, indefeasible in class warfare, with a privileged capacity for historical comprehension, and (according to Marxist historical laws) bound to triumph. Other classes, by comparison, were regressive, selfish, purblind and ordained to fail.

The ideas that Gordon Walker assimilated and upheld after 1933 are encapsulated in his preface to the book that he published before the outbreak of war in 1939:

This book is written for the workers. They, more than any other class, are able to approach history with honesty, clarity, and freedom from inhibitions. For they, alone, as a class, have nothing to fear but everything to gain from . . . the process of historical change. Their thoughts, actions and understanding of to-day will make the history of to-morrow. The working class alone has the duty and the interest, and therefore the ability, to *understand* the history not only of the suppressed classes but of the ruling classes of the present and the past.

His book may have derived, at least remotely, from Winwood Reade's *The Martyrdom of Man*, which Masterman recommended to his pupils. Certainly, it was as ambitious as its title *An Outline of Man's History* suggests. Yet, while Feiling, Harrod and Trevor-Roper turned to the august house of Macmillan to publish their books, Gordon Walker wrote for a series issued by the Fulham-based Plebs League. The Plebs Outline series bore the slogan 'Candid but not impartial', and targeted working-class autodidacts. It is a measure of the violent changes wrought by the European political crisis of the 1930s that a Student of Christ Church became a man of Marx and an educator of the plebs.[1]

Gordon Walker's Englishness was ineradicable from his Marxism, as his writings show. His lack of sympathy with Stalinist communism was so evident that he was refused a visa to visit the Soviet Union in 1936. When the Labour party disaffiliated the university Labour Federation in 1940, on the grounds that it was a communist front organization, Gordon Walker became Senior Treasurer of the substitute Democratic Socialist Club, which issued a rousing promotional leaflet: 'We don't like Hitler and we're rather coy with Stalin. We have NOTHING in common with the Stalinist anti-war policy of the old "Labour" club.' His early trust in the benefits of proletarian rule and historical change was sundered by his wartime experiences and post-war observations. Human nature seemed to him suspect. The ease with which totalitarian governments established themselves in the twentieth century made him charier of talking at large about progress.[2]

Collingwood, Woodward and Hancock, among other Oxford-trained historians, urged that the initial task for a young historian must be to get closer to people, to get inside situations, to engage in the contemporary crisis. Hancock identified *attachment*, not detachment, as the primary virtue that a historian must seek.

Subsequently, in the 1960s, the word 'attachment' was superseded by 'commitment'. Gordon Walker's commitment was horribly intensified after the collapse of Hitler's regime. In April 1945 he travelled in a BBC recording van into Germany. He first visited the Gestapo prison at Wolfenbüttel, where he saw torture chambers, a guillotine and grievous malnutrition. Next, on 21 April, he entered Belsen. This horrendous experience, which he described in BBC broadcasts and in a published diary, informed the most ambitious of his books, *Restatement of Liberty*. That treatise was partly written in snatched intervals while a busy Cabinet minister, and lacks literary grace: it is, at once, grinding, thoughtful and significant. The history of several millennia is covered in 400 pages. Gordon Walker's selection, arrangement and ordering of historical evidence is that of a good man who is struggling to explain, in an orderly manner, what Belsen means.

Gordon Walker was part of a group of Oxonians who arrived in the university between 1925 and 1928, and emerged as the coming generation of young Labour leaders in the 1930s. All the others were undergraduates of New College, pupils of G. D. H. Cole, and won first-class honours in Greats or PPE. Douglas Jay, whose father possessed what used to be called 'independent means', won a prize fellowship at All Souls in 1930, but spent most of the following decade in London as a journalist on *The Times* and the *Economist*. Richard Crossman, son of a judge, was elected in 1931 as a Fellow of New College, where he proved to be a negligent tutor in PPE. Two other New College socialists, Hugh Gaitskell and Evan Durbin, became political economists within the University of London. Gaitskell, a future party leader, was (like Gordon Walker) the son of an official in the Indian Civil Service.

In Britain there was no radical intelligentsia, which might be compared to those of other European powers, until the Oxford generation of 1925–8 mustered themselves in 1931–3. The Fabian Society put a lulling emphasis on gradualness rather than disruption. Moreover, the Labour party leadership customarily disparaged the graduate intelligentsia. Ramsay MacDonald, the Labour Prime Minister of 1924 and 1929–31, likened the university at Oxford to 'a painted lady, from whom Labour has nothing to expect'. His

Cabinet colleague Arthur Greenwood found it a 'benighted' place still stuck in 'the dead middle ages'. In 1931, accordingly, the Labour government introduced legislation to abolish the English and Scottish university constituencies, but it fell from power a few months later before the bill's enactment. The workers mistrusted the intelligentsia. A working-class audience cheered a speaker who told them that the only good proletarian leader was one 'whose arse stuck out of the seat of his pants'. The party leadership's mistrust of academic thinking had an unhappy product: the unsystematic notions, the reliance on emotion and brawn over brainpower, the inchoate policy-making that resulted in the collapse of the Labour government in 1931 and the trouncing of Labour candidates at the polls.[3]

The general election of 1931, held at a time of global economic crisis, turned on such issues as the balance of trade, the desirability or otherwise of tariffs, monetary policy, prices and the perils of inflation. Yet few parliamentary candidates, Labour or otherwise, could venture beyond old party cries, or speak intelligibly on such subjects as the causes of boom and slump. Labour needed knowledge, expertise, prevision, analysis, constructive internal criticism and revisionism in order to regain its appeal after the electoral wreck of 1931. In an effort to satisfy this need, Cole wrote *The Intelligent Man's Guide through World Chaos* (published by Gollancz in 1932). He argued that the traditional policies of British socialism had been 'washed out' by the world's economic depression. Labour supporters must rethink their ideas, clarify their purposes and redirect their efforts if the party was to regroup as an effective political force. Labour's economic programme must be overhauled so as to meld national efficiency with equalitarianism in the same bundle of policies. The cycle of boom and slump must be regulated if not eliminated. Sound measures must be taken to lower levels of unemployment. Social justice must be improved by stricter planning and coordination. It is striking that after the publication of Cole's *Intelligent Man's Guide* it was Oxford-trained activists, rather than Cambridge Keynesians, who took the lead in grafting Keynes's ideas on to Labour party thinking. Schemes were laid for taking manufacturing industries, mining and transport and other services into state ownership.[4]

The New College intelligentsia shirked confrontation in one

crucial area: the restrictive practices of trade unionism. Since 1902 British productivity had fallen as the result of tightening trade union controls. Scottish workers upheld the 'ca' canny' (or go-slow) doctrine, and their English counterparts cleaved to the identical 'loomp o' labour' theory. This prejudice, which had no grip in other European nations, maintained that there was a fixed optimum of work to be done in any workplace. Accordingly, the less work done by any individual worker, the more there would be for others to do. Trade union rules therefore aimed to increase the number of men on a job, and to lower output per man. There was a gulf between actual and potential output. By the 1950s, in the three industrialized regions of Europe where restrictive practices were hallowed, namely England, Scotland and Wales, working hours were longest, paid holidays were the shortest, real incomes the slowest to rise and per capita output the most meagre.[5]

The Oxford careers of Gordon Walker and his New College contemporaries betokened a more tolerant mood in the university. Gilbert Murray had been shunned by some of his fellow Students of Christ Church during the political strife before 1914. His support for George Whale, a solicitor who was Liberal parliamentary candidate for Oxford City in 1910, had brought him snubs in the common room. Fifteen years later, though, Murray found Christ Church less fraught. 'It is so safe in its conservative and aristocratic and clerical tradition that it can afford to be surprisingly open-minded and tolerant.'[6]

Sir Thomas Gordon Walker, grandfather of our historian, was a son of the manse from Morayshire. His first official appointment in the ICS, as an assistant commissioner in Punjab, came in 1872. He rose through the administrative hierarchy to become a senior judge, a Knight Commander of the Indian Empire and (at the close of his official career) Lieutenant Governor of Punjab. He and his wife retired to a house on the Grand Avenue in Worthing, a coastal resort with a large community of ICS pensioners. Their household favoured regularity, self-effacement and assiduity. Duty and responsibility were the gauges of success: not fortune or fame. Sir Thomas's son Alan and Alan's son Robin both married into Worthing families with Indian connections.

Alan Gordon Walker, who was born in Bengal, matriculated at Balliol in 1901. After achieving a fourth-class degree in classics, he transferred to the School of Law and took his final degree more successfully in 1904. A year later, when aged only twenty-two, and a pupil barrister in the Middle Temple, he married Dora Chrestien, whose family lived in Worthing. The young couple moved to the Punjab at the start of Alan's ICS career in 1907. 'As the vast task of Indian administration expanded,' reported Reginald Coupland, who served on a Royal Commission inquiring into the upper grades of the ICS during the 1920s, 'as government became more complicated, technical and efficient, it was progressively more difficult for its authors and managers to imagine the safe transfer of it all to inexperienced hands.' Although Alan Gordon Walker learnt to speak Urdu, Persian, Arabic and Turkish, and meted out justice as a judge in Lahore, he never reached his father's official altitude: he left the ICS before he was fifty, retired to the Canary Islands and died in Paris in 1934.[7]

Dora Chrestien, his wife, had been born at Marseille in 1885. Her father Fernand François Chrestien was of French stock: born in Bengal in 1838, he became a merchant dealing in mica (silicate mineral used in cosmetics, paints, glue and varnish) and was ultimtely one of the largest mica producers in the world. When he died in 1923, he left an estate that a century later was the equivalent of millions of pounds sterling. His wife, Eliza Day, whom he married in Bengal in 1876, was Patrick Gordon Walker's maternal grandmother: he must have known her well, for she died at Worthing in 1933 at the age of eighty, when he was twenty-six. Her origins were rural and impoverished. She was the fourth daughter of Uriah Day, described as a 'horsekeeper' in the Ilminster census of 1861. Her sisters toiled as glove makers. She became a servant in the household of an Ilchester civil engineer, accompanied her employer's family to India and thus came to marry a Franco-Bengali businessman fifteen years her senior.

Patrick Gordon Walker was born in 1907, and went to board at Wellington College in 1921. The school had been founded to educate, at little or no charge, the orphan sons of army officers. Eighty pupils were originally envisaged: by the 1920s the numbers exceeded 500, and few of them orphans at reduced rates; remnants of the military

orphanage mentality nevertheless remained. Obedience and virility
were prized. Privations were seen as spurs to hardihood. Meals were
frugal and monotonous. Freezing classrooms and boarding houses
left pupils too cold to think in winter. Yet Rollo St Clare Talboys,
who was Gordon Walker's history master at Wellington, regarded
the 1920s as an apex. 'The Public Schools, secluded within their
walls and playing-fields, entered upon a period of eminent prosperity,
renewal, and expansion. Here, if anywhere, in what was perhaps a
disintegrating world, were the strongholds of survival and orderly
tradition.' Post-war Wellington pupils became more thoughtful and
questioning than their predecessors, Talboys found, and more aware
of events in the outside world.[8]

Talboys requires a detour in this book because, when Masterman
took a sabbatical year in 1938, at a time when Feiling had renounced
teaching in order to concentrate on writing his history of England,
he went to the House as a supernumerary tutor in modern history
and remained a mainstay of the teaching there for eight years. He
was a Hampstead clergyman's son, stepson of an official at the War
Office and nephew of Edward Carus-Wilson, a schoolmaster and
private tutor, who was prosecuted for murdering a pubescent boy
and for sexually assaulting adolescent pupils while Rollo Talboys was
a junior member of Christ Church in 1897–1900. Perhaps this scandal
contributed to the wary flippancy and hard, crisp, unassailable irony
with which he faced the world. After coming down, he worked as a
cramming coach, became a mentor of the epicene railway heir Ronald
Firbank and then joined the staff at Wellington. There he preferred
brawny, naive, homespun boys for his pupils. While encouraging
verbal thrust-and-parry in the classroom, he disliked emotional
scenes or explicitness. In his universe, there was a world of difference
between the braves who showed their feelings with terse restraint
and the vulgarians who expose their every raw nerve. His manner
was calm, urbane, prudent and perhaps mistrustful. History he treated
as a branch of literature and unfit for philistines. He knew the need
for calculated disrespect in education: one family had their son
described, in an end-of-term report, as 'dirty, lazy, ill-tempered, and
stupid: he should, in due course, make a typical parent'.[9]

After the declaration of war in 1939, Christ Church's tutors in
modern history went away to the armed forces or government

departments. As their replacement, Talboys taught young men who had one or two terms in Oxford before starting their service in the air force or army. He made a special subject of military history, and instructed them in the strategy and battle tactics of the American civil war. 'What he most loved was the ordinary, plain, country boy, for whom he could open windows on the wonders of history and literature and art in a manner given to few teachers,' Dundas wrote after his death in 1953. 'They mostly came from small local grammar and day schools, with no great claims to scholarship, but were simple and manly and receptive. Them he taught and mothered and had up to his house, and showed them the sights and meaning of Oxford.' It was at Talboys's prompting that a star Christ Church pupil, Raymond Carr, went to Wellington in 1941 to teach history. The digressive liveliness of his lessons delighted brighter pupils: flapping his hands all the while, he veered from seventeenth-century religious and parliamentary topics into paeans to Flaubert, Stendhal, Goncharov, Turgenev and other Russian masters.[10]

Wellington was denounced in memoirs by two old boys, Esmond Romilly and Constantine FitzGibbon, and by a former master Cuthbert Worsley; but Gordon Walker did not resent his schooldays. He played rugby, cricket and hockey; he won the half-mile and mile races; during his final year, he was head of his house, and company sergeant-major in the school's officer training corps (OTC). Talboys liked his type, and helped him to win an open scholarship to Christ Church in 1925.

There Gordon Walker became a conscientious pupil of Feiling and Masterman. They were disappointed when he failed to get first-class honours in their subject in 1928 – perhaps because his prose tended to be leaden and congested. His second-class degree was neither mentioned nor forgotten by his Oxford contemporaries: Crossman, Gaitskell and Jay ranked him as a shade below themselves; specks of deprecation were flicked at him and left their mark; arrogant youngsters and spiteful old men in Christ Church liked to make snide references to him as a second-class man. Gordon Walker nevertheless passed a test of palatability in 1931 by giving the customary formal oration at the Christ Church gaudy (college feast) on the subject of the Marquis of Dalhousie, a mid-nineteenth-century Governor-General of India whose portrait hung in Christ

Church hall. He spoke as an Anglo-Indian: there were no provocations in his speech; and he was soon afterwards elected as a Student. Ayer, Pakenham and Trevor-Roper felt that he owed his studentship to Masterman's belief that sports all-rounders like himself would be a healthy influence on young men.

Like a good son of Worthing, Gordon Walker read the *Daily Telegraph*. In 1928 he began sending it short letters for publication on such subjects as Varsity sports and the level of municipal rates. His earliest article for the newspaper praised the refacing of Peckwater Quad, repairing of the balustrade in Tom Quad and restoring of the statue of Mercury. Other contributions reported theatrical or musical performances: none of them showed any trace of interest in the proletariat. His vocabulary was that of someone who had been head of a school boarding house. 'The old virtues of fidelity, honesty and gentleness are, perhaps, no longer admired,' he wrote in 1929. 'Frankness, manliness and even, perhaps, ruthlessness, have taken their place.' The repetition of 'perhaps' showed a tentativeness that was never found in cocksure Crossman with his double first.[11]

Gordon Walker began his studentship as the understudy for Feiling and Masterman. He found that undergraduates across the university, including many thoughtful ones, were questioning the traditional assumptions of the School of Modern History. Richard Southern, who was at Balliol in the early 1930s, decided at an early stage of the course that the curriculum skirted most of the important elements in people's lives:

The universal usefulness of the past as a guide and model for future development suddenly and catastrophically appeared to be outdated; the system of thought which held everything together was itself becoming a piece of the past: the broadening down of freedom from precedent to precedent, the slow emergence of democratic assemblies from the Anglo-Saxon Witans and the Anglo-Norman *Curia Regis*; the great providential growth of freedom, which Acton had so inspiringly seen as the key to universal history, began to appear, not as a universal rule of human development, but as the invention of the nineteenth century, nearer indeed to our own in time, but as remote . . . in thought and feeling from the present as the thirteenth century. When this happened, the historical programme which had dominated the universities from about 1880 to 1930 was widely seen to satisfy neither the past which it had attempted to put at our service, nor the present which it had aimed at serving.

Southern rejected the 'absurd delusion' that present times are a climax of public integrity, personal morality, scruples and wisdom. The study of history, which means the appreciation of past beliefs and images, should convince students of the comparative poverty of their own times in contrast to the wealth of the past. 'This imaginative participation is a first step towards taking seriously our own shortcomings,' Southern said. 'The mere thought of what we have lost is a challenge to explain, perhaps to replace, the defects of the present.'[12]

Probably the most formative influence on Gordon Walker at Christ Church was an exact contemporary there named John Hampden Jackson. The pair talked, disputed, developed Marxist interpretations, explained historic losses and laid plans to remedy the defects of the present. Born at Wallasey in 1907, Hampden Jackson was the son of a salt salesman. At Christ Church he was Fell Exhibitioner of 1927. Following his graduation in 1929, he taught at the former ICS college, Haileybury. 'His teaching was fluent, with unexpected but profitable digressions and exchanges of view, swiftly forcing me to revise ingrained attitudes to patriotism, rebellion, heroes, war, literature, and my prose style,' recalled one Haileybury pupil. Another called him 'a genius as a teacher'. His best ideas were offered obliquely. He infiltrated rather than force-fed facts: some of them memorably obscure, such as that the utopian socialist Charles Fourier had identified forty-nine varieties of cuckold. Jackson loved À la recherche du temps perdu, and lent bright boys the newest volumes from Aldous Huxley, Arthur Koestler, Ezra Pound and Virginia Woolf. He believed that irrationality was a robust, often overwhelming political force, and that the left weakened itself by denying or downplaying the appeal of unreason. He loved France, which was, he declared, the foremost country in Europe in everything except loving-kindness and mass production.[13]

Attitudes to Europe in the university were generally remote, wary, tendentious and ill-informed. There was pride rather than shame in being a monoglot in anything other than dead languages. In 1929 Kenneth Diplock of University College lumped the School of Modern Languages together with those of chemistry, physics and engineering as inimical to ideals of general culture. These were practical, specialist schools, which attracted people who treated university as a place to prepare themselves for grubbing after salaried work. Linguists were mere job hunters. The learning of modern European languages required classification and memory to be used almost to the exclusion of reasoning, Diplock argued. It was therefore inferior in character formation, reasoning power and cultural value to Greats, PPE, history, English and jurisprudence.[14]

Hampden Jackson and Gordon Walker rejected such dilettante nativism. They determined to monitor the problems of historic nationalities, new nation states and rising nationalism. Jackson was drawn to the Baltic, and wrote about Finland, Estonia and Soviet encroachments thereon. Christ Church encouraged Gordon Walker, as it had Masterman in 1913 and Harrod in 1923, to gain experience by visiting German universities: in Gordon Walker's case that at Heidelberg particularly. Some of his expenses were covered by acting as a correspondent of the *Daily Telegraph*. He reported the turmoil of July 1932 when Franz von Papen and his Cabinet of Prussian Junkers destabilized German constitutionalism and the Nazis won the largest number of seats in the Reichstag election. Twice he saw Goebbels addressing supporters, and once Hitler. As a reporter of these historic events, he concluded that by splitting their votes among social democrats, communists and the 'pseudo-radical' National Socialists, rather than combining together in one cohesive movement to control capitalism, the German proletariat failed to take responsibility for its political destiny.[15]

The part played in German politics by young people, and the gulf between the generations, was prominent in Gordon Walker's *Telegraph* coverage. The older generation of the English governing class claimed to have masterminded victory in 1918, and could stand with satisfied airs at the Cenotaph and soothe the nation into docility. In Germany, though, the authorities of the Weimar Republic were tarnished by defeat, and young Germans set up a vengeful clamour for national vindication. 'Politics are largely in the hands of the young: the universities are extremely political, and often have to be shut because of disorder,' Gordon Walker reported. Student violence during this period left ineradicable marks on his thinking. People of university age are 'the easiest prey for the devils of irrationality', he warned twenty years later. 'That is why all totalitarian movements, whether communist or fascist, make a deeper appeal to youth than to any other section of society.'[16]

Gordon Walker told *Telegraph* readers that Germans retained a tradition of political fury that had been unknown elsewhere in Europe since the sixteenth-century religious strife. Anti-Semitism was a violent political force in Germany rather than a pervasive social prejudice as in England. Jews were reviled with 'hysterical hatred' by the parties of the right. 'Hitler has pocketed for his party the deep Jewish hatred, putting the loss of the war down to Jewish "November traitors"', Gordon Walker reported. 'This racial feeling is the main binding-link between the very ill-suited elements in the party.' He saw a man greeted by cries of 'Heil Hitler!' in a wine shop because he had knocked down a Christian girl for consorting with a Jew. Such incidents convinced him that brutality was admired as 'a quality' in Germany.[17]

Nazi bullying was at the root of a dream that Gordon Walker recorded in October 1932 after returning to Oxford. Christ Church undergraduates were rioting against him. He took refuge in Masterman's rooms. A man told him that he was unpopular because of his conceit: 'playing rugger with a pot belly'. When the rioters renewed their onslaught, Masterman ushered him into another room, barred the door and hustled him out of a window. Dream analysis was a popular habit among Christ Church intellectuals of the 1930s (Trevor-Roper covered pages of his notebooks with records of his nightmares and reveries): Gordon Walker interpreted his dream as expressing his fear of men in a mass, which ill-fitted his keen desire to influence their minds. He could infuse individuals with his convictions, but felt too self-conscious to sway groups effectively. 'In private intercourse my feet move of their own: in public I have to move them.' These anxieties, and his difficulty in moving spontaneously under public scrutiny, contributed to his failure in the Smethwick and Leyton parliamentary elections of 1964–5.[18]

Gordon Walker's politicization had different origins from those of Crossman, Durbin, Gaitskell and Jay. The New College quartet were affronted by the poverty, deprivation and social injustice that arose from unregulated capitalism. They decried the supposed inviolability of the free price mechanism, the unequal distribution of income among the population, the existence of 'idlers' living off what was called 'unearned incomes', the perpetuation of class privileges, the sacrosanctity of inherited wealth and the view that taxation is a form of confiscation. Economic reconstruction was the throttle that drove their socialism; but Gordon Walker's activism, which began in the autumn of 1932 and proceeded apace during 1933, was provoked by thuggish political gangsterism in Germany. He was set on forming in Britain a strong working-class movement which would protect constitutional propriety and resist totalitarianism of any political hue.

Labour candidates had been trounced in the general election of 1931 by the candidates of the coalition National government, which was mainly composed of Conservatives but led by a renegade Labour prime minister. This defeat had different sequels in the two ancient universities. There were few factories in Cambridge, which was surrounded by dispiriting fen villages, and few industrial workers ripe for enlistment in socialist campaigns. The Labour Club there was so demoralized by the election results that it collapsed. This enabled the flourishing of Communist Party of Great Britain (CPGB) cells in which the Soviet spies Philby, Maclean, Burgess, Blunt and Cairncross were involved after 1933. By contrast, the City of Oxford constituency contained the Morris motorcar plant, the Pressed Steel works and other factories. The core Labour support was too solid for party activism to evaporate as in Cambridge. Indeed, Labour candidates in the constituency and in council wards discouraged university members from campaigning for them: the working class were easily irritated by educated people presuming to join their cause.

The CPGB, with such volatile MPs as Cecil L'Estrange Malone and Walton Newbold, failed as a parliamentary force in the early 1920s. Accordingly, young Oxford men with progressive plans and parliamentary ambitions planned their careers in the largest, most promising of the leftward parties, Labour. Cole, moreover, had a paramount influence on Oxford's socialist aspirants. Although at times he seemed to defend Soviet state terrorism and to deny the existence of slave labour camps, he upheld the values of European social democracy, defended the personal and group freedom available under parliamentary capitalism, deplored Stalinism, and disfavoured (in his words) 'the all-European victory of Communism à la Russe.'[19]

Cole's disciples drew on Marxist analysis without becoming communists or apologists for Stalinism. Durbin, for example, advocated the nationalization of industrial sectors, but denied that modern capitalism was pure exploitation. He disavowed the dictatorship of the proletariat and saw that the British proletariat was undergoing embourgeoisement by the accelerating process of home ownership, Post Office savings and such like. Similarly, neither Hampden Jackson nor Gordon Walker had the communist faith that the proletariat could provide political leadership and solve socio-economic problems, by some instinct rooted in class consciousness, and regardless of their level of intelligence, education and knowledge. The two friends sought to build a frame of mind in the 'newspaper-reading public' that would repair the ravages of laisser-faire and level class inequalities. These part-time students, outside university life, had scant interest in the old forms of constitutional, parliamentary and patriotic history. Study circles of working men almost invariably opted for 'economic history' when asked what subjects they preferred to take. They reasoned that political history, as Namier reported in 1928, 'is about kings and statesmen and wars, while they want to learn about "the likes" of themselves.'[20]

Jackson's brief and lucid work, *Europe since the War: A Sketch of Political Development, 1918–1932* (1933), explained the trinity of ideals which vied with one another for paramountcy during those fifteen years: communism, nationalism (which Jackson also called 'fascism') and internationalism. He treated Lenin as a genius, Keynes as a sage and Mussolini as responsible for 'one of the greatest national revivals in history', which made Italy 'the most united, the most efficient and almost the most prosperous nation in Europe'. Ireland's experience as the first country to break free from the British Empire, and the prospects of India following suit, were brought to the fore by Jackson. 'Gandhi in India and de Valera in

Ireland', he maintained, 'are leading a spiritual revolt of their people against the materialist standards of Great Britain.' His overall message was insistently statist. 'Government is a business for experts,' he wrote: 'only when the central government is powerful can the best be achieved for the good of the community.'[21]

Gordon Walker, of course, had strong ancestral reasons for being a centralizing *dirigiste*. His father and grandfather had been administrators of British India. They were cogs in an apparatus of centralized government which they believed was working for the betterment of humanity and for the common good. The S in the acronym ICS denoted Service, after all, and three generations of Gordon Walkers found fulfilment in public service.

There was a consensus among Cole's Labour acolytes in Oxford, including Gordon Walker, that forward strides towards social justice and economic stability were possible only after the taking of careful measurements. Goodwill and energy were not enough. A minutely calibrated yet comprehensive scheme of national economic planning was required to counter world depression. Market activity, prices and incomes must be regulated by central authorities. Goods and services must be provided in accordance with a national plan. Some older dons apprehended that the ubiquity of state controls and fixed standards would produce a society of reductive and uniform mediocrity. George Gordon, President of Magdalen, speaking in 1934, warned progressive-minded young members of the university against becoming passengers 'in the political train, the world-wide express, heading for the land of universal and contented Beta-minus'.[22]

The Labour party drew its strength from the ethical fervour of its rank-and-file membership. Their certainty that their aspirations for social justice, economic equality and community solidarity put them on a superior level to dog-eat-dog individualists and to avid materialists sustained the party's morale and stoked its astounded indignation at times of electoral defeat between 1931 and 1959. Party leaders expected continuous electoral successes because they represented the majority class. The proletariat, if it combined but did not try to dictate, would be undefeatable, they believed. They could not accept that the working classes were as snobbish in their way as the middle class in Worthing. The trade union strikes to preserve the 'differentials' between different grades of workers, which were rife until the 1980s, should have disabused them. So, too, should the race for status symbols.

There was a patriotic tint in Gordon Walker's decision to join the Labour party. In the Westminster parliament, so it seemed to him, the Old Gang were pursuing their inflexible, deadbeat courses. In his view, the nation was being degraded by the Conservative party; and he wanted to revive national pride. When Cole, at a Pink Club lunch in 1932, mused on the need to evolve internationally applicable socialist doctrines, Gordon Walker felt uneasy. Discussion of abstractions and fundamental principles was allowable, he conceded, 'but . . . we are Englishmen. There is no harm in discovering the common factors for all practical socialisms, but our particular concern is English socialism for England.' Theoretical talk about socialist purity 'will lead nowhere except possibly to the production of an infallible scripture which even then will be open to contradictory interpretations'. The Marxist–Leninist insistence that capitalism must be destroyed by warfare was too annihilating for Gordon Walker to accept. The semi-feudal conditions that had made the Russian revolution were far different from those prevailing in England which, although ostensibly capitalist, was already 'half socialist' in its provision of pensions, savings, public housing, increasing home ownership, hospital facilities and other social services. 'Even if the Marxist inevitable end is a true reading of history, England has half-escaped its applicability to her,' Gordon Walker wrote. The class war in England had been only a hand-to-hand skirmish. The electoral franchise had not been extended as a concession after riots or revolutionary demonstrations. The nearest to civil war in the British Isles had come in 1912–14 in Ireland. That crisis had stemmed from religious sectarianism, not class strife.[23]

Gordon Walker's socialist tactics rested on his belief that people travel boldly and furthest when they know their general direction but not their destination. Socialism might be achieved in England by people who were glad to work together on similar courses; but the movement would split asunder if it was too tightly bound to unanimity in policy or ultimate ends. He saw the Labour party as a broad coalition. The consent of the electorate to a programme of progressive change must be won by persuasion: attempts at compulsion would provoke angry reaction. Labour's purpose was to end economic exploitation rather than to impose collective ownership. 'It may well be that a good deal of private endeavour and enterprise will be left. If it is found to carry out the main ends as well as or better than state control, it must be left. There can be no question of damning the private exploitation of labour as such: but only if it defeats socialist ends.'[24]

The English meaning of equality was concerned with legal rights and not personal wealth. Magna Carta in 1215, the Petition of Right in 1628 and the various emancipation acts after 1829 provided equality under the law, free speech, free conscience, free association. Equality in England, like *égalité* in France, did not connote equal standards of living or equal pay. Equal rewards and living conditions were the lot of prisoners and conscripts, but not of free men and women. Even in prison, bribes, favours and extortion stopped any true levelling standard. 'There must be no running after a vague equality,' Gordon Walker declared. In his ideal state, as in the medieval Church, men would be 'chosen and promoted for their subservience to the main end'. Their remuneration would reflect the value of their work, but such wealth as they accumulated would be only a life tenure and non-inheritable. Citizens would be kept from poverty and assured of reasonable leisure, but (wrote Gordon Walker) 'there can be no question of all men being in fact equal in wealth or office.'[25]

Cole's pupils acknowledged the difficulties that were posed to socialist societies by the human need of financial incentives and money differentials. 'One has to admit', wrote Douglas Jay, 'that in a socialist society – which is not a Utopia but a collection of normally self-seeking human beings – the prestige of money incomes will be with the mass of men great. Let us therefore exploit their semi-sublimated worship of Mammon by ceremoniously paying high salaries with one hand and discreetly taking them away with another.' The second hand, of course, was that of high taxation.[26]

By 1934, when Gordon Walker became Secretary of the Oxford University constituency Labour organization, his political engagement was permeating his teaching. In Michaelmas term of that year he invited Christ Church undergraduates reading modern history to a talk in his room on the Marxist philosophy of history. One of

them was Hugh Trevor-Roper, who recalled the event in his valedictory lecture as Regius professor in 1980.

> He explained that, theoretically, it should be possible to discover
> the objective laws of historical change, and that the way to test
> such laws, once discovered, was to see whether they enabled one
> to predict the next stage in the historical process. The Marxist
> interpretation, he assured us, had survived this test; it had
> predicted the course of events since Marx's own time with remark-
> able accuracy; and therefore it could now be regarded as
> scientifically valid.[27]

In 1934 Gordon Walker married Audrey Rudolf, whose family had
owned plantations in Jamaica for several generations. Thereafter,
although he saw tutorial pupils in his rooms in Canterbury Quad,
he preferred an uxorial existence with his wife in their house in
Museum Road (between Rhodes House and Keble). Some Students,
including Harrod, regretted his fleeting attendance at high-table
dinners and common-room colloquies. He took pleasure in domes-
ticity, and was funny, loving and supportive to his wife and five
children. His son Alan has only the happiest memories of him: he
loved to read humorous novels to his children, those of P. G.
Wodehouse, Jerome's *Three Men in a Boat* and *The Diary of a Nobody*
by the Grossmith brothers.

In 1935 Gordon Walker's first book, *The Sixteenth and Seventeenth
Centuries, 1494–1714*, was published in the Gollancz series entitled
'An Outline of European History' under the general editorship of
Hampden Jackson. The series, with its *Marxisant* slant, repudiated
the opinions and emphases of the old Oxford gang of Marriott,
Oman, Grant Robertson and their like. 'The stress is no longer on
military and diplomatic manoeuvres', Jackson declared, 'but on
economic conditions and on ideals and institutions created to express
them.' It was the implicit philosophy of Jackson's series that a sound
knowledge of historical facts was not an end in itself, but a grounding
in the more important aim of acquiring a historically informed
mental attitude. The 'Outline' method of historical teaching, with
its mild indoctrination, would produce a socially aware citizenry,
which put the common good before selfish personal interests.

Hampden Jackson quoted with approval a saying of Lord Acton: 'Liberty is a self-determined, self-chosen perseverance in the way we deliberately think the best.' He and Gordon Walker were committed to helping their pupils and readers to persevere in trying to think in the best ways. Although Gordon Walker's volume gave more prominence to economics than was then customary in textbooks, its pages are not overweighed with statistical data. The overall tone is reliable and accessible: one reviewer called Gordon Walker's prose 'homely but scholarly'. The homeliness is that of a puritan home: there are no ornaments or fripperies.[28]

At the age of twenty-eight, Gordon Walker stood as Labour parliamentary candidate for the City of Oxford at the general election of 1935. Labour had not bothered to contest the seat at the previous election in 1931: it remained a forlorn chance for a Labour candidate. Gordon Walker's speeches called for the socialization of the major extractive and manufacturing industries and of transport and other services, so that production and profits could be controlled by the working classes. He wanted redistribution of wealth and less disparity in incomes. He advocated arms limitation and the abolition of aerial bombing rather than expansion of the armed forces and rearmament. He maintained, too, that capitalism fomented international tension: the striving for private profit led to aggressive rivalry for foreign markets among capital-intensive industries.

Two antithetical groups within the Oxford constituency Labour party began to grumble at Gordon Walker after the general election of 1935. Communist sympathizers mistrusted him because he had been refused a Soviet Union visitor's visa. Stalin's officials apprehended that he would emulate Walter Citrine, the head of the Trades Union Congress, who had visited the Soviet Union in 1935 and then published a pedestrian but unflattering diary of his tour entitled *I Search for Truth in Russia*. Fellow-travellers in the Oxford party begrudged a candidate who seemed to be anti-Stalinist. At the opposite pole, party members who had voted Liberal in the 1920s were alarmed by his support for the Unity campaign of 1936–7. This had been launched by Sir Stafford Cripps, with the backing of such members of the Labour intelligentsia as Cole, Laski and John Strachey. Unity was a coalition drawn from the Labour party,

Socialist League, Independent Labour Party (ILP) and CPGB: while ostensibly anti-fascist, its driving force was anti-capitalism; some of its organizers intended that it serve the ends of Stalinism.

Christ Church was as important in Oxford elections of the 1930s as it had been in the eighteenth century. At the by-election for one of the two university seats in 1937, the official Conservative candidate Sir Farquhar Buzzard, the Regius Professor of Medicine, who was a congenial member of the Christ Church common room, faced an Independent Conservative candidate who was a less popular member of the same community, Lindemann. There was public support for Buzzard from the historians of Christ Church: Feiling and Masterman rallied to him; Dundas too. While Buzzard supported the Chamberlain government, Lindemann was the rebel Churchill candidate advocating heavy and immediate rearmament. Finally, Sir Arthur Salter, Gladstone Professor of Political Theory and Fellow of All Souls, announced his candidature.

G. M. Young listed Salter's *Security: Can We Retrieve It?*, together with Strachey's *The Theory and Practice of Socialism* and Laski's *Parliamentary Government in England*, as three books of the 1930s which gave the clearest insight into that sombre period. Salter was a technocrat who believed that the world had been transformed by international telegraphy, telephone cables and aviation. He envisaged a sovereign world government, which would limit the right of member states to erect tariffs, to raise armed forces and to amass weapons. Salter added that tax uniformity and standardized global regulations governing foreign travel and residence would be advantageous. His proposed world government would be organized on a federal basis, with national governments reduced to the status of the separate federated states of Germany and the United States if not to that of English county councils. The endorsements of Salter from the Labour and Liberal thinkers Cole and Murray prompted Churchill to call him the 'Popular Front' candidate. In the event, Salter won the election by a majority of nearly 4,000 votes.[29]

In May 1938 the Oxford Union resolved that its members wished the ruling National Government to be replaced by a Popular Front government. Three months later the Conservative MP for the City of Oxford dropped dead in a graveyard. His constituency association hastened to adopt a young Fellow of All Souls and former scholar of Christ Church, Quintin Hogg, as their candidate for the by-election. Following his defeat in the general election of 1935, Gordon Walker had been readopted as Labour candidate by the Oxford City constituency party. After the Nazi remilitarization of the Rhineland in 1936, he had become an advocate of rearmament, who wanted Chamberlain's government to protect the integrity of Czechoslovakia's borders and to help the survival of the Spanish republic. He had a further hope that a future Labour government would join with the Roosevelt administration in America to herd aggressor nations into what he called a quarantine of embargoes and sanctions.

Then came the September crisis over Nazi designs on Czechoslovakia. The country went on to a war footing: 85,000 gas masks were distributed in Oxford. On 15 September Chamberlain flew to Munich to assuage Hitler and returned with an agreement that Gordon Walker called 'a sell-out of Czechoslovakia'. Three weeks later, on 8 October, Crossman appeared in Gordon Walker's rooms at Christ Church to announce the intention of running Lindsay, the Master of Balliol, as a Popular Front candidate and urging Gordon Walker to withdraw his candidature. This was the first that Gordon Walker knew of manoeuvres which had begun a fortnight earlier and which, as he learnt by telephoning Gilbert Murray's wife, were an open secret in Oxford.[30]

Crossman was drawn by 'the vision of a new order', applauded the 'will to power' and deplored 'the humane, gentlemanly powerlessness' of constitutional European states. Isaiah Berlin, who was briefly his underling at New College, found him cynical, contemptuous, authoritarian and indeed a 'left-wing Nazi'. Another New College colleague, the legal philosopher H. L. A. Hart, hated him. Once, when Crossman jeered, 'Still worrying about the truth, I suppose', Hart retorted, 'I'm sure *you're* not.' Other dons found Crossman over-assertive, egotistical and devious. The *Oxford Magazine*, under Max Beloff's editorship, called him 'Double-Crossman' and 'Slick-dick'. Crossman had continued to live in Headington and to lead the Labour group on Oxford City Council after he had been deprived of his fellowship in 1937 following an affair with a colleague's wife. He disliked the thought of any of his circle getting ahead of him into parliament. At a Pink Lunch, from which Gordon Walker was absent, he recalled Salter's success as a Popular Front candidate a year earlier and convinced most of his listeners of the need to find a non-partisan candidate to stand against Hogg.[31]

Two of Gordon Walker's colleagues in the House, Pakenham and Harrod, supported Crossman's moves. Pakenham, who was a Labour councillor under Crossman's leadership, claimed fifteen years later that he had been duped by communist sleepers within the constituency Labour party and that he regretted urging Gordon Walker to withdraw. But the CPGB was not responsible for him behaving like an excitable busybody, rushing between tête-à-têtes, giving assurances that he quickly forgot, refusing on one occasion to share a platform with Gordon Walker and supplanting him by a ruse. After Walker had acceded with reluctance to a request from his constituency party to resign his candidature, Pakenham cajoled Lindsay into announcing that he would not stand for re-election at the next general election, which was due within eighteen months. This declaration harmed his candidature: some voters disliked a here-today, gone-tomorrow MP who was pledged to be finished with constituency work by 1940. Pakenham was soon adopted in Gordon Walker's place as the Labour candidate. He hoped to retain some of Lindsay's supporters, and thus to win the seat in 1940. In these circumstances, it was bogus and self-deluding for one of Lindsay's supporters to claim the Popular Front campaign as 'the creative, the generous, the imaginative side' and to attribute blanket 'selfishness, stodginess, and insincerity' to Hogg voters.[32]

Lindsay had made Balliol into a 'puritan, high-minded, Little-Cambridge-in-Oxford, where serious undergraduates cultivated the moral basis and studied the niceties of personal relations' – the description is Trevor-Roper's. Although Philip Toynbee claimed that the governing principle of Balliol intellectuals in the 1930s was 'an almost harsh demand for emotional integrity', the probity in Lindsay's campaign swiftly frayed. Among younger dons, Isaiah Berlin condemned the intrigues of Crossman and Pakenham, while the staunch organizer of Labour in Oxford, Geoffrey Hudson, the All Souls expert on Sino-Japanese affairs, thought Lindsay's candidacy 'deplorably mismanaged' throughout. E. R. Dodds, a Christ Church attendee at the Pink Lunches, found Lindsay 'ponderous' on the hustings and Hogg 'nimble'. While Hogg took bold leaps from high ground, Lindsay was apt to pick as a jumping-off place some low tump of well-worn platitude.[33]

The rejection by the Trades Union Congress, and by Ernest Bevin of the Transport & General Workers Union, of the Popular Front scheme was decisive for Gordon Walker. Everything that he had seen in Germany in the early 1930s had convinced him that socialist ideas were futile unless they had persuaded the working classes and were channelled through organized labour. It infuriated him that, although Lindsay fought the election on the issue of Chamberlain's foreign policy, there was no mention of the Spanish civil war. He thought, as did many young Christ Church men including Trevor-Roper, that Spain's legitimate republican government should be defended from Franco's fascist rebels and deplored Chamberlain's policy of non-intervention. A Popular Front, which included English supremacists such as Winston Churchill and Lord Lloyd, must contain men who favoured the Falangists and others who did not mind them much.

In Gordon Walker's analysis, the Czechoslovakia crisis had induced hysteria among Oxford's bourgeoisie (whether ex-Liberals, Left Book Club socialists or members of the CPGB). 'We must *do* something!' they cried, but they had only a hazy programme. They convinced themselves that dislodging Chamberlain from Downing Street was an all-important and constructive policy. 'Any talk of the importance of holding the Labour Movement together, of building up its strength, of looking not only to Oxford but to the whole series of by-elections & to the General Election – all these were swept away by the agreement that nothing else mattered but the next 6 months, & some defeat of Chamberlain, however achieved.' None of the social reforms in Labour's programme were brought before the electorate either.[34]

The Oxford bourgeoisie's errors were set by Gordon Walker in a continuum with those of Germany and France. The German middle-class revolution of 1848 failed because its leaders were impractical, overly theoretical, perhaps even too softened by ideals. Germany did not become a unified federal state until 1870: accordingly, throughout the nineteenth century, its 'native middle-class' had been more politically fissiparous, more 'deficient' and 'backward' than its

English or Scottish counterparts. 'The middle-class never attempted to take over its nation as our middle-class did – never tried to assume the responsibility of leadership for its entire nation.' Accordingly, much of the responsibility in commerce, education, the arts, sciences and the law was delegated to Jewish people. 'Civic courage . . . was never rated as high in Germany as in England.' Germany had a distinctive political phenomenon in the Junker class. These were militant frontiersmen of a type that had disappeared in the British Isles after the merger of the kingdoms of England and Scotland in 1603. But the eastern borders of Prussia were mobile: sometimes Hohenzollern armies pushed outward to the east; sometimes they resisted ingressions from the east. The result was that after 1870 socially regressive militarist forces were overdeveloped in Germany.[35]

The English gentry were the saviours of their nation in Gordon Walker's historical analysis. He used the word 'gentry' to denote the leading classes in towns and the countryside and attributed their force for good to their adherence to that English species of Protestant Christianity called 'puritanism'. The English gentry, unlike the continental bourgeoisie, 'did not achieve power in a sudden and complete sweep', argued Gordon Walker. 'It acquired, therefore, no taste for violent, dramatic or doctrinaire solutions.' Its journey to political power, under a constitutional monarchy, depended on its gradualist temper, its tenacity and its talent for negotiation. The English gentry was, he said, 'the politically wisest and most practical of any corresponding class in Europe'. English literature, so he further claimed, 'was the literature of an assured people without hidden political inferiorities, the literature of the politically most experienced and practical people in Europe'. Neither the Germans nor the French could vie with it.[36]

As a proficient German-speaker, Gordon Walker was recruited to the BBC's wartime European Service after the outbreak of war. He never returned to teach at Christ Church, where Talboys shouldered his duties. By 1942 he was in charge of daily broadcasting to Germany. His programmes reiterated the unity of English workers, their free trade unions, the affiliation of those unions to the Labour party and their devotion to victory in the war. Tangye Lean, author of the undergraduate manifesto *Storm in Oxford* (1932), showed the efficacy of Gordon Walker's programmes in his wartime study *Voices in the Darkness*. He quoted a weaver with a heavy Yorkshire accent addressing his fellow workers in Germany on a Gordon Walker programme in 1941:

> We work in cotton mills where the noise of machinery is so deafening that we cannot hear each other speak unless we shout into each other's ears, and so we have learnt to talk across the looms by reading each other's lips. In the dusty light amid the forest of belting, we wave our shuttles to and fro to each other to attract attention, and then we discuss the news. I have learnt your language painstakingly, writing my translations in the china-clay dust on my loom-frames, and so I am able to listen in to your German broadcasts. You are being *misled* as far as we British working people are concerned. We are solid and united behind Churchill . . . He expresses our will.[37]

In September 1944 the BBC seconded Gordon Walker to help in the resumption of free broadcasting by newly liberated Radio Luxembourg. It was during this secondment, in mid-April 1945, that he was driven across Germany, seeing released slave workers and Gestapo prisoners on the roads, to witness the atrocities of Belsen concentration camp. His chief contact there was a military intelligence officer and BBC programme maker called Derrick Sington, who had been his contemporary at Wellington. In December 1945 Gollancz published Gordon Walker's shocking diary of his time in Belsen under the title *The Lid Lifts*. Subsequently Sington, who spent a total of five months in the camp, published his longer record, *Belsen Uncovered*. He married one of the captives.[38]

Concentration camps had arisen in the heart of Europe, Gordon Walker wrote in *The Lid Lifts*, as the result of the twentieth-century trend to dehumanization. They expressed the root 'evil' of the century of total war: 'Never have human beings been brought so low.' The camps constituted a 'deliberate, coldly calculated and coolly executed assault' on European civilization. But rather than clamour for vengeance the English must acknowledge their share in 'the long descent into degradation from the Boer War camps, through the Spanish civil war, through the occupation of the Rhineland, through Munich, through the phoney war'. The glee that followed Mussolini's execution by partisans on 28 April alarmed him. To people who said that the Duce's death had avoided messy complications, he countered that the argument of convenience was the first step towards accepting 'mob-murder' as a political resource. He expected the trend towards dehumanization would resume with invigorated power. 'As new nations, and new social systems come into being, all uncertain of themselves and of their inner strength . . . we may find in the world a spread of one-party dictatorships.' As tyrannies are cruel persecutors of minorities, 'that means the constant danger of concentration camps.'[39]

During the election campaign of 1945, Gordon Walker remained the apolitical Assistant German Service Director at the BBC. He was not among the ruck of Labour parliamentary candidates whom Iris Murdoch found 'ignorant, opinionated, careerist, insensitive'. But a day after the election results were announced, Alderman Alfred Dobbs, who had been Labour MP for Smethwick for less than twenty-four hours, was killed in a motoring accident on the Great North Road at Doncaster. After a by-election, Gordon Walker reached the House of Commons as Dobbs's successor. He felt confident ('I think we've got twenty years of power ahead of us'), but 'more appalled by the consequences of failure than fired by the prospects of success'. The worst that could happen if Labour succeeded in government was that it would be criticized for not achieving more. 'If we fail, democracy fails in Britain. And that means in the world.'[40]

The new MP stood well with the Labour party leaders. Attlee found him diligent and industrious. Cripps remembered his support of the pre-war Unity campaign. Herbert Morrison thought that he had acted impeccably at the time of the Oxford by-election. He had in turn praised Morrison, the former leader of London County Council, as personifying 'Labour's record of splendid efficiency in local government. In London – a city with greater population, wealth, and far more complex problems than those of many sovereign states – Labour has set the standard for the world in efficient, progressive and incorruptible government.' In October 1946, after only a year in the Commons, Gordon Walker was appointed by Morrison as his Parliamentary Private Secretary.[41]

A year later he was promoted to be Under Secretary of State at the Commonwealth Relations Office. His tenacity in arduous desk work resulted in his further promotion to Cabinet rank, as Secretary of State for Commonwealth Relations, in 1950. A newspaper profile at this time described him as 'a man who puts the strength of his party before the brilliance of its ideas, a devotee of the sensible compromise, a student of practical ways and means'. It spoke, too, of his 'decent-mindedness and common sense'. These were the reasons that Attlee considered appointing him as Bevin's successor as Foreign Secretary in 1951. Gaitskell discouraged the idea, partly to protect his own pre-eminence among the younger members of the Cabinet; perhaps partly because he agreed with the *Observer* that Gordon Walker 'is not at [his] best when faced with a dire choice'.[42]

Gordon Walker finished his most ambitious book, which he gave the plain title of *Restatement of Liberty*, in the summer of 1950. It had been planned and prepared when he was a Student of Christ Church, and attempted to provide a historical theory of liberty for use by the British Labour movement in a century of encroaching industrialized totalitarianism. 'Millions in possession of freedom have freely, before our eyes, consented to be made unfree.' Germans, Italians and Spaniards, among other European peoples, had 'revolted against the appalling responsibilities of freedom [and] sought refuge in a dictator who would lift the burden from them'. Some of those who abhorred freedom, and millions of others who had never known it, set up 'the Total State as an ideal infinitely preferable to freedom, worthier of strong and purposeful men, more capable of achieving men's highest aims'.[43]

Crucial sections of *Restatement of Liberty* derive from Gilbert Ryle, who had been Gordon Walker's Christ Church colleague throughout the 1930s and had become 'the reigning professor' among Oxford philosophers with the publication of *The Concept of Mind* in 1949. Gordon Walker's *Restatement* follows Ryle's *Concept* in treating dualism – Descartes' notion that the body and mind are separate substances – as faulty. People who give primacy to human reason, those who uphold the prospects of human perfectibility or cleave to the 'comforting illusion of progress', those who believe that parliamentary constitutionalism and technology are inherently progressive, are falsifiers (according to Gordon

Walker) because they fail to acknowledge the force of evil. He was in accord with the recent warning in Herbert Butterfield's *Christianity and History*: 'the hardest strokes of heaven fall in history upon those who imagine that they can control things in a sovereign manner, as though they were kings of the earth, playing Providence not only for themselves but for the far future . . . and gambling on a lot of risky calculations'.[44]

Arthur Hassall, who taught his last pupil in 1924, is the only one of the modern historians of twentieth-century Christ Church treated in this book to have held to the tenets of the Church of England. His successors had no Christian faith, or placed such corollaries on their beliefs as to secularize their meaning. Yet Christian ideas are ineradicable in European historiography. The proper study of historians is Original Sin. Arnold Toynbee became convinced of the reality of Original Sin by his knowledge of the Turkish genocide of Armenians in 1915. 'Human nature has in it an inherent vein of abominable wickedness; but then it also has in it an inherent vein of lovable goodness,' wrote Toynbee. 'Every human soul is a battlefield on which these two irreconcilable spiritual forces are perpetually contending for mastery.' Everyone with a conscience must try to probe the moral inconsistency of humankind, said Toynbee. 'This is not just to satisfy an intellectual curiosity, but in order to grapple with Original Sin with intent to subdue it. One must probe human nature in oneself; one must probe it in one's neighbours.' Evan Durbin, Gordon Walker's Oxford contemporary, had argued in *Personal Aggressiveness and War* (1939) that neither capital-intensive industrialism nor nationalism provided the root cause of war: the innate violence of human nature was to blame; individuals harboured a secret, unconscious aggression to which they often gave group expression; hatred and animosity, or what Christians had once termed devilry, can be stirred in the populace by impulses of which they are unaware.[45]

Gordon Walker's thinking, after his experience of Belsen, resembled Toynbee's. In a section of *Liberty* headed 'Terms with the Devil', he presented the root fallacy of the Cartesian view of humanity as its failure to give a proper account of evil. The age of totalitarian states, of total wars and of death camps had convinced him that 'no political philosophy can safely enshrine liberty and stability and progress that does not come to terms with the devil, [and] that does not recognize sin as a constituent part of man's nature'. The capacity for wickedness is the abomination that distinguishes humans from all else in nature. 'Sin is unique to man: for sin entails not merely the doing of harmful acts, but the awareness that the acts are harmful. Sin is the awareness of evil [and] therefore an essential attribute of man – distinguishing him from the animals and uniting him with all his fellow humans.' Gordon Walker did not use the phrase 'Original Sin' in the doctrinal sense of Adam and Eve, originally perfect, falling from grace and discovering shame. Instead, he attached a societal meaning to the phrase. 'The recognition of evil as a part of human nature . . . guards against the enormities inseparable from setting up heaven on earth,' as totalitarian regimes promised to do.[46]

Society could be improved, Gordon Walker insisted, only once its leaders had acknowledged the violence and beastliness of the world and stopped their cowardly skulking in a bogus peace of mind. Bertrand Russell and his kindred forsook morality and all standards of justice when they flinched 'from the arduous and unpleasant task of pursuing good by opposing evil in an imperfect and defective world'. These were strong epithets to launch at Russell, who had only a year earlier become a Nobel laureate. Similarly, Gordon Walker thought it was cant for academics to promote intricate systems of state planning while advocating notions of absolute individual liberty. He found it senseless for Harold Laski to argue in *Liberty in the Modern State* (1930) and Barbara Wootton in *Freedom under Planning* (1945) that the concept of 'liberty' is valueless unless it means the unimpeded ability to do what one likes.[47]

Liberty bears the strong imprint, in every section, of Julien Benda's *La Trahison des clercs* (Paris, 1927, and best known in English translation under the title *The Treason of the Intellectuals*). The German sociologist Norbert Elias was another influence on *Liberty*. Raymond Carr, Gordon Walker's pupil at Christ Church, recalled his enthusiasm for Elias's two volumes on the process of civilization (the volumes were published in German in 1937–9, but remained little known to Anglophone readers until their translation into English in 1969). Gordon Walker had respect, even reverence, for the frame of mind of Jewish intellectuals from twentieth-century *Mitteleuropa*: Benda and Elias pre-eminently, but also Franz Borkenau, Isaac Deutscher, Karl Mannheim and Karl Polanyi.[48]

Restatement of Liberty is the testament of Christ Church's first socialist tutor in modern history. Tawney and Toynbee are praised. Lenin, Marx and Engels as well as Bacon, Hobbes and Locke are cited. Lord Hewart's *New Despotism* and Collingwood's *New Leviathan* help Gordon Walker's arguments. Ideas are tapped from Darwin's *On the Origin of the Species*, Dicey's *Introduction to the Study of the Law of the Constitution*, Eliot's *Murder in the Cathedral*, Mead's *Coming of Age in Samoa*, Mumford's *Technics and Civilization*, Ortega's *The Revolt of the Masses*, Sorel's *Reflections on Violence*, Spengler's *The Decline of the West* and Weber's *The Protestant Ethic and the Spirit of Capitalism*. Sadly, Gordon Walker's book is too much of a stodge of ideas to be digestible. The reviews were neither plentiful nor appreciative: its reception must have disappointed him.

Cole's janissaries of the late 1920s brought a new mentality to the Commons front bench after Gaitskell replaced Attlee as Labour leader in 1955. Gordon Walker joined Jay and Pakenham as the best trusted by Gaitskell of the parliamentary intelligentsia. He became, indeed, a champion Gaitskellite, who later wrote a meticulous account of his old colleague in the *Dictionary of National Biography*. Although Anthony Eden, Prime Minister in 1955–7, had won first-class honours while at Christ Church, he was not an intellectual and felt baffled when political decisions were taken on the basis of abstract principles rather than changing circumstances. Gordon Walker's cast of mind and approach to problems were inimical to Conservative frontbenchers: thus Harold Macmillan, a literary intellectual who never joined the intelligentsia, found him insincere, charmless, arrogant and lacking in compassion, 'with a certain sour superiority which socialist dons affect', treating 'voters as merely instruments of his ambition'. This was unfair. Journalists were more accurate in likening Gordon Walker to a trusted family solicitor, to a kindly uncle and to Stanley Baldwin.[49]

After Gaitskell's death in 1963, Harold Wilson and George Brown contended for the party leadership. A government led by Brown would be 'solid, sometimes truculent, very English, though not always in the best way, strongly influenced by the trade unions', William Rees-Mogg noted at the time. 'It would be hearts-of-oak loyal on defence, on the Atlantic alliance and on Europe . . . It would not be a middle-class government or an intellectual's government. But it might, for better or worse, be something closer to government by the people than Britain has ever known before.' That was the sort of Labour party that Gordon Walker wanted: accordingly, he acted as Brown's campaign manager, but was not wily enough to best Wilson's team.[50]

At the general election of 1964, Gordon Walker was defeated at Smethwick by a Conservative candidate whose supporters chanted in the streets, 'If you want a nigger neighbour, vote Labour.' He was nevertheless installed as Foreign Secretary by Wilson, and a by-election in the safe Labour seat of Leyton was arranged with him as candidate. White supremacists distributed neo-Nazi propaganda in the Leyton constituency, dressed as monkeys and gave Hitler salutes. He was muddled with Aloysius 'Lucky' Gordon, the Jamaican-born jazz singer who had raped Christine Keeler a few years earlier. Churchill was known to be dying on polling day in January 1965, and some of the sillier electors voted in a spirit of Dunkirk nostalgia. Gordon Walker was defeated, left the Cabinet and was treated for a time by the Labour leadership as if he had 'a hoodoo'. Crossman, watching the announcement of the Leyton result on television, for once saw his old rival without bias: 'acting with melancholy dignity, and also revealing his deep inner defeatism.'[51]

Leyton returned Gordon Walker to the Commons a year later, in the general election of 1966. He served briefly as Secretary of State for Education, but Wilson asked him to retire from the Cabinet in 1968, and gave him the small solace of being appointed a Companion of Honour. He did not seek re-election in the general election of February 1974, and later was granted a life peerage. He was in a taxi, on his way to attend the House of Lords, when he died suddenly in 1980.

As an historian Gordon Walker did no more primary research for his books than Hassall, which is to say none; but his secondary reading was extensive. He engaged himself as a scholar to resist the Nazis, and never detached his work from the times in which he lived or from his responsibilities to the society of which he was part.

Christ Church, as seen from the chaplains' court, in 1802.

Christ Church kitchens in Georgian times.

The West front of Christ Church, on St Aldates, in the 1830s.

Henry Halford Vaughan saw his subject as a study of evolutionary change. His inaugural lecture as Regius Professor (1849) contrasted the brevity of human history with the aeons of natural history.

William Stubbs, in his inaugural lecture as Regius Professor (1867), reverted to the doctrine that history shows God's overruling providence in the world's workings.

Frederick York Powell's inaugural lecture as Regius Professor (1894) was a mess. He remained a Christ Church original: gregarious, lovable, persuasive and provoking.

Arthur Hassall dedicated his working life to the 'private hours' with his tutorial pupils and to readying them for examination success.

A Christ Church undergraduate, William Robinow (1883–1958), on the river with friends. He became a barrister, and served as a tank officer in the First World War.

An Edwardian idyll: Robinow's friends picnicking.

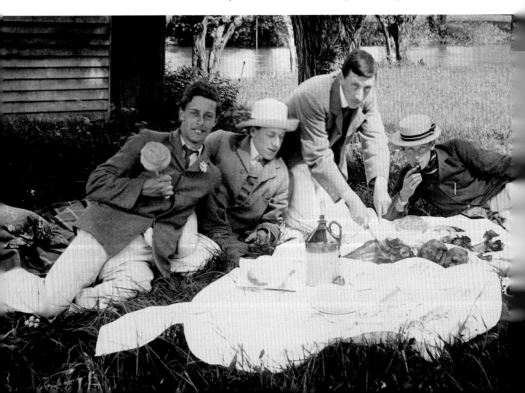

An undergraduate room in Tom Quad in 1906. It was occupied by Geoffrey Radcliffe, afterwards a barrister at Lincoln's Inn, and Fellow and Bursar of New College.

An Edwardian undergraduate's cheaper attic room.

Thomas Banks Strong, of whom an admirer said 'emotional utterances appeared to him utterly indecent, a form of nudism for which he had a deep detestation'.

The undergraduate reading-room at Christ Church around the time that Feiling and Masterman came to the college.

Keith Feiling, historian of Toryism and organizer of Oxford conservatism.

J. C. Masterman, historian, prisoner-of-war, counter-espionage officer, grey eminence.

Roy Harrod, the staunchest of Christ Church men, became Oxford's leading economist despite hankering to be a philosopher.

Patrick Gordon Walker relinquished his studentship of Christ Church following his election to parliament in 1945.

Hugh Trevor-Roper after returning from Germany to become a student of Christ Church, 1946.

Robert Blake, the tutelary genius of post-war Oxford conservatism, near the end of his twenty years as Provost of the Queen's College, Oxford.

His ideas were original, conscientious, far-reaching and committed. He strove, sometimes awkwardly, to make sense of good and evil in his own age and in the remote past. How did Belsen arise, he asked; that neat, scrupulous, methodical work of man, that extermination centre with huts aligned like entries in a ledger? As the Oxford poet Jonathan Price wrote in 'The Camp',

> All human nature
> Shares the account of what went on in there.[52]

CHAPTER 11

Hugh Trevor-Roper: Drawn to Convulsions

'Modern history', Hugh Trevor-Roper told readers of the *Sunday Times* in 1952, 'is replacing the ancient classics as the intellectual training of our century.' Partly this was because *Literae Humaniores* was in decline. Some tutors teaching Classical Moderations (Mods) bored their pupils, he felt, by treating ancient literature with a trivializing crossword-puzzle mentality. Others handled texts with austere and sterile pedantry. Worse still, when pupils came to study ancient classical philosophy and history in the second part of their course, Greats, they encountered philosophers who insisted that their subject had no concern with improving character or teaching statecraft. Given the decline of *Literae Humaniores*, Trevor-Roper believed that the historical frame of mind provided the most apt training for twentieth-century conditions. The spirit of keen criticism animates historical practice and gives it value. Critical vitality was essential in an epoch of nihilistic anger, procrustean intellectual categorization and murderous totalitarianism.[1]

History was not, for Trevor-Roper, a matter of transcribing, accumulating and translating documents: written evidence was lifeless and personal testimony remained suspect until they had been subjected to judicious scrutiny and criticism. The eleven volumes of *British Documents on the Origins of the War, 1898–1914*, compiled by the 'learned and conscientious' G. P. Gooch, ever 'indefatigable with his scissors and paste', were 'not very illuminating on causes', Trevor-Roper wrote in a review of A. J. P. Taylor's *The Course of German History* (1945). Taylor had written a *pièce d'occasion*, in a spirit of 'lively antipathy', which was 'being widely read by people who are interested not in the past, which it analyses, but the present, which it may explain. Taylor's approach represents historical writing at its strongest, Trevor-Roper said.[2]

This chapter is confined to the years when Trevor-Roper received his training as a modern historian in the House and then formulated his historical philosophy. His experiences in wartime and in the second half of his life are left aside. He entered Christ Church with a classical scholarship in 1932, and spent two years there reading Classical Moderations before transferring to the School of Modern History. In 1936, after the award to him of first-class honours, he secured a two-year university senior studentship, which entitled him to use the Christ Church senior common room. Before the expiry of that studentship he was elected to a research fellowship at Merton. There he worked on a biography of William Laud, the primate who had been beheaded by the order of parliament in 1645. War work kept him from his scholarly avocations until 1946, when he returned to Christ Church as a Student. Thereafter he was a vital force in collegiate life until his Crown appointment as Regius Professor of Modern History in 1957. The Regius chair was attached to Oriel, and his studentship therefore lapsed. Christ Church remained, though, the Oxford institution for which he cared most.

Previous studies have attested to the influence on Trevor-Roper of his elderly American mentors Logan Pearsall Smith, who was a man of letters, and Smith's brother-in-law Bernard Berenson, who was an art appraiser. Both men entertained him in their homes, recommended books and practised at high altitude what Auden called, in *Journey to a War*, the conversation of the highly trained. Neither Smith nor Berenson was an academic. This chapter stresses the formative inspiration that Trevor-Roper took from senior men working as university professors, notably Namier in Manchester and Pieter Geyl in Utrecht. Their ideas, procedures and example spurred him to master the historical essay as an art form, and to become, in Sir John Elliott's judgement, 'the greatest historical essayist' of twentieth-century England.[3]

Born in 1914 in Northumberland, Trevor-Roper was son of a physician with a general practice in Alnwick. He never heard his parents speak any words of affection to one another or to their three children. They regarded a show of emotion as unbecoming, abnormal and ridiculous. As a result, he grew a social carapace which served to conceal and protect his feelings. He never could show affection or excitement either spontaneously or publicly. In company, his manner was sceptical, deflationary and dismissive. Even when he drank deep with trusted friends, he remained opaque, impersonal, reticent. It was hard for him to believe that people liked him. If they made a show of friendliness he suspected that they were being polite at best, and at worst insincere. Praise from people whom he did not know and trust put him on guard or made him morose. The world was a hostile place, which must be kept under close scrutiny, and full of people – some friendly, but the majority of them careless, indifferent or adversarial – against whom pre-emptive moves were required. Despondency overcame him easily. To the extent that his recurrent dejection was a form of self-disgust he cured it by expressing disgust in others.[4]

During his first six terms at the House, Trevor-Roper was awarded three scholarships in classics, and first-class honours in Mods. He never read Greats, because during his second year as an undergraduate he determined to transfer to the School of Modern History. This meant that although he studied the creative writers of the ancient world in Mods, he never reached classical historians, such as Thucydides or Herodotus, in Greats. The trigger for his decision to change school was, he said, reading a tedious epic poem by Nonnus; but more than that he had become irked by the reverence accorded to the classical scholars Wilamowitz and Housman. He had learnt German in order to read Wilamowitz in his native language, but then, with undergraduate insolence, dismissed Germany's greatest humanist scholar as 'a fraud'. 'He symbolized to me the barrenness of a purely literary and philological approach to the classics, and indeed to literature in general, and the absurd pretentiousness of assuming that so narrow an approach can have any wider meaning.' Housman, too, seemed arid, sour, grim, infertile and nitpicking in his scholarship.[5]

Yet the primary influence on Trevor-Roper of the ancient Greeks was ineradicable. 'If history is ultimately the history of the human mind and not of mere human organization, then we can never escape from the Greek experience,' he wrote in 1957. The clarity of the Greek language, and the consequent clarity of Greek thought, was responsible for the intellectual advances of classical Greece. These sentiments come from his review of Maurice Bowra's *The Greek Experience*, which stressed that ancient Greek literature – even the most exalted – was meant to be heard rather than read. 'Every sentence had to be forceful, carry its full load of meaning, and leave no doubt of its purpose,' wrote Bowra. Ancient Greek was the medium of 'an energetic, enterprising intelligence, which is impelled by the expansion of experience and the birth of ideas to find words for them; which likes fine distinctions and insists upon making them; which appreciates the nuance of the spoken word and employs effective means to get it right; which forces its way beyond habitual concepts to others more rarefied and more abstract and does not in the process lose its nerve or loosen its grip'. Trevor-Roper's sentences were vigorous, carried a weight of meaning and drew fine distinctions. His prose was meant to be heard as much as read. Many of his most striking essays evolved from lectures. He studded his writings, as Rory Allan noted, with exclamations, questions asked aloud of his audience and other rhetorical devices. 'In his writing,' Allan showed, 'he *speaks* to us, in prose that profits from being read aloud, so that what we read on the page echoes in our ears as a chorus of written and oral harmony.'[6]

Long after Trevor-Roper ducked away from reading Greats, classical literature enriched his imaginative intelligence. During the early 1940s he reread all of Homer, Pindar, Lucretius and Horace. Virgil was his constant resource. He relished, too, the vengeful Greek elegist Theognis, with 'his bitter, introverted pride', 'his hatred of humanity and disgust with life'. During a low point in his career and marriage, in 1962–3, he determined to reread the Greek tragedians, beginning with Sophocles, even if it meant neglecting the latest issues of historical journals. As to Latin, 'the majestic Cicero, the virtuous Livy, the sententious Seneca, the judicious Quintilian, the elegant Pliny', he had read them all, so he wrote in 1944, but did not expect to do so again. 'Latin prose literature consists of two works only: the Metamorphoses of Apuleius, and the Confessions of St Augustine. These two old Africans I could read every year.'[7]

Trevor-Roper ranked Michael Rostovtzeff as the greatest of twentieth-century ancient historians. The first English edition of his masterwork, *The Social and Economic History of the Roman Empire*, had been bought by Christ Church library as early as May 1926. Bright students in the leading universities of Europe devoured the book in the years after its publication: Rostovtzeff delighted them, as Momigliano recalled, 'by what seemed to us his uncanny gift of calling things ancient to life. He guided us through the streets of Rome, Pompei, Nîmes, and Trèves and showed us how the ancients had lived'. Rostovtzeff drew his ideas on social stratification and authority from the writings of Max Weber: in Gooch's estimate, no other scholar could match the Russian's range, erudition and imagination. Peter Brown found Rostovtzeff's massive olive-green volume to be thrilling, chilling and magnificent.[8]

Rostovtzeff's *chef-d'œuvre* pleased Trevor-Roper by virtue of its visual wealth, its lustiness and above all its being a product of its author's personal situation as a refugee from the Bolshevik revolution. The Russian's magnitude as a scholar had been made by the crisis of exile: he learnt from it to adapt *Marxisant* historical concepts for his own use while loathing Leninism. His creative reformulation of ideas resembled the procedure that made Trevor-Roper for a time into the leading exponent in Christ Church of Tory Marxism. Both men recognized historical determinism, and the notion that humankind can rule its destiny, as ideas that empowered tyrannies. Neither of them could tolerate the contortions necessary to believe that 'civilizations', like a species of animal or plant, have a predetermined life cycle. Rostovtzeff's dire experiences and Trevor-Roper's vinegary observance of the twentieth century made it impossible for them to regard history as a progressive advance towards the perfect knowledge and ethical superiority of the present. Rostovtzeff, whose birthdate was 1870, was infuriated by the complacent and presumptuous notion that twentieth-century culture and ethics were richer, not poorer, than those of the past.[9]

'The main phenomenon which underlies the process of decline', wrote Rostovtzeff, 'is the gradual absorption of the educated classes by the masses and the consequent simplification of all the functions of political, social, economic, and intellectual life, which we call the barbarianization of the ancient world'. He saw a warning lesson for twentieth-century Europe in the evolution of the ancient world. 'Violent attempts at levelling have never helped to uplift the masses. They have destroyed the upper classes, and resulted in accelerating the process of barbarization. But the ultimate problem remains like a ghost, ever present and unlaid: Is it possible to extend a higher civilization to the lower classes without debasing its standard and diluting its quality to the vanishing point? Is not every civilization bound to decay as soon as it begins to penetrate the masses?'[10]

Trevor-Roper stinted his praise of his Christ Church tutors in modern history, Feiling, Masterman, Gordon Walker and Nowell Myres. Feiling's liking for semi-mystical allusiveness was unappealing. Gordon Walker's Marxist determinism impressed him briefly by its proselytizing fervour; but no scheme that declared itself infallible could hold his respect for long. He reached an easier understanding with Masterman, whose Whig inclinations were congenial to him. Oliver Franks's biographer went astray when he described Trevor-Roper as 'a luxuriant High Tory'. Peregrine Worsthorne was nearest to the truth in calling him 'an infidel Scottish Whig'; Neal Ascherson comes close with the phrase 'an anti-clerical Whig with a preference for free speech over superstition'. During the 1930s Trevor-Roper felt part of a university generation that was, in his words, 'consciously opposed to the conservative orthodoxy of the time [and to] the inherited residue of Victorian social values'. He felt contempt for the complacent impercipience of nineteenth-century opinion makers. 'They moved comfortably forward in their lush meadow, loudly and complacently cropping its abundance, confident in their strength, pleased with their liberty, satisfied with their explanations of it, blind to the future.' Similarly, his elders in the England of George V were risible figures: 'the convictions of one generation become the joke of the next', he wrote in 1939.[11]

After the award of his university senior studentship in 1936, Trevor-Roper began to research the influence of the puritan revolution on the character and organization of the Church of England. As Feiling declined to act as his supervisor, Claude Jenkins, who was a Canon of Christ Church by virtue of being Regius Professor of Ecclesiastical History, was able to annex Trevor-Roper as a pupil. Jenkins was grubby and malodorous in person, miserly and filching in his habits, archaic and untidy in his erudition.

The Cambridge scholar Joseph Needham had recently tried to promote what he called 'Laudian Marxism', whereby the High

Churchmen of the Anglican communion tempered and Anglicized dialectical materialism for the betterment of communities. But Trevor-Roper's anti-clericalism had been accentuated by Jenkins: godly influences were bogus and unreal to him, and it was absurd to think that churchmen might mitigate the crises of the 1930s. His approach as a postgraduate researcher was accordingly irreligious. He sought the moneyed interests behind the spiritual and institutional schemes of Stuart England, evaluated the Church of England in secular terms and remained mindful of the ideological afflictions of the 1930s as he studied those in the reign of Charles I.[12]

Oxford historians shrank from abstract thought in the 1930s, and continued to do so in the 1950s. On his arrival in the university as a refugee in 1939 Arnaldo Momigliano found that he had only to utter the word 'idea' to be given the address of the Warburg Institute in London. Momigliano's pupil Peter Brown, who matriculated at New College in 1953, found Oxford tutors were prone to 'a narrow emphasis on political and institutional history and a deeply philistine avoidance of grand topics such as religion and the history of ideas'. To Brown it seemed in retrospect that Oxford's historical imagination was cramped by the colleges' traditional function of training the members of the governing class. The syllabus and examinations, because they were a preparation for future politicians and officials, gave priority to political and institutional history. There was little room for the history of ideas on a degree course which 'amounted to the study of power by the future wielders of power'. High honours in examination results went to those who could write fluent and confident papers without any hint of imprudence or impracticality.[13]

The isolated exception to this shirking of intellectual boldness was Collingwood, who held the post of university lecturer in both philosophy and Roman history when Trevor-Roper was an undergraduate. In his writings Trevor-Roper makes no reference to Collingwood: Blair Worden, who knows his mind best, thinks he would have found Collingwood's writings too abstract; Collingwood's biographer, in turn, accuses Trevor-Roper of 'hard-boiled . . . philistinism' and of being 'ennobled as Lord Dacre for services to cynicism'. It is clear, though, that Collingwood in the 1940s and Trevor-Roper in the 1950s asked similar questions and took similar directions. Collingwood's posthumous book *The Idea of History*, which was published in the year of Trevor-Roper's election as a Student, was a classic of its kind. 'All history is the history of thought,' it stated. The academic disciplines of philosophy and history were akin to one another. Both were animate, evolving subjects, asking different questions in each generation and finding different answers, and needing perpetual revision. 'The chief business of twentieth-century philosophy is to reckon with twentieth-century history,' Collingwood declared.[14]

'More & more, as I read history,' Trevor-Roper told Logan Pearsall Smith in the late 1940s, 'I believe in the Whig historians. There is no getting away from the fact that they are right.' Macaulay stood foremost in the pantheon. He had taught that Whigs had proven more successful than republicans, Levellers or Jacobins in bettering societies, and would for the foreseeable future be more successful than English utilitarianism, French socialism or American populism in the same task. In an essay written in 1968, at a time of illiberal turmoil in the universities, Trevor-Roper commemorated Macaulay's trust in 'the continuing political capacity of a practised liberal, historically educated ruling class'. Progress would, in his summary of Macaulay's tempered meliorism, 'be far more painlessly achieved, and far more securely based, under the leadership of whig magnates than by the direct action of political pedants'.[15]

Acton, who stood second behind Macaulay in the pantheon of Whig historians, was in Trevor-Roper's presentation a member of that nineteenth-century elite, 'the aristocratic historical pessimists', men like de Tocqueville and Burckhardt who could not forgive democracy for fostering dangerous, imbecilic optimism. Many of Acton's axioms were appealing to Trevor-Roper: 'No trusting without testing', for example; or 'Judge talent at its best and character at its worst; suspect power more than vice, and study problems in preference to periods.' Trevor-Roper, who was never on easy terms with political, religious and academic orthodoxies, shared Acton's mistrust of power: it has (he said) 'the same tendencies and the same evils, whether it is wielded by prince or parliament, demagogue or pope'.[16]

Trevor-Roper followed Acton in his belief that the study of

historical processes, rather than of historical events or of historical periods, kept historians from the pettiness, opacity and futility of overspecialization in subject matter. 'To me,' he declared in 1957, 'the interest of history lies not in its periods but in its problems, and, primarily, in one general problem which is its substance in all times and all places: the interplay between heavy social forces or intractable geographical facts and the creative or disruptive forces which wrestle with them: the nimble mind, the burning conscience, the blind passions of man.' In the history of humanity, the most dynamic element is 'the human mind, which sometimes triumphs, sometimes destroys, sometimes founders'. The decisions taken by responsible and informed leaders can only be effective – the determining circumstances of history can only be understood – if (as he said during a BBC broadcast on historical imagination in 1958) account is taken of 'the intangibles of politics, the illusions, the frustrations, the resentments, the interests and passions', the 'moods, prejudices and fears, the deep unspoken assumptions of anonymous men, below the level or outside the field of normal politics'.[17]

The Whig creed of Macaulay and Acton was enriched, Trevor-Roper believed, by being adapted for twentieth-century conditions by Tawney. The book that the latter wrote during his brief fellowship of Balliol, *The Acquisitive Society* (1921), is Macaulay's creed remade in the aftermath of a total war. 'Social institutions are the visible expression of the scale of moral values which rules the mind of individuals,' Tawney said. 'It is impossible to alter institutions without altering that moral evaluation.' He spurned the Fabian faith in the benefits of centralized planning and state control. Mental adjustments by communities, rather than the push of political leadership or the pull of theoreticians, and psychological adaptation rather than the resetting of administrative machinery, would bring wholesome progress to people's lives. The conditions needed for a just society were (wrote Tawney) 'capable of being apprehended by the most elementary intelligence, provided it will read the nature of its countrymen in the large outlines of history, not in the bloodless abstractions of experts'.[18]

Bradley, Collingwood, Woodward and others in Oxford had insisted that critical historians must draw inferences and reach conclusions based on their own experience. Trevor-Roper maintained that the contemporary conditions in which history books were researched, planned and written added to their value. He himself was committed to understanding the turmoil and instability both of his own time and of the seventeenth century. He prepared his biography of Laud, who was executed after three years of convulsive civil wars, while 'one of the most barbarous civil wars in history', as he called it, was being fought in Spain. *Archbishop Laud* is, in its way, as much a product of that time as *For Whom the Bell Tolls* or *Homage to Catalonia*. The Spanish civil war was 'an extraordinary experience which transcended politics and became for many an almost religious experience'. For Trevor-Roper's university community in the late 1930s, anti-fascism was the commanding new religiosity. There was little reckoning with the Christian creed in *Archbishop Laud*.[19]

Trevor-Roper, who had learnt the Spanish language at school, did not agree with his friend Sir Richard Rees, the driver of a Republican military ambulance, that the Spanish war was *the* capital event of the twentieth century; but he did hold that it was *the* great European crisis before the Munich agreement of 1938, and more momentous, for example, than the German annexation of Austria. He saw Spain's war, as it raged, as the prelude to a greater struggle against European totalitarianism. The communists in the Soviet-organized International Brigades seemed to him auxiliaries in the defence of the British Empire against encroaching fascist tyranny. Like many reflective young Oxford men, he deplored the British government's policy of non-intervention – especially its refusal to supply weapons to the legally constituted Republican government – as cowardly and shameful.[20]

When Picasso's painting *Guernica* was exhibited in Oxford in October 1938, Trevor-Roper queued to see its depiction of bombing atrocities. Twenty years later he said that he hoped to see it hanging one day in the Prado in Madrid. His partisanship was such that twelve years after Franco's victory he defended the Republican razing by fire of Spanish churches. 'I am on the side of the burners, not of the churches,' he wrote in 1951. The arsonist mobs, whether led by anarchists or communists, were, he thought, 'a *jacquerie* against the outward symbols of a hated system which merely happen to be works of art beyond their comprehension'. Thirty years later, as Master of Peterhouse in the 1980s, he was disgusted to find that one of the Fellows, David Watkin, wore black armbands on the anniversary of Franco's death.[21]

Trevor-Roper's lifelong historical philosophy was formed by the anxiety, exasperation and despair aroused in him by the dictators of his early manhood, by the cruelty and sycophancy of their entourages and by the ineffectual responses of parliamentary democracies to bellicosity. He recognized appeasement as a populist policy, which originated in insularity, ignorance and political make-believe. The Munich agreement of 1938 remained 'clear and vivid still', he wrote twenty years later, 'not merely a political arrangement, good or bad, but a moral experience'. A moral experience, moreover, that was transformative. His generation learnt grim lessons, 'the easy atrophy of the human conscience', 'the ease and speed with which, in certain circumstances, barbarism can break through that thin crust and even, if backed by power and sanctified by doctrine, be accepted as the norm'.[22]

During the war Trevor-Roper reached the military rank of major, and headed a section in the Secret Intelligence Service (SIS) called the Radio Security Service, which specialized in the collation and analysis of intercepted radio traffic. Many other Christ Church men were involved, at a high level of responsibility, in espionage, counter-espionage, surveillance and intelligence gathering. Dick White, the only man to be head of both the Security Service (MI5) and SIS (MI6), had been a pupil of Feiling and Masterman in the 1920s and trusted Trevor-Roper as a friend. Masterman, Ryle, Ayer, Page, Lloyd-Jones, Blake and Stuart were sometime Students of Christ Church who worked for the secret services. Another Christ Church modern historian, and protégé of Feiling's, Bill Deakin, reached the rank of brigadier in wartime military intelligence, and afterwards worked for British security at the United Nations. Robert 'Robin' Zaehner, who had been both an undergraduate and lecturer at the House, was a vital SIS agent in Iran. These were all first-class-honours men who had grown deft at handling a double life: the type whom J. I. M. Stewart found throughout post-war Oxford and dubbed 'the true Secret Service boy'.[23]

From the outset of his work at the Radio Security Service Trevor-Roper showed the traits which he later attributed to the Naval Intelligence officer Ewen Montagu: 'does not suffer fools too gladly, and has a certain sympathy with rogue characters'. He recruited to his small department the startlingly intelligent trio of Stuart Hampshire, Ryle and (at Masterman's suggestion) Stuart. Patrick Reilly, the liaison officer between the Foreign Office and SIS, called them 'a team of brilliance unparalleled anywhere in the intelligence machine'. Guy Liddell of the Security Service thought their product was excellent. 'Trevor-Roper has a scholarly approach,' he noted in his diary in 1941, 'and perhaps a better understanding of the system than anybody else. He is, however, somewhat of an intellectual snob.' The accomplishments of the RSS heightened Trevor-Roper's already robust self-confidence. As noted by Michael Howard, the historian of wartime intelligence who succeeded him in the Regius Chair of Modern History, he brought his skills in bureaucratic infighting and his zest in defeating Whitehall adversaries to the post-war business of his colleges, his faculty and his university.[24]

Stuart Hampshire described the mentality of Christ Church dons in 1945 as 'pedantic and silly'. Yet Trevor-Roper was glad to return there in 1946 as a Student teaching English and European history from 1500 to 1715, and nineteenth- and twentieth-century European history. For eleven years, together with Blake and Stuart, he led a cabal in the governing body of Christ Church which targeted prudes and pedants and styled itself as 'the Party of Gaiety and Light'. Trevor-Roper described his allies as 'secular, anti-hierarchical, pluralist, tolerant, even (in the original sense of the word) libertine'. His party, Bowra's Immoral Front and their Cambridge counterparts identified themselves as rationalists who flouted unreasonable dictation from politicians, churchmen, moralists and professors. Authority seemed to them too often rigid, complacent and sterile. They teased prigs, incited irreverence and exercised a disinterested malice. In an epoch of peacetime state rationing of food and comforts, they ridiculed frugality and celebrated pleasure – or at least the pleasures of the arts, the table and the bottle. Women were not close kindred to them. When they plotted to get their friends into jobs, the friends were always men.[25]

Although the Party of Gaiety and Light tried to enlist the sympathies of their fellow Student Stewart, he would not engage with them. Probably he found them disruptive and fractious. One of his characters, in his Oxford college novel *The Guardians* (1955), complains of the 'intolerance' of the younger dons. 'They tend', he says, 'to congregate in corners, plotting petty subversions, and sharing small primitive jokes. It is a pity.' Certainly, the Party of Gaiety and Light shows the extent to which Trevor-Roper, as Peter Ghosh noted, treated Christ Church before 1957, as he did Oriel and Peterhouse afterwards, 'not as a united community but as a divided, political entity made up of parties, specifically clericals and reactionaries against liberals and progressives'. Always he upheld the anti-clerical and liberal party.[26]

It is dismaying to realize how often Trevor-Roper was unhappy during his eleven years as a Student. During the war Ryle had instructed him, as he did other intellectuals-in-the-making, that it is possible to be both earnest and happy; but the lesson did not last. After 1946, Trevor-Roper's pervading moods were anxiety, overwork, frustration, weariness and depression. He felt oppressed by collegiate administration, by niggling and uncongenial colleagues, by deadlines, and by the deceit, self-delusion and chicanery that beset humanity. His sabbatical year was wasted by the pressing need to help his future wife to obtain a divorce from a husband of whom she was frightened. After his marriage in 1954, partly to earn the fees that paid for the expenses of married life, Trevor-Roper broadcast on BBC radio, became a panellist on the influential *Brains Trust* television programme and its later non-BBC equivalent *Dinner Party*, acted as a special overseas correspondent of the *Sunday Times* in Israel, Spain, Morocco, Iraq, Iran and Mexico, had the confidence of a seasoned pundit in assessing such topics as Stalin's death, Adenauer's Germany or the Geneva Summit talks, and was a prolific book reviewer and essayist. Some Oxford colleagues deprecated these activities as ostentatious grabs for attention. Woodward thought that Trevor-Roper, like Taylor, was trying to shock the public with sensationalism.[27]

Trevor-Roper was usually on the move, and always had another journey in prospect. Despite his introversion he was as inveterate a party-goer as the extrovert Bowra: socializing tired him, and yet to parties he went again and again. The week before the coronation in

1953 was busier than most, but not atypical. He dined at Denham with Lord Vansittart, the pre-war Permanent Under Secretary of the Foreign Office. In Oxford he lunched with William Walton, who was an honorary Student of Christ Church, and later attended a performance of Walton's cantata *Belshazzar's Feast*. He took a party of Belgians to hear Thomas Armstrong play the Christ Church organ and the cathedral choir to sing Handel's *Zadok the Priest*. On that same day he entertained two visitors from Soviet Russia at Christ Church and brought Isaiah Berlin and Dimitri Obolensky to dine with them. He attended a lunch for the Vice-President of Bolivia, for whom he was expected to act as interpreter. He participated in the ceremonial roasting, by the nuclear physicist Hans Halban, of an ox presented by the Rector Magnificus of the University of Copenhagen. For a man with a reputation for obduracy, Trevor-Roper had a weak power of refusal. His time and energies were depleted by inessential diversions.

A heart-cry from Trevor-Roper in 1953 shows the peculiar strains of being a well-known figure living in an architectural masterpiece. He yearned to spend his coming Sunday resting in bed, but instead the Ambassador in Cairo, Sir Ralph Stevenson, together with his wife and the Yugoslav Ambassador in London, were due in mid-morning and expecting to be shown the sights of the college and university.

> However busy one is people descend upon one and assume that one is free to see them, at all hours; they treat Oxford as a comfortable, restful place, where *they* can relax by claiming hours of one's time; and because there is a convention that one must always *appear* to be at ease & delighted to see them, they assume that they are conferring a positive benefit upon one by their visits & interruptions.

The day visitor in the hallway is the enemy of achievement.[28]

After his period at Merton, Trevor-Roper was never at peace with his colleagues in any Oxford or Cambridge college: not Christ Church, not Oriel, not Peterhouse. Nor was he satisfied with the social environment of the university. He praised Ernest Gellner for condemning 'the Narodniks of North Oxford', the 'intelligentsia-without-ideas', in his contentious book *Words and Things*. It was, for Trevor-Roper as for Gellner, 'the cult of meticulousness, the dislike of ideas . . . the insistence on practical irrelevance' that was dismaying about university life. He could not, or so it seems, allow himself to feel fulfilled or tranquil in his workplace. Always there was some rankling anxiety. He found solace and content only when away from Oxford: tramping in remote and picturesque countryside – in Northumberland or the Scottish Borders, in Greece and Iceland – or basking in the cultivated luxury of Bernard Berenson's Tuscan villa I Tatti. He cherished the remark of Charles Fisher, on returning to Christ Church from a Borders holiday, 'that the cry of the Old Etonian in Peckwater is a poor substitute for the wail of sea-birds in Northumberland'. It was easier for him to exult in the architectural beauties of Christ Church than to feel corporate pride in the Students, Dean and Canons. He wrote an official guidebook to the college, which was given to incoming undergraduates from 1950. The history of the institution is recounted through its fabric: there is lyricism and exactitude in his descriptions of its quadrangles and interiors; but of the human element he says little.[29]

The Worthing shopkeeper's son David Hopkins, an undergraduate who lacked academic and social confidence, found Trevor-Roper considerate and appreciative. He was capable of protective kindliness towards the disadvantaged or downcast. But a protégé of Ryle's, Antony Flew, who had gained first-class honours in Greats at St John's, was crushed by the Party of Gaiety after his appointment in 1949 as a lecturer in philosophy at Christ Church. Most unusually, he was not confirmed in a studentship after his probationary year as a lecturer, and he left the House in 1950. It is not clear why Blake and Trevor-Roper determined to oust Flew: perhaps he was truculent or had an excess of self-belief. Gellner later depicted his linguistic philosophy as 'a trivial exercise', 'making nonsense of all intellectual advance' and 'immensely silly'. Possibly Flew was too cocksure in expressing the perplexity of philosophers at, in Ryle's words, 'the pretensions of historians to interpret the actions and words of historic personages as expressions of their actual thoughts, feelings, and intentions'. Historical investigation, it seemed to linguistic philosophers, can never reach the inward mainsprings of their subject: 'historians', says Ryle, 'may describe the signals, but they can never begin to interpret them as effects of operations in the eternally sealed signal-boxes'.[30]

As Flew's replacement, and again at the instigation of Ryle, Peter Herbst was appointed to a lectureship in philosophy. Herbst had been born in Heidelberg, came as a refugee to England and underwent schooling at Haileybury. After the outbreak of war, he was shipped as an enemy alien to Australia, where he endured internment. Following his election, a dinner was held to introduce him to his new colleagues at the House. He was seated beside Dundas, who made a short speech introducing him, and then posed some public questions. 'Tell me, Herbst, are you a Jew?' was the first. Herbst admitted that he was. 'Tell me, Herbst, are you a bugger?' was the second question. 'I'm afraid not,' he replied. 'Oh, here again we are quite tolerant,' Dundas retorted. Herbst realized that he was undergoing an initiation ceremony. If he parried these questions with unruffled grace, he would be accepted; but if he showed unease he would become a social reject among the Students.[31]

Trevor-Roper's detestation of Dundas intensified after the old man made him the butt of his malice in a gaudy oration of 1953. Gaudies should be moments to savour the magnificence of the college hall, the ceremonial robes, the saying of grace, the candlelight, the college silver, the circulation of wines and snuff, the venerable portraits. In 1953 Christ Church's guest of honour was Gordon Walker's political mentor Herbert Morrison, then a Visiting Fellow at Nuffield College, coarse, self-satisfied and a champion Labour pugilist in parliamentary knockabout. 'Mr Herbert Morrison', said Dundas in his oration, 'seemed the sort of man – or perhaps I should say chap – who was not likely to remain a stranger for long in any company so fortunate as to include him.' Then, as his speaking notes show, he likened the Labour bruiser to a striking Christ Church personality,

[a] colleague, not a pupil – anything but – Mr. Trevor-Roper, if I may compare great things – with great. Both, I am sure, are profound lovers of peace, political or academic: both fight like mad to get it, and seem to extract some pale unselfish pleasure from the mere act of fighting. When the battle is over, and Mr M. is Prime Minister and Mr T.-R. Archbishop, perhaps of Canterbury, but surely more likely of Westminster – after all, he

is still celibate – they will be as peaceable as you and I are: meanwhile they are both warriors, and not, I should guess, notably
unhappy warriors.

Three years later Trevor-Roper besought Stuart, as Curator of the
common room, which, he said, 'used to be a gay, convivial, conversational meeting-place', to restrict Dundas's attendance there. The
old man had become a thorough pest:

> Shuffling about in his squalid clothes, maddening everyone by his
> perpetual querulity and egotism, permanently half-tight and sniv-
> elling, he . . . does great damage by using Christ Church as a base
> from which to go a-peeping round school swimming-baths. He
> is a nuisance in undergraduate societies. He is unpleasant to the
> servants. In fact he is unpleasant to everyone.[32]

Little wonder that after a student of the college, Michael Foster,
gassed himself in his college rooms at the start of Michaelmas term
in 1959, his former pupil Quintin Hailsham inveighed against
common-room malice. 'Dons', he told Harrod, 'are all . . . beasts to
one another.' Herbst thought that Trevor-Roper was as objectionable
as Dundas in devising social tortures. He described how the Student
in modern history liked to select a victim at high table, preferably
a cleric, and best of all an American cleric, and would then set about
embarrassing him. On one occasion Trevor-Roper offered snuff to
an American bishop sitting beside him. The ecclesiastic inhaled
powdered tobacco up his nostrils, began to dribble and made a mess
of himself. At this Trevor-Roper feigned dismay. 'It's nothing,' he
told the bishop in a carrying voice, 'it's just that there is a superstition around the House . . . that to be able to sneeze heartily to snuff
is a sign of chastity.' Such humiliating japes were, recalled Herbst in
old age, part of the House style. He had seen enough of such behaviour with the result that, after four years, although he could have
continued in post, he forsook Christ Church for a job in the Gold
Coast (Ghana).[33]

There was a belief, which sometimes may have been justified, that
American universities sought temporary relief from the bores on
their campuses by encouraging them to apply for travel grants from

the Ford, Guggenheim and Rockefeller foundations to fund sabbatical years in Oxford. Certainly, in J. I. M. Stewart's university novel of 1956, *Old Hall, New Hall*, there is a champion bore, first laughable and finally sinister, visiting from a mid-western American campus. When W. H. Auden returned to the House from New York as Oxford's newly elected Professor of Poetry in 1956, his tendency to deliver repetitive and dogmatic monologues made him an object of resentful raillery. He had, as his friend Stephen Spender noted, 'a hard time in the Common Room at Christ Church, where several of the dons twit him about America, and where he is half-fascinated, half-bored by the endlessly cliquey Oxford donnish conversation'. When he first entered the common room after dinner, Cherwell, who was presiding as the senior Student, ostentatiously turned his back on the poet, and thereafter refused ever to acknowledge him. After a few months of these animosities Auden felt so 'attacked' that he produced his poem of paranoia, 'There will be no peace', with stanzas that can be read as a commentary on the Students and Canons of Christ Church.

> What have you done to them?
> Nothing? Nothing is not an answer:
> You will come to believe – how can you help it? –
>   That you did, that you did do something;
> You will find yourself wishing that you can make them laugh:
>   You will long for their friendship.
>
> There will be no peace.
> Fight back, then, with such courage as you have
> And every unchivalrous dodge that you know of,
>   Clear in your conscience on this:
> Their cause, if they had one, is nothing to them now;
> They hate for hate's sake.[34]

Combativeness was, for Trevor-Roper, an admirable trait. He admired Namier for entitling one of his volumes of essays *Conflicts*, Lucien Febvre for calling his essay collection *Combats pour l'histoire*, and Geyl for choosing a similar title, *Tilts and Tourneys*. By contrast, when he reviewed a volume of essays by Sir Maurice Powicke, Regius

Professor at Oxford until 1948, he seized on a few demure phrases and teased the old man for wishing that Oxford historians might recover the 'serene certainties of our predecessors', and for describing scholarly controversy as a '*malaise* or discomfort which oppresses the thoughtful study of history'. Powicke's historical philosophy was expressive of the age of Beveridge and of the chastened hopes of the generation of social democrats who had been confounded by the European dictators. History lessons in schools should teach empathy, he told the Historical Association in 1944. 'The greatest social virtue', he said, 'is consideration for others': 'systematic drilling' by history teachers in this quality was more valuable to communities and individuals than 'doing the Tudors'.[35]

Many people disliked Trevor-Roper. As early as 1936 Bowra urged Isaiah Berlin to discourage All Souls from electing him to an examination fellowship. Billa Harrod thought him bombastic. Several of his wife's Scottish friends found his nagging anti-clericalism and reiterative anti-Catholicism so objectionable that they would no longer have him to stay. He lost his tenancy of a Queen Anne house on the Bruern estate in Oxfordshire because his sneers offended his landlord Michael Astor and provoked an angry scene at dinner. His brusque iciness to Hamish Hamilton's wife was the subject of complaints to Berenson. H. J. Habbakuk, Chichele Professor of Economic History, said that his conversational manner resembled that of the prosecutor in a law court. Sir Arthur Norrington, President of Trinity from 1954, found him 'infernally uncivil' in his writings. Noël Annan relished his company, but called him 'appallingly unkind'. To George Lyttelton he seemed 'conceited', and 'generally . . . at someone's throat'. His pleasure in making trouble in departmental business was painful and incomprehensible to less complicated colleagues. After giving thoughtful and affectionate encouragement to the young scholar Alan Macfarlane, he offended him by ironical remarks about the inhabitants of Essex whose activities Macfarlane was investigating. Overall Macfarlane liked and admired him, and attributed his 'spitefulness' to a 'mixture of arrogance and insecurity'. The animosities even led the biographer of the Hispanist historian Raymond Carr to apply the adjectives 'cruel' and 'murderous' to him.[36]

The clubland gossip Kenneth Rose, who enjoyed his company,

found him boastful and prone to the 'elevated bitchiness in which most dons talk about each other'. He failed to persuade his fellow judges of the Wolfson Prize for History to give a lifetime award to Trevor-Roper: although the panel of judges changed regularly, it always included one or two people who disliked or resented him too much. Trevor-Roper's London publishers felt that his unpopularity inhibited him from producing an ambitious book from which they could earn money. 'He has made so many enemies', said Maurice Macmillan in 1969, 'that he is reluctant to expose himself. But, as his publishers, we suffer.'[37]

Macmillan took a thumping profit, though, from Trevor-Roper's second book, *The Last Days of Hitler*. The book was the brainchild of the former Christ Church historian Dick White, who was then head of Counter-Intelligence in the British zone of occupied Germany. He first proposed that the Oxford philosopher and intelligence officer J. L. Austin should pursue and interrogate the survivors of Hitler's Berlin bunker and confirm the circumstances of the Führer's death. After Austin had declined this suggestion, White turned to Trevor-Roper, who set to work with relish. Extracts from the finished book were serialized in the *Daily Telegraph* in November and December 1946 under such headlines as 'The Demon of Destruction and his Court' and 'Doomed Marionettes' Hopes and Horoscopes'. *The Last Days of Hitler* has never gone out of print since its publication early in 1947. The book secured for Trevor-Roper a place among the public intellectuals or pundits who led so much of public discourse in the quarter-century after the war.[38]

The Last Days was published at the dawn of the golden age of the English public intellectual. New respect for elite intelligence and dispassionate expertise arose partly from the discomfiting, unarticulated knowledge that the appeasement of the dictators in the 1930s had been, supremely, a populist policy. The success of Oxford and Cambridge dons as emergency officials of wartime government departments made post-war ministers, programme makers and editors welcome their rationality and sense of responsibility in opinion forming and decision taking. 'The good old Oxford and Cambridge clearness of thought and expression' and 'solid ferro-concrete intelligence', as Iris Murdoch called it, was finally recognized as highly invaluable. Nineteen-forty-eight was the launch year in this phase of intellectual ascendancy. Bertrand Russell gave the BBC's inaugural Reith lectures on 'Authority and the Individual'. Other BBC lecture series have been recounted in the chapter on Roy Harrod. Thereafter BBC audiences, and readers of the *Observer* and the *Sunday Times* too, welcomed explanations, predictions and conclusions from Oxbridge dons such as Annan, Ayer, Berlin, Asa Briggs, Alan Bullock, Anthony Quinton, Taylor and Trevor-Roper. These men, for they were seldom women, differed in their political allegiances, academic disciplines and social intentions; but they all believed in public service, and held that the free interchange of ideas and hardiness in argument conduce to responsible citizenship.[39]

No living scholar, perhaps, had so much unintended influence on Trevor-Roper's recession in the 1940s from *Marxisant* thought as Christopher Hill. Special Branch began monitoring Hill as a member of the CPGB in 1935, and had his luggage searched when he disembarked at Harwich after a visit to the Soviet Union in 1936. Trevor-Roper thought him matchless among the Marxist historians of his generation, but baulked at the way that his analysis and inferences were subject to party rules of thinking. While Hill surrendered to the absolutism of Marxist dogma and was thrilled by revolutionary action, Trevor-Roper saw class mobilization, Agitprop and mass insurrection as likely to be destructive, dishonest and despotic.[40]

Trevor-Roper was sent by the *Observer* in 1947 to report on Stalinist tactics in Italy, France and Czechoslovakia, and concluded that the communist parties in those countries made pledges to the peasantry and urban proletariat, and coined slogans about increased production, but had no policies, no expertise in trade agreements, tariffs and foreign exchanges, cared only for gaining control and then downing other left-wingers. Hill, by contrast, wrote in 1947 that the successes of the Bolshevik revolution 'demonstrated that the common people of the earth . . . can take over power and run the state infinitely more effectively than their "betters"'. Trevor-Roper countered a few years later that it was the Red Army, not the will of the people, that had imposed the Soviet single-party system on eastern Europe: a dictatorial system that Hill insisted was setting an example for the industrialized countries of the world by achieving 'rational planning, full employment and universal economic security'.[41]

Although Trevor-Roper's essay 'Karl Marx and the Study of History' dates from 1955, its arguments were roused by reading *The English Revolution* and similar works. 'The more one looks at the technical method of Marxist historians,' Trevor-Roper declared, 'the more one is driven to the conclusion that the evidence is simply selected to buttress up immutable and unsubstantiated dogma.' Marxism was a blight on scholarly standards. Gifted historians such as Hill and Eric Hobsbawm, perpetually toying with the Marxist concepts of 'feudalism', 'bourgeoisie' and 'capitalism', made themselves practitioners of a mortifying, inward-looking pedantry. 'Marxist historians, when they write as Marxists, are now like . . . the inhabitants of Lilliput fighting as to which end of a boiled egg should be broken.' Their school of history has produced, Trevor-Roper concluded,

an army of obscure scholiasts busily commenting on each other's *scholia* and loudly claiming to have inspired the work of other historians who have long ago left them behind in their barren, circuitous, resonant cave of Adullam. In the dim past of the nineteenth century, when the Marxist dogma was new and untested, it may have inspired some historical research, as new ideas often do, even if they are in fact erroneous. For historical knowledge, like other knowledge, is advanced by theory and only disciplined by facts. But now we are in the mid-twentieth century . . . Disproved by all intellectual tests, it is Russian power alone which now sustains and irrationally seems to justify the Marxist interpretation of history.[42]

Yet, throughout the petrifying chill between the Berlin airlift of 1948 and the building of the Berlin wall in 1961, Trevor-Roper flinched at the crudity of Red-baiters. Repentant ex-communists, such as the former Comintern agent Franz Borkenau or the ex-Trotskyite James Burnham, were (to him) shrill, unseemly, vindictive and untrustworthy. He liked to remind British conservatives, too, of their eager gratitude after 1941 for the alliance with the Soviet Union in Europe. Always he showed magnanimity towards gifted Marxist scholars.

When in 1980 Robert Blake and the Cambridge historian J. H. ('Jack') Plumb indulged in unpleasant antics to expel the Soviet spy Anthony Blunt from his fellowship of the British Academy, Trevor-Roper wrote to the Academy's President that although he despised Blunt, 'he was elected a Fellow for his scholarship, not for his politics, morals, or patriotism; and I think that the Academy will only make itself ridiculous if it now expels him'. Hobsbawm had confided to him that Plumb, the chief stirrer of the agitation, was himself a former member of the CPGB. 'I do not think the Academy should be used to purge the guilt of old Cambridge communists!'[43]

The worst schism in the Party of Gaiety and Light occurred in 1955 because of Trevor-Roper's latitude in such matters. He had been excited by reviewing *The World of Odysseus*, in which the American classicist Moses Finley drew on sociology and anthropology, rather than textual criticism, to interpret Homeric epics. Finley, he wrote, has 'reconstructed an era, a society, a culture that seemed lost, and done it – what adds a relish to his achievement – not in a remote Polynesian island or from the mute evidence of stones, but in a crucial stage of our European history, and from the two greatest, best-known epic poems in the world'. Trevor-Roper was fascinated by Finley's analysis of the giving of gifts and the storing of treasure: never with the aim of economic profit, but to affirm status, which, Trevor-Roper wrote, 'in spite of all that Marx has said, perhaps still remains the *primum mobile* of social man, at least of those who are above the starvation line'. Finley had been penalized for his former communist party membership by dismissal from Rutgers University, and had settled in England as a fugitive from Red-baiting: Blake and Stuart were enraged when Trevor-Roper tried to obtain a studentship for him. (While Christ Church prevaricated, Denys Page bagged Finley for Cambridge, where he was later elected to a chair and became head of a college.)[44]

The journal *Past and Present*, which was founded in 1952 with Hill on the editorial board and Hobsbawm as assistant editor, was appreciated by Trevor-Roper at a time when the Institute of Historical Research refused to stock the periodical because of its communist affiliations. He recommended *Past and Present* to Geyl, and regarded it as a promising cadet version of Braudel's *Annales*. When Maurice Ashley wrote a captious and unjust *TLS* review of Hill's *Puritanism and Revolution* in 1959, Trevor-Roper defended Hill. He respected Hobsbawm's historical work, and in 1960 helped this member of the CPGB in tricky negotiations with the US border force. He continued to praise the intellectual excitement of Joseph Needham's *Science and Civilization in China* even after discovering its author's turpitude as the apologist-collaborator for Maoism.[45]

In national politics, he was enraged by obtuse semi-fascistic Tory patriotism during the Suez crisis of 1956. He thought Ulster Unionists were no better than Turkish Cypriots. Michael Oakeshott, author of the classic essay 'On being Conservative', was to him a 'prophet of darkness', whose fostering of irrationality was an encouragement to 'desperate bigotries'. Although Trevor-Roper sat on the Conservative benches in the House of Lords after Margaret Thatcher nominated him for a life peerage in 1979, she complained to Woodrow Wyatt in 1986 that, like other dons, he was susceptible to 'the *Guardian* trend of thinking'. Certainly, he had scant respect for disenchanted liberals, such as Max Beloff, who defected to neo-conservative Thatcherism. Moreover, when he was Master of Peterhouse in the 1980s, he abominated the reactionary obscurantism of a few of its Fellows. They were not honest Tories, he maintained, but fascists, ultra-clerical, troglodytes, Jacobites and Adullamites. Their use of the word 'liberalism' in a pejorative sense affronted him.[46]

At intervals during the 1940s Trevor-Roper reflected on Spanish imperial power, and on the nation's literature and arts. Marcel Bataillon's *Erasme et l'Espagne* (1937) and Fernand Braudel's *La Méditerranée et le monde méditerranéen à l'époque de Philippe II* (1949) convinced him that a knowledge of Spanish history was indispensable for an understanding of early modern Europe. He first visited Spain in 1951:

> I was delighted with the place, – with those infinite golden uplands: everything was golden, – stubble-fields, golden hillocks of grain being winnowed on every village floor, golden corn-dust suspended in the air of those hard, cold, impersonal sierras; with those vast

churches echoing night and day (as it seemed to me), like some
Tibetan lamasery, with the interminable, hieratic, nasal mumble
of bald-headed priests immobile in their huge carven stalls; and
above all, with the antique dignity of even the poorest peasants
when one spoke to them among those vast empty fields.

The 'Homeric simplicity' of Spanish culture set the country apart as
'an incongruous, accidental, isolated appendage to Europe', he wrote.
Like Pascal he thought truth was respected north of the Pyrenees,
and error beyond them. His fascination with the country is plain in
the lengthy report 'The Secret of Franco's Rule' that he contributed
to the *Sunday Times* after an investigatory visit in 1953.[47]

Spain was in Trevor-Roper's mind in 1952–3 as he formulated his
thinking about court and country parties for a major essay about
the Elizabethan gentry. 'I can find no Spanish *social* historians,' he
wrote to Gerald Brenan, author of *The Spanish Labyrinth*, 'and yet
just as English history would be to me unintelligible without some
understanding of the puritan squires, so I suspect that the Castilian
hidalgos [lesser nobility] must have had some greater significance
in Spanish social history than merely as soldiers & colonists abroad.'
He wanted to study the Spanish gentry as he developed his thesis
of a general crisis in seventeenth-century Europe. 'It seems to me,'
he told Brenan,

> that in the 16th and 17th centuries there is, in Western Europe,
> on the one hand, a general cult of 'the court', represented socially
> by the great scramble for offices, the competition for titles, the
> character of education, the waste and display of official life . . .
> and, on the other hand, an opposite cult which can conveniently
> be called 'the country': a cult (often also nurtured among failed
> courtiers and officials) of self-respecting parsimony and idealisa-
> tion of an aristocratic attitude.

During the 1950s he taught an undergraduate course on sixteenth-
century Spain and its impact on the rest of Europe. Among the
younger Oxford scholars of that decade he trusted best the judgement
of John Elliott, with whom he visited Catalonia in 1956. 'Oh, the
struggle to get anything done in this Arab country! The crowds, the

inefficiency, the slow, sullen bigotry, the seediness, the slow, dusty, creeping, devitalised spirits of the place: the thin laymen, the fat priests!' The riches of the Prado re-emphasized to him the exceptionalism of Spain. 'Other national galleries oppress one with the continuity of tradition, but Spanish painters are individual: they stand out so suddenly, breaking tradition rather than continuing it, that one gets a far more vivid impression, or rather discontinued series of impressions, from going through those rooms.'[48]

Trevor-Roper used the phrase 'general crisis' to describe events in seventeenth-century Europe. He also applied it when praising Rostovtzeff's account of the privileges and wealth of Roman office holders, and his charting of the ascendancy and decline of different sections of the nobility and gentry. The enlarged powers of urban elites, the expansion of officialdom, the enhanced power and prosperity of office holders, the counterblasts from the countryside and the ensuing factious rivalry between country and court are recurrent themes in Rostovtzeff's account of the third and of Trevor-Roper's version of the seventeenth centuries. Trevor-Roper's court–country antithesis is Rostovtzeff remade.[49]

Such was the Russian's importance to him that in 1958 he convinced Janet Adam Smith, redoubtable literary editor of the *New Statesman*, to allow him a page and a half of small print to review a revised edition of *The Social and Economic History of the Roman Empire* (prepared by P. M. Fraser of All Souls). 'How can one possibly summarize such a work,' Trevor-Roper asked, 'or extract its conclusions, so tightly and subtly bound with the visible and invisible filaments of powerful erudition?' Rostovtzeff argued that the rural proletariat and the military combined to overturn the supremacy of the cities of the Roman Empire, as they later did to imperial Russia. His further judgement that 'the driving forces were envy and hatred, and those who sought to destroy the rule of the bourgeois class had no positive programme', together with Trevor-Roper's gloss – 'the third century AD is not the only time when the blind envy and hatred of a previously oppressed class was suddenly and destructively and disastrously armed' – were unpalatable to more doctrinaire *New Statesman* readers. Still less savoury for them was Trevor-Roper's conclusion that 'the gradual absorption by the masses of the educated classes is the main feature of the process of national decline, because it entails the simplification of all political, social, economic, and intellectual functions: a process which Rostovtzeff called "barbarization".[50]

When in 1947 Masterman consulted twenty-five members of the Modern History Faculty on their preferences for a successor to Powicke as Regius Professor, Trevor-Roper told him that Namier was 'easily first' among the candidates: Namier also had strong support from the impressive trio of Bullock, Deakin and Taylor. He was resisted by others who detested his abrasive manners (that overriding determination that Trevor-Roper called 'megalon-amier'): as also by Richard Southern, who recognized Namier's accomplishments but backed the candidature of his mentor Vivian Galbraith. A good number of modernists favoured Woodward. The names of Myres, Hancock and Rowse were also mooted. Galbraith bested Namier and the rest, and succeeded Powicke as Regius Professor in 1948. He had been, Powicke thought, too brazen in pushing to secure the Crown appointment. Woodward agreed, and added that once ensconced in Oxford, Galbraith had turned into 'a flâneur'.[51]

Galbraith was a palaeographer and producer of documentary records rather than a medieval historian. He studied chronicles and charters, and made a fetish of attendance at the Chancery Lane buildings of the Public Record Office. Indeed, he had been an appa-ratchik of the imperious and complacent regime that, until the PRO's removal to Kew in 1977, made it such an ill-managed, grimy, incon-venient and disheartening institution. His ideas, foibles, prejudices and objections rushed from him in a heedless, headlong, unrestrain-able flow. He was malicious and sly: it pleased him to hurt and demoralize younger Oxford scholars; he had a devious trick of uttering ostensibly impersonal and generalized remarks that were, in truth, crafted and humiliating jibes aimed at people in his hearing; he liked to exert power, too, by snubbing or insulting the wives of younger colleagues. His love of feuding was shown in his treatment of the Christ Church medievalist E. F. Jacob. 'Galbraith expressed himself with obscene contempt about Ernest,' Rowse noted. 'He obviously not only despised him but hated him.' Jacob's equivocal and guarded manner, 'his eternal camouflage' as Rowse called it, exasperated Galbraith, 'with his rude, abrasive candour'. When giving lectures Galbraith approached the lectern like a scratch golfer at his tee and swore like a bloke in a pub. He appreciated 'every quality except formality and a prudent reserve', recalled his protégé Southern. His brutal extroversion ill-matched Trevor-Roper, whose remote, politic, restrictive manner was never coarsened by manly expletives.[52]

Galbraith was vexed by Trevor-Roper's championing of Namier's candidature for the Regius chair in 1948. He was further riled by the younger man's open dismay at Galbraith's appointment by the Attlee government. 'Namier – who on any account must surely be admitted to be England's greatest living historian – has been kept out of every Oxford chair in turn,' Trevor-Roper lamented. This exclusion was a protective comfort to the quiet lives of timid mediocrities whom Gellner later called the intelligentsia-without-ideas. As a jab at Galbraith Trevor-Roper described Namier's essays, although only by-products of his studies, as a 'solider achievement than the whole work of many highly placed historical professors'. In these essays, of which Macmillan had been publishing selections with increasing rapidity since 1939, Namier gave paramountcy to the contextures of time and place, and to small accidents of environment. He dismissed doctrinaire ideas as the 'subterfuge of those who . . . try to enclose life into abstract words and meaningless descriptions, so that they master it, measure it, and juggle with it'. His causeries, as they accumulated, provided a distinctively Namierite historical philosophy by bringing a single, integral and cohesive intelligence to bear on such diverse subjects as eighteenth-century English parliamentary history, the French revolutions, the Napoleonic emperors, nationalism, peasant revolts, twentieth-century European diplomatic crises, Ukraine, Judaica and Zionism, Masaryk, Lawrence of Arabia, Trotsky, the Third Reich, prose style. Namier's essays never fail, Trevor-Roper wrote in 1952, 'to give us some new insight, some brilliant surprise which, once uttered – and this is the test of profundity – suddenly seems obvious: a truism which had previously occurred to nobody'.[53]

Pieter Geyl, too, passed Trevor-Roper's test of profundity. He had been born in 1887, and worked as London correspondent of a Rotterdam newspaper from 1913 until his appointment to a newly created chair in Dutch history and institutions at University College, London in 1919. Fifteen years later he obtained the chair of modern history at the University of Utrecht despite influential opponents, including the regnant Queen of the Netherlands, who mistrusted his brand of Flemish nationalism. His histories of the Netherlands in the sixteenth and seventeenth centuries were, in G. P. Gooch's judgement, 'at once warmly patriotic and scrupulously critical'. After the Nazi occupation of the Netherlands in 1940 Geyl was incarcerated for thirteen months in Buchenwald, where he wrote sonnets and a detective novel. While held captive in other prisons, he turned to the study of historiography and prepared 'his brilliant book', as Trevor-Roper called it, *Napoleon, For and Against*. 'One of the best of living historians,' so Trevor-Roper told Berenson, 'indeed in a class by himself, or perhaps a class which he shares with Namier, and one or two others.'[54]

In 1952 Trevor-Roper asked Geyl for a meeting, and journeyed to Utrecht for that end. A friendship ensued: never intimate but based on mutual encouragement, their veneration of truth for its own sake, their dislike of regimentation and their exacting standards of scholarly integrity. For Geyl and Trevor-Roper the understanding of what European societies had lost as well as gained – the feat of explaining the grief and anger as well as the ideals and imaginations of the past – was a means to put in proportion, and perhaps to remedy, present failings. 'The first duty of historical scholarship, criticism, again criticism, and criticism once more,' said Geyl. 'After giving to criticism its full due, we can by the spectacle of history feel fortified in our love of life, in our respect for life.' History was for him 'not an inventory of dead people and of dead things, but a key to life – as literature, too, is a key to life.'[55]

Geyl published his earliest criticisms of Toynbee's panoptic historical theories of civilization in 1946, and held a broadcast debate with him in the launch year of the intellectual re-empowerment of the BBC in 1948. Throughout the 1950s he published essays that decried Toynbee's methods, determinism, intentions, errors and prophecies. He also criticized the partiality of Taylor, the sycophancy of E. H. Carr towards the Soviet Union, and Geoffrey Barraclough's dismissal of Napoleon and Bismarck as 'Neolithic figures' without relevance to current problems. Trevor-Roper's growing interest in historiography was stimulated by meeting Geyl. He published his earliest strictures on Toynbee, which followed Geyl's lead, in 1954, and a year later persuaded the *Sunday Times* to let him review Geyl's *Debates with Historians*, which contained four critical essays on Toynbee. He extolled his Dutch friend as 'a cosmopolitan scholar . . . a liberal and a rationalist [who] has no use for the worship of power, whether conservative or revolutionary'. Subsequently he followed Geyl in publishing critical essays on Barraclough, Carr and Taylor.[56]

Trevor-Roper's reflections on 'Human Nature in Politics', which the BBC broadcast in 1953, were honed by his contacts with Geyl. 'Political theory which does not start from a theory of man is in my view quite worthless,' said Trevor-Roper. Besides constant basic necessities, such as physical security, material sufficiency and religion, 'the *mind* of man' can vary greatly from time to time and place to place. The different attitudes to acquiring, spending and saving money through the centuries, and the varied senses of national glory, are examples of the fluctuating and evolving mentality of the human race. If this imperative point is not understood, said Trevor-Roper, historians may easily ascribe to one century the motives and priorities of another. In the most offensive case, dialectical materialism dismissed the professed motives, ideals, aims and rules of life of historic figures and movements as cant which masked their capitalist imperatives. 'It seems to me vulgar and parochial thus to deny to our ancestors the right to think differently from ourselves – even to tell them that they do not mean what they say when they protest that they did think differently.' As human motivation varies so greatly, even within the same epochs and nationalities, 'there can be no ideal or permanent political system, only a series of political philosophies which succeed or fail according as they are appropriate or inappropriate to the changing psychological as well as to the permanent basic needs of humanity'. Accordingly, Trevor-Roper told his BBC audience, the proper task of political philosophers is not to plan the ideal arrangements of society, but to devise a political system that is sufficiently adjustable to meet changes of social need and human motivation. 'If that is done, we can profitably dispense with such dreary and disastrous prophets as Jean-Jacques Rousseau and Karl Marx.'[57]

Geyl marked his retirement in 1958 from his chair at Utrecht with a valedictory lecture entitled 'The Vitality of Western Civilization'. Europe had for centuries held the central directing power in world events; but Eurocentric historical writing was under increasing reproach, he said. Historians were expected to apologize for their nation's past errors which were, in truth, inseparable from human nature. An academic at Leyden University was advocating that extra-European history should be a compulsory part of the school syllabus, 'at the expense, inevitably, of the study of the Greek and Roman world out of which our own civilization has partly sprung'. The study of Chinese, Arab and Russian civilizations might be inform-ative for students at university level, but to extend this to schoolchildren could only fill the pupils' heads with hotchpotch. 'To all of us,' said Geyl, 'the history of our Western cultural community must provide a point of departure and always a point of orientation.' After reading this Parthian shot, Trevor-Roper wrote to its author: 'may you long continue to preach liberalism, rationalism, and the virtue of European intellectual values against these obscurantist doctrines of universal history, according to which the blind migrations and abject superstitions of Huns and Hottentots are as significant as the European Renaissance and Enlightenment!'[58]

Twenty years later, writing the introduction to a book about the vulnerability of planet earth, with contributors including the Nobel laureate Konrad Lorenz and the polymath Roger Caillois, Trevor-Roper reiterated these points. 'Now that it has been cut down to size, now that the other countries have mobilized their greater natural resources, and overshadow it, why should we remember Europe, except as the exploded laboratory of a not very brave new world?' He had his ready answer. Because the geographical fragmentation of Europe, its internal complexity and linguistic multiplicity, had fostered a polit-ical and intellectual history of unique and abundant variety.

Europe is the source of all modern ideas. It has been the motor of history. It has surpassed all other continents in the richness of its literature and its arts. These are a function of its extra-ordinary dynamism. For human vitality is indivisible. The same energy which overturns ancient traditions, invades and conquers other peoples, transforms and destroys other elements, is also the driving-power which creates the works of the spirit.[59]

Like Namier and Geyl, Trevor-Roper intended that his essays would endow the reading public with insights into the exercise of power and enlarge historical perspectives in a century circumscribed by total wars. There was nothing cursory or fleeting in these pieces, many of which seem freshly written and thought-provoking after seventy years. He assembled forty-two of them in his *Historical Essays*, published by Macmillan in 1957. All but nine of them had previously appeared in the *New Statesman* by arrangement with Janet Adam Smith. The others had appeared in such non-academic periodicals as *Commentary*, *Encounter* and the *Spectator*.

In the preface to his collection Trevor-Roper signalled his distance from academic historians who have a static outlook and narrowing format: 'they choose a period, sometimes a very brief period, and within that period they strive, in desperate competition with ever-expanding evidence, to know all the facts'. *Historical Essays* offers a panoply of different territories, climates, epochs, sovereignties, religions and ideals. It begins with an essay on George Adam Smith's *Historical Geography of the Holy Land*: a nod of acknowledgement to the *Annalistes* and other geographically informed historians. Later chapters evaluate Finley's *The World of Odysseus*, Muhsin Mahdi's *Ibn Khaldoun's Philosophy of History*, Charles Boxer's study of Jesuit proselytizing in Japan, *The Letters of Peter Paul Rubens*, Michael Roberts's biography of the Swedish monarch Gustavus Adolphus, and assessments of Clarendon, Macaulay, Burckhardt and Marx as historians.[60]

The scholarly masterpieces of Trevor-Roper's time were, he thought, mostly the work of expatriates or foreign illuminati. After staying for three days in Brenan's Málaga cottage in 1954 he wrote: 'I venerate him more, I think, than any other scholar-writer, or at least among English writers.' He extolled Henri Pirenne for using 'antiquarian exactitude in the service of historical generalization – a gift which seems to me the real test of a historian, or at least of a historian's historian'. The works of Émile Mâle were 'wonderful' in illuminating human motives. Giorgio de Santillana, classical scholar and historian of scientific ideas, had imagination as well as erudition: 'Whatever problem he faces in the long history of human ideas, he never sees it in isolation. He sees it as a moment in an unending process; and he sees the process too.' Fernand Braudel's *La Méditerranée et le monde méditerranéen à l'époque de Philippe II* seemed to him 'the greatest work on the 16th century produced in my memory', as he told Berenson. 'Only the French can write history: Marc Bloch and his disciples have made all the other historians seem trivial.' He extolled the *Annales* School in France, attended their seminars in Paris, attempted a rapprochement between English and French historians and laid plans for a historical research institute in Oxford following the French model. It was at Roland Mousnier's suggestion that he turned to the study of witchcraft. He urged the young John Elliott to read François Simiand, and Werner Sombart too. Trevor-Roper had barely heard of Burckhardt until Berenson recommended him in 1949. In the next few years he read, 'with ever-increasing admiration', all of Burckhardt's published work. He promoted Burckhardt, who was almost unknown to English readers, as 'one of the profoundest of historians', and truly prophetic, for warning that the overthrow of the French monarchy after 1789 had created two alternative forms of European government, Caesarism or revolutionary radicalism, both born 'out of the blind assent of the masses, a hideous ideological tyranny'.[61]

Trevor-Roper gave the kernel of Burckhardt's historical philosophy in his preface to a volume of the Swiss scholar's lecture notes: 'It is, fundamentally, that human civilization, which he valued so highly for its variety and creative strength, is in reality a delicate, precarious thing which only an educated ruling class can effectively protect against the revolt of the masses with their numerical strength, their materialism, their indifference to liberty, their readiness to yield to demagogic power.' This was close to the message of Rostovtzeff, which Trevor-Roper also endorsed. Burckhardt, he continued, dismissed the nineteenth-century doctrine of infinite progress as 'unwarranted, immature, half-baked: not an idea but a parrot-cry'. If Burckhardt was 'unreasonably timid' about popular enthusiasm, which he depicted always as an emanation of 'the blind, undifferentiated, resentful, brutalized, impersonal mob', it was not, wrote Trevor-Roper, because he was afraid of material loss: 'it was fear of a renewal of barbarism through social discontinuity'. Burckhardt strove to conserve whatever had existing value. He grieved when ideals, objectives and works of art or imagination were discarded or doctored in the hope of obtaining some marginal or temporary advantage. 'Experience teaches us', Trevor-Roper quoted him as saying, 'that the human race has over the ages achieved very little of supreme excellence, and will do no better in the future; we may well mourn when things of excellence are destroyed.'[62]

Pirenne and Mâle, Burckhardt and Bloch, Clarendon and Gibbon knew themselves to be under the ineradicable influences of the literature and ideas of ancient Greece and Rome. So, too, did Trevor-Roper. He gave a heartfelt profession of his intellectual creed in his presidential address to the Joint Association of Classical Teachers in 1973. 'The study of history is not merely of politics but of civilization; and since literature and society are so closely and indeed essentially interwoven, a study of history which ignores literature must be completely inadequate,' he declared.

> How can anyone understand a society who does not read its literature? The professional historian goes back to the original documents: the documents of state. But what documents are more original than the art and literature of any people, the still living documents of society? Historical writing which is not nourished from such sources is dry and dead – as most academic theses, and most textbooks, too dismally testify. To study Elizabethan England without reading Shakespeare, or Puritan England without reading Milton, or Restoration England without reading Dryden – the idea is to me grotesque. All great historians have been students of literature too; for, as a great living French historian [Braudel] writes, art and literature are the true witnesses of all history that it is worth our time to study.[63]

The human mind mattered to Trevor-Roper: even the human mind at its worst. In 1951, during the same weeks that he read Bataillon's study of Erasmus in Spain, Trevor-Roper studied the German edition of Hitler's *Tischgespräche* ('Table talk'). 'The vulgarity of his mind is dreadful,' he told Berenson; 'but the fashionable view that he was a pure charlatan, only accidentally placed in a position of absolute power, seems to me not only wrong but, by its inevitable political consequences, disastrous. Whoever, from nothing, acquired absolute power, & kept it, by accident?' He shared Namier's 'anguished conviction', expressed in 1947, 'that Hitler, Goebbels, and Streicher, the Third Reich with its doctrines, powers, and conquests, its torture-chambers, death-trains, and vivisection practised on human beings, may not have been a gruesome accident or a gruesome aberration', but the planned outcome of human minds. When, in 1952, Trevor-Roper hailed Bullock's biography of Hitler as 'masterly', he added a rider that Bullock knew how to find facts, how to test and present them, but seemed less interested in ideas.[64]

He developed this argument in the prefatory essay, 'The Mind of Adolf Hitler', which he contributed to the English edition of *Hitler's Table Talk* published by the rising house of Weidenfeld & Nicolson in 1953. He maintained that Hitler was not 'a mere illiterate, illogical, unsystematic bluffer and smatterer'. The Führer's lust for dominion was served by a system of thought which should be no less important to the critical historian than the mentalities of Bismarck or Lenin. Certainly, Hitler's thinking was 'coarse, turbid, narrow, rigid, cruel', and obsessed by historical cataclysms, but it was directed at the basic questions of history and politics, revolution and ideology, strategy and power.[65]

Trevor-Roper was not displeased when contemporaries joined issue with this view and provoked him to reassert it. 'Combat', says Worden, 'upheld his spirits.' His displeasure was aroused instead by people, especially members of his university, who were afraid of thinking or seemed to devalue the intellect. Tom Boase, the art historian President of Magdalen, was condemned by him in 1954 as 'a smooth, urbane, cultivated, civilised man of the world, who, underneath his polished surface, is intellectually empty'. Boase was not ignorant, for he had written learned books: 'He merely can't *think* very hard!' Similarly, his objection to Rowse's books was 'their positive fear of profundity', as he wrote in 1955. 'He faces no problems, plumbs no causes, is ostentatiously content with quick, sharp, trite judgments.' There was in Rowse a 'harsh persistent flavour of intellectual nihilism' which kept him from greatness as an historian. The teaching in Oxford of classical literature, and of medieval and modern European languages (including English), was 'dangerously' anti-intellectual because of its excessive concentration on texts, he warned. 'It can lead too easily to conservatism of the spirit, to pedantry – or, alternatively, to that opposite refuge from pedantry, which is triviality.' Indeed, 'All occupations have their diseases, and this, I believe, is the occupational disease of the student of literature: it makes a man frightened of thought.'[66]

Pedantry and triviality were descried by Trevor-Roper in other Oxford faculties. His friendship with Ryle, which must have been impaired by the Flew affair in 1950, shrivelled away in the harsh glare of his contempt for the Oxford exponents of linguistic philosophy. He was exasperated by 'their esoteric triviality, their mumbo-jumbo (Logical Positivism at least was *clear*!), and, in many cases, their personal and intellectual silliness, which is particularly obvious if one lives among them', as he told the sociologist and anthropologist Ernest Gellner. Overspecialization was to blame. 'Like the Jesuits and the Communists,' he wrote of Oxford's linguistic philosophers, 'they have now created such an army of themselves that they can all build themselves up by learnedly quoting each other. Criticism from outside, from those who haven't mastered their private language, they, like all initiates, naturally despise.' In 1959 he persuaded the books editor of the *Sunday Times* to let him review Gellner's attack on linguistic philosophy, *Words and Things*. 'Mr Gellner is out to kill,' Trevor-Roper said by way of praise before joining in the massacre. Plato, Aristotle, Descartes, Hume, Hegel, Marx thought that philosophy meant understanding, even changing, the world. They wrote for laymen because they recognized that philosophy affected politics, history, religion, science. By contrast, linguistic philosophers, like medieval schoolmen, wrote for each other, in jargon that excluded laymen. Certainly, they seemed more parochial than the logical positivists of Vienna or the existentialists of Paris. Trevor-Roper endorsed the pith of Gellner's attack on linguistic philosophy: 'The minuteness, pedantry, lack of obvious purpose, in brief, the notorious triviality of these discussions, or many of them, can only be explained in Veblenesque terms. Conspicuous Triviality is a kind of Conspicuous Waste.'[67]

The rancour aroused by *Words and Things* provoked an editorial in *The Times* and acidulous exchanges in its correspondence pages. The only recent comparable commotion among dons had been raised by 'the Gentry controversy' in which Trevor-Roper ranged himself against Tawney and Lawrence Stone in 1951–7. Both his motives in this dispute and the personal cost to him have been misunderstood or overlooked. Coupled with his praise of Namier, this episode damaged his prospects in the Modern History Faculty of mid-twentieth-century Oxford.

In 1941 Tawney had published in the *Economic History Review* a thought-provoking *ballon d'essai* entitled 'The Rise of the Gentry, 1558–1640'. This article, which was composed under wartime conditions and might have been revised by its author in other circumstances, argued that the economic and political power of the aristocracy declined during Elizabeth's reign. 'The Rise of the Gentry' was read with eagerness and respect by many young scholars, including two of Masterman's most erudite students, Lawrence Stone and Trevor-Roper.

Stone had begun to read modern history at Christ Church in 1938, four years after Trevor-Roper transferred to that school. His studies were suspended in 1940, but completed after war service. In 1947 he obtained his first academic job as a lecturer in modern history at University College, Oxford. Stone was 'one of the most buoyantly invigorating figures in the contemporary historical scene', as Keith Thomas wrote a quarter of a century later. He possessed 'a striking capacity for synthesis, and an ability to write vivid, continuously interesting prose'. His work exhibited, Thomas continued, 'carelessness about details, a tendency to exaggerate, and an eagerness to push recalcitrant facts into unduly schematic categories'. The carelessness was inevitable given Stone's attitude to primary sources. 'When you work in the archives,' he later said, 'you're far from home, you're bored, you're in a hurry, you're scribbling like crazy. You're bound to make mistakes. I don't believe any scholar in the Western world has impeccable footnotes. Archival research is a special case of the general messiness of life.'[68]

In the late 1940s Trevor-Roper began to assemble a book, which he never completed, on four millionaires whose enterprises would, he thought, illustrate the social and economic forces at work in the period covered by Tawney's article. The moneylender Thomas Sutton, who had founded Charterhouse, was set to be one of them. Trevor-Roper lent Stone, as a fellow Carthusian, his notes on documents concerning Sutton that he had found in the Public Record Office.

Stone next consulted the archival material on which these notes were based, and on the basis of this and other sources, published an article 'The Anatomy of the Elizabethan Aristocracy' in the *Economic History Review* of 1948. He went much further than Tawney in arguing that the Elizabethan peerage was teetering on the brink of bankruptcy.

Some scholars were wary of Stone's 'Anatomy' from the outset. Conyers Read, President of the American Historical Association in 1949–50, felt 'great distress' at its categorical tone and unreliability. 'Of course,' said J. E. Neale (whom Trevor-Roper ranked as the greatest living authority on Elizabethan England), 'Stone's article should never have been published, and it would not have got past an editor like A. L. Poole, or Pollard.' The article had been submitted to the journal's co-editor Michael ('Munia') Postan, a Cambridge medievalist who was then engaged on writing a Whitehall history of *British War Production*. Postan combined 'not merely great knowledge and mental power but a very rare unselfishness', in the words of Sir Keith Hancock. Apparently, he did not consult any scholarly referees about the text of Stone's 'Anatomy'. He later admitted to his co-editor H. J. Habbakuk that he regretted sending Stone's unamended text to the printers 'without remitting it to him for revision', especially as he had 'misgivings' about Stone's handling of some statistics. Tawney held the presidency of the Economic History Society, which published the quarterly journal, and had been 'very insistent' on publication, Postan said, 'and I regard myself as a babe in 16th century matters'.[69]

Initially Trevor-Roper did not share the misgivings of Neale and Read. He praised the article's excellence both to its author and to Oxford friends. In the winter of 1949–50, he was glad to act as Stone's referee in a successful application to succeed Deakin as a Fellow and tutor in modern history at Wadham. But he also began to check Stone's citations of PRO manuscript sources and printed sources after noticing 'gigantic statistical errors' in the article. He found discrepancies which were not, he decided, the product of 'haste and inexperience but deliberate falsification on a shocking scale'. This poisoning of the wells of truth was a capital offence: he resolved, as he told the American scholar Wallace Notestein, 'to liquidate Stone'. He undertook his task of annihilation for the same motives and in the same spirit as his biography of the fantasist Sinologue Sir Edmund Backhouse or his lampoon, which the *Sunday Times* did not dare to publish, of the mendacious letters of Harold Laski. In all these cases, equally for Stone, Laski and Backhouse, the former head of the wartime Radio Security Service was determined by fierce scrutiny and persevering analysis to expose errors, misdirection and falsehood. The aspersion that Trevor-Roper began a campaign of jealous retribution against Stone because he was galled by the younger man's publishing success, or felt afflicted by some meagreness in his own *curriculum vitae*, is unworthy.[70]

'I think the truth matters,' Trevor-Roper told Harrod after publication of his Stone article. 'If people write for other purposes they must take the risk therein entailed.' He might have 'exposed the wretch earlier, but as long as he had no job I thought the effect might be ruinous to him'. Once Stone was secure in Wadham, he shed his compunctions. 'His article has by now become the doctrine of the Schools and is quoted in printed works as canonical. It was given pride of place dominating the whole issue of the *Economic History Review* which contained it; and on the strength of it Stone was put onto the Economic History Council.' Stone's candidature had even been mooted when Hancock vacated the Chichele chair in economic history. 'For these general reasons I judged that the bubble had to be pricked,' he told Harrod. There was also a more particular motive: 'I am writing a book which will include, from the same evidence, conclusions so different from those of Stone that questions would have been asked unless the controversy were first disposed of.'[71]

Trevor-Roper pursued truth as an absolute good, without ulterior purpose. Falsification riled him. The side to his character that liked to dent the authority of Regius professors also liked to build the confidence of the young. His generosity to doctoral students – John Elliott, Alan Macfarlane, Felix Raab, John Robertson, Blair Worden – is well attested. He regaled them with irreverent talk, made indiscreet confidences, gave mischievous accounts of university vicissitudes and spoke with disinfectant irony of the traditions, methods and personal myths of fellow historians in Oxford and elsewhere. He loved eager mental ferment when it was purposive and disciplined; felt refreshed and vitalized by the best young scholars; was seldom too busy to see them; felt no edge of grievance when they published. 'The past to Raab was always living, always modern: ideas were ideas, of whatever date,' Trevor-Roper wrote of one of his star pupils. 'Always he would come with work in his hand, and ideas in his head.' Raab's written work was well planned and punctually executed. 'But his efficiency was never mechanical: it was always accompanied and enlivened by the ideas which had inspired it, or had emerged from it, and which still hovered around it, demanding.'[72]

It was not envy of a younger man that incited Trevor-Roper to furious work in the autumn of 1950, 'scribbling away, night and day, deleting in the evening all that I have written in the morning, in the usual manner of authors, emptying inkpots and filling waste-paper baskets'. He circulated drafts and consulted colleagues before sending the final text, which was entitled 'The Elizabethan Aristocracy: An Anatomy Anatomized', to Postan. His article, in a phrase, disproved the thesis that the English gentry rose on the profits of the land and at the expense of the nobility, and discredited both the evidence and the inferences in Stone's article. 'I have received from Trevor-Roper an article containing a very damaging refutation of your article on the Elizabethan aristocracy,' Postan wrote to Stone on 2 November. 'Editorial ethics compel me to publish it and prevent me from even showing it to you before publication, but I am trying to do all I can to get the rudeness out of it.' The haggling over Trevor-Roper's eviscerating phrases continued for some months.[73]

In March 1951, when publication of 'The Elizabethan Aristocracy' was imminent, Woodward resigned the chair of modern history. He chafed at the conditions of post-war Oxford and wished to give his wife, who had recently survived major surgery, the recuperative experience of life at Princeton. The scramble to succeed him became, he thought, unseemly. Taylor and Trevor-Roper, as he wrote, 'left no stone unturned to get my chair when I resigned, and each thinks himself badly treated by the electors – hence T-R's indirect kicks at G. N. Clark, Galbraith & other senior Oxford historians!' Woodward had been an early mentor to Taylor, who had repaid him with an anonymous but readily ascribable attack on his work in the TLS. Taylor and Trevor-Roper, with their broadcasting and journalism, made Woodward feel 'uneasy' about the Oxford History School. 'There is too much clever and unscrupulous "push", and too much flashy plausibility in it at present. This wasn't so in the days of Firth, Barker, Fisher, Davis, etc. However, these pushers tend to devour one another, and behind them there is another group of much healthier-minded men.'[74]

Taylor aside, there was a broad field of candidates. Alfred Cobban and Albert Goodwin, then Vice-Principal of Jesus College, were both historians of the French revolutions of more or less liveliness. William Medlicott, Max Beloff and Ernest Passant had assembled and edited diplomatic documents: those anthologies of information, without critical intelligence, which were the twentieth-century equivalent of medieval annals. In contrast to these men, who specialized in short historical periods in particular realms, Trevor-Roper preferred to study recurrent historical problems, in different centuries and involving different nationalities. He presented himself to Masterman, Provost of Worcester College, to which the chair was attached, as the clarion of the Christ Church band that included Blake and Stuart. 'We view with apprehension', he told his former tutor, 'the tendency in the History School at present towards narrow specialisation within single centuries. This creates an artificial division between medieval and modern studies, and reduces research to disconnected fragments, at least in the modern field.'[75]

Of the seven electors for the chair, three were committed to Trevor-Roper: Masterman, Feiling and H. V. F. Somerset, who was Fellow in modern history at Worcester. Somerset had published nothing but a small book of his juvenile epigrams a quarter of a century earlier, cared little for history and everything for music. Dean Lowe of Christ Church, who was in his final months as Vice-Chancellor of the university, was considered to be a neutral voice. The three hostile electors were Galbraith, Sir G. N. Clark, Provost of Galbraith's college Oriel, who told Rowse that *Archbishop Laud* was 'a dud book' which had skimped the religious faith at the heart of the primate's being, and Austin Lane Poole, the dipsomaniac President of St John's, who considered Trevor-Roper's part in Flew's failure to obtain a studentship of Christ Church to be unforgivable. 'Like every good medievalist I have ever known,' Galbraith wrote in a fulsome appreciation of Poole, 'he was an out-and-out conservative, regretting the necessity for change, and anxious to reduce it to a minimum.' Poole's scholarship was solemn and specialist: Trevor-Roper's dispersed and novel interests were anathema to him.[76]

The publication of Trevor-Roper's article marked the outbreak of the 'gentry controversy' which raged through the 1950s among historians in Oxford and elsewhere. It developed from a bout of 'donnish fisticuffs' in 1951 to a full-scale 'academic slaughter-fest' a few years later. This description comes from the great historian of late antiquity Peter Brown, who thought all of the disputants underrated the power of religious thought and overrated socio-economic factors. It was easier, he says, 'to count manors and to tot up mortgages than to read sermons'.[77]

After the first and inconclusive meeting of electors, in early May, Feiling hastened to All Souls, where he asked for a copy of the latest issue of the *Economic History Review* containing 'The Elizabethan Aristocracy'. Dean Lowe did the same at Christ Church Library. 'From this evidence,' Trevor-Roper deduced, 'it seems clear that the two parties are locked in indissoluble engagement over my candidature, and have only separated in order to read my article on Stone, which, no doubt, has been praised as intellectually cogent by my referee, J. E. Neale, and denounced as morally reprehensible by Galbraith.' Trevor-Roper doubted that deadlock would be breached by the electors reading his article, 'for who, in politics, has ever been converted by argument or reason or even facts?' He spoke of slaying the Regius Professor as recently he had spoken of liquidating Stone. 'If I could advance into that chair over the dead body of Galbraith, what heaven it would be! The journey to the chair would then be infinitely sweeter than the mere occupation of it, and I should linger and dawdle on the way to savour its sweetness.'[78]

For two months Galbraith and Poole insisted that the language of 'The Elizabethan Aristocracy' was unpardonable and Trevor-Roper unfit for the chair. Lowe and Feiling writhed at the continuing demands for their hard-pressed time. Somerset quietened the jarring din of the electoral meetings by playing harmonies in his head. In June Masterman sought the advice of Neale (Namier's 'only peer in scholarship', as Trevor-Roper called him). Had Trevor-Roper gone too far in 'crushing' a fellow historian? Did Neale consider that Stone deserved such condign criticism, 'and that in the interests of truth it was desirable that Trevor-Roper should expose the mistakes which he had made?'[79]

'It would be a grave injustice to regard Trevor-Roper's article as in a way a disqualification for the Chair,' Neale replied. 'Even more important, it would be a serious disservice to scholarship.' Stone's article had only been published because of the laxity of Postan. 'Once published, its interest, lucidity and appearance of scholarship gave it a weight with all but a few specialists that disturbed me (as it disturbed Conyers Read in America) and made me consider, long before I heard about Trevor-Roper's answer, that in the interests of truth and scholarship its methods and inaccuracies called for public criticism.' Neale had been 'shocked' by Stone's work, 'not only because of the extraordinary ignorance it displayed, but because when one looked up his footnote references they so often did not bear out his statements. I felt that there was an egregious lack of integrity.' Richard Pares and other fine minds had been duped. Trevor-Roper had not exaggerated the faults in Stone's scholarship. The great historians of a previous generation, Thomas Tout and Albert Pollard, both of whom were known for their irritable roughness with incompetents and mountebanks, would, wrote Neale, 'have dealt much more drastically with a similar article in their day'.[80]

Early in July the electors finally settled on a compromise candidate, Bruce Wernham, a modest, likeable and unproductive scholar whose official history of RAF Bomber Command was never published. 'I am of course very disappointed: it is no good pretending that I didn't want it very much – I did,' Trevor-Roper admitted to Masterman. 'An Oxford chair seems to me the only chance of being able to do the work I want to do.' As to Galbraith's animosity, 'I can only say that he has never spoken to me, never recognised me, never shown the least interest in my work; so I simply don't know why he has denounced me so violently, even, beyond their patience, to my closest friends.'[81]

Trevor-Roper had many consolatory letters from colleagues in his college together with a letter from one Student who was intent on wounding. Dundas supposed that he must be 'angry' at being bested by a candidate who was far from brilliant: to outsiders, he continued, 'it does seem shocking that learned persons who don't like you should vote against you *for that reason*, for I can imagine no other'.

There was deadly truth in Dundas's remark.[82]

In an attempt to rally from this reverse, Trevor-Roper applied in 1956 to give the next year's six Ford lectures. He proposed Anglo-Spanish relations 1604–60 as his subject, and intended to parallel Geyl's work. Appointment as Ford lecturer was one of the highest distinctions that the University of Oxford could confer on historians: it was little surprise that Galbraith duly mustered the medievalists on the Board of Electors to reject his application. Woodward was appointed instead, but when he asked for the timing of the lectures to be altered to accommodate his annual pilgrimage to Princeton, Charles Stuart and the Party of Gaiety successfully defeated this reasonable proposal. Trevor-Roper was on the shortlist of five candidates to replace Woodward, but was again bested by the medievalists. 'After a tremendous struggle,' as he reported in 1957, 'in the course of which Galbraith twice left the room in clownish dudgeon, the board compromised on Norman Sykes, a boring Cambridge clergyman.' Trevor-Roper's ideas and conclusions about seventeenth-century Spain 'sadly remained unwritten', as John Elliott recalled. 'The world was thus deprived of what surely would have been a scintillating survey.' A little of this shine can be found, though, in the vivid and perceptive chapter 'Spain and Europe, 1598–1621', which Trevor-Roper wrote in the 1960s for the New Cambridge Modern History.[83]

The mustered opposition of medievalists to Trevor-Roper aroused modernists to press his claims to the Regius chair as the year of Galbraith's statutory retirement approached. 'There is a dearth of good candidates for the Regius Chair – that is of candidates of the right age, academic stature and authority . . . both inside and outside Oxford,' Asa Briggs told Masterman in 1956. 'By far the most impressive candidate, I would say, is Hugh Trevor-Roper. He has an acute analytical power and a commanding historical knowledge: he has chosen to write rather than to keep silent, and what he has written is of the highest quality.' The School of Modern History needed a historian who had competence in European as well as British history if it was to maintain its status among the Oxford disciplines. Southern of Balliol and Bruce McFarlane of Magdalen were both too narrow, Briggs said. Taylor was disqualified by his 'academic irresponsibility, [and] the irresistible tendency to make the bright rather than the considered judgment'.[84]

While soundings were being taken, after the installation of Masterman as Vice-Chancellor and Trevor-Roper's publisher Harold Macmillan as Prime Minister, Berlin was elected to the Chichele chair of social and political theory in March 1957. Replying to Trevor-Roper's congratulations Berlin wrote of his relief that the tension was over, but also of his depression. '*Why* should I have so eagerly stuck my head into a noose that every professorship necessarily is? with the duty to revive a moribund subject? and all those teeming American & Nigerian & Indian graduates?' He felt pleased to have been elected instead of Oriel's candidate, John ('Jack') Gough, a busy, dutiful college man. By besting Gough he had foiled, as he explained in an exuberant stream of consciousness,

> a whole generation of pre-1914 Balliol worthies – G. N. Clark – Sumner, Toynbee, actual & assimilated Wykehamists – who include Woodward & Sumner's Epigoni, Christopher Hill, Hancock, & other non-conformist fanatics, who find me instinctively distasteful: They dominated Oxford in the thirties, and are now on the way out: . . . piously atheistical persons[,] solemn, self-conscious, inferiority-ridden, and deeply resentful of almost all forms of spontaneity & life. I cd not bear them: the mixture of secularised protestant sentimentality, tame public school 'leftism', and appalling priggishness created an air in which I suffocated much more quickly than the wildest excesses of Conservatism or Communism: on the whole it was Asquith worshipping, naturally more at home in Germany than in France, pro-Arab & conscientiously anti-anti-semitic, excited by pseudo-revolté figures like Rowse or Crossman, and deeply craven and empty aside. Sir G. Clark is . . . particularly characteristic: & to be elected to anything in his teeth is almost a duty for those who oppose necrophily in academic life.[85]

Trevor-Roper replied in agreement with all that Berlin had written about the 'academic necrophily' of 'pseudo-Wykehamists'.

> It may be that we shall live in vain; but let us at least try, by the time that Black Death unwraps us in his soporific mist, to have

ruined *them* in Oxford! The more I think of professorial chairs, the less I want to fill them; but if we – i.e. people who think as we do – can fill them *all*, then perhaps, though at our own expense, we shall do something to expel from Oxford this grim, timid, meaningless, virtuous spirit which has extinguished life for so long in the place.

As he enjoyed teaching his Christ Church pupils and valued the college's amenities, he dreaded his obligatory move to Oriel if appointed to the Regius chair. 'But if it is offered to me, I shall take it, much as a prosperous business man accepts an ill-paid and wearisome ministry of state: for the sake of the status, the power, the social advance, and, above all, *doing down the rival claimant!*' Downing Street now understood, he continued, 'that the fanatical opposition of Galbraith and his miserable army of poisonous-toothed mice is utterly unrepresentative' of Oxford feeling. Macmillan intended to intervene in Crown appointments because he thought it was important that the universities were led by sound men. The recent choice of a new Provost for King's College, Cambridge had been 'disastrous', Trevor-Roper reported Macmillan as saying: 'that fellow Noël Annan will be there for 30 years: he doesn't believe in God & will corrupt all the Etonians who go to King's'.[86]

There was one doubt. Following Geyl's example, Trevor-Roper had written an essay condemning Toynbee, which had been accepted for publication in the monthly magazine *Encounter*. Blake and Stuart, recalling that his attack on Stone had been used to baffle his candidature in 1951, insisted that it would be fatal to publish the piece before the Regius chair had been allocated. 'What, oh what shall I do?' Trevor-Roper mock-wailed to Berlin. 'It is *very* wicked, but documented and (I am sure) true. It will cause great pain – but to those to whom we *want* to cause pain.' The article, entitled 'Arnold Toynbee's Millennium', caused all the pain that its author wanted when published by *Encounter* a few days after Trevor-Roper's appointment to the Regius chair was announced in June 1957. Toynbee's 'huge, presumptuous, and utterly humourless work' was 'not merely erroneous . . . but hateful', he wrote. 'For Toynbee does not only utter false arguments and dogmatic statements, calling them "scientific" and "empirical"; he does not only preach a gospel of deliberate obscurantism; he seems to undermine our will, welcome our defeat, gloat over the extinction of our civilization, not because he supports the form of civilization that threatens us, but because he is animated by what we can only call a masochistic desire to be conquered.' When the article was recycled in *Encounter*'s German sister-magazine *Der Monat*, it was prefixed, as Trevor-Roper told Geyl, by 'an extraordinarily sanctimonious statement saying that whereas they deplored such an article, they nevertheless, out of their sense of public duty, thought it necessary to show their readers what was . . . exciting controversy abroad'.[87]

Trevor-Roper's inaugural lecture, delivered in November 1957, remains a joy to read: rich in playful irony, perfectly proportioned, inspiring and with a long perspective. It presents history as a humane subject: 'the study not of circumstances, but of man in circumstances'. The humanities exist to enlarge the comprehension of the laity, to make telling contrasts and to trace hidden affinities; and if they lose touch with the lay mind, they deserve to perish. In this respect the humanities are antithetical to sciences, which require onerously trained professionals to converse with one another in language of technical exactitude. Oxford historians should be useful and provocative scholars, providing a general education for their students and enlivening their teaching by controversy rather than mortifying their subject with overspecialization – that deplorable 'private expertise which carries the details of a subject progressively farther away from lay comprehension'. Trevor-Roper applauded pure, concentrated research, which could lead to bold, questing new ideas, but decried niggling expertise. 'I should like to think that in our historical research at Oxford we might pay a little more attention to fertile error, even at the expense of our zeal for unimportant truth.' He wanted an expansive interdisciplinary approach rather than narrowing compartmentalization. Modern history, he said, should be inconceivable 'without the contributions of economists like Adam Smith, Simiand, and Keynes, sociologists like Marx, Weber, and Sombart, philosophers like Hume and Hegel, scholars of culture and art-history like Burckhardt and Mâle, even anthropologists and psychologists like Frazer and Freud'. Historical scholarship was most fertile when rooted in the anxieties and distress of the years in which it was researched, drafted and revised.

'The greatest professional historians of our century – a Bloch, a Rostovtzeff, a Namier – have always been those who have applied to historical study not merely the exact, professional discipline they have learned within it but also the sciences, the hypotheses, the human interests which – however intermixed with human error – have been brought into it by the lay world outside.'[88]

Trevor-Roper sent a heartfelt message to his audience, some of them the 'intelligentsia-without-ideas' from North Oxford, by naming his trio of greatest twentieth-century historians: Rostovtzeff born in the Ukraine, who had been required to prove that he was neither Jewish nor a communist before gaining an academic post at the University of Wisconsin, Bloch born in Lyon, and Namier in Poland; two of them refugees from the Soviet system, two of them secular Jews who affirmed their ancestral identities in the face of persecution. Bloch – tortured by the Gestapo, and shot by a firing squad – is commemorated on his gravestone with the epitaph of his choice: *dilexi veritatem* – I have loved the truth.

CHAPTER 12

Robert Blake: The Busy Hum of Rumour and Intrigue

In 1969 Enoch Powell, the incendiary spokesman of backstreet anger, visited Oxford to address the Oxford University Conservative Association. OUCA's President, Stephen Milligan, who was reading PPE at Magdalen and was later to be elected as an MP, had advocated latitude in immigration policy when addressing a recent Conservative party conference. The distance between Powell and Milligan, within the Conservative party, prompted a thoughtful article in *The Times* by Robert Jackson, who was also later a Conservative MP. Following the study of backbench opinion by his All Souls colleague Samuel Finer, Jackson depicted Oxford-trained Conservatives – the cohort of opinion that Feiling had marshalled in the thirty years before his retirement in 1950 – as predominantly internationalist and pro-European, libertarian in their approach to social policy, chary of economic regulation, less punitive in penal matters and less attached to the Commonwealth than the rest of the party. The attitudes of those who went to Oxford after 1950 and began to rise in the Conservative party during the 1960s were little different, said Jackson:

> Conservatives at Oxford like to think of themselves as detached, sophisticated, and internationally minded. Many of them are conscious of an aristocratic Conservative tradition in which Christ Church counts for at least as much as Nuffield, and rather more than Balliol. They maintain that they are more interested in the method of politics than in the formulation of policy: they learn

Parliamentary manners at the Union and intrigue in the OUCA caucuses.

The inflation, deflation and revival of individual reputations, the drifts of party sentiment and the tactical uses of particular issues to advance the party's general standing were the stuff of Oxford's young Conservative activists. The play of personalities interested them more than such topics as new technological innovation or monetary policy. Their thinking, said Jackson, 'is suffused with an historical awareness, and their pundits are not economists but historians like Mr Robert Blake'.[1]

Blake had taken Feiling's mantle as a mentor of undergraduate caucus politicians. He taught that politics is the art of the piecemeal. Political motives, allegiances and decisions are seldom as staunch and coherent as most politicians and some political historians wish to think. A pure motive was for Blake a barren theme. He relished the muddle of aspiration, foreboding, regret, benevolence, anger, craving for novelty, anxiety, insincerity, destructiveness, imbalance, egotism, ignorance, prejudice and spite that provide the mainsprings of political action. 'Drudgery, pretentious commonplace, dense prejudice, invincible dullness', Acton had written in 1890, 'make up the larger half of average politics.' Not so for Blake. Average politics for him, and for his Christ Church pupils, and for the readers of his books, was spirited, capricious, disorderly and never drab. Deviousness, he thought, is more interesting than simplicity. The political instincts to snatch and to spoil and to waste are ineradicable. Timely ideas or well-chosen catchphrases matter more to electors than a record of administrative efficiency. Blake agreed with Lord Hailsham, who was elected an Honorary Student of Christ Church in 1962, that there must be strong government, but preferably less of it. State intervention and official oversight may be obtrusive, inessential and misguided in many circumstances; but a robust state, with decisive and durable leadership, was essential for national defence, institutional stability, the maintenance of law and order and the preservation of the value of the currency.[2]

Blake recognized that university-trained activists had, by their policy planning, boosted the majority by which Labour won power in the general election of 1945. The authority of Laski, Cole and

Gordon Walker's fellow socialists from New College, the influence of Victor Gollancz's Left Book Club and the spur of Keynes and Beveridge, were crucial in the electoral surge that thrust Frank Pakenham from his studentship of Christ Church to ministerial office. Yet it was astonishing, Blake felt, how swiftly the intellectual fashion turned against socialism. By 1947–8, university Conservatism was attracting undergraduates and some younger dons. This revival, in which he was a central figure, received a fell blow, Blake thought, from the Suez humiliation of 1956. Feiling, indeed, resigned his membership of the party in protest at Eden's collusion with France and Israel.

Iain Macleod, Chairman of the Conservative party in the early 1960s, told Blake that the party lost university voters in the three general elections held between 1959 and 1966 because of Suez. It mattered little in the short term, Blake felt, that the universities bombinated against Eden's conduct. The party can win general elections, after all, without the prop and brace of professors. The word 'intelligentsia' bore the same relation to 'intelligent' as 'gent' does to 'gentleman', he said. Nevertheless, the difficulties in nourishing thoughtful Oxford Conservatism after 1956 contributed to the narrow defeat of the party in the election of 1964 and to its vanquishing in 1966.[3]

In the period from 1964, when Blake began to contribute a regular column on Westminster politics to the *Illustrated London News*, and especially after the publication of his biography of Disraeli in 1966, he gave intellectual sinews, strategical acumen and a philosophical continuity to the Conservative party leadership of Edward Heath. Robert Jackson identified him in 1969 as the pundit of reflective Conservatism. The political historian Kenneth Morgan, a Labour member of the House of Lords, praised him as the custodian of mid-twentieth-century Conservatism. In the aftermath of Suez, when almost no other academic historian found a proud or pleasant subject in the history of the Conservative party, Blake renewed and redefined that history both in his Ford lectures of 1968 and in scholarly, gracefully written and widely read biographies of prime ministers.[4]

Few people were interested to read Lord Coleraine's shrewd study of political convictions and leadership, *For Conservatives Only*, when it was published in 1970. It was not until 1976–7, when Ian Gilmour,

Victoria Rothschild and Dick White encouraged William Waldegrave to begin writing *The Binding of Leviathan: Conservatism and the Future*, that any member of Blake's dreaded intelligentsia resumed a searching, methodical and memorable interest in the political ideas and cultural basis of conservatism. Waldegrave argued that politicians who apply abstract principles to partisanship and policymaking are misusing their powers and misunderstanding the nature of state authority. The Conservative turn of mind was, wrote Waldegrave, 'never afraid of swift state action to relieve injustice or defend the weak; always afraid of fashionable theory and exclusive claims to truth; always aware of the reality of irrationality and Original Sin; always frightened of the dark side of the human psyche dressed up in political clothes, as Jacobinism, Bolshevism, Stalinism, Fascism or racism'. The preservation of authority, trust in tradition, hostility to dogma and fear of change were the four roots of Conservatism. All of this Blake had been teaching since he took Feiling's baton a quarter of a century earlier.[5]

Historically Blake was a Peelite, and in contemporary politics he was a wary adherent of Peel's twentieth-century counterpart Heath: both leaders had stubborn principles which nearly broke their party. He was on the fringe rather than at the core of the 'Heathmen' of 1966–74, but had sufficient standing to be gazetted, at Heath's recommendation, with a life peerage in 1971.[6]

Robert Blake was born in Norfolk in 1916. His paternal ancestry was Cornish: his grandfather was a tailor and outfitter in Truro; his father began his working life as the village schoolmaster at Kenwyn, and (after marrying the daughter of a Norwich solicitor) became senior history master at King Edward VI Grammar School in Norwich. His mother's family, which bore the surname of Daynes, was rooted in Norfolk. Patricia Waters, whom he married in 1953, was a Norfolk farmer's daughter. He retired to a converted coach house on the banks of the River Yare near Norwich, and died there. His attachment to Oxford never exceeded his pride in his native county and its county town. He resented the Conservative politician Duff Cooper taking the title of Norwich for his peerage in 1952.[7]

Blake was the only grammar school boy among the historians who are the subjects of this book; the only schoolmaster's son, too.

His father, indeed, was his history master at King Edward VI School. There was some thought of the boy trying for a King's Scholarship at Eton, but his father felt that the emphasis there on classics would not suit him. His uncle Norman Daynes, who had won a first in Greats at Magdalen in 1906 and became a county court judge, chose his nephew as his heir. He followed this uncle to Magdalen in 1935 on an Eldon law scholarship, but then determined to read PPE and gained first-class honours. The attitude to examination success had long been ambivalent at Magdalen. George Gordon, who became President of the college in 1928, was always depressed by examining schoolboys and undergraduates. 'The gross uniformity of it all – down to handwriting – is painful,' he told his wife. 'A boy from Jarrow should *not* do everything on paper in exactly the same way as a boy from Eastbourne or a boy from Hounslow. What is the *use* of breed and locality – those fine things – if he does?' Similarly, a sour Magdalen man, E. H. W. ('Eddie') Meyerstein, reckoned that Oxford examinations were a test to ascertain whether examinees had mastered 'a peculiarly political type of intellectual insincerity'.[8]

Gordon set a fine example to alert, clever and gregarious undergraduates such as Blake: 'a rare companion', recalled Sir Desmond MacCarthy, and as 'a talker animated, accurate, familiar (in the best sense), and direct'. Gordon and J. M. Thompson, who was Vice-President of the college in Blake's time, were attuned, as Blake became, to the process of historical change as a series of psychological shocks and losses. Progress, they felt, as often as not entails human devaluation and emotional coarsening. 'We lived on loyalties this age disowns,' Thompson wrote in 1940 of the college's Edwardian undergraduate generation.[9]

Magdalen's traditional indifference to standardized measurements of academic skills had been redressed in the college, since the 1920s, by Blake's tutor in philosophy T. D. ('Harry') Weldon. If Gordon gave Blake an instructive example of social leadership, it was Weldon who instilled in him the importance of both academic prowess and ruthless, prudential tactics in college meetings. Weldon, supremely, was a war-damaged man. In 1915, at the age of eighteen, he had begun four years' service as an artillery officer on the Western Front. There he was blasted, wounded, traumatized, decorated for his courage and knocked off-balance. Thereafter he chainsmoked through an ivory cigarette holder, sometimes soaked himself in whisky and suffered a nervous ailment which covered his face with red blotches. Gilbert Ryle thought that, for Weldon, the Armistice of 1918 represented a tunnel mouth through which he could not allow himself to look back. Certainly, in peacetime Oxford, Weldon sought tranquillity in a canalized life, in which the waters never overflowed. He was a Freemason who disliked the influence of clergymen, and a cynic who nevertheless upheld proprieties. His campaign to raise Magdalen's academic standing brought the philosopher J. L. Austin into fellowship at the college in 1935: Austin's biographer speaks of Weldon as 'a seasoned plotter and schemer'.[10]

Ryle judged Weldon to be a jovial rather than a happy man, who yearned to quell any echoes of the past in his mind. Weldon preferred tutoring to lecturing: nonchalant young men who struck sophisticated attitudes bored him; those with 'native fire in their bellies' had his appreciative attention. He believed that tutorial hours were best spent in demolition work. He wanted to shake and break the preconceptions of undergraduates, leaving them for a time lost in the rubble of their thinking, before goading them to build their mental city anew. He struck at their religious beliefs, at their conventional assumptions and at their immature certainties. 'In his expression of his views on affairs and policies – though seldom in his comments on persons – Weldon liked to sound callous,' Ryle recalled. 'There seemed to be something self-protective in his sedulous harshness of expression. It was as if he had to jeer in order to drown a very different voice that, for some reason, he could not bear to hear again.' This tone is not evident in Weldon's major work, his *Introduction to Kant's Critique of Pure Reason* (1945), but is manifest in his heartfelt book of 1946, *States and Morals,* and its successor, *The Vocabulary of Politics* (1953). Traces of Weldon's mentality pervade Blake's writings. There is little talk of fairness, good intentions, disinterested friendship, the benefits of consistency or of immutable standards in the political domain that Blake studied. The pace is set by contingency, imperfections, inadequacy, contradiction and urgency.[11]

In 1942–5, after Blake had left Magdalen, Weldon served at RAF Bomber Command in Buckinghamshire as personal staff officer to Air Marshal Sir Arthur Harris. He became a staunch admirer of Harris's ruthless, roughshod leadership, which earned him the nicknames among contemporaries of 'Butch' and, for posterity, 'Bomber'. After helping in the saturation bombing of German cities, Weldon returned each night to college, where he played post-prandial bridge by candlelight. He peppered *States and Morals* with allusions to bombing. 'How many lives is Cologne cathedral worth?' he would ask pupils. C. S. Lewis, his Magdalen colleague, thought him diabolical, and said that having seen through and demolished everything, he lived at rock bottom.[12]

Blake followed Weldon into Freemasonry. His elections as President of the junior common room of Magdalen and to member-ship of the exclusive Gridiron Club (Grid) were early signs of his sociability. He liked evenings of good talk and right-thinking. In middle age he became a stalwart of The Club, an Oxford fraternity (including Berlin, Bowra, Raymond Carr, Masterman and Trevor-Roper) who called one another 'Brother' and recruited new members with the covertness associated with enlistment in the Security Service. In London Blake joined two genial clubs: the Beefsteak, a sanctum lit by a large bay window overlooking the hurly-burly of Charing Cross Road, where members eat and talk with gusto at a single long table; and Pratt's, occupying a small house in St James's, run under the benevolent proprietorship of the Duke of Devonshire, where members dine hugger-mugger and boisterously. He did not persist in his membership of the Whiggish club Brooks's, where the staidness was said to resemble a ducal house in which the old duke was lying dead in a bed upstairs. Trevor-Roper described Blake in 1980 as 'enflamed with claret and port' after lunching at the Beefsteak when he intervened at a meeting of the British Academy disputing the fellowship of the art historian and Soviet spy Anthony Blunt. Blake's manipulation of the press and his menacing words during this episode marked a nadir in his academic career.[13]

After gaining first-class honours in PPE, Blake reverted to the study of law with the intention of following his uncle into practice at the Chancery bar. Following the declaration of war, Blake was offered work in the Security Service (MI5). He preferred, however, to enlist in a fighting regiment, the Royal Artillery, which was posted to the Middle East. In June 1942 he was captured by Italian troops: his first month as a prisoner-of-war, spent in a camp at Bari, he reckoned as the most hateful of his life. 'The humiliation, the squalor, the despair of being a prisoner, the heat, the revolting food, the sheer boredom, the indefinite prospective period of incarceration, all combined to produce a mood of black despondency, such as I have never experienced before or since,' Blake recorded in his unpublished memoirs.[14]

For fifteen months Blake was held captive at Chieti in the Abruzzi. While there he read the Bible, Shakespeare, Gibbon and Macaulay to keep himself from mental stupor. In the autumn of 1943, after escaping, he spent eighteen days in the rafters of a hut (an episode which gave him nightmares for the rest of his life) and lived on the run, during the winter of 1943–4, from wolves as much as from enemy pursuit. After finally reaching England, he needed six months' sick leave. Once his strength was regained he worked for the Security Service from October 1945 to April 1946. During these seven months he learnt to appreciate Lewis Namier's dictum that all secrets are already in print if you know where to look for them.[15]

At the prompting of Trevor-Roper and Charles Stuart, whom he had met while on secret service, he was brought to Christ Church in April 1946 to fill the vacant political lectureship created by Pakenham's departure to serve as a Labour government whip in the House of Lords. In 1947 he was confirmed as a Student. 'Robert is', Trevor-Roper wrote afterwards, 'a first-class hunter-bred beast: not one of your Pegasean, flashy, fidgety, incalculable, temperamental, prima-donna-ish thoroughbreds, all high speed, frayed nerves, and unpredictable excitability, but a sound, reliable, almost infallible hunter, guaranteed to perform with equal competence in every point-to-point for years.'[16]

In 1953 Blake married, and moved from his set of college rooms to a college house in Headington. Unfortunately, in his generation, Students were intolerant of each other's wives. Billa Harrod, Alexandra Trevor-Roper, Pamela Stuart and Patricia Blake cannot have been impervious to the felinity with which they were discussed: they must have felt as if they were being tested at college events, and marked down too. The discomfiting temper of college life indeed led Billa Harrod to leave Oxford and to make her homes in Campden Hill Square and Norfolk. Probably the men were unkinder than the women: but some wives became expert in acidulous condescension to others. This was, after all, an age when, as Blake noted in 1964, women were not the most successful Conservative candidates, 'because the majority of Conservative voters are women, and women do not like voting for their own sex'.[17]

The privations of college life in the years of rationing and socialist government were 'dismal', Blake recalled to Trevor-Roper in 1960. 'No food, precious little drink, a general hatred of fun and learning, morose bigots denouncing one at the slightest hint of gaiety, an appallingly large number of undergraduates, exiguous salaries, medieval dirt, squalor and discomfort.' Both men wanted the college to remember that it was rich, and to behave like a rich college. They disliked the penny-pinching of Dean Lowe, whom Blake regarded as a curmudgeon, believing neither in God nor in learning, gorging himself on bureaucratic paperwork. Blake and Trevor-Roper had scant respect for Oxford clergy, favoured the laicization of Christ Church and formed an anti-decanal faction within the governing body which voted against Lowe whenever reasonable. Although Lowe's health failed in 1952, he did not resign until 1959.[18]

Blake was not a relentless anti-clerical in Weldon's mould. He felt protective of the Church of England, as by law established. 'The young should always be brought up in the Established Faith,' he told Trevor-Roper in 1958. 'They can then have all the more fun in deviating from it later. Few figures are more pathetic than children conscientiously educated in virtuous agnostic principles.' The familiar description of the Church of England as the Conservative party at prayer lost its aptness in the 1950s. It was no longer possible, he noted in 1961, 'to combine Conservatism with a polite, rational, moderate – perhaps sceptical – above all non-proselytising and anti-clerical Anglicanism'. When he received a life peerage in 1971, he took the territorial designation of Braydeston, because he liked to attend services in its small hilltop church above the Yare valley. In 1977 he initiated a debate in the House of Lords regretting the diminution of Christian content and the 'mish-mash' of comparative religion given in the religious education of schoolchildren. The process was, he felt sure, a cultural impoverishment, and perhaps a source of political immorality.[19]

Blake, Trevor-Roper and Stuart set about promoting (in Blake's words) 'progress, sense, liberty and good living' in mid-twentieth-century Christ Church. They spread mischief too. 'Now that the season of Good Will on Earth and Peace towards Men – or whatever they say – is over,' he wrote to Trevor-Roper on New Year's Eve of 1962, 'I feel I can write to you. Who, I ask myself – and you – can we ruin next?' His answer was Brian Young, the Headmaster of Trevor-Roper's old school, Charterhouse, who had applied for the headmastership of Eton. The two men joined Masterman in convincing Eton's governors to appoint Anthony Chenevix-Trench, a Christ Church man who had achieved a brilliant first in Greats in 1947 and had returned as a tutor in classics there in 1951–2. Chenevix-Trench, who was an alcoholic thrasher of boys, proved to be a startling failure at Eton.[20]

When Blake succeeded Trevor-Roper as Senior Censor in 1953, Christ Church men were performing poorly in Greats, modern history, English, law and PPE. He thought the college had laxer standards of admission than Magdalen, New College and Balliol, and that Trevor-Roper had been susceptible to the surface charm of some young men. 'You cannot', he wrote in a post-mortem on the dismal finals results of 1956, 'make a silk purse out of a sow's ear – and there were some pretty tough and gristly (and deaf) old ears among that lot.' Standards of spelling, grammar, punctuation and intelligibility fell, he judged, among Christ Church undergraduates during his twenty-two years there. This long antedated the conversion of grammar schools into comprehensive schools, and in his opinion reflected a general slackness in post-war classroom teaching of literacy.[21]

There was an additional and specific administrative problem at Christ Church. The criteria for selection were inconsistent and disunified because the Senior Censor was in charge of picking each year's successful candidates, and that office changed hands every three years. Moreover, Senior Censors were too busy with other college business, which had grown insupportably onerous, to sift each year's entrance applications with sufficient attention. Subsequently, Blake supported the creation of a new post of Tutor for Admissions, and took a leading part in securing the appointment of Paul Kent, 'an enlightened and progressive Conservative' (he said), and the Reader in Chemistry. Kent was fit for a new age: he had been educated at Doncaster Grammar School, Birmingham University and Princeton, was an expert in carbohydrate chemistry and wrote two historical monographs, *Einstein in Oxford* and *History of Science at Christ Church*. An improved phase in Christ Church history began when Kent took the reins as Tutor for Admissions in 1965.[22]

Although Blake had no patience with slackers, he was sympathetic to able young men who flunked their finals. Thus, in 1952, he feared that Antony Acland's poor results would preclude him from joining the Foreign Office, to which he was eminently suited. After hasty remedial work, Acland qualified for a diplomatic career and rose to be Ambassador in Washington and Permanent Under Secretary of the FO. He was one of a generation of Christ Church PPE men – Robert Armstrong and Crispin Tickell were among the others – which provided lustrous national service in Whitehall. Blake was also set on jettisoning slothful youths who recurred on the lists of examination failures. In 1954 his recommendation to send down a 'clearly worthless man', who had repeatedly failed Responsions, was outvoted in the governing body after an intervention by Harrod. Afterwards he reproached Harrod for 'a regrettable surrender to sentimental emotionalism and moral blackmail, and a deplorable betrayal of the intellectual standards which a great institution like Christ Church ought to preserve'. He expected the Canon professors and the college chaplain Eric Mascall to be heedless of intellectual merit, but not Harrod.[23]

In 1959 Blake was installed as Senior Proctor of the university. His deputy, Marcus Dick, was an erratic and discontented Fellow and tutor in philosophy and politics at Balliol. The proctorship was an admirable apprenticeship for a man like Blake who wished to become a leading power-broker and wire-puller in the university, for proctors were required to attend every university committee so as to ensure that academic business was undertaken with efficiency and that major decisions were compatible with one another. Proctors also maintained university discipline: undergraduate magazines could not be published, nor universities clubs and societies started, without proctorial consent; rowdy infractions were punishable by the proctors too. Undergraduates in the 1950s had been children and adolescents during the world war and at the time of the atomic bombing of Japan. These chastening experiences had produced a prudent and pragmatic generation, in Dick's view. Mindful that their lives were subject to adventitious forces, they never made far-ahead plans. University was for them an interval in which to ready them-selves to adapt to whatever compulsions were imposed on them by world events. There was little rejoicing, little idealism and little cynicism among Oxford students of the 1950s. The ideal was to seem dispassionate and steady with an underlay of decorous oppor-tunism. Shoplifting in Blackwell's bookshop, requiring discreet moves and steely self-sufficiency, was the preferred delinquency of undergraduate rebels during Blake's proctorial time. Drugs, sex and Mao were too showy and febrile. [24]

Weldon once told Blake that, as Dean of Magdalen in 1928, he had rusticated John Betjeman and Alan Pryce-Jones, a future editor of the *Times Literary Supplement*, when their love affair became too open. Blake, like Weldon, was concerned to repress any public signs of impropriety. In 1962 he became indignant at the behaviour of 'fornicating teenagers of both sexes and every nationality, Scandinavians predominating', who had summer school bookings at Christ Church. For once he sympathized with Mascall, who had succeeded to Dundas's role as the college's querulous and prurient fusspot. Mascall complained to Dean Simpson that 'sported oaks', that is outer doors to college rooms which had been shut to casual visitors rather than left ajar, were a sure sign of fornication behind them. Simpson, a wise man who regarded Mascall as an irritant, countered that shut doors to college rooms could also be a sign of studious work in progress. 'Although there may indeed be some hard work practised by the young men,' Blake commented, 'it is not of the sort unconvincingly alleged by the Dean. From behind those decorously closed doors, so I am told, the noise of amorous squeaks and the creaking of college beds, which are ill designed for these lamentable purposes, makes it all too clear that the college has been turned into something little better than a bawdy house.'[25]

A decade later the insalubrious regime of celibate monasticism was moribund. In a Christ Church novel of the 1970s J. I. M. Stewart pictured the dons conversing about their motorcars and television sets as they dined at High Table, rather than performing yesteryear's arch pieces of characterful, exacting and perhaps malicious dialogue. Meanwhile, on the benches in the body of the hall, undergraduates discuss politics, vacation jobs, the need to skimp on their student grants, and (Stewart fancies) 'their lengthening sexual histories', which were no more, as in Dundas's day, 'exclusively of an old-fashioned auto-erotic order'.[26]

After the close of his proctorial term Blake contemplated leaving Oxford. In 1961 he applied for the vice-chancellorship of the University of East Anglia, which was then being built on a spacious campus at Norwich. Harrod, he suspected, was to blame for him being runner-up for the appointment. 'Roy has driven people almost insane by pressing my claims in and out of season upon everyone who has had anything to do with this,' he confided to Trevor-Roper. His lobbying 'has put up the backs of the neutrals and the waverers'.[27]

Five years later the acclaim of *Disraeli* established Blake as a public intellectual. When, in 1968, Lord Florey's death left the provostship of the Queen's College vacant, Alastair Parker, a Fellow and Director of Studies in modern history there, received a deft hint from his former Christ Church tutor Trevor-Roper. Given the national stature of the author of *Disraeli*, surely the Fellows of Queen's should choose him as Florey's successor. Blake took office as Provost in October 1968, and his shrewd geniality began to work its charm in a new college; but he ceased to be an historian in the House.

It seemed to Blake that the influence of Ayer, Ryle and other linguistic philosophers devalued the philosophical parts of Greats and PPE in Oxford. Semantic play and focus on 'category mistakes' had little use in the study of virtuous rulers, statecraft and sovereignty. But the School of PPE was not worth preserving if, as he believed should happen, the philosophical segment were dropped and the tripartite syllabus reduced to bipartite. In his view, politics tutors, if they were to do any good, must be historically minded, even if they had not read history as undergraduates. Otherwise, the teaching of politics at undergraduate level would deteriorate into 'half-baked socio-political-theoretical guff'. By the late 1960s he urged that the economics side of PPE should be accepted as a subject on its own; and that politics should be subsumed in the schools of either modern history or law. Modern history was, for the average undergraduate, the best-rounded subject to read. The School of English was too soft: that of law too starchy.[28]

Blake remained a true pupil of Weldon. Weldon, until his death in 1958, liked to organize colloquia in which PPE undergraduates and tutors met and held discussions with their counterparts in the sciences. Interdisciplinary thinking mattered as much to him as examination results. 'Philosophy withers', Weldon warned Ryle, 'if preserved for philosophers only.' Blake similarly thought that the universities of his time were being blighted by insular overspecialization, with 'scholars writing for scholars, historians for historians, philosophers for philosophers, etc.' He deplored parochialism, pomposity, jargon or sacerdotalism in university life. As he wrote in 1960,

> The main reason for boys (and girls) going to a university is that they should at the end (1) be rather better suited to doing whatever job they are to do simply because they have had an education which enables them to use their minds and adapt their brains to the problems that they have to face; (2) be capable of getting more out of life than the moronic television admass world which can do nothing except gape; and (3) have had three highly enjoyable years. For all these reasons the subjects which they read must provide enough scholarly discipline to toughen their minds but at the same time not degenerate into mere exercises in technical expertise.

Yet too many of his colleagues behaved as if their main teaching duty was to train fresh dons, and accordingly designed a syllabus to that end.[29]

Blake served as a Conservative councillor on the City of Oxford Council in 1957–64. This was partly to enable him to muster opposition to the Ministry of Transport's scheme to build a dual carriageway through Christ Church Meadow. Partly, also, because he was imbued with a tradition of civic responsibility and social service, which is why he also became an Oxford magistrate. As a councillor, magistrate and member of non-academic committees he seemed 'a real heavyweight, who isn't afraid to give a forthright opinion, whether asked for or not', as an official of the university press noted. The City Council and the magistrates' court provided perspectives on educational policy which were not vouchsafed to many educationalists, as is clear from his informed and dissentient reactions to two official reports on education which were published in October 1963.[30]

The report of Sir John Newsom's committee on the education of schoolchildren of average and below-average ability was, Blake wrote, essential reading for anyone who wished to understand how the squalor of secondary modern schools was generating aimless, disobliging young adults and disruptive teenagers. He deplored the way that political leaders, understanding that there were no swift satisfactions or easily measurable improvements to be had from Newsom's recommendations, preferred to give the fanfare to Lord Robbins's report on the universities. Michael Stewart and Anthony Crosland, the two men with first-class honours in PPE who were the Labour government's Secretaries of State for Education in 1964–7, prepared and issued a directive against selective state education in 1965. They did not, however, allot funds to meet the priorities identified by Newsom's committee. Newsom's recommendation to raise the school-leaving age from fifteen to sixteen was implemented nine years later by the Heath government in 1972.

Although the Robbins committee members drew on papers submitted by their two chief researchers, Richard Layard and Claus Moser, eminent academics who both later received peerages, they were not themselves impressive to Blake. He wished they had included a college fellow from one of the ancient universities, a lecturer from a redbrick university, head teachers from a grammar school and a secondary modern school. Instead, as he complained, the committee members were 'grave faceless figures who, having long ceased to be concerned with actual teaching or research, move silently through the corridors of power, relaxing occasionally at the Athenaeum'. (Like Robert Bridges, Blake felt distaste for the 'great intellectual nobs and literary nobs / scientific nobs and Bishops *ex officio*' of that Pall Mall club.) He thought the panjandrums on the committee, with their aim of providing the highest education for the highest number, were guilty of 'sour Benthamite egalitarianism', as he termed it. He wished there had been dissentient voices to test the general confidence that university independence would not be compromised if 80 per cent of university income came from government grants, with 20 per cent derived from tutorial fees. As the *gratin* of educational administrators, in touch with government departments and state agencies at a high level, the panjandrums never considered that state funding would lead to intrusive, harrying and politicized state regulation, or that such regulations would injure academic work. Private funding of higher education was uncountenanceable to them.[31]

The Robbins committee annoyed Blake by laying plans for the future based on statistics and fixed targets rather than considering the anomalies and limits of young people's educational capacities. They assumed, he wrote, 'that a great increase in the university population must be secured somehow at almost any cost – though there is little discussion as to why – and further that it can be secured without lowering the admittedly high standards of British universities today'. Although the committee expected scant difficulty in finding additional university teachers, Blake rightly predicted that the enlarged university system would struggle to recruit academic staff of true ability. He thought the Wilson government's espousal of an expanded university system was a meretricious misspending of money. It heralded a crude, impatient drive for universities to become sources of quick, concerted and perhaps intellectually compromised innovation.[32]

Trevor-Roper's introduction of Blake to 'Dawyck' Haig, a Scottish earl and landscape artist, resulted in the first book with Blake's name on the title page. *The Private Papers of Douglas Haig, 1914–1919, Being Selections from the Private Diary and Correspondence of Field Marshal the Earl Haig of Bemersyde, K.T., G.C.B., O.M.* etc. was published by Eyre & Spottiswoode in 1952. It is, like several of Blake's later works, a study in intrigue. 'English political history during the First World War', as he explained in his introduction, was:

> compounded of . . . patriotic emotion, noble self-sacrifice, and high endeavour, of personal ambition, furious vendettas, and implacable resentments. It is not only a history of courageous action and devotion to duty, it is also a history of plot and counter-plot, obscure manoeuvre, and tortuous intrigue. Policy and decisions only emerged as the result of a complicated conflict of forces which are not easy to analyse. The personal antipathies of powerful men, the political animosity provoked by the clash

between the old aristocratic order and the new democracy, the strains of total war itself, all in varying degrees shaped the actions of the principal leaders.

Many readers were shocked to learn how the commanders squabbled while the battlefields were strewn with dead. Startled, too, to find how seldom Haig mentioned the casualties.[33]

Blake's introductory essay is a masterpiece in political interpretation. Lloyd George, 'the first portent of the new mass age', as he put it, 'had been delighting one half of the nation – and enraging the other half – with a display of political acrobatics unsurpassed since the days of Disraeli'. Lloyd George's political life, from the night in 1901 when, after delivering an anti-war speech, he had to flee in disguise from the patriotic fury of a Birmingham mob, 'had been a whirl of publicity and excitement'. As shown by his denunciations of the hereditary wealth of the nobility,

in another land and a later time Lloyd George, with his skill as a demagogue and his hatred of the aristocratic way of life, might have been an exponent of the new Caesarism, the creator of a dictatorship based upon the radicalism of the masses and directed against the established order of society. Yet, such is the all-absorbing power of the British political tradition, he who began as the bitter enemy of property and privilege was destined to end his days . . . a landowner and an earl.

The necessity for breakneck mobilization of industry to supply the munitions required by a total war brought newspaper proprietors such as Beaverbrook, shipowners such as Inverforth, engineers such as Eric Geddes, coal owners such as Rhondda, accountants such as Hardman Lever and retailers such as Devonport into ministerial office. 'It was Great Britain Ltd with a managing director of formidable power', wrote Blake. 'Lloyd George was the nearest thing to a popular dictator since Cromwell, and at times he treated parliament almost as contemptuously.' Yet Lloyd George was weaker politically when he supplanted Asquith in 1916 than was Churchill when he replaced Chamberlain in 1940. On all critical wartime issues, Conservative parliamentarians were more united than Liberals, and their traditions were better suited to waging war. The Liberals 'were the party of liberty, and liberty is the first casualty of war', as Blake noted. 'They were the party of moral conscience, and that is another casualty of war. They were the party of legalism, parliamentary forms, constitutional propriety, and these also are casualties of war.'[34]

It had been expected that Richard Law, Lord Coleraine would write the official biography of his father Andrew Bonar Law, Lloyd George's replacement as Prime Minister in 1922. But 'Dick' Law had put his literary energies into writing a polemical Conservative testament, *Return from Utopia*, which had been hailed by G. M. Young as essential reading to understand post-war England. Accordingly, after the publication of Haig's *Private Papers*, Bonar Law's boon companion Lord Beaverbrook proposed that Blake should write the biography which filial devotion had not produced.[35]

This task fitted Blake's abilities well, for (in his words) 'the busy hum of rumour and intrigue' was never still in Bonar Law's public career. Law achieved the party leadership by well-timed opportunism, by recalling old favours, by wire-pulling and by sharp jabbing with his elbows. He was a narrow, hardened partisan who held that the preservation of party unity was more important than winning elections. In every crisis he checked first what party loyalists wanted. He and Disraeli were the only Conservative leaders chosen while the party was in opposition until Edward Heath in 1965: all three of them might be ranked as outliers. Law was a Presbyterian who had been born and reared in Canada, and whose business life had been spent mostly in Glasgow, yet he became, wrote Blake, 'leader of the Party of Old England, the Party of the Anglican Church and the country squire, the Party of broad acres'.[36]

Electors who were angry and suspicious felt drawn to Law as a man who was sombre, fatalistic, incurious, indifferent to new ideas, uncultured, and kept the same impassive countenance at times of adversity and of success. He encouraged his followers in violent courses. No party leader was as ready to foster furious divisions for quick electoral advantage until Johnson in the next century. In 1912 Law pledged that the newly renamed Conservative and Unionist party would follow, without question, whatever line the faction of Irish Protestants resisting Irish Home Rule chose to take. 'I can imagine no length of resistance to which Ulster will go, which I shall not be ready to support, he declared. He endorsed – so too did his allies, including privy councillors and former Crown law officers – armed resistance to the London government. He seemed, indeed, ready to foster an army mutiny in order to thwart the Government of Ireland Act of 1914. The passion, hatred and melodrama that Irish aspirations brought into English public life were thrilling to Blake. 'The whole story of Ireland in those years is an extraordinary compound of crime, intrigue, romance and murder,' he wrote. Such elements played to his strengths as an historian. Law had recurrent dealings with Field Marshal Sir Henry Wilson, the Protestant Irish activist who was assassinated on his doorstep in Belgravia in 1922. Wilson was the subject of one of the pen portraits in which Blake excelled:

His very appearance was unusual: the enormously tall and bony frame; the intelligent, ugly and curiously enigmatic countenance. His conversation was equally unorthodox – a compound of gravity and buffoonery; for even discussing issues of life and death he would frequently introduce into his discourse the language and antics of the clown. These characteristics did not endear him to his Army colleagues, by whom he was, indeed, profoundly mistrusted as a schemer. Had they been familiar with the poets they might well have applied to him Dryden's famous couplet:

For close designs and crooked counsels fit
Sagacious, bold and turbulent of wit.

. . . Wilson all his life was devoted to the art of secret intrigue. Intrigue was the very fibre of his being. He was never more at home than in the atmosphere of plot and counterplot and labyrinthine manoeuvre, which prevailed in high Army circles at this time.

No wonder that Blake understood Law and Wilson. 'My own natural instinct when engaged in promoting some good, or dishing some bad, cause is to work by intrigue,' he told Trevor-Roper some years later: 'thro'. . . "close designs" and, as one's foes might perhaps allege, "crooked counsels".[37]

The Unknown Prime Minister is a fine work of history as well as a biography which has not been superseded in seventy years. After its completion, Blake tried to persuade the Rhodes Trustees to let him write a biography of Cecil Rhodes. Perhaps they withstood his approaches because they sensed the relish with which he would have examined the temerities, dodges and vainglories of South African mining millionaires. Blake's interest in miscreant capitalism is evident in his decision, as co-editor of the volume of the *Dictionary of National Biography* covering the 1970s, to include three ignoble entrepreneurs, Sir Eric Miller, Lord Brayley and Lord Plurenden, who had been ennobled on Harold Wilson's recommendation.

Once his hopes of Rhodes had been quenched, Blake determined to write a biography of the fourteenth Earl of Derby, a Christ Church man who had thrice been Prime Minister between 1852 and 1868 – and incidentally the richest Prime Minister of all time until Sunak, richer even than Rosebery or Peel. Blake liked politicians to be impious, and Derby, who had vandalized the statue of Mercury during an undergraduate riot in Tom Quad, was certainly that. The steady routines of government office bored him. Points of honour were decisive with him: points of principle were nugatory. His manners were casual and sarcastic. He halted the House of Lords resistance to the Oxford University Act of 1854 because he wanted to get away in time for a horse race. The noblemen whose names he submitted for political appointments to the Royal Household were rejected by the Prince Consort as dandies, roués and racecourse bankrupts. Despite the verve of his oratory, he had no fixed convictions, and was by turns a Whig, a Canningite, a Peelite, leader of the Tory squires. He never headed a government with a parliamentary majority and was always beset by hostile Commons combinations. Before the enlargement of the electorate by his Reform Act of 1867, political power was not won by netting the small number of floating voters in the constituencies. Instead, between 1846 and 1868, political allies gained office together by manoeuvres which captured the unaligned or equivocating voters in the House of Commons. Blake, though, finally decided that he did not want to devote years to a prime minister who was even less known than Law.[38]

Meanwhile Blake had written a telling essay on Law's successor as party leader and Prime Minister, Stanley Baldwin. He praised

Baldwin for fumigating public life after Lloyd George had made it stink with corruption. He preferred 'dreamy, mystical, impetuous and intuitive' Baldwin to his successor as party leader, 'brisk, efficient, executive and unimaginative' Neville Chamberlain. He admired Baldwin for moderating social tensions. 'Baldwin discerned that the British – or perhaps it is safer to say the English – people are not by nature addicted to class warfare. Hunger, unemployment, or an arrogantly repressive attitude on the part of the possessing classes might drive them into it. But the various elements of society, though they had grievances enough to voice, did not feel themselves oppressed or insulted in their capacity as members of a particular class.' The Labour party was impervious to this truth, Blake believed. Most of its leaders continued to speak and plan in terms of class struggle long after Butler, Eden and Macmillan in the 1950s, building on Baldwin's pre-war achievement, had quelled class antagonism among most Conservatives. 'When the Labour party, too, has had its Baldwin,' Blake predicted, 'it may become something more than a discounted pressure group whose main hope of office lies in some national disaster.' Labour's Baldwin was called Blair.[39]

Blake's weekly column in the *Illustrated London News* provided a political historian's commentary on contemporary events. Time and again, in an apt and arresting manner, for a small but influential readership, Blake used political history to show the axis on which parliamentary parties rotate. He understood that if the governments of 1951–64 had not shied away from domestic political excitement, they would not have won the general elections of 1955 and 1959. They kept to the consensus-building aim of full employment and to the state provision of medical services and pensions. They did not dare to confront the overweening and arbitrary exercise of power by trade unions. They avoided the trouble of reversing the public ownership of extractive industries, manufacturing, transport and other public services – the process that the Labour government of 1945–51 cannily called nationalization rather than socialization so as to imply that it was in the national interest – a strategy that signally failed as a means of renewal or invigoration. They adhered to a restrictive, inefficient system of state regulation of capital invest-ment and commodities. The new *dirigisme* was presented as part of an apparatus of immovable state power exercised in the national interest, but was really expressive of a frantic anxiety to control. There was more concern to remove social grievances than to remove disincentives to new enterprises. The provision of state-funded health care and welfare benefits had attained, Blake argued, the status of religion in a theocracy. Retail price fixing continued until 1964. Most culpably of all, the Conservatives maintained for thirteen years a level of taxation that was oppressive, demoralizing, punitive and corrupting. When they left office in 1964, maximum death duties were 80 per cent, and the maximum rate of tax on personal incomes stood at 90 per cent.

Among post-war Conservative leaders, Eden was 'the ideal political figure for the television age', Blake judged. He spoke in terms that electors understood. He drove himself hard and was irritable with his entourage if they faltered in keeping pace. 'In appearance he might well have stepped out of one of the brittle, glittering plays of Noël Coward. His habit of addressing his friends as "My dear", which annoyed virile, barbecue-loving statesmen across the Atlantic, confirmed this impression.' An Italian newspaper called him 'Lord Eyelashes'. He had a discerning interest in the visual arts and was well read. 'In matters of food and wine he could be described as an abstemious gourmet who ate and drank little himself, but provided an admirable table for his guests.' John Foster Dulles, whom President Eisenhower appointed US Secretary of State in 1953, was, in Blake's presentation, impractical and devious in foreign affairs and prone to adopting a contentious legalistic tone in negotiations. 'These characteristics,' wrote Blake, 'together with a fondness for the high moral line on "colonialism", and a remarkable capacity for thinking aloud in a slow voice at interminable length, was not calculated to endear him to Eden, any more than Eden's superior expertise, long experience and fashionable upper-class English mannerisms endeared him to Dulles.' These personal antipathies had their part in the failure of the Anglo-French invasion of Egypt in 1956.[40]

Blake was relieved that Macmillan rather than Butler succeeded Eden as Prime Minister. 'I profoundly mistrust Butler,' he told Trevor-Roper on the day that Macmillan kissed hands. 'There is something cold, smooth, scaly, and slightly repellent about his demeanour.' Blake preferred gaudy buccaneers to monochromatic pillars of respectability. Disraeli, Lord Randolph Churchill, Sir Winston

Churchill and F. E. Smith had the audacity that he relished. For this reason, he preferred Macmillan to Gaitskell. 'There was no love lost between *them*,' he wrote. The antipathy was as strong as that between Disraeli and Gladstone. 'Each tended to regard his rival as the embodiment of what he most disliked – prickly morality on the one hand, and cynical slipperiness on the other.'[41]

Blake felt that in the ten years after 1956 Britain came to resemble the Fourth Republic of France, which had come to an inglorious end in 1958. 'A country with a healthy political system can recover from isolated incidences of political mendacity,' he wrote. The Jameson raid in 1895 and the Marconi scandal in 1912 had left no lasting effects. But 'the evasions, the subterfuges, the accusations and counter-accusations involved in the Suez affair' in 1956 delivered an underlying shock. The Profumo affair of 1963 was a bogus stunt, without significance to national security, but it enabled Labour politicians such as Crossman and Wilson, and scurrilous newspapers like the *Daily Mirror*, to launch a fusillade of rumour and suspicion against established authority and thus delivered a fell blow to the politics of deference. British politicians never regained the full trust of the electorate. The dominant political mood, as Blake reported in 1966, was disillusion.[42]

Blake held that hostility to Conservativism was fuddy-duddy. 'Dons of our age group upwards tend to be not exactly left-wing but rather anti-Conservative,' he told Trevor-Roper in 1960. They were stuck in past habits of thinking, based on their dislike of policies and parliamentary leaders of twenty or thirty years ago. 'Most of our contemporaries and immediate seniors remain emotionally fixated in the era of unemployment, appeasement, the hungry 'thirties, the Spanish Civil War, etc., and although they realise intellectually that there is not much point in voting for Mr Gaitskell's inanities in the nineteen-sixties, nevertheless the spectacle of the very embodiment and personification of the new successful conservatism is more than they can bear.'[43]

In 1957 Blake took sabbatical leave from Christ Church to begin archival research on a biography of Disraeli. There were abundant but unsatisfactory books on the subject already. G. E. Buckle, sometime editor of *The Times* and Fellow of All Souls, had (with the journalist W. F. Monypenny as his coadjutor) produced a marmoreal tribute in six volumes, totalling 1,250,000 words, in 1910–20. They presented the first and last Earl of Beaconsfield as a political wizard, who charmed the Conservatives into power after long durance in the wilderness; as the oracle of One-Nation Conservatism; and as a statesman who preserved the peace of Europe. Any unsavouriness was suppressed. 'Victorian convention seems to have dictated an altogether undue discretion despite the fact that the authors wrote long after the passing of the Victorian era,' Blake told Harrod. In 1925–7, at the acme of Baldwin's second government, when his party was fumbling after One-Nation Conservativism, there had been a flurry of Disraeli biographies targeted at general readers. Sir Edward Clarke, André Maurois and E. T. Raymond wrote books that Blake considered facile and superficial because their authors had not bothered to consult Disraeli's papers and had pillaged their material from the six official volumes. Blake, though, intended to subject the political structure of mid-Victorian England to a searching reconsideration.[44]

While preparing the Disraeli book, Blake taught the political part of the PPE curriculum to a German undergraduate. His pupil's shrewd questions about the Tory party's springs of action brought him (he said) to a full realization, for the first time, of 'the difficulty of defining any consistent set of Conservative principles handed down from the past to the present', which is what Feiling had tried to do for both Christ Church pupils and members of the Oxford political caucuses. English Conservatism stood apart from both the European right and the 'doctrinaire atavism and sheer incompetence' represented in America by Senator Barry Goldwater, the Republicans' presidential candidate in 1964. (Goldwater was a libertarian, anti-communist enragé, and advocate of low taxation whose influence eliminated eastern seaboard Rockefeller liberalism from the Republican party.) 'English conservatism', Blake maintained in 1964, 'is essentially empirical, adaptable, and non-doctrinaire. It is a style of politics, a way of doing things, rather than a specific set of beliefs, let alone dogmas.' No one was drummed out of the Conservative party on a matter of belief until the expulsions of 2019. 'As long as you do not advocate total nationalisation on the one hand, or, say, militant racialism on the other, you can maintain almost anything and remain a Conservative.'[45]

'No one', Blake wrote, 'can understand Disraeli if he thinks in terms of a person actually trying to *do* things, like Peel, Churchill, Attlee, Heath; or even of someone trying to stop things being done – alas all too few – Melbourne, Salisbury, Callaghan.' Disraeli was intent on acting his part upon the stage of history: 'more like Harold Macmillan and Harold Wilson than anyone after him, more like Charles James Fox than anyone before him', as Blake wrote. Insincerity was basic to Dizzy's system. 'The people have their passions,' he told the electors of High Wycombe, 'and it is ever the duty of public men occasionally to adopt sentiments with which they do not agree, because the people must have leaders.'[46]

Blake's *Disraeli*, published in 1966, stands in the first rank of political biographies. He depicted an avid opportunist, an incorrigible poser, somersaulting in his opinions, bouncing colleagues into risky commitments, jockeying for place, snatching short-term party advantages, keeping a sharp eye for loopholes and basking in renown. 'There was an ornate effrontery about him,' Blake wrote. For engineering the second Reform Act of 1867, which enlarged the electorate, Disraeli deserved 'to go down to history as a politician of genius, a superb improviser, a parliamentarian of unrivalled skill, but not as a far-sighted statesman, a Tory democrat, or the educator of his party'. His performance at the Congress of Berlin, his pounce on the controlling shares in the Suez Canal Company, his staunch loyalties and occasional vindictiveness were all weighed and evaluated by Blake in the 766 pages of his text.[47]

It was at Queen Victoria's request that Disraeli prepared the Royal Titles Act of 1876 which bestowed the title of Empress of India on her. He said at the time that there was no reason against her younger sons Prince Arthur and Prince Alfred being created Duke of Canada and Duke of Australia respectively. Disraeli also favoured the proposal of the Viceroy, Lord Lytton, to create a separate peerage in India. This measure was thought likely to please, together with the imperial title, the princely class in India. That class had only slight political power, admitted Lord Salisbury, but was the only one with which the London government had hope of attaining useful influence. The Disraelian view of the Indian Empire, as a congeries of alliances between an aristocratic government in London and similarly princely societies in the subcontinent, was attractive to

Blake. Social order in the colonies should rest on the intertwining sympathies and harmonious interests of ruling classes separated by oceans. Talk of racial supremacism seemed overdone to him.[48]

Blake disliked the speed with which, after relinquishing the Indian Empire in 1947, the London government withdrew from sovereignty in Asia and Africa. 'Of course, a great deal of pious guff was talked about liberty and democracy,' he wrote. 'There was much self-congratulation on the peaceful way in which power has been transferred. But the truth is that power would not have been transferred if Britain had possessed the resources and – no less important – the will to retain it.' He was infuriated by the Wilson government's announcement, in 1968, that three years hence British troops would be withdrawn from bases east of Aden, that is from Malaysia, Singapore and the Persian Gulf. 'Nothing can excuse the way in which this last retreat has been conducted,' he raged. 'Not a single ennobling feature, not one flicker of courage or vision or generosity illumines the dismal scene. Second-rate politicians jabbering under the chairmanship of the most blinkered prime minister since Neville Chamberlain, the most dishonest since Lloyd George and the most ineffective since Goderich, have produced a package which . . . double-crosses our friends.' The withdrawal was a cost-cutting exercise at a time of economic crisis and sterling devaluation, but Blake presented it as a sop to 'the fanatics and ninnies of the Left' who resented anything patriotic. He consoled himself with the reflection that the loss of Empire might make the British 'more commercially minded, more efficient, in fact more American in our attitude, at the same time less paternalistic, less welfare-minded, less moralistic.'[49]

When President Richard Nixon introduced a guaranteed annual minimum income in the United States in 1968, he claimed that he had been prompted to this by reading Blake's *Disraeli*. Undoubtedly the book was read and discussed by Conservative leaders in England as they tried to rally from defeat by the Labour party in the general election of 1966.[50]

When the Conservatives chose Heath as their party leader in 1965, they thought they were getting an equivalent to Wilson: a grammar school boy who had been set on course at Oxford to become a professional-minded politician rather than a playful amateur. 'They have really done nothing of the sort,' Blake said in his tart way. 'Mr Heath is far more like a Conservative equivalent of Hugh Gaitskell – a man of sincerity, intellectual principle, and straightforward character, seeking power for the sake of putting specific policies into practice.' What is more, in the general election of 1966, he repeated Gaitskell's error in 1959 and announced too many detailed policies on too many topics. Blake sympathized with Heath's aim to overturn the passive domestic policies that masqueraded as Conservative paternalism: as he wrote in the *Illustrated London News* in 1965, this amounted to 'featherbedding every declining industry which made enough fuss, and generally encouraging a sort of cosy live-and-let-live sloppiness, which has been largely responsible for our economic ills'.[51]

The revisionism in *Disraeli* heartened the radical corporatists, or 'Heathmen' as one commentator dubbed them, who formed the phalanx for their party leader. Although Blake seemed in close enough affinity with them to receive a peerage within a year of Heath taking office, his inclination was to put a firm foot on the brake while the Heathmen trod nervously on the accelerator. A core belief of Oxford Conservatism, which Blake followed Feiling in instilling in politically minded undergraduates, was that electorates dislike sudden and alarming measures. 'It has never paid the Conservatives to come forward as a party of avowed change,' Blake insisted. 'They can successfully be a party that quietly brings about change when in office, but they have not yet won an election on a platform of change, and they have almost always fared badly when they have sought to appear in this implausible guise.' Yet Heath avowed his intention 'to embark on a change so radical, a revolution so quiet and so total that it will go far beyond the programme of a Parliament'. His government, he said in 1970, had been 'returned to office to change the course and the history of this nation, nothing else'. Blake admired Heath for taking initiatives that were as bold as Peel's. He approved Heath's agenda: 'lower direct taxation; less governmental interference; reduction in public expenditure; selectivity in the social services, and a shift of the burden from the Treasury to the employers; legislation to restrain the power of the unions; and entry into the European Economic Community'. But Heath's government became vulnerable because, as Blake realized, it pursued draconian reforms with a precipitate impatience which affrighted the electorate.[52]

At times the Conservative party seemed to offer no larger ideal than the liberty of consumers to go on shopping sprees with full pockets. Its primary purpose by the end of the 1950s seemed to be the provision of retail satisfaction. Once the party had been the bulwark of Empire; but imperialism was defunct, and the Macmillan government transmogrified the colonies into a 'Commonwealth of Nations' which, as Blake wrote, 'continually dissolves into ever stranger shapes, and surely cannot last much longer in a form that has any real meaning'. The Conservatives had always been the party of the shire counties. English rural districts, but not Scottish or Welsh, stayed loyal to the party of Sir Harry Legge-Bourke, Sir Harry d'Avigdor-Goldsmid, Sir Oliver Crosthwaite-Eyre, Sir Walter Bromley-Davenport and the other hyphenated squires. 'Home Rule for England would not be a bad Tory slogan,' Blake advised after Heath's election as party leader. Yet the Heath government was to deal a mortal blow to the composure of the shires in the form of the meretricious Local Government Act of 1972. This tampered with county boundaries, created new metropolitan counties such as Tyne & Wear, created non-metropolitan counties such as Avon, abolished three English counties, merged Herefordshire with Worcestershire, replaced the thirteen historic counties of Wales with eight newfangled ones. These quick, nervous changes shook trust in Heath's staunch Conservatism, Blake concluded, more than anything else.[53]

Blake was an historian with a lust for life. Both his research and his skill in the selection and organization of evidence were masterly. The non-academic experiences of soldiering, of secret service work, of conspiratorial planning sessions in college, and his engagement with contemporary politics honed his scholarly acumen. The patterns that he found in history were the patterns to which his own mind was disposed. Everyone agreed that he had a robust nature and a sturdy philosophy of life. He was never apologetic, and sometimes he proved ruthless. Although he could be aggressive in college business and public affairs, he had a precautionary subtlety in his opening tactics and never rushed heedless into battle. His general disposition was intolerant, but tempered by an amused, half-cynical sufferance.

No one who had, like him, profited from the undermining and refortifying tutorial methods of Harry Weldon could think that a purpose of university education is to leave pupils feeling unchallenged, comfortable, safe. He was fascinated by risk takers and rule breakers, though he was disposed to repress unruliness in the young.

Blake ascended from a studentship of Christ Church to the provostship of the Queen's College in 1968 at a time when colleges, faculties and the university were changing apace. Two new honours schools in natural sciences were inaugurated in Oxford in 1968 alone: five others had been founded in previous years; for the first time in university history the sciences became weightier in administrative importance, and better funded, than the humanities. Although arts faculties could not satisfy the new clamour for technological utility, their syllabuses were widened after 1960 and their staffs enlarged. The proliferation of dons, and the variegation of their remits, made once again stark the divergence between teaching and research, which had provoked Hassall's hostile reaction to Firth's inaugural Regius lecture in 1904. In Christ Church, as in other colleges, the status of those teaching fellows, such as Charles Stuart, who worked only for their pupils, was shaken. With more Students teaching the new and widened curricula, there were more opinions vouchsafed and more votes to be solicited at college meetings. The techniques of college management, which had been practised since 1919 by such Censors as Masterman, Harrod, Trevor-Roper and Blake, no longer answered. The traditional propensity of key individuals to dither and prevaricate was replaced in the enlarged governing body by a more collective infirmity of purpose. Havering, of course, is sometimes less foolhardy than overconfidence.

The publication of the Robbins report on higher education in 1963 had intensified equalitarian resentment of the University of Oxford as an incorrigible champion of privileges and as a cocksure finishing school for the future governing class. Elitism began to be decried as an offence against social justice and democracy. Doubtless democracy is the most palatable political system, but it should have traction over only a limited ground. 'It pertains to politics exclusively, and has no other application in any other domain,' as the Belgian commentator on totalitarianism Simon Leys has argued. 'When applied anywhere else, it is death – for truth is not democratic, intelligence and talent are not democratic, nor is beauty, nor love – nor God's grace. A truly democratic education is an education that equips people intellectually to defend and promote democracy within the political world; but in its own field, education must be ruthlessly aristocratic and . . . shamelessly geared towards excellence.'[54]

Moreover, in the generation after the Robbins report, acquisitive people, with high-pressure, full-time commitment to moneymaking, complained that there was no respect for enterprise or profit in the colleges. They wanted to bring the rat-race mentality into the heart of teaching. Within a startlingly short period, the combination of equalitarian scolds and profit-and-loss record keepers made it seem either reactionary and shameful or frivolous and spoilt to speak of the duty of the two ancient English universities to train the next generation of the nation's rulers in truth telling or other virtues. The consensus about the purposes and techniques of teaching modern history, which had been upheld for centuries in Oxford colleges, was broken within a few years. Lessons in statecraft or in character-building for public responsibilities were abruptly seen as obsolete, presumptuous and even offensive. 'Our men have been pretty well running the country since before Honours Schools and so forth were invented', admits a don in J. I. M. Stewart's Christ Church novel of 1974. But this no longer holds, he adds. 'Oxford isn't, and this place isn't, a glorified public school – building character, and codifying manners, and raising hymns of praise for the gifts of all-roundedness and leadership.' Historical knowledge that derived from religious, political, community and corporate experience, that acknowledged traditional doctrines of the Church or of the law, that was embodied in still operative institutions – these forms of recognition and learning were increasingly traduced as supportive of existing power structures and thus complicit in the misdemeanours of authority.[55]

Many upcoming scholars had their thinking sent askew by the schematizing yet destructive ideas of Michel Foucault. He was obsessed with power and control, and wrote in a coercive style of prose that had the effect of quelling independent thinking that might enable his readers to wriggle free from his domination. For Foucault knowledge and truth were not the outcome of diligence, skill, awareness, comprehension and discernment: there was no room for playfulness or rejoicing in the pursuit of knowledge and truth. All he could see were distorted patterns of thought and restrictive terminology which served the interests of malevolent controlling forces. Painstaking expertise was decried as a swindle by people who were complicit in the abusive misuse of conspiratorial powers. The momentous subject matter of history, 'struggle and suffering, short glories and long miseries, wars and intermittent peace', the historic consciousness 'of action and pain, of power and pride, of sin and death' as outlined by Karl Löwith in 1949, was reduced, like human sexuality, to a set of mere social constructions. Post-modernism degraded human destiny and responsibility. It provided a safe form of delinquency for dons who wished to show their radicalism without the strenuous dangers of revolutionary action. 'Structures do not take to the streets,' as Oxbridge graffiti declared in chalk. A significant number of university teachers in non-science subjects began to betray their vocation by belittling the idea that the truth can be found and taught. Some indeed held that it is naive to believe in the possibility or value of absolute truth.[56]

Increasingly specialized research interests, in the history departments of universities, produced parochial work that could not enlarge the curiosity and imagination of any student or help her to think well about the bigger issues of human motive and conduct. 'Shards of the past delivered to us by so many microhistories', as the French historian Pierre Nora wrote in 1989. How meagre in insight these shards would have seemed to Camden and Clarendon, to Acton and Stubbs, to Feiling and Masterman. How timid and selfish an approach compared with that of Gordon Walker, who tried as an historian to better the present and future prospects of humanity by explaining the development of human nature and social discipline over a millennium. Excessive specialization and the writing of unreadable microhistories were the outcome of a period when the higher culture of western Europe and north America, not just of Christ Church or of Oxford University, had been jolted apart. By 1989 it was clear to Nora that many precious elements of human experience – 'the warmth of tradition', 'the silence of custom' and 'the repetition of the ancestral' – were being lost.[57]

Rules and orders, as well as misrule and disorder, are the stuff of historical studies. Blake had been a notable disciplinary force within Christ Church, and preserved university regulations as a Proctor. Yet with his taste for mischievous derring-do, he would have been fascinated by the twenty-first-century Prime Minister whom

Ferdinand Mount has called 'a seedy, treacherous chancer' and by the party leader who was characterized as 'a disingenuous grifter'. Blake's ambivalence about discipline was reflected across the university by 1967–8. Undergraduates were asserting their maturity, winning their release from the traditional strictures of proctorial and college discipline, chafing at the old forms of moral tutoring and beginning to participate in the administrative decisions of colleges and university. At the same time, and by an odd discrepancy, they also began to expect to be kept safe – at first from emotional risks, then from jeopardy of disappointment in the Schools, and finally from ill-expected or unfriendly opinions. Colleges had to accept safeguarding and therapeutic roles, and to arrange access to counsellors and other protective shields and services, for people who in other ways, it was claimed, should be respected as adults.[58]

Blake's installation as Provost of Queen's came at a time of undergraduate demonstrations against the American war in Vietnam, occupations of university buildings, barricades and chants, mucky stencilled pamphlets and the discovery that wanton political resentment can have aphrodisiac effects. 'I do not doubt', wrote the American sociologist Philip Rieff, who returned annually for a term in an Oxford college in this period, 'that English high culture has declined with the decline of empire. With the dissolution of the Pax Britannica, the manners of young Oxonians grow visibly more American, especially among those who, suffering identity-shrinkage under the retreat of English authority, talk themselves into easy hostilities to its callow successor, American power.' Blake would not have disagreed.[59]

This was the period when it became a virtue to be pleased with oneself. In 1969 W. H. Auden, by then an Honorary Student of the House and soon to return to live there, heard of someone shouting *We are ALL of us marvellously gifted*. Sorry, he thought, but you have just proved that you ain't. During that same year Barbara Castle, with the authority of a First Secretary of State in the Labour government, addressed a Cambridge audience. 'It is not enough to end the misery of poverty,' she declared. There was an urgent need to end what the German educationalist Kurt Hahn had called 'the misery of unimportance'. Workplaces, schools and universities must acknowledge the right of every man and woman, Castle said, 'to express their personalities, to control their own environment, to be

taken into account as individuals'. Namier, in a heartfelt essay of
1941, had alluded to such sentiments as leading to 'a democracy of
conceit', based on 'self-adoration', frothing with an egocentric confidence in 'the omnipotence of human thought, and the infinite
perfectibility of human nature'. The platform cries of Barbara Castle
and the street cries of Oxford narcissists encouraged a new frame
of mind. Naivety, fervour and optimism are its governing emotions,
Namier said. He might have added that it generates the misery of
self-importance.[60]

The loss of control over one's environment, so often aggravated
by mass production and hyper-consumerism, has indeed done irreversible harm to the planet and to mental health. But the
expectation to be heard, even if one has nothing coherent or useful
to say, and the making of self-expression as one's main stock-in-
trade, however callow one may be, stands at odds with centuries
of modern history teaching. Truth is the paramount aim of the best
of modern historians, but the truth about power, religious passion,
rulers, nations, cliques, geographical influences and acquisitiveness,
not the personal truths that supposedly help individuals towards the
paltry aim of self-affirmation. To live in constant awareness of one's
own self-fabricated image, or to regale oneself with a continuous
narrative of one's feelings and actions, does not conduce to a proper
awareness of other people, or to resolution, fulfilment, gratitude in
life. The notion that everyone is marvellously gifted, and has a right
to express their importance, prevents individuals from having a just
sense of their value in the world or a proportionate view of their
relations to their fellow citizens. The overprizing and commodifica-
tion of individuality, which has intensified in Britain since the 1980s,
makes a citizenry of isolated, competitive, self-absorbed, dissatisfied,
fractious and wayward social atoms. The demand that everyone
should be able to express their personalities and opinions on equal
terms raises the senseless clamour that balkanizes localities and
nations. Often, too, the expression of personality fosters histrionics
at the expense of self-respect, and narcissism instead of true
self-awareness. Personal melodrama is sought as a cure for the misery
of unimportance. To be oneself, people are told, is a paramount
need. But does the full value of being one's self justify the effort?

Self-love and self-recognition are among the motive forces for acts of remembrance, as Philip Rieff's son David has shown in his opusculum *In Praise of Forgetting*. Driven by his experiences as an American observer of the Bosnian war in 1992–5 and the Rwanda genocide of 1994, David Rieff is uneasy about the potentially violent disjuncture between memory and history. Acts of remembrance, by nations, ethnic communities, social classes and minorities, are now promoted as a salubrious priority by educationalists and political practitioners. Yet such acts lack historical method, and ought to be recognized as *anti-history*. 'Memory, insofar as it is affective and magical, only accommodates those facts that suit it; it nourishes recollections that may be out of focus or telescopic,' says Nora. Human memory, whether private or collective, is notoriously fallible. It is subject to tricks, distortions and self-censorship, which may be deliberate or unintentional. It can assume sacred airs or demand unchallengeable reverence. Acts of remembrance are acritical, emotive, wilful, pliant, readily manipulated, an easy tool of malpractice, often capable of giving wrongful incitement. Historical thought is a critical activity. It is undertaken by scholars who amass evidence and ideas, splice and quicken them, analyse and interpret. They raise difficult questions, spread reasonable doubts and honour the truth as exactly they can. Their mission is to deny, correct, lambast, demystify and disempower what Nora calls 'the terrorism of historicized memory'.[61]

Schoolchildren in developed countries are, David Rieff finds, increasingly ignorant of contemporary politics, geography and history. 'And what little history they do know is not history in the proper sense of the term but remembrance,' he continues. Often remembrance reduces the past to a congeries of personal memories and pretends that individual sincerity, or it may be a taste for self-absorbed melodrama, is a fit substitute for historical truth. It is concerned with providing a fit decor for wallowing in past triumphs or past injuries. Essentially, Rieff argues, remembrance is narcissistic, and more concerned with finding amenable feelings than with establishing accurate truths about the past. For him, 'the over-valuing of collective memory and the under-valuing of history is a perfect fit with the spirit of an age that is itself dominated by instant gratification'. Acts of remembrance serve the ends of identity politics, and empower those individuals and communities that thrive in the contemporary domain of grievance and victimhood. 'There are few phenomena more uncontrollable socially and, hence, more dangerous politically than a people or a social group that believes itself to be a victim,' as Rieff warns. He quotes the Polish poet and Nobel laureate Wisława Szymborska marking the coming apotheosis of anti-history:

> Those who knew
> what was going on here
> must make way
> for those who know little.
> And less than little.
> And finally as little as nothing.[62]

Neither the synthetic Americanism of Oxford's revolutionary children nor the indulgence of grievance and victimhood posed the worst threat to the integrity of the university system that Blake had cherished: most menacing was state sponsorship. In 1960 a well-meaning official committee, chaired by the shipping magnate and artistic patron Sir Colin Anderson, had recommended that all British students on full-time, first-degree university courses should receive government grants that provided for the payment of college fees plus a standard sum for maintenance. Within a few years the set figures for the fees were outstripped by the rising costs of university education. The widening shortfall came to be covered by a block grant from the University Grants Committee. Politicians – unjustifiably – treated this block grant as if it was a financial rescue of improvident and irresponsible spenders. The predominant new reliance on state funding, rather than on income from student fees, put the universities under the suzerainty of government ministers and their officials in London. There were two reasons, as 'Monty' Woodhouse, Fellow of Nuffield and MP for Oxford understood, why dons, as subordinate workers in this new regime, felt puny and beset under the welter of dockets and questionnaires: 'One is that intellectuals can only thrive on truth; the other is that they detest bureaucratic organization.'[63]

A line of Arthur Hugh Clough's describes the procedures and choices of state-controlled universities: 'Foolish delays, more foolish evasions, most foolish renewals'. University administration came to resemble the managerialism of nationalized industries: centralized regulation, indiscriminate standardization, meaningless gauges of research productivity and targets set by an obtuse state were its predominant features. The Education Reform Act, enacted by the Thatcher government in 1988, was acknowledged by Robert Jackson (then a minister in the Department of Education) as having the effect of nationalizing university funding. Central political control – that is, the allotment of funds by government bureaucracies to hidebound university administrations – allows little respect for academic expertise, mental play and the search for pure but commercially inapplicable truths. It has no respect at all for enquiring, imaginative and abundant minds which are not bent on serving the needs of a nation fixated by mass consumption.[64]

Blake relinquished his studentship at a time when dons stopped saying aloud, or thinking to themselves, that in modern history they were teaching prudence in the management of change. Instead, from the late 1960s, they burrowed into scholarly specialization, often but not invariably ripe and interesting, which yielded no precepts for the practical betterment of their pupils as citizens. After the 1980s, throughout the British universities, increasing numbers of pupils, who had often been assured that they were marvellously gifted, expected first-class honours, and raised outcries if they were awarded anything else. The politicization of personal and community memories, and the formalization of acts of remembrance, sometimes elicits feel-good complacency and sometimes nourishes the culture of complaint; but always it blotches and smudges the clear truths of modern history. This is a sad time. The shades of past historians of Christ Church, undergraduates and Students alike, watch agape. One can only recall lines from Laurence Binyon's poem 'The Burning of the Leaves':

> Let them go to the fire, with never a look behind.
> The world that was ours is a world that is ours no more.

Acknowledgements

History in the House is written on my own initiative, without the sponsorship, oversight or approval of any Oxford institution or individual. The opinions and emphasis are mine alone: no inferences should be drawn or ascriptions attempted that involve anyone else.

I thank Tanya and Henry Harrod, Alan Gordon Walker and Blair Worden for their generous and time-consuming criticism, corrections and encouragement of chapters 9, 10 and 11 respectively. They have kindly granted me permission to quote from the published and unpublished writings of Roy Harrod, Patrick Gordon Walker and Hugh Trevor-Roper.

Further thanks are due to the archivists of the institutions that provided the primary sources for this book:

All Souls College, Oxford, papers of John Sparrow.
Balliol College, Oxford, diaries of Sir Harold Nicolson.
Bodleian Library, Oxford, papers of Isaiah Berlin, the Canning Club, Sheila Grant Duff, Sir Patrick Reilly and Lord Simon.
Borthwick Institute for Archives, University of York, papers of Lord Halifax.
British Library, papers of George Canning, Roy Harrod, Lord Liverpool and Sir Robert Peel.
British Library of Political and Economic Science, papers of Ernest Gellner, and of the Economic History Society.
Christ Church, Oxford, papers of R. V. Dundas and Hugh Trevor-Roper.
Churchill College, Cambridge, papers of Patrick Gordon Walker.
Eton College Library, papers of Victor Cazalet.
Exeter University Library, papers of A. L. Rowse.

King's College, Cambridge, papers of Noël Annan.

National Archives, Kew, papers of the Security Service and of the Treasury.

University of Utrecht, papers of Pieter Geyl.

Wadham College, Oxford, papers of Maurice Bowra.

Worcester College, Oxford, papers of J. C. Masterman and E. L. Woodward.

Quotations from John Sparrow's papers are reproduced by permission of the Warden and Fellows of All Souls College, Oxford. Quotations from the published and unpublished writings of Isaiah Berlin are used with the permission of the Trustees of the Isaiah Berlin Literary Trust. I apologize to other literary representatives whom I have been unsuccessful in contacting.

In writing this book, I have felt the guiding hands or in some cases, alas, the hovering shades of my past teachers: Gerald McCarthy, who taught me English literature at school; and †Owen Chadwick, Roderick Floud, †Clive Linehan, John Morrill, Richard Overy, Quintin Skinner, †Norman Stone, Gillian Sutherland, †Clive Trebilcock and Blair Worden, all of whom taught me modern history at Cambridge.

This book could not have been written without the mental infusions, friendship and amenities that I enjoyed during my membership of All Souls College, Oxford. Two of its former Visiting Fellows, Michael Kremer and Simon Malloch, gave notable help in providing references and citations. The thinking of my All Souls friend Dmitri Levitin inspired this book. Dmitri first interested me in the history of educational institutions and showed me the importance of intellectual communities and corporate affiliations, rather than lone minds, in the advancement of knowledge. The passion and imaginative daring of his scholarship delight me: his ideas, so far as my hapless crudity allows me to understand them, have become a motive force. He read chunks of the manuscript and suggested timely improvements.

I thank Jenny Davenport and Christopher Phipps for keeping me in my place, and making it so agreeable. Several twenty-first century undergraduates at Christ Church have enlivened me with their energy, initiative, curiosity and affection: †Rory Allan, Felix Hale,

Darian Murray-Griffiths, Tom Perrin and Timothy Pleydell-Bouverie. I am grateful, too, for the generous actions and spirit of Hugo Davenport-Hines, Andrew Roberts, Charles Sebag-Montefiore, James Stourton and William Waldegrave.

For two decades Brian Young, Professor of Intellectual History and Student of Christ Church, has given me friendship, laughter, balance and arresting notions. John Drury, Dean of Christ Church from 1991 to 2003, and subsequently Chaplain of All Souls, has renewed my sense of truth, gladdened me by his talk and shown new ways to think, watch and rejoice. His wife, the art historian Caroline Elam, astute and amusing and omnicompetent, became, by the medium of Zoom, a sustaining figure to me during the English lockdown and French *confinement* of 2020–1. My book is dedicated to this trio with admiration and gratitude.

Le Meygris, December 2023

Notes

Abbreviations

BL   British Library, London
BLPES   The British Library of Political and Economic Science, London
Bodleian   Bodleian Library, Oxford
EUL   Exeter University Library
NA   The National Archives, Kew

Chapter 1: The Historian Needs a Lust for Life

1 *Vindication of the English Constitution in a Letter to a Noble and Learned Lord, by Disraeli the younger* (London: Saunders & Otley, 1835), 181; Mandell Creighton, *Thoughts on Education* (London: Longmans Green, 1903), 198–9.

2 Bertrand Russell, *Collected Papers*, vol. 12 (London: Routledge, 1985), 66.

3 David Douglas, 'William Dugdale: The "Grand Plagiary"', *History*, vol. 20 (1935), 194.

4 Arnaldo Momigliano, *Essays in Ancient and Modern Historiography* (Oxford: Blackwell, 1977), 161–9; Momigliano, *The Classical Foundations of Modern Historiography* (Berkeley: University of California Press, 1990), 29–53.

5 Waldo Hilary Dunn, *James Anthony Froude*, vol. 1 (Oxford: Clarendon Press, 1961), 48–9.

6 Stephen McKenna, *While I Remember* (London: Thornton Butterworth, 1921), 63.

7 F. H. Bradley, *The Presuppositions of Critical History* (Oxford: James Parker, 1874), ii, iii, 15, 19, 26.

8 Edith Sichel ed., *Gathered Leaves from the Prose of Mary E. Coleridge*

(London: Constable, 1910), 232; Charles Whibley, *The Letters of an Englishman*, vol. 2 (London: Constable, 1912), 38–9; E. L. Woodward, *The Twelve-Winded Sky* (London: Constable, 1930), 75, 77, 78–9; R. G. Collingwood, *The Idea of History* (Oxford: Clarendon Press, 1946), 202.

9   Marc Bloch, *The Historian's Craft* (Manchester: Manchester University Press, 1954), 43–5, 80.

10 Keith Hancock, *Country and Calling* (London: Faber & Faber, 1954), 95, 213, 216, 220; Hugh Trevor-Roper, 'Lost Generation', *Sunday Times*, 1 November 1959.

11 Pieter Geyl, *Debates with Historians* (The Hague: Martinus Nijhoff, 1955), 1; Bloch, *Historian's Craft*, 25–6; Edward Hallett Carr, *The New Society* (London: Macmillan, 1951), 11.

12 Keith Thomas, *The Ends of Life: Roads to Fulfilment in Early Modern England* (Oxford: Oxford University Press, 2009), 207.

13 W. J. K. Diplock, *Isis, or the Future of Oxford* (London: Kegan Paul, 1929), 62.

14 Gilbert Ryle, *The Concept of Mind* (London: Hutchinson, 1949), 144, 284, 312.

15 Stuart Hampshire, *Modern Writers, and Other Essays* (London: Chatto & Windus, 1969), xi–xiii.

16 Lillian Quiller-Couch ed., *Reminiscences of Oxford by Oxford Men, 1559–1850* (Oxford: Oxford Historical Society, 1892), 150; Harold Laski, *The Danger of being a Gentleman* (London: Allen & Unwin, 1939), 54.

17 Hugh Lloyd-Jones, *Blood for the Ghosts: Classical Influences in the Nineteenth and Twentieth Centuries* (London: Duckworth, 1982), 294.

18 *The Complete Works of W. H. Auden: Poems, 1940–1973*, ed. Edward Mendelson (Princeton: Princeton University Press, 2022), 574.

19 Diplock, *Isis*, 27, 31–2.

20 J. I. M. Stewart, *Full Term* (London: Gollancz, 1978), 7–9.

Chapter 2: A College for State Men

1   *Letters and Papers, Foreign and Domestic, of the Reign of Henry VIII*, vol. 2 (London: Her Majesty's Stationery Office, 1864), 1182; William Camden, 'Wise Speeches', in *Remains Concerning Britain* (London: John Russell Smith, 1870), 298.

2   Earl of Northumberland, *Advice to his Son*, ed. George Harrison (London: Ernest Benn, 1930), 114. I owe my sense of virtue politics and much that follows in this chapter to John Hankins, *Virtue Politics: Soulcraft and Statecraft in Renaissance Italy* (London: Harvard University Press, 2019).

3 Judith Curthoys, *The Cardinal's College: Christ Church, Chapter and Verse* (London: Profile, 2012), 12.

4 *Death Repeal'd by a thankfull memoriall sent from Christ-Church in Oxford celebrating the noble deserts of the Right Honourable Paule, late Viscount Bayning of Sudbury* (Oxford: Leonard Lichfield, printer to the university, 1638), 3.

5 Burton, preface 'Democritus Junior to the Reader', *Anatomy of Melancholy* (first published in 1621 and enlarged by its author in successive editions over the next thirty years).

6 Sir Humphrey Gilbert, *Queene Elizabethes Achademy*, ed. Frederick Furnivall (London: N. Trübner, 1869), 11; Henry Peacham, *The Compleat Gentleman*, ed. George Gordon (Oxford: Clarendon Press, 1906), 18. This section follows Mervyn James, *Society, Politics and Culture: Studies in Early Modern England* (Cambridge University Press, 1986) and Susan Bryson, *From Courtesy to Civility: Changing Codes of Conduct in Early Modern England* (Oxford: Clarendon Press, 1998).

7 James McConica, 'The Rise of the Undergraduate College', in McConica ed., *The History of the University of Oxford*, vol. 3 (Oxford: Clarendon Press, 1986), 40–1; George Gascoigne, *A Hundreth Sundrie Flowers*, ed. George Pigman III (Oxford: Clarendon Press, 2000), 315; Stephen Alford, *The Early Elizabethan Polity: William Cecil and the British Succession Crisis, 1558–1569* (Cambridge: Cambridge University Press, 1998), 16, 20–3, 41, 116; Peacham, *Compleat Gentleman*, 45; Norman Jones, *Governing by Virtue: Lord Burghley and the Management of Elizabethan England* (Oxford: Oxford University Press, 2015), 64; Haly Heron, *The kayes of counsail: a newe discourse of morall philosophie (1579)*, ed. Virgil Heltzel (Liverpool: University of Liverpool Press, 1954), 3, 79; Elizabeth Strutt, *Practical Wisdom; or, The Manual of Life. The Counsels of Eminent Men to their Children* (London: Henry Colburn, 1824), 247; John Locke, *Some Thoughts Concerning Education*, ed. John and Jean Yolton (Oxford: Clarendon Press, 1989), §185.

8 Thomas Starkey, *A Dialogue between Pole and Lupset*, ed. T. F. Mayor, Camden 4th series, vol. 37 (London: Royal Historical Society, 1989), 74–5; William Harrison, *The Description of England*, ed. Georges Edelen (Ithaca, NY: Cornell University Press, 1968), 114.

9 Burton, *Anatomy of Melancholy*, part 2, section 3, mem 2.

10 Starkey, *Pole and Lupset*, 124–5.

11 Historical Manuscripts Commission, *Calendar of the Manuscripts of the Marquis of Salisbury KG Preserved at Hatfield House*, part 1 (London: Her Majesty's Stationery Office, 1883), 163; Stanley Bindoff, Joel Hurstfield and Charles Williams eds, *Elizabethan Government and Society: Essays Presented to Sir John Neale* (London: Athlone Press, 1961), 80–1.

12 Gilbert, *Queene Elizabethes Achademy*, 10.

13 Sir John Neale, *The Elizabethan House of Commons* (London: Cape, 1949), 16, 302–3.

14 Francis Bacon, 'Of Negociating', section 47 of *Essays or Counsels Civil and Moral* (published in revised editions of 1597–1625); Bacon, *The Essays and Advancement of Learning* (London: Macmillan, 1906), 119; Strutt, *Practical Wisdom*, 45; Ronald McKerrow and F. P. Wilson eds, *The Works of Thomas Nashe*, vol. 1 (Oxford: Blackwell, 1958), 9–10, vol. 3 (Oxford: Blackwell, 1958), 311, 315; Paul Jordan-Smith ed., *Robert Burton's Philosophaster* (Stanford: Stanford University Press, 1931), 33, 223.

15 Kenneth Fincham, 'Oxford and the Early Stuart Polity', in Nicholas Tyacke ed., *The History of the University of Oxford*, vol. 4 (Oxford: Clarendon Press, 1997), 180.

16 Millicent Barton Rex, *University Representation in England, 1604–1690* (London: Allen & Unwin, 1954).

17 Burton, *Anatomy of Melancholy*, part 2, section 2, mem 4; Henry Morley, *Character writings of the seventeenth century* (London: Routledge, 1891), 206–7; S. T. Irwin ed., *Microcosmography: or, A piece of the world discovered in essays and characters, by John Earle D.D.* (Bristol: Crofton Hemmons, 1896), 66–7, 112–13.

18 Historical Manuscripts Commission, *Thirteenth Report* (London: Her Majesty's Stationery Office, 1892), 56–8; John Fell, biographical preface to Richard Allestree, *Forty sermons whereof twenty one are now first publish'd* (Oxford: Scott, Wells, Sawbridge, Bentley, 1684), 3–4.

19 Frederick Varley ed., *Mercurius Aulicus: a diurnall communicating the intelligence and affaires of the Court to the rest of the Kingdome . . .* (Oxford: Blackwell, 1948), 57; Fell, preface to Allestree, *Forty sermons*, 18–19.

20 Fell, preface to Allestree, *Forty sermons*, 8–9; Andrew Clark ed., *The Life and Times of Anthony Wood, antiquary, of Oxford, 1632–1695*, vol. 1 (Oxford: Oxford Historical Society, 1891), 299.

21 Richard Allestree, *The Gentlemans Calling* (London: Timothy Garthwaite, 1660), unpaginated preface.

22 Sir Walter Raleigh ed., *The Complete Works of George Savile, First Marquess of Halifax* (Oxford: Clarendon Press, 1912), 188–9.

23 Fell, preface to Allestree, *Forty sermons*, 18, 19–20.

24 Maurice Exwood and H. L. Lehmann eds, *The Journal of William Schellinks' Travels in England, 1661–1663* (London: Royal Historical Society, 1993), 97; Robert Beddard, 'Restoration Oxford and the Remaking of the Protestant Establishment', in Tyacke ed., *History of the University of Oxford*, vol. 4, 804.

25 Beddard, 'Restoration Oxford', 803.

26 Clark ed., *Life and Times of Anthony Wood*, 348.

27 Sir William Holdsworth, *A History of English Law*, vol. 6 (London: Methuen, 1924), 540–1, 543; Holdsworth, *Sources and Literature of English Law* (Oxford: Clarendon Press, 1925), 193–6; Basil Duke Henning ed., *The House of Commons, 1660–1690*, vol. 1 (London: Secker & Warburg, 1983), 4.

28 Edward Hyde, Earl of Clarendon, *The History of the Rebellion and Civil Wars in England*, book IV (describing the events of 1641, and written at intervals in 1646–8; first published 1702–4). See edition published by Oxford University Press in 1840, 130–1.

29 Allestree, *Gentlemans Calling*, 22, 26, 27.

30 Historical Manuscripts Commission, *Report on the Manuscripts of Allan George Finch, Esquire, of Burley-on-the-hill, Rutland*, vol. 1 (London: His Majesty's Stationery Office, 1913), 212, 216, 218, 237, 443.

31 John Nichols ed., *The Miscellaneous Works of Bishop Atterbury*, vol. 2 (London: J. Nichols, 1799), 2.

32 Locke, *Some Thoughts Concerning Education*, 156–7, 241–3.

33 Ibid., §94.

34 Amelia Heber, *The Life of Reginald Heber, D.D., Lord Bishop of Calcutta*, vol. 1 (London: John Murray, 1830), 470.

35 Alexander Allardyce ed., *Letters from and to Charles Kirkpatrick Sharpe*, vol. 1 (Edinburgh: Blackwood, 1888), 121, 442–3.

36 Lord Holland, *Further Memoirs of the Whig Party: 1807–1821*, ed. Lord Stavordale (London: John Murray, 1905), 116; William Anthony Hay, *Lord Liverpool: A Political Life* (Woodbridge: Boydell Press, 2018), 28–33; R. G. Thorne ed., *The House of Commons, 1790–1820*, vol. 5 (London: Secker & Warburg, 1986), 510; BL Add ms 38580, f. 16, Cyril Jackson to Lord Hawkesbury, 6 May 1787; BL Add ms 59772, ff. 5 and 11, Robert Jenkinson to Lord Hawkesbury, 26 April and 4 June 1787.

37 Peter Jupp ed., *The Letter-Journal of George Canning, 1793–1795* (London: Royal Historical Society, 1992), 49, 112, 131.

38 BL Add ms 89143/1/1/78, Cyril Jackson to George Canning, 1 September 1788.

39 BL Add ms 40605, f. 12, Cyril Jackson to Robert Peel, 28 January 1810; E. G. W. Bill, *Education at Christ Church, Oxford, 1660–1800* (Oxford: Clarendon Press, 1988), 72–3; Laurence Brockliss, *The University of Oxford: A History* (Oxford: Oxford University Press, 2016), 335.

40 Edward Copleston, *A Reply to the Calumnies of the Edinburgh Review against Oxford: containing an account of studies pursued in that university* (Oxford: printed for the author, 1810), 159–60, 169, 176–7.

41 Lord Acton, *Lectures on the French Revolution*, ed. J. N. Figgis and R. V. Laurence (London: Macmillan, 1910), 94, 97.

42 Lucy Sutherland and Leslie Mitchell eds, *History of the University of Oxford*, vol. 5 (Oxford: Clarendon Press, 1986), 622.

43 Allardyce ed., *Letters from and to Charles Kirkpatrick Sharpe*, vol. 1, 111.

44 James Bryce, *Studies in Contemporary Biography* (London: Macmillan, 1903), 301–2.

45 Angus Hawkins, *The Forgotten Prime Minister: The 14th Earl of Derby*, vol. 1 (Oxford: Oxford University Press, 2007), 19–22.

46 Copleston, *A Reply to the Calumnies of the Edinburgh Review against Oxford*, 152.

47 Robert David Anderson, *European Universities from the Enlightenment to 1914* (Oxford: Oxford University Press, 2004), 3.

48 Edward Nares, *Heraldic Anomalies*, vol. 2 (London: G. and W. B. Whitaker, 1824), 151, 155–6.

49 J. C. Masterman, *To Teach the Senators Wisdom, or an Oxford Guide-Book* (London: Hodder & Stoughton, 1952), 180–1; Geoffrey Faber, *Oxford Apostles: A Character Study of the Oxford Movement* (London: Faber & Faber, 1933), 129; John Ruskin, *Praeterita and Dilecta* (London: Everyman, 2005), 229; Thomas Huxley, *Aphorisms and Reflections* (London: Macmillan, 1908), 26.

50 Robert Beaken ed., *Faithful Witness: The Confidential Diaries of Alan Don, Chaplain to the King, the Archbishop and the Speaker, 1931–1940* (London: S.P.C.K., 2020), 163; Lawrence Goldman, *The Life of R. H. Tawney: Socialism and History* (London: Bloomsbury, 2013), 22; Richard Southern, *History and Historians: Select Papers* (Oxford: Blackwell, 2004), 171.

Chapter 3: *The Tigers of Old Time*

1 R. G. Collingwood, *The Idea of History* (Oxford: Clarendon Press, 1946), 204; Benedetto Croce, *History as the Story of Liberty*, trans. Sylvia Sprigge (London: Allen & Unwin, 1941), 15, 17, 18, 32–3.

2 Edward Hall, *The History of England during the Reign of Henry the Fourth and the Succeeding Monarchs to the End of the Reign of Henry the Eighth* (London: Rivington, 1809), 46–7, 112–13 (usually known as *Hall's Chronicle*); David Womersley, *Divinity and State* (Oxford: Oxford University Press, 2010), 100–1, 104–5, 107.

3 Katherine Duncan-Jones and Jan van Dorsten eds, *Miscellaneous Prose of Sir Philip Sidney* (Oxford: Clarendon Press, 1973), 83–4.

4 John Hale ed., *Guicciardini: History of Italy and History of Florence*, trans. Cecil Grayson (New York: Washington Square Press, 1964), vii.

5 John Addington Symonds, *Renaissance in Italy: The Catholic Reaction*, part 1 (London: Smith Elder, 1904), 233–7.

6 Francesco Guicciardini, *Maxims and Reflections of a Renaissance Statesman (Ricordi)*, trans. Marco Domandi (New York: Harper Torchbooks, 1965), C1, C125, C140, C157, B32; 39, 72–3, 76, 81, 104.

7 Hugh Trevor-Roper, *Renaissance Essays* (London: Secker & Warburg, 1985), 123.

8 Hugh Trevor-Roper, *Europe's Physician: The Various Life of Sir Theodore de Mayerne* (New Haven: Yale University Press, 2006), 120–1.

9 William Camden, *Britain, or a chorographicall description of the most flourishing kingdomes*, vol. 1 (London: George Bishop & John Norton, 1610), 377.

10 Trevor-Roper, *Renaissance Essays*, 135.

11 William Camden, *Remains Concerning Britain* (London: John Russell Smith, 1870), 2.

12 Trevor-Roper, *Europe's Physician*, 194.

13 William Camden, 'Author to Reader', prefatory essay to *Annales of Great Britain under Queen Elizabeth* (Camden wrote the book in 1607–17; his Latin text was published in 1615–25; English translations were published, after his death, in 1625–9).

14 *The Works of the ever memorable John Hales of Eaton*, vol. 1 (Glasgow: Foulis, 1765), 170–1.

15 Sir Charles Firth, *Essays: Historical and Literary* (Oxford: Clarendon Press, 1938), 42, 54, 57; Sir Keith Thomas, 'A Puritan Jihadi', *New York Review of Books*, 23 June 2022, 54.

16 Thomas Fuller, *The History of the Holy War* (London: William Pickering, 1840), vi.

17 Blair Worden, *God's Instruments: Political Conduct in the England of Oliver Cromwell* (Oxford: Oxford University Press, 2012), 376–9, 388–9.

18 Ibid., 373, 376, 377, 378.

19 Clarendon, *History of the Rebellion and Civil Wars in England*, book IV.

20 Leopold von Ranke, *History of England, principally in the seventeenth century*, vol. 6 (Oxford: Clarendon Press, 1875), 29; Worden, *God's Instruments*, 373; *Lord Macaulay's History of England*, vol. 1 (London: J. M. Dent, 1906), 129–30; Henry Hallam, *The Constitutional History of England from the accession of Henry VII to the death of George II* (London: John Murray, 1850 edn), vol. 1, 496–7; Lord Morley of Blackburn, *Oliver Cromwell* (London: Macmillan, 1921), 84.

21 Henry Peacham, *The Compleat Gentleman*, ed. George Gordon (Oxford: Clarendon Press, 1906), 51–3.

22 Joseph Mordaunt Crook, *Brasenose: The Biography of an Oxford College* (Oxford: Oxford University Press, 2008), 89; Basil Henning Duke ed., *The House of Commons, 1660–1690*, vol. 3 (London: Secker & Warburg, 1983),

123–4; Thomas Fuller, dedicatory epistle of *The History of the Holy War* (first published in 1639), vi.

23 Daniel Defoe, *Augusta Triumphans: or, the way to make London the most flourishing city in the universe* (London: Nutt, Dodd & Stagg, 1728), 5; Chesterfield, letter to Samuel Madden, 15 April 1749, in Lord Mahon ed., *The Letters of Philip Dormer Stanhope, Earl of Chesterfield*, vol. 3 (London: Richard Bentley, 1845), 340; Hallam, *Constitutional History*, vol. 2, 413.

24 Historical Manuscripts Commission, *Report on the Manuscripts of His Grace the Duke of Portland, K.G.*, vol. 7 (London: His Majesty's Stationery Office, 1901), 224; Viscount Bolingbroke, *Letters on the Study and Use of History* (London: Capell, 1779), 14.

25 Sir Charles Firth, *Modern Languages at Oxford, 1724–1929* (London: Oxford University Press, 1929), 5–6.

26 William Ward, *Georgian Oxford: University Politics in the Eighteenth Century* (Oxford: Clarendon Press, 1958), 132.

27 Bill, *Education at Christ Church*, 279.

28 Ibid., 58–9, 281; J. R. H. Weaver, *Henry William Carless Davis, 1874–1928, and a Selection of his Historical Papers* (London: Constable, 1933), 66–7.

Chapter 4: The Great Charm of Lucid Order

1 Edmund Sheridan Purcell, *Life of Cardinal Manning, Archbishop of Westminster*, vol. 1 (London: Macmillan, 1895), 43; Stephen Paget, *Henry Scott Holland: Memoir and Letters* (London: John Murray, 1921), 50; Falconer Madan, 'Oxford', in *Encyclopaedia Britannica*, vol. 18 (Edinburgh: Adam & Charles Black, 1885), 94.

2 E. Geoffrey W. Bill, *University Reform in Nineteenth-Century Oxford: A Study of Henry Halford Vaughan, 1811–1885* (Oxford: Clarendon Press, 1973), 17. I follow chapter 3 of Bill's book closely in these paragraphs.

3 H. J. C. Grierson ed., *The Letters of Sir Walter Scott*, vol. 8 (London: Constable, 1935), 300–1; Arthur Hassall, *Christ Church, Oxford: An Anthology in Prose and Verse* (London: Hodder & Stoughton, 1911), 97.

4 Mark Pattison, *Memoirs* (London: Macmillan, 1885), 21–2; 'Death of Lord Conyers Osborne', *The Times*, 22 February 1831.

5 Sir Llewellyn Woodward, *The Age of Reform, 1815–1870* (Oxford: Clarendon Press, 1938), 489.

6 Keith Feiling, *A History of England: From the Coming of the English to 1918* (London: Macmillan, 1950), 801; Augustus and Julius Hare, *Guesses at Truth by Two Brothers*, vol. 1 (London: Taylor & Walton, 1848 edn), 54–5.

7 Walter Bagehot, *Complete Works*, vol. 3, ed. Norman St John-Stevas (London: The Economist, 1968), 213.

8 Charles Cooper, *Annals of Cambridge*, vol. 4 (Cambridge: Warwick, 1853), 581–2; Lewis Campbell, *On the Nationalization of the Old English Universities* (London: Chapman & Hall, 1901), 43.

9 George Russell ed., *Letters of Matthew Arnold, 1848–1888*, vol. 1 (London: Macmillan, 1895), 206.

10 'Parliamentary Intelligence', *The Times*, 2 August 1834.

11 Henry Offley Wakeman, *An Introduction to the History of the Church of England: from the earliest times to the present day* (London: Rivingtons, 1896), 468; Lyulph Stanley, *Oxford University Reform* (London: Simpkins Marshall, 1869), 11–12; Geoffrey Faber, *Oxford Apostles: A Character Study of the Oxford Movement* (London: Faber & Faber, 1933), 136, 399; Harold Anson, *T. B. Strong: Bishop, Musician, Dean, Vice-Chancellor* (London: S.P.C.K., 1949), 12.

12 Pattison, *Memoirs*, 236–7; Andrew Lang, *Oxford: brief historical and descriptive notes* (London: Seeley, 1890), 240, 242–3; Evelyn Abbott and Lewis Campbell eds, *The Life and Letters of Benjamin Jowett, M.A.: Master of Balliol College, Oxford*, vol. 1 (London: John Murray, 1897), 190–1.

13 Arnold Haultain ed., *A Selection from Goldwin Smith's Correspondence . . . between the Years 1846 and 1910* (London: T. Werner Laurie, 1913), 1, 6.

14 Goldwin Smith, *Reminiscences*, ed. Arnold Haultain (New York: Macmillan, 1910), 103.

15 Richard Southern, *History and Historians: Selected Papers*, ed. P. J. Bartlett (Oxford: Blackwell, 2004), 89.

16 Henry Parry Liddon, *Sermons on some words of Christ* (London: Longmans Green, 1892), 264–5; Lord Redesdale, *Memories*, vol. 1 (London: Hutchinson, 1915), 95; Edward Talbot, *Memories of Early Life* (London: A. R. Mowbray, 1924), 41–2, 44.

17 Edward Dowden, *Shakespere, a critical study of his mind and art* (London: Henry King, 1875), 34.

18 Mandell Creighton, *Historical Lectures and Addresses*, ed. Louise Creighton (London: Longmans Green, 1903), 215–16; Louise Creighton, *Life and Letters of Mandell Creighton D.D. Oxon and Cam* (London: Longmans Green, 1905), vol. 2, 501; Sir John Marriott, *Memories of Four Score Years* (London: Blackie, 1946), 57; Lord Acton, *Historical Essays and Studies* (London: Macmillan, 1907), 428.

19 Creighton, *Mandell Creighton*, vol. 1, 74; James Kirby, *Historians and the Church of England: Religion and Historical Scholarship, 1870–1920* (Oxford: Oxford University Press, 2016), 3–4.

20 Richard Jenkyns, *The Victorians and Ancient Greece* (Oxford: Blackwell, 1980), 14; A. V. Dicey, 'Blackstone's Commentaries', *National Review*, vol. 54 (December 1909), 653–75.

21 Southern, *History and Historians*, 122–3; William Holden Hutton, *William Stubbs, Bishop of Oxford, 1825-1901* (London: Constable, 1906), 95; Philippa Levine, *The Amateur and the Professional: Antiquarians, Historians and Archaeologists in Victorian England, 1838-1886* (Cambridge: Cambridge University Press, 1986), 37.

22 G. Cecil White, *A Versatile Professor: Reminiscences of the Rev. Edward Nares D.D.* (London: Brimley Johnson, 1903); V. H. H. Green, 'An Early Regius Professor', *Oxford Magazine*, 4 December 1958, 155–7.

23 Edward Nares, *Views of the Evidences of Christianity at the End of the Pretended Age of Reason: in eight sermons preached before the University of Oxford* (Oxford: University Press, 1805), 23, 475.

24 Edward Nares, *Elements of General History, Ancient and Modern*, vol. 3 (London: T. Cadell, 1822), 205, 231, 235, 483–4, 487.

25 White, *Versatile Professor*, 239–40; Hare and Hare, *Guesses at Truth by Two Brothers*, vol. 1, 50.

26 White, *Versatile Professor*, 240–3; Edward Nares, *Heraldic Anomalies*, vol. 2 (London: G. and W. B. Whitaker, 1824), 157; Henry Halford Vaughan, *Oxford Reform and Oxford Professors: A reply to certain objections urged against the report of the Queen's commissioners* (London: John Parker, 1854), 49.

27 Thomas Arnold, *Introductory Lectures on Modern History delivered in Lent Term, MDCCCXLI* (London: Longmans Green, 1874), 23–4, 25, 28, 31.

28 Hassall, *Christ Church, Oxford*, 99.

29 George Valentine Cox, *Recollections of Oxford* (London: Macmillan, 1868), 180–1.

30 Jenkyns, *Victorians and Ancient Greece*, 15; John Antony Cramer, *An Inaugural Lecture on the study of Modern History: delivered in the Clarendon, Oxford, March 2, 1843* (Oxford: T. Combe, 1843), 18, 28–30.

31 Cramer, *Inaugural Lecture*, 8, 19–20.

32 See generally Bill, *University Reform*.

33 Evelyn Abbott and Lewis Campbell eds, *Letters of Benjamin Jowett, M.A.: Master of Balliol College, Oxford* (London: John Murray, 1899), 164–5; Henry Halford Vaughan, *Two Lectures on Modern History, delivered on inauguration, October 1849* (Oxford: John Henry Parker, 1849), 8, 16–17.

34 Bill, *University Reform*, 185; Michael Brock and Mark Curthoys eds, *The History of the University of Oxford*, vol. 7, part 2 (Oxford: Clarendon Press, 2000), 41.

35 Countess Cowper, *Earl Cowper, K.G.: A Memoir* (Panshanger: privately printed, 1913), 35, 669, 710–11.

36 Goldwin Smith, *Lectures on Modern History, delivered in Oxford, 1859-61* (Oxford: J. H. Parker, 1861), 13–17; A. L. Smith, *Frederic William Maitland:*

two lectures and a bibliography (Oxford: Clarendon Press, 1908), 3, 38, 47; J. Horace Round, *Peerage and Pedigree: Studies in Peerage Law and Family History*, vol. 1 (London: St Catherine Press, 1910), ix.

37 Abbott and Campbell eds, *Life and Letters of Benjamin Jowett*, vol. 1, 176–7.

38 Vaughan, *Oxford Reform*, 29, 90–1; Lewis Farnell, *An Oxonian Looks Back* (London: Hopkinson, 1934), 33.

39 Southern, *History and Historians*, 92; Sir Sidney Lee, *King Edward VII*, vol. 1 (London: Macmillan, 1925), 77; Brock and Curthoys, *History of University of Oxford*, vol. 7, part 2, 42; Goldwin Smith, *The Reorganization of the University of Oxford* (Oxford: James Parker, 1868), 34; Arnold Haultain ed., *A Selection from Goldwin Smith's Correspondence . . . between the Years 1846 and 1910* (London: T. Werner Laurie, 1913), 24, 33; Lord Acton, *The History of Freedom and Other Essays*, ed. John Neville Figgis and Reginald Vere Laurence (London: Macmillan, 1909), 236.

40 George Russell ed., *Letters of Matthew Arnold, 1848–1888*, vol. 1 (London: Macmillan, 1895), 157; Haultain, *Goldwin Smith's Correspondence*, 17; James Bryce, *Studies in Contemporary Biography* (London: Macmillan, 1903), 76.

41 Frederick York Powell, 'William Stubbs, Bishop of Oxford', *Manchester Guardian*, 23 April 1901.

42 William Stubbs, *Seventeen Lectures on the Study of Mediaeval and Modern History* (Oxford: Clarendon Press, 1900), 15–16; William Stubbs, *The Constitutional History of England: in its origins and development*, vol. 1 (Oxford: Clarendon Press, 1875), 224.

43 William Stubbs, *Lectures on European History*, ed. Arthur Hassall (London: Longmans Green, 1904), 11; Stubbs, *Seventeen Lectures*, 465; John Hale ed., *The Evolution of British Historiography: From Bacon to Namier* (London: Macmillan, 1967), 58.

44 Stubbs, *Seventeen Lectures*, 465–6.

45 Henry Scott Holland, *Personal Studies* (London: Wells, Gardner, Darton, 1905), 222; Stubbs, *Seventeen Lectures*, 19, 31, 471.

46 Stubbs, *Seventeen Lectures*, 239, 258, 271–2.

47 William Stubbs, *Lectures on Early English History*, ed. Arthur Hassall (London: Longmans Green, 1906), 370–2; Stubbs, *Seventeen Lectures*, 255.

48 Stubbs, *Early English History*, 336–7; Stubbs, *Seventeen Lectures*, 470–1.

49 William Stubbs, *Historical Introductions to the Rolls Series*, ed. Arthur Hassall (London: Longmans Green, 1902), 91–2.

50 Stubbs, *Early English History*, 237.

51 Ibid., 211, 369–70.

52 Ibid., 370; Stubbs, *European History*, 96.

53 Abbott and Campbell eds, *Letters of Benjamin Jowett*, 243; John Morley,

On Compromise (London: Chapman & Hall, 1874), 31; Farnell, *Oxonian*, 57; Mary Smith, *Arthur Lionel Smith, Master of Balliol (1916–1924)* (London: John Murray, 1928), 75–6.

54 Morley, *On Compromise*, 90; John Octavius Johnston, *Life and Letters of Henry Parry Liddon* (London: Longmans Green, 1904), 239; Thorold Rogers, 'Oxford Professors and Oxford Tutors', *Contemporary Review*, vol. 56 (1889), 930.

55 Stubbs, *Seventeen Lectures*, 442–3.

Chapter 5: Frederick York Powell: Heathen, Anarchist and Jingo

1 Oliver Elton, *Frederick York Powell* (Oxford: Clarendon Press, 1906), vol. 1, 203.

2 *The Complete Tales of Henry James*, vol. 8 (London: Rupert Hart Davis, 1963), 27.

3 Robin Darwall-Smith, *A History of University College, Oxford* (Oxford: Oxford University Press, 2008), 369; Elton, *York Powell*, vol. 1, 14.

4 Lord Redesdale, *Memories*, vol. 1 (London: Hutchinson, 1915), 100; E. G. W. Bill and J. F. A. Mason, *Christ Church and Reform, 1850–1867* (Oxford: Clarendon Press, 1970), 135–6; 'Death of the Duke of Hamilton K.T.', *Daily Telegraph*, 18 May 1895; Cecil Day Lewis and Charles Fenby eds, *Anatomy of Oxford* (London: Cape, 1938), 235.

5 Edward Talbot, *Memories of Early Life* (London: A. R. Mowbray, 1924), 31–2.

6 Harold Anson, *T. B. Strong: Bishop, Musician, Dean, Vice-Chancellor* (London: S.P.C.K., 1949), 10–12.

7 Elton, *York Powell*, vol. 1, 264.

8 Algernon Stedman, *Oxford: Its Social and Intellectual Life* (London: Trübner, 1878), 20–1; Elton, *York Powell*, vol. 1, 15.

9 Henry Thompson, *Henry George Liddell: a memoir* (London: John Murray, 1899), 181; Elton, *York Powell*, vol. 1, 16–17.

10 Elton, *York Powell*, vol. 1, 162; Evelyn Abbott and Lewis Campbell eds, *Letters of Benjamin Jowett, M.A.: Master of Balliol College, Oxford* (London: John Murray, 1899), 154.

11 Stephen Paget and John Crum, *Francis Paget, Bishop of Oxford, Chancellor of the Order of the Garter, and Sometime Dean of Christ Church* (London: Macmillan, 1912), 21–2; Andrew Lang, *Oxford: brief historical and descriptive notes* (London: Seeley, 1890), 244; William Whyte, *Redbrick: A Social and Architectural History of Britain's Civic Universities* (Oxford: Oxford University Press, 2015), 151.

12 Louise Creighton, *Life and Letters of Mandell Creighton D.D. Oxon and Cam* (London: Longmans Green, 1905), vol. 2, 503–5.

13 Thompson, *Liddell*, 206.

14 Elton, *York Powell*, vol. 2, 20.

15 Clare Hopkins, *Trinity: 450 Years of an Oxford College Community* (Oxford: Oxford University Press, 2005), 279.

16 Elton, *York Powell*, vol. 2, 84, 89.

17 Ibid., 82–3, 89–90.

18 William Stephens, *The Life and Letters of Edward A. Freeman*, vol. 1 (London: Macmillan, 1895), 112; Elton, *York Powell*, vol. 1, 86–8.

19 Elton, *York Powell*, vol. 1, 116–17, 254; John and Florence MacCunn, *Recollections of W. P. Ker, by Two Friends* (Glasgow: MacLehose, 1924), 6; Laurie Magnus, *Herbert Warren of Magdalen: President and Friend, 1853–1930* (London: John Murray, 1932), 113–16.

20 Elton, *York Powell*, vol. 1, 163, and vol 2, 365–6; Roy Harrod, 'Dodgson of Christ Church', *Times Literary Supplement*, 11 December 1970; Claude Blagden, *Well Remembered* (London: Hodder & Stoughton, 1953), 118.

21 Elton, *York Powell*, vol. 1, 22, 427; David Ogg, *Herbert Fisher: A Short Biography* (London: Arnold, 1947), 34–5; Lewis Farnell, *An Oxonian Looks Back* (London: Hopkinson, 1934), 125.

22 Elton, *York Powell*, vol. 1, 92, 177, 440.

23 Farnell, *Oxonian*, 125.

24 Elton, *York Powell*, vol. 1, 166–7.

25 Sir Charles Oman, *On the Writing of History* (London: Methuen, 1939), 243.

26 Elton, *York Powell*, vol. 1, 170, 300.

27 Ibid., 199.

28 Ibid., 201–2.

29 Ibid., 447–8.

30 Ibid., vol. 2, 422–3; Lady Raleigh ed., *The Letters of Sir Walter Raleigh (1879–1922)*, vol. 2 (London: Methuen, 1926), 310.

31 Elton, *York Powell*, vol. 1, 107–8.

32 Ibid., 423–4.

33 Ibid., 117, 172, 214, 289; vol. 2, 339.

34 Ibid., vol. 2, 1–2, 4, 12, 94–5.

35 Ibid., vol. 1, 498; Thomas Huxley, *Aphorisms and Reflections* (London: Macmillan, 1908), 24, 158.

36 Elton, *York Powell*, vol. 2, 11, 334–5; William Stubbs, *Seventeen Lectures on the Study of Mediaeval and Modern History* (Oxford: Clarendon Press, 1900), 466–7, 468, 470.

37 Elton, *York Powell*, vol. 1, 417; vol. 2, 85.

38 Elton, *York Powell*, vol. 2, 9–10.

39 Ibid., 325–6, 331.

40 Ibid., vol. 1, 282.

41 Ibid., vol. 2, 183, 186–7.

42 Ibid., 334–5.

43 Ibid., vol. 1, 262–3, 396; vol. 2, 13. Emphasis in original.

Chapter 6: Arthur Hassall: The History Ring

1 William Courthope, 'Women at Oxford and Cambridge', *Quarterly Review*, vol. 186 (October 1897), 540; Lord Charnwood ed., *Discourses and Letters of Hubert Murray Burge, Bishop of Oxford, 1919–1925* (London: Chatto & Windus, 1930), 7; Sir Charles Tennyson, *Life's All a Fragment* (London: Cassell, 1953), 13.

2 Edward Thring, *Theory and Practice of Teaching* (Cambridge: Cambridge University Press, 1883), 80.

3 C. R. L. Fletcher, *Mr Gladstone at Oxford 1890* (London: Smith Elder, 1908), 51; Edward Dicey, editorial, *Observer*, 7 January 1872.

4 Algernon M. M. Stedman [later Methuen], *Oxford: Its Social and Intellectual Life* (London: Trübner, 1878), 22.

5 'Mr Arthur Hassall, An Oxford Tutor for Forty Years', *The Times*, 24 November 1930.

6 Stephen Paget and John Crum, *Francis Paget, Bishop of Oxford, Chancellor of the Order of the Garter, and Sometime Dean of Christ Church* (London: Macmillan, 1912), 22; J. C. Masterman, *On the Chariot Wheel: An Autobiography* (Oxford: Oxford University Press, 1975), 59.

7 Stedman [Methuen], *Oxford*, 27–8.

8 John Henry Newman, *The Idea of a University, defined and illustrated*, discourse v, section 9 (1852) (London: Longmans Green, 1891 edn), 120–1; Claude Colleer Abbott ed., *The Letters of Gerard Manley Hopkins to Robert Bridges* (London: Oxford University Press, 1935), 175–6.

9 Henry Scott Holland, *A Bundle of Memories* (London: Gardner, Darton, 1915), 63, 66–7; Henry Nevinson, *Changes and Chances* (London: Nisbet, 1923), 43.

10 Harold Anson, *T. B. Strong: Bishop, Musician, Dean, Vice-Chancellor* (London: S.P.C.K., 1949), 33; Claude Blagden, *Well Remembered* (London: Hodder & Stoughton, 1953), 150.

11 Anson, *Strong*, 24–6.

12 Anon., 'How to choose a college in Oxford', *National Review*, 48 (1906), 285.

13 Stephen McKenna, *While I Remember* (London: Thornton Butterworth, 1921), 57, 60–1.

14 A. V. Dicey, *Introduction to the Study of the Law of the Constitution* (London: Macmillan, 1885), 14.

15 Laurie Magnus, *Herbert Warren of Magdalen: President and Friend, 1853–1930* (London: John Murray, 1932), 51; Arnold Haultain ed., *A Selection from Goldwin Smith's Correspondence . . . between the Years 1846 and 1910* (London: T. Werner Laurie, 1913), 188.

16 Cecil H. King, *Strictly Personal: Some Memoirs* (London: Weidenfeld & Nicolson, 1969), 47.

17 Blagden, *Well Remembered*, 116–17.

18 Masterman, *Chariot Wheel*, 116.

19 Andrew Lang, *Oxford: brief historical and descriptive notes* (London: Seeley, 1890), 246–9; Hastings Rashdall, *The Theory of Good and Evil: A Treatise on Moral Philosophy*, vol. 1 (Oxford: Oxford University Press, 1907), viii; Stephen Leacock, *My Discovery of England* (London: Bodley Head, 1922), 81.

20 Thorold Rogers, 'Oxford Professors and Oxford Tutors', *Contemporary Review*, vol. 56 (1889), 934; Charles Firth, *A Plea for the Historical Teaching of History* (Oxford: Clarendon Press, 1904), 19.

21 Christ Church Library, ms 580/1, Strong to Dundas, 29 October 1917.

22 Arthur J. Engel, *From Clergyman to Don: The Rise of the Academic Profession in Nineteenth-Century Oxford* (Oxford: Clarendon Press, 1983), 83–4; Margaret Lodge, *Sir Richard Lodge: A Biography* (Edinburgh: Blackwood, 1946), 32; Elsa Richmond ed., *The Earlier Letters of Gertrude Bell* (London: Ernest Benn, 1937), 119, 124, 135, 142; Sir John Marriott, *Memories of Four Score Years* (London: Blackie, 1946), 57; Sir Ernest Barker, *Age and Youth: Memories of Three Universities* (Oxford: Oxford University Press, 1953), 19–21, 26–8.

23 *The Times*, 1 May 1899 and 24 November 1930; Richmond, *Earlier Letters of Gertrude Bell*, 113, 115, 119, 125, 138, 160, 171.

24 Henry Offley Wakeman, *Essays introductory to the study of English Constitutional History by Resident Members of the University of Oxford* (London: Longmans Green, 1891), 2, 267.

25 Harold Steinhart, *The History of the Canning Club, from 1861 to 1911* (Oxford: privately printed for the club by Hart, 1911), 233; Henry Offley Wakeman, *An Introduction to the History of the Church of England, from the earliest times to the present day* (London: Rivingtons, 1896), 384–6, 446–8.

26 *Oxford House Papers: a series of papers for working-men, written by members of the University of Oxford*, first series (London: Rivingtons, 1890), 213, 214, 225.

27 Marriott, *Memories*, 61; Lord Curzon of Kedleston, *Principles & Methods of University Reform, Being a Letter Addressed to the University of Oxford*

(Oxford: Clarendon Press, 1909), 46; Masterman, *Chariot Wheel*, 150.

28 Reba Soffer, *Discipline and Power: The University, History, and the Making of an English Elite, 1870–1930* (California: Stanford University Press, 1994), 34, 37, 47, 56.

29 Arthur Hassall, *Life of Viscount Bolingbroke* (Oxford: Blackwell, 1915), 71, 171.

30 Arthur Hassall, *Louis XIV and the Zenith of the French Monarchy* (London: Putnam's, 1910), 83, 85, 96–7.

31 Arthur Hassall, *The History of British Foreign Policy from the Earliest Times to 1912* (Edinburgh: Blackwood, 1912), 281–2, 284, 344.

32 George Saintsbury, *A Scrap Book* (London: Macmillan, 1922), 45–6, 49.

33 Richmond, *Earlier Letters of Gertrude Bell*, 115; William Stubbs, *Seventeen Lectures on the Study of Mediaeval and Modern History* (Oxford: Clarendon Press, 1900), 472.

34 Steinhart, *Canning Club*, 290.

35 Ibid., 332.

36 Christ Church Library, ms 580/1, John Murray to Dundas, two undated letters [soon after 24 February 1915] on notepaper of the headmaster of Eton and of the Christ Church Oxford Mission, Faraday Road, Notting Hill; Kumar P. S. Menon, *Many Worlds: An Autobiography* (London: Oxford University Press, 1965), 49–52.

37 J.N.H.M. in *Oxford Magazine*, 27 November 1924.

38 David Fleming, *Hellfire: Evelyn Waugh and the Hypocrites Club* (Cheltenham: History Press, 2022), 40–1; EUL 113/2/2, diary of A. L. Rowse, 5 December 1922 and 14 March 1923; Keith Winter, *Other Man's Saucer* (London: Heinemann, 1930), 120, 125.

39 John Betjeman, *An Oxford University Chest* (London: John Miles, 1938), 41.

Chapter 7: Keith Feiling: Never Hurry, Never Pause

1 Sir John Masterman, *On the Chariot Wheel: An Autobiography* (Oxford: Oxford University Press, 1975), 152–3; John McManners, *Fusilier: Recollections and Reflections, 1939–1945* (Wilby: Michael Russell, 2002), 23.

2 Keith Feiling, 'Victorian England', *Observer*, 6 December 1936.

3 Keith Feiling, *The Life of Neville Chamberlain* (London: Macmillan, 1947), 83; Keith Feiling, *The Study of the Modern History of Great Britain, 1862–1946: An Inaugural Lecture Delivered on 1 February 1947* (Oxford: Clarendon Press, 1947), 5–6, 17–19.

4 Mary Smith, *Arthur Lionel Smith, Master of Balliol (1916–1924): A Biography and Some Reminiscences by his Wife* (London: John Murray, 1928), 305–9.

5 Cyril Bailey, *Francis Fortescue Urquhart: A Memoir* (London: Macmillan, 1936), 39–45, 104.

6 J. R. H. Weaver and Austin Lane Poole eds, *Henry William Carless Davis, 1874–1928* (London: Constable, 1933), 77–9; 'The Regius Professor', *Oxford Magazine*, 5 February 1925.

7 Keith Feiling, 'Government of Free Men', *Sunday Times*, 25 November 1945; Sir Ernest Barker, *Age and Youth: Memories of Three Universities* (London: Oxford University Press, 1953), 58, 187; Julia Stapleton, *Englishness and the Study of Politics: The Social and Political Thought of Ernest Barker* (Cambridge: Cambridge University Press, 1994), 123–4.

8 Thomas Case, 'Greek at Oxford', *The Times*, 22 November 1911; Thomas Case, *Letters to 'The Times', 1884–1922* (Oxford: John Johnson, 1927), 83; George Binney Dibblee, *The Psychological Theory of Value* (London: Constable, 1924), 226.

9 J. W. Mackail, *James Leigh Strachan-Davidson, Master of Balliol: A Memoir* (Oxford: Clarendon Press, 1925), 81; Richard Symonds, *Oxford and Empire: The Last Lost Cause* (London: Macmillan, 1986), 52.

10 Charles Whibley, *The Letters of an Englishman*, vol. 1 (London: Constable, 1911), 209–11; Mackail, *Strachan-Davidson*, 91.

11 Peter Brown, *Journeys of the Mind* (Oxford: Princeton University Press, 2023), 39, 43, 46.

12 Lord Curzon of Kedleston, *Principles & Methods of University Reform: Being a Letter Addressed to the University of Oxford* (Oxford: Clarendon Press, 1909), 210–11.

13 Norman Douglas, *South Wind* (London: Martin Secker, 1917), chapter 6; Keith Feiling, *A History of England: From the Coming of the English to 1918* (London: Macmillan, 1950), 1041.

14 Christ Church Library, ms 580/1, Dean Strong to Robin Dundas, 18 August 1914, Keith Feiling to Dundas, 2 September 1914.

15 Christ Church Library ms 580/1, Strong to Dundas, 27 February and 17 August 1917; A. J. Ayer, *Part of my Life* (London: Collins, 1977), 81; Hugh Trevor-Roper, *The Letters of Mercurius* (London: John Murray, 1970), 105.

16 Harold Anson, *T. B. Strong: Bishop, Musician, Dean, Vice-Chancellor* (London: S.P.C.K., 1949), 32; Ronald Jasper, *Arthur Cayley Headlam: Life and Letters of a Bishop* (London: Faith Press, 1960), 136.

17 Samuel Eliot Morison, 'An American Professor's Reflections on Oxford', *Spectator*, 7 and 14 November 1925.

18 George Gordon, *The Discipline of Letters* (Oxford: Clarendon Press, 1946), 15–16.

19 Morison, 'An American Professor's Reflections on Oxford', 7 November 1925.

20 Charles Firth, *A Plea for the Historical Teaching of History* (Oxford: Clarendon Press, 1904), 15.

21 Richard Davenport-Hines, *Conservative Thinkers from All Souls College Oxford* (Woodbridge: Boydell Press, 2022), 71-4; Keith Feiling, *Toryism: A Political Dialogue* (London: Bell, 1913); Feiling, 'What is Conservatism?', *Criterion Miscellany 14* (London: Faber & Faber, 1930); Feiling, 'Principles of Conservatism', *Political Quarterly*, vol. 24 (1953).

22 Wallace Notestein, 'Feiling: A History of the Tory Party', *History*, vol. 11 (April 1926), 69; Robert Blake, 'Keith Feiling', *Spectator*, 24 September 1977.

23 Peter Quennell, *The Marble Foot: An Autobiography, 1905-1938* (London: Collins, 1976), 115; Harold Acton, *More Memoirs of an Aesthete* (London: Methuen, 1970), 24; Dacre Balsdon, *Oxford Life* (London: Eyre & Spottiswoode, 1957), 257-8.

24 G. M. Trevelyan, 'Charles II's Foreign Policy', *Observer*, 28 September 1930, and 'Century of Party History', *Observer*, 17 July 1938; Keith Feiling, 'The Missing Muse Found', *Observer*, 21 February 1932.

25 Edward Armstrong, *Poems* (Oxford: Oxford University Press, 1931), 5; McManners, *Fusilier*, 23.

26 Feiling, *Study of the Modern History of Great Britain*, 13-14.

27 Notestein, 'Feiling', 70.

28 Keith Feiling, 'History without Bias', *Listener*, 21 October 1931.

29 G. M. Young, *Victorian England: Portrait of an Age* (London: Oxford University Press, 1936), 99.

30 Keith Feiling, *A History of the Tory Party, 1640-1714* (Oxford: Clarendon Press, 1924), 14-15, 17; *Oxford Magazine*, 25 February 1926.

31 Ibid., 61-2, 68-9, 493.

32 Basil Williams, 'Review of Books', *English Historical Review*, vol. 47 (January 1932), 121.

33 Feiling, *Toryism*, 51-2.

34 Bodleian, Ms Dep. d. 782, f. 177, 1137th meeting of the Canning Club, 27 January 1926; Alan Lennox-Boyd, 'The Attitude of the University towards Conservatism', *Oxford Magazine*, 10 June 1926.

35 Philip Murphy, *Alan Lennox-Boyd: A Biography* (London: I.B. Tauris, 1999), 12-13, 17.

36 Henry Channon, *The Diaries*, vol. 1: *1918-38*, ed. Simon Heffer (London: Hutchinson, 2021), 831, 868.

37 Tom Harrisson, *Letter to Oxford* (Wyck: Hate Press, 1933), 32, 47; Derek Walker-Smith, 'International Snobbery', in Richard Comyns Carr ed., *Red Rags: Essays of Hate from Oxford* (London: Chapman & Hall, 1933), 64-5.

38 Derek Walker-Smith, *Coming This Way? The Politics of Plenty* (London: Sampson Low, Marston, 1948), 4-6.

39 Feiling, 'What is Conservatism?', 8.

40 EUL 113/1/2/4/1, Rowse notes on Feiling and Oman, November 1962; EUL 113/1/2/4/4, Rowse notes on Feiling, October 1974.

41 Feiling, 'What is Conservatism?', 5–7.

42 Keith Feiling, *Sketches in Nineteenth Century Biography* (London: Longmans Green, 1930), 89, 105.

43 Keith Feiling, 'Coleridge as Politician: A Conservative Forerunner', *The Times*, 22 September 1925; Feiling, *Sketches*, 88, 90, 92–3.

44 Feiling, *Sketches*, 4, 6–7, 9.

45 Ian Gilmour [Lord Gilmour of Craigmillar], *Memoirs, 1926–1957* (London: Umbria Press, 2014), 112–16.

46 Keith Feiling, 'Landings in Egypt', *The Times*, 6 November 1956.

47 Samuel Finer et al., *Backbench Opinion in the House of Commons, 1955–59* (Oxford: Pergamon Press, 1961), 90, 92, 119–20.

48 Feiling, *History of England*, 813–14.

49 Keith Feiling, 'The Story of 1936', *Observer*, 2 June 1940; Feiling, *Chamberlain*, 297; Feiling, 'Chiel Amang Them', *The Times*, 25 April 1961; Reba Soffer, *History, Historians and Conservatism in Britain and America: The Great War to Thatcher and Reagan* (Oxford: Oxford University Press, 2009), 95.

50 Churchill Archives Centre, Cambridge, CHAR 1/205/55–6, Keith Feiling to Winston Churchill, 5 May 1929; Martin Gilbert ed., *Winston S. Churchill: Documents*, companion vol. 5, part 1 (London: Heinemann, 1979), 1418–19 and companion vol. 5, part 2 (London: Heinemann, 1981), 246; Maurice Ashley, 'Sir Keith Feiling', *The Times*, 24 September 1977; Keith Feiling, 'Mr Churchill on British Policy', *Observer*, 25 June 1939.

51 Feiling, *Chamberlain*, 150, 197, 458.

52 Keith Feiling, *In Christ Church Hall* (London: Macmillan, 1960), 6.

Chapter 8: J. C. Masterman: Doyen of the Modern History Corps

1 J. C. Masterman, *On the Chariot Wheel: An Autobiography* (Oxford: Oxford University Press, 1975), 1; Harry Pitt, '"I Think You'll Find": A Portrait of J. C. Masterman', *Worcester College Record* (1999), 53; Willie Elmhirst, *A Freshman's Diary, 1911–1912* (Oxford: Blackwell, 1969), 5.

2 Michael Innes [J. I. M. Stewart], *Death at the President's Lodging* (London: Gollancz, 1936), 10; *The Complete Works of W. H. Auden: Prose, 1926–1938*, ed. Edward Mendelson (Princeton: Princeton University Press, 1996), 31.

3 Paul Roberts, 'Francis Lys', *Oxford Magazine*, 16 October 1947, 8–10.

4 Masterman, *Chariot Wheel*, 56; Sir John Marriott, *Memories of Four Score Years* (London: Blackie, 1946), 91–3.

5   'Death of Lord Morley', *Manchester Guardian*, 24 September 1923; J. C. Squire, 'John Morley as a Writer', *Observer*, 30 September 1923.

6   John Morley, *On Compromise* (London: Chapman & Hall, 1874), 4–5; Sir Duncan Wilson, *Gilbert Murray OM* (Oxford: Oxford University Press, 1987), 61, 78.

7   Sir John Masterman, *Bits and Pieces* (London: Hodder & Stoughton, 1961), 83–7; Masterman, *Chariot Wheel*, 76; Winwood Reade, *The Martyrdom of Man*, 17th edn (London: Kegan Paul, Trench, Trübner, 1903), 543–4.

8   Meredith Dewey, *Diaries, Letters, Writings*, ed. A. V. Grimstone and M. C. Lyons (Cambridge: Pembroke College, 1992), 209; Anon., *Letters of Arthur George Heath, Fellow of New College, with Memoir by Gilbert Murray* (Oxford: Blackwell, 1917), 126.

9   Arreen Grundy (Brasenose), 'The Religion of the Undergraduate, by an Oxford Undergraduate', *Nineteenth Century*, vol. 97 (May 1925), 672; Masterman, *Chariot Wheel*, 77; 'Sir John Masterman: Service in MI5 and Oxford', *The Times*, 7 June 1977.

10 Masterman, *Chariot Wheel*, 85.

11 Masterman, *Bits and Pieces*, 42; Worcester College archives, Masterman papers 10/1/24, Arthur Hassall to Masterman, 24 May 1914.

12 Masterman, *Bits and Pieces*, 44–5.

13 Sir John Balfour, *Not Too Correct an Aureole: The Recollections of a Diplomat* (Wilton: Michael Russell, 1983), 10; Ben Rogers, *A. J. Ayer: A Life* (London: Chatto & Windus, 1999), 252; Frederic Raphael, *Last Post* (Manchester: Carcanet, 2023), 409.

14 Worcester College archives, Masterman papers 10/1/17/15, lecture in German prisoner-of-war camp.

15 Pitt, 'Portrait', 55.

16 Masterman, *Chariot Wheel*, 128–9; Worcester College archives, Masterman papers 10/1/24.

17 Michael Ramsey, *From Gore to Temple: The Development of Anglican Theology between Lux Mundi and the Second World War, 1889–1939* (London: Longmans, 1960), 147; see generally Keith Briant and George Joseph eds, *Be Still and Know: Oxford in Search of God* (London: Michael Joseph, 1936); *Oxford Magazine*, 15 October 1920.

18 Sir John Masterman, 'Late Duke of Norfolk', *The Times*, 1 March 1975; Christ Church Library, ms 580/1, James Butterwick to Robin Dundas, 21 May 1928; Sir Roy Harrod, *The Prof: A Personal Memoir of Lord Cherwell* (London: Macmillan, 1959), 150; Bodleian, Ms Dep. d. 782, minutes of Oxford Canning Club meeting 1125, 4 May 1925.

19 Masterman, *Chariot Wheel*, 67; J. C. Masterman, *To Teach the Senators Wisdom, or an Oxford Guide-Book* (London: Hodder & Stoughton, 1952), 44–5, 175.

20 Masterman, *Chariot Wheel*, 125–6.

21 Solomon Bandaranaike, *Speeches and Writings* (Colombo: Department of Information & Broadcasting, 1963), 5, 7, 9, 10.

22 Percy Matheson, *The Life of Hastings Rashdall D.D.* (Oxford: Oxford University Press, 1928), 95; Eton College Library, VAC 7, diary of Victor Cazalet, 8 October, 6 November and 2 December 1919, 4 and 10 March 1920.

23 Robert Rhodes James, *Victor Cazalet: A Portrait* (London: Hamish Hamilton, 1976), 69, 73, 78; Bandaranaike, *Speeches*, 37; Stuart Ball ed., *Parliament and Politics in the Age of Churchill and Attlee: The Headlam Diaries, 1935–1951* (London: Cambridge University Press, 1999), 374; Henry Channon, *The Diaries*, vol. 2: *1938–43*, ed. Simon Heffer (London: Hutchinson, 2021), 1038–40.

24 'Portrait Gallery', *Sunday Times*, 19 October 1958; Anon., *C. H. Wilkinson, 1888–1960* (Oxford: Oxford University Press, 1965), 58; 'Danger of Orthodox Mediocrity', *The Times*, 29 November 1956; 'Bigger Universities Terrifying', *The Times*, 27 August 1958.

25 Worcester College archives, Masterman papers 1/17/10, Lecture 7, 'Burke and the French Revolution'.

26 Worcester College archives, Masterman papers 10/1/21; W. K. Hancock, *Ricasoli and the Risorgimento in Tuscany* (London: Faber & Gwyer, 1926), 205, 224, 229.

27 Worcester College archives, Masterman papers 10/1/21.

28 Worcester College archives, Masterman papers 10/1/17/10 and 10/1/21.

29 Worcester College archives, Masterman papers 10/1/17/30.

30 Ibid.

31 Ibid.

32 Masterman, *Senators Wisdom*, 160, 174.

33 Worcester College archives, Masterman papers 10/1/70, J. C. Masterman, memorandum on Alec Dunglass at Christ Church, n.d. [January 1964]; Masterman, *Senators Wisdom*, 175.

34 Worcester College archives, Masterman papers 10/1/17/10, lecture on the growth of democracy in England.

35 Worcester College archives, Masterman papers 10/1/22, Advice to candidates sitting Schools [n.d., c. 1934].

36 Worcester College archives, Masterman papers 10/1/24, Masterman's private memorandum to members of the research committee, 1931.

37 Masterman, *Senators Wisdom*, 20.

38 Masterman, *Bits and Pieces*, 8–9, 86; Isaiah Berlin, *Flourishing: Letters 1928–1946*, ed. Henry Hardy (London: Chatto & Windus, 2004), 142.

39 Masterman, *Chariot Wheel*, 204; Pitt, 'Portrait', 60.

40 Edward Harrison, 'J. C. Masterman and the Security Service, 1940–1972', in Harrison, *Secret Service against the Nazi Regime* (Barnsley: Pen & Sword, 2022), 155–90; Pitt, 'Portrait', 54.

41 Berlin, *Flourishing*, 502; Robin Darwall-Smith, *A History of University College, Oxford* (Oxford: Oxford University Press, 2008), 501.

42 Worcester College archives, Masterman papers 10/1/74.

43 NA PREM 8/1144, Sir Stafford Cripps to Clement Attlee, 17 January 1948, and LMET to Attlee, 23 January 1948; NA T 215/90, Sir Edward Bridges to Cripps, 16 June 1947.

44 Pitt, 'Portrait', 56, 59.

45 'Sir John Masterman: Service in MI5 and Oxford', *The Times*, 7 June 1977.

Chapter 9: Roy Harrod: Keynesian on a Slum Island

1 An excellent biographical memoir, which I have followed gratefully, is Henry Phelps Brown, 'Henry Roy Forbes Harrod, 1900–1978', *Proceedings of the British Academy*, vol. 65 (London: British Academy, 1981), 656, reprinted from *Economic Journal*, vol. 90 (March 1980). For a shorter study, see Walter Eltis, 'Roy F. Harrod (1900–1978)', in Robert Cord ed., *The Palgrave Companion to Oxford Economics* (Cham: Springer Nature Switzerland, 2021), 309–29.

2 Roy Harrod, 'Economics, 1900–1950', in Alan Pryce-Jones ed., *The New Outline of Knowledge* (New York: Simon & Schuster, 1956), 471.

3 'Stained Wings', *Daily Telegraph*, 4 March 1930.

4 Merlin Holland and Rupert Hart-Davis eds, *The Complete Letters of Oscar Wilde* (London: Fourth Estate, 2000), 782, 1022; Roy Harrod, 'Oscar Wilde', *Times Literary Supplement*, 27 July 1962, and 'Wilde's De Profundis', *Times Literary Supplement*, 30 August 1963.

5 Roy Harrod, *The Prof: A Personal Memoir of Lord Cherwell* (London: Macmillan, 1959), 21.

6 Roy Harrod, 'A New University: A. D. Lindsay and the Keele Experiment', *Listener*, 22 December 1960; Drusilla Scott, *A. D. Lindsay: A Biography* (Oxford: Blackwell, 1971), 237; Roy Harrod, 'Lord Nuffield's Foundation in Oxford', *Economic Journal*, vol. 47 (December 1937); G. N. Clark, 'Alexander Dunlop Lindsay', *Oxford Magazine*, 8 May 1952, 304–6.

7 Anon., *Letters of Arthur George Heath, Fellow of New College, Oxford* (Oxford: Blackwell, 1917), 60; Lionel Robbins, *Autobiography of an Economist* (London: Macmillan, 1971), 111.

8 Harrod, *The Prof*, 19, 21.

9 M. W. Rowe, *J. L. Austin: Philosopher and D-Day Intelligence Officer*

(Oxford: Oxford University Press, 2023), 82, 87; Harrod, *The Prof*, 23, 24, 26; Sir Hans Krebs, *Reminiscences and Reflections* (Oxford: Clarendon Press, 1981), 200.

10 Roy Harrod, *Sociology, Morals, and Mystery: The Chichele Lectures Delivered in Oxford under the Auspices of All Souls College, 1970* (London: Macmillan, 1971), 6; Roy Harrod, *The Life of John Maynard Keynes* (London: Macmillan, 1951), 59; Harrod, *The Prof*, 40–1.

11 Beverley Nichols, *Patchwork* (London: Evergreen/Heinemann, 1940 edn), 46–7, 91, 151–2, 188.

12 Anon. [Roy Harrod], 'A Brilliant Oxford Figure', *The Times*, 3 July 1971; Hugh Lloyd-Jones ed., *Maurice Bowra: A Celebration* (London: Duckworth, 1974), 9–15; Sir Maurice Bowra, *The Greek Experience* (London: Weidenfeld & Nicolson, 1957), 71.

13 All Souls archives, Sparrow papers 59, Roy Harrod to John Sparrow, 25 November 1961; BL Add ms 72775, Roy Harrod, memorandum 'Walter Runciman: a crucial link', n.d. [1975?]; Michael Bloch and Susan Fox, *Bloomsbury Stud: The Life of Stephen ('Tommy') Tomlin* (London: M.A.B., 2020), 31–3, 210; Nigel Nicolson and Joanne Trautmann eds, *The Letters of Virginia Woolf*, vol. 3 (London: Hogarth Press, 1977), 155; Maurice Bowra, *New Bats in Old Belfries, or Some Loose Tiles*, ed. Henry Hardy and Jennifer Holmes (Oxford: Robert Dugdale, 2005), 73.

14 Henry Channon, *The Diaries*, vol. 3: *1943–57*, ed. Simon Heffer (London: Hutchinson, 2022), 856.

15 S. E. Morison, 'An American Professor's Reflections on Oxford', *Spectator*, 7 November 1925.

16 'Dr Joseph Wells', *The Times*, 1 March 1929; Dame Margaret Cole, *The Life of G. D. H. Cole* (London: Macmillan, 1971), 141.

17 Harrod, 'Economics, 1900–1950', 469, 471.

18 Roy Harrod, 'John Maynard Keynes and the Power of Reason', *Listener*, 5 February 1948.

19 BL Add ms 72728, Robin Dundas to Roy Harrod, 30 August 1923; Harrod, *Maynard Keynes*, 319–20, 321–2.

20 Harrod, *Maynard Keynes*, 321; Cheryl Misak, *Frank Ramsey: A Sheer Excess of Powers* (Oxford: Oxford University Press, 2020), 111, 195, 220.

21 BL Add ms 72728, Robin Dundas to Roy Harrod, 30 August 1923; Roger Venables, *'D': Portrait of a Don* (Oxford: Blackwell, 1967), 2; Sir John Masterman, *On the Chariot Wheel: An Autobiography* (Oxford: Oxford University Press, 1975), 117.

22 BL Add ms 71616, John Masterman to Roy Harrod, 25 July 1924.

23 BL Add ms 71611, Keith Feiling to Roy Harrod, 22 July 1924; BL Add ms 72728, Robin Dundas to Harrod, 18 December 1926; Harrod, *The Prof*,

41; Robert Blake, 'A Personal Memoir', in Walter Eltis, Maurice Scott and James Wolfe eds, *Induction, Growth and Trade: Essays in Honour of Sir Roy Harrod* (Oxford: Clarendon Press, 1970), 2.

24 Michael Davie ed., *The Diaries of Evelyn Waugh* (London: Weidenfeld & Nicolson, 1976), 188; Henry Channon, *The Diaries*, vol. 1: *1918–38*, ed. Simon Heffer (London: Hutchinson, 2021), 711.

25 William Plomer ed., *A Message in Code: The Diary of Richard Rumbold, 1932–60* (London: Weidenfeld & Nicolson, 1964), 29; Hugh Thomas, *John Strachey* (London: Eyre Methuen, 1973), 5. Strachey substituted the forename of John for Evelyn when he changed his affiliation to the Labour party.

26 Tangye Lean, 'A Proust Gap Bridged', *Spectator*, 20 February 1953; L. P. Hartley, *Sixth Heaven* (London: Putnam, 1946), 56; Henry Green, *Pack my Bag* (London: Hogarth Press, 1940), 210–11; Bodleian, Ms Dep. d. 783, Canning Club minutes of meeting 1195, 28 November 1928.

27 Harrod, *The Prof*, 149, 155.

28 Ibid., 41; Roy Harrod, 'A New University', *Listener*, 22 December 1960; Blake, 'Personal Memoir', 11.

29 Sir Maurice Bowra, *Memories* (London: Weidenfeld & Nicolson, 1966), 115; Isaiah Berlin, *Flourishing: Letters, 1928–1946*, ed. Henry Hardy (London: Chatto & Windus, 2004), 58.

30 Christ Church Library, mss 580/1, Roy Harrod to Robin Dundas, 12 August 1925; Roy Harrod, 'The Spare Chancellor', *Listener*, 5 November 1959; BL Add ms 72775, Roy Harrod to Frances Harrod, 24 April 1929.

31 Misak, *Frank Ramsey*, 305.

32 Cecil King, *Strictly Personal: Some Memoirs* (London: Weidenfeld & Nicolson, 1969), 47; BL Add ms 71617, Frederick Lindemann to Roy Harrod, 27 February 1926; BL Add ms 72731, Gilbert Ryle to Harrod, 6 and [11?] March 1931; A. J. Ayer, *Part of my life* (London: Collins, 1977), 142, 231.

33 Jacob Bronowski, 'The Legendary Prof', *Observer*, 27 September 1959; Angus Wilson, 'Harrod and Hero-Worship', *Spectator*, 9 October 1959; C. P. Snow, 'Lord Cherwell', *New Statesman*, 26 September 1959.

34 Christ Church Library, mss 580/1, Roy Harrod to Robin Dundas, 12 August 1925; Roy Harrod, *Liberal Plan for Peace* (London: Gollancz, 1944), 10; Roy Harrod, *And So It Goes On: Further Thoughts on Present Mismanagement* (London: Rupert Hart-Davis, 1951), 120.

35 Candida Lycett Green ed., *John Betjeman: Letters, 1926–1951* (London: Methuen, 1994), 224; EUL 113/1/3, Roy Harrod to A. L. Rowse, 16 July 1932.

36 Frank Pakenham, *Born to Believe: An Autobiography* (London: Cape, 1953), 86–7.

37 Lycett Green, *Betjeman Letters*, 223–4.

38 Nigel Nicolson ed., *The Letters of Virginia Woolf*, vol. 5 (London: Hogarth Press, 1979), 248; Anne Olivier Bell ed., *The Diary of Virginia Woolf*, vol. 4 (London: Hogarth Press, 1982), 188; Herbert Hensley Henson, *The Group Movement* (Oxford: Oxford University Press, 1933), 48; Cecil Day Lewis, *Starting Point* (London: Cape, 1937), 83; Richard Crossman ed., *Oxford and the Groups* (Oxford: Blackwell, 1934).

39 Harrod, 'Peace Aims and Economics', *Horizon*, vol. 1 (1940), 155–7, 160–1.

40 Harrod, *The Prof*, 167; Ayer, *Part of my Life*, 177.

41 Winston S. Churchill, *Documents: The Wilderness Years, 1929–1935*, ed. Martin Gilbert (London: Heinemann, 1981), 1305–7; BL Add ms 71183, Winston Churchill to Roy Harrod, 5 November 1935.

42 Harrod, *The Prof*, 168; Bodleian, papers of Viscount Simon 100/118, G. M. Trevelyan to Simon, 10 June 1952; Simon 100/126, Trevelyan to Simon, 13 June 1952.

43 Harrod, 'The End of an Experiment?', *Spectator*, 21 August 1936.

44 Harrod, *The Prof*, 171.

45 Ayer, *Part of my Life*, 217–18.

46 Ben Pimlott ed., *The Second World War Diary of Hugh Dalton, 1940–45* (London: Cape, 1986), 41; Harrod, *The Prof*, 227–8; Roy Harrod, *A Page of British Folly* (London: Macmillan, 1946), iii.

47 Roy Harrod, *Liberal Plan for Peace* (London: Gollancz, 1944), 113; Peter Catterall ed., *The Macmillan Diaries*, vol. 2 (London: Macmillan, 2011), 362.

48 Harrod, *British Folly*, 58–9.

49 Roy Harrod, *Towards a Dynamic Economics: Some Recent Developments of Economic Theory and their Application to Policy* (London: Macmillan, 1948), 146, 148, 149, 152, 155.

50 NA KV 2/4116, Roy Harrod to Guy Burgess, 23 July 1956; KV 2/4120, serial 939a, Harrod to Burgess, 12 April 1957; KV 2/4132, serial 1329a, Harrod to Burgess, 15 March 1960; KV 2/4606, serial 296a, Harrod to Burgess, 24 October 1960; KV 2/4138, serial 1556a, Harrod to Burgess, 18 January 1963.

51 'Liberal's Gloomy View of our Trade Prospects', *Manchester Guardian*, 31 July 1948.

52 Anon., *The Challenge of our Time* (London: Percival Marshall, 1948), 11, 14; Max Beloff, 'University of the Air', *Oxford Magazine*, 1 November 1956, 57–8.

53 Roy Harrod, 'Freedom and the New Society', *Listener*, 27 September 1951.

54 Harrod, *Towards a Dynamic Economics*, 150; Harrod, *And So It Goes*, 121; BL Add ms 72765, Quintin Hogg to Roy Harrod, 25 August 1950; Balliol College archives, diary of Harold Nicolson, 29 December 1952.

55 G. D. H. Cole, 'A Modern Epic', *Oxford Magazine*, 3 May 1951, 377–8; Noël Annan, 'John Maynard Keynes', *Times Literary Supplement*, 23

February 1951; Isaiah Berlin, *Affirming: Letters, 1975–1997*, ed. Henry Hardy and Mark Pottle (London: Chatto & Windus, 2015), 94.

56 'The Motor Car Problem', *Oxford Magazine*, 19 February 1931; Bodleian, Grant Duff papers 45/2, Goronwy Rees to Sheila Grant Duff, 21 January 1932; Michael Innes [pseudonym of J. I. M. Stewart], *Death at the President's Lodging* (London: Gollancz, 1936), 8; Day Lewis, *Starting Point*, 39; J. M. Thompson, *Collected Verse, 1939–46* (Oxford: Blackwell, 1947), 106–7; Edmund Wilson, *The Fifties* (New York: Farrar, Straus & Giroux, 1986), 134; Frank Costigliola, *Kennan: A Life between Two Worlds* (Oxford: Princeton University Press, 2023), 395.

57 BL Add ms 71196, Robert Blake to Roy Harrod, 27 September 1956; Judith Curthoys, *The Cardinal's College: Christ Church, Chapter and Verse* (London: Profile, 2012), 29–32; Robert Blake, 'Westminster Scene', *Illustrated London News*, 29 January 1966.

58 BL Add ms 72765, Roy Harrod to Edward Boyle, n.d. [c. 5 November 1956]; Add ms 71618, Harrod to James Stuart, 6 December 1956; Add ms 71196, Robert Blake to Harrod, 27 September 1956, Harrod to Anthony Eden, 17 July 1959, Eden to Harrod, 25 July and 7 December 1959.

59 J. I. M. Stewart, *A Use of Riches* (London: Gollancz, 1957), 11; Nicholas Davenport, 'Economic Tract for the Times', *Times Literary Supplement*, 20 March 1959.

60 Roy Harrod, 'Why I shall vote Conservative', *Observer*, 20 September 1959.

61 John Carey, *The Unexpected Professor: An Oxford Life in Books* (London: Faber & Faber, 2014), 150.

62 BL Add ms 72804, Hugh Trevor-Roper to Roy Harrod, 21 February 1963; information from Stephen Keynes; Phelps Brown, 'Harrod', 696; Thomas Balogh, 'Are these harrodships really necessary?', *Oxford Magazine*, 2 March 1961, 273.

63 Roy Harrod, 'Britain, the Free World and the Six', *The Times*, 2 January 1962; BL Add ms 71194, Roy Harrod to Lord Selborne, 31 March 1962; Robert F. Dewey, *British National Identity and Opposition to Membership of Europe, 1961–63: The Anti-Marketeers* (Manchester: Manchester University Press, 2009), 105.

64 John Vaizey, 'Essays in Expansionism', *Times Literary Supplement*, 26 October 1967.

Chapter 10: Patrick Gordon Walker: Writing for the Workers

1 Patrick Gordon Walker, *An Outline of Man's History: Plebs Outline Number 7* (London: National Council of Labour Colleges, 1939), iii.

2   John Campbell, *Roy Jenkins: A Well-Rounded Life* (London: Cape, 2014), 40.

3   Cecil Day Lewis and Charles Fenby eds, *Anatomy of Oxford* (London: Cape, 1938), 23; Neal Wood, *Communism and British Intellectuals* (London: Gollancz, 1959), 29–30, 37.

4   G. D. H. Cole, *The Intelligent Man's Guide through World Chaos* (London: Gollancz, 1932), 611; R. H. Tawney, 'Labour Party History', *Times Literary Supplement*, 10 March 1950.

5   Sir Robert Ensor, *England, 1870–1914* (Oxford: Clarendon Press, 1936), 502.

6   Sir Duncan Wilson, *Gilbert Murray OM* (Oxford: Oxford University Press, 1987), 318.

7   Sir Reginald Coupland, *The Empire in These Days* (London: Macmillan, 1935), 111.

8   Rollo St Clare Talboys, *A Victorian School: Being the Story of Wellington College* (Oxford: Blackwell, 1943), 61, 63, 74; Talboys, 'Teaching as a University Function', *Oxford Magazine*, 3 March 1927.

9   Sir Griffith Williams, 'Mr R. St. C. Talboys', *The Times*, 6 October 1953; Sir Michael Howard, *Captain Professor* (London: Continuum, 2006), 28, 33; Miriam J. Benkovitz, *Ronald Firbank: A Biography* (London: Weidenfeld & Nicolson, 1970), 33–5.

10 Robin Dundas, 'Mr R. St. C. Talboys', *The Times*, 30 October 1953; another version in *Christ Church Annual Report* for 1953; María Jesús Gonzáles Hernández, *Raymond Carr: The Curiosity of the Fox* (Brighton: Sussex Academic Press, 2013), 79–82; obituary of Gordon Stevens in *The Times*, 28 September 2019.

11 P. C. Gordon Walker, 'Varsity Sports and the Age Limit', 'De-Rating' and 'New Haloes for Old', *Daily Telegraph*, 5 November and 6 December 1928, 25 February 1929.

12 Richard Southern, *History and Historians: Selected Papers*, ed. P. J. Bartlett (Oxford: Blackwell, 2004), 129, 133.

13 Peter Vansittart, 'An extra-muralist of wisdom and wit', *Guardian*, 21 September 1989; Wolfgang Liebeschuetz, 'William Hugh Clifford Frend, 1916–2005', *Proceedings of the British Academy*, vol. 150 (Oxford: Oxford University Press, 2007), 38.

14 W. J. K. Diplock, *Isis, or the Future of Oxford* (London: Kegan Paul, 1929), 36, 49–50.

15 Patrick Gordon Walker, 'The Historical Background', in *The Future of Germany*, Peace Aims pamphlet 19, 1943, 3–5, 8.

16 Patrick Gordon Walker, 'Real Factors Governing German Politics To-Day', *Daily Telegraph*, 25 July 1932; Patrick Gordon Walker, *Restatement of Liberty* (London: Hutchinson, 1951), 281.

17 Gordon Walker, 'Real Factors'.

18 Patrick Gordon Walker, *Political Diaries, 1932–1971*, ed. Robert Pearce (London: Historians' Press, 1991), 57.

19 G. D. H. Cole, *The Intelligent Man's Guide through World Chaos* (London: Gollancz, 1932), 559, 568; Cole, *Europe, Russia and the Future* (London: Gollancz, 1941), 15–17.

20 Lewis Namier, *Skyscrapers, and Other Essays* (London: Macmillan, 1931), 44; Arthur Koestler, *The Invisible Writing* (London: Collins, 1954), 32.

21 J. Hampden Jackson, *Europe since the War: A Sketch of Political Development, 1918–1932* (London: Gollancz, 1933), 40, 94, 140.

22 George Gordon, *The Discipline of Letters* (Oxford: Clarendon Press, 1946), 113.

23 Gordon Walker, *Political Diaries*, 57–8.

24 Ibid., 58–9.

25 Ibid., 59.

26 Douglas Jay, *The Socialist Case* (London: Faber & Faber, 1937), 318.

27 Hugh Lloyd-Jones, Valerie Pearl and Blair Worden eds, *History and Imagination: Essays in Honour of H. R. Trevor-Roper* (London: Duckworth, 1981), 358.

28 J. D. Griffith Davies, 'Modern History', *Times Literary Supplement*, 4 April 1935.

29 G. M. Young, 'Testament of Faith', *Sunday Times*, 3 December 1950; Earl of Birkenhead, *The Prof in Two Worlds: The Official Life of Professor F. A. Lindemann, Viscount Cherwell* (London: Collins, 1961), 151, 153.

30 Gordon Walker, *Political Diaries*, 78.

31 R. H. S. Crossman, 'Freedom and the Will to Power', *Horizon*, vol. 1 (May 1940), 323–7; Michael Ignatieff, *Isaiah Berlin: A Life* (London: Chatto & Windus, 1998), 59; Nicola Lacey, *A Life of H. L. A. Hart: The Nightmare and the Noble Dream* (Oxford: Oxford University Press, 2004), 24; *Oxford Magazine*, 1 March 1956, p. 318.

32 Peter Conradi, *A Very English Hero: The Making of Frank Thompson* (London: Bloomsbury, 2013), 114.

33 Hugh Trevor-Roper, 'Understudy', *Sunday Times*, 14 March 1954; Philip Toynbee, *Friends Apart: A Memoir of the Thirties* (London: MacGibbon & Kee, 1954), 48; Churchill College, Cambridge archives, GNWR/2/1/1, Ian Bowen to Patrick Gordon Walker, 19 October 1938, and Geoffrey Hudson to Gordon Walker, 13 October 1938; E. R. Dodds, *Missing Persons: An Autobiography* (Oxford: Clarendon Press, 1977), 131.

34 Churchill College, Cambridge archives, GNWR/2/1/1, Patrick Gordon Walker, 'The Lindsay candidature in Oxford, Oct. 1938'.

35 Gordon Walker, 'The Historical Background'.

36 Gordon Walker, *Liberty*, 252, 253, 255–6.

37 Tangye Lean, *Voices in the Darkness: The Story of the European Radio War* (London: Secker & Warburg, 1943), 84–5; Thomas Harding, *The Maverick: George Weidenfeld and the Golden Age of Publishing* (London: Weidenfeld & Nicolson, 2023), 34–5.

38 'Mr. D. Sington', *The Times*, 19 February 1968.

39 Patrick Gordon Walker, *The Lid Lifts* (London: Gollancz, 1945), 69–72; Alan Gordon Walker, *Patrick Gordon Walker: A Political and Family History* (London: Umbria Press, 2022), 40, 156–72.

40 Iris Murdoch, *Living on Papers: Letters, 1934–1995*, ed. Avril Horner and Anne Rowe (London: Chatto & Windus, 2015), 44; Gordon Walker, *Political Diaries*, 165–6.

41 Churchill College, Cambridge archives, GNWR/2/1/2, Patrick Gordon Walker, 'Labour's Chance: The Lesson of Oxford', 30 October 1938.

42 'Profile: Patrick Gordon Walker', *Observer*, 26 March 1950; Philip Williams ed., *The Diary of Hugh Gaitskell, 1945–1956* (London: Jonathan Cape, 1983), 173, 236, 238.

43 Gordon Walker, *Liberty*, 13.

44 Murdoch, *Living on Papers*, 120; Gordon Walker, *Liberty*, 182, 309; Herbert Butterfield, *Christianity and History* (London: G. Bell, 1950), 104.

45 Arnold Toynbee, *Acquaintances* (London: Oxford University Press, 1967), 242; Evan Durbin and John Bowlby, *Personal Aggressiveness and War* (London: Kegan Paul, 1939), 17, 74.

46 Gordon Walker, *Liberty*, 115–17.

47 Ibid., 13–14, 126.

48 Ibid., 178–80.

49 Earl of Avon, *The Memoirs of the Rt. Hon. Sir Anthony Eden: Full Circle* (London: Hodder & Stoughton, 1960), 320; Peter Catterall ed., *The Macmillan Diaries*, vol. 2 (London: Macmillan, 2011), 519, 652.

50 William Rees-Mogg, 'The Heirs Apparent', *Sunday Times*, 27 January 1963.

51 Gordon Walker, *Patrick Gordon Walker*, 101, 104, 106; Tony Benn, *Out of the Wilderness: Diaries, 1963–67* (London: Hutchinson, 1987), 234; Janet Morgan ed., *The Backbench Diaries of Richard Crossman* (London: Hamish Hamilton, 1981), 1022; Cecil King, *Diary, 1965–70* (London: Jonathan Cape, 1972), 109, 141; Richard Crossman, *The Diaries of a Cabinet Minister*, vol. 1 (London: Hamish Hamilton, 1975), 135.

52 Jonathan Price, *Everything Must Go* (London: Secker & Warburg, 1985), 23.

Chapter 11: Hugh Trevor-Roper: Drawn to Convulsions

1 Hugh Trevor-Roper, 'Namierana', *Sunday Times*, 1 June 1952. For the life and ideas of Trevor-Roper, see Adam Sisman, *Hugh Trevor-Roper* (London: Weidenfeld & Nicolson, 2010), and Blair Worden, 'Hugh Redwald Trevor-Roper, 1914–2003', *Proceedings of the British Academy*, vol. 150 (2007), 247–84.

2 Hugh Trevor-Roper, 'Selected Notices', *Horizon*, vol. 12 (November 1945), 353, 355.

3 Sir John Elliott, *Spain, Europe and the Wider World, 1500–1800* (New Haven: Yale University Press, 2009), xiii, 25; Elliott, 'The "General Crisis of the Seventeenth Century"', in Blair Worden ed., *Hugh Trevor-Roper: The Historian* (London: I.B. Tauris, 2016), 45.

4 Hugh Trevor-Roper, *One Hundred Letters from Hugh Trevor-Roper*, ed. Richard Davenport-Hines and Adam Sisman (Oxford: Oxford University Press, 2014), 43–4, 47–8; and a distillation from unpublished letters in Dacre papers 17/1/1.

5 Hugh Trevor-Roper, 'Apologia transfugae', *Spectator*, 14 July 1973.

6 Hugh Trevor-Roper, 'The Glory that was Greece', *Sunday Times*, 27 October 1957; Sir Maurice Bowra, *The Greek Experience* (London: Weidenfeld & Nicolson, 1957), 16–17; Rory Allan, 'The Historian as Public Intellectual', in Worden, *Hugh Trevor-Roper*, 260.

7 Hugh Trevor-Roper, *Wartime Journals*, ed. Richard Davenport-Hines (London: I.B. Tauris, 2012), 27–8; S. J. V. Malloch, 'The Classicism of Hugh Trevor-Roper', *Cambridge Classical Journal*, vol. 61 (2015), 52; Dacre papers 113/29/3.

8 Arnaldo Momigliano, *Studies in Historiography* (London: Weidenfeld & Nicolson, 1966), 91; G. P. Gooch, *History and Historians in the Nineteenth Century*, 2nd edn (London: Longmans Green, 1952), xxv; Peter Brown, *Journeys of the Mind* (Oxford: Princeton University Press, 2023), 129, 172.

9 Hugh Trevor-Roper, 'Wrack and Crumbling', *New Statesman*, 12 April 1958.

10 Michael Rostovtzeff, *The Social and Economic History of the Roman Empire* (Oxford: Clarendon Press, 1926), 486–7; (vol. 1, 541 of 1958 edition).

11 Alex Danchev, *Oliver Franks: Founding Father* (Oxford: Clarendon Press, 1993), 151; Hugh Trevor-Roper, 'The liberal tide', *Spectator*, 22 December 1990; Neal Ascherson, 'The Liquidator', *London Review of Books*, 5 January 2016; Trevor-Roper, *One Hundred Letters*, 274; Hugh Trevor-Roper, 'The Torments of Lord Acton', *Sunday Times*, 7 October 1956; Hugh Trevor-Roper, *Archbishop Laud, 1573–1645* (London: Macmillan, 1940), 3.

12 Joseph Needham, 'Laudian Marxism: Thoughts on Science, Religion and Socialism', *Criterion*, vol. 12 (October 1932), 56–72.

13 Arnaldo Momigliano, *Essays in Ancient and Modern Historiography* (Oxford: Blackwell, 1977), 1; Brown, *Journeys of the Mind*, 95, 137.

14 Fred Inglis, *History Man: The Life of R. G. Collingwood* (Oxford: Princeton University Press, 2009), 337; R. G. Collingwood, *The Idea of History* (Oxford: Clarendon Press, 1946), 215.

15 John Russell ed., *A Portrait of Logan Pearsall Smith Drawn from his Letters and Diaries* (London: Dropmore, 1950), 164; Hugh Trevor-Roper, *History and the Enlightenment*, ed. John Robertson (New Haven: Yale University Press, 2010), 199 (reproducing an essay first published in 1968).

16 Trevor-Roper, 'The Torments of Lord Acton'; Trevor-Roper, 'When World History Ceases Being European', *International Herald Tribune*, 10 June 1974; Trevor-Roper's introduction to Acton, *Lectures on Modern History* (Gloucester, Mass.: Peter Smith, 1975), 8; Lord Acton, *Lectures on Modern History*, ed. J. N. Figgis and R. V. Laurence (London: Macmillan, 1906), 23-4; Acton, *Lectures on Modern History*, ed. Hugh Trevor-Roper (New York: Meridian Books, 1961), 37.

17 Hugh Trevor-Roper, *Historical Essays* (London: Macmillan, 1957), vi; Trevor-Roper, 'Historical Imagination', *Listener*, 27 February 1958; A. F. Scott ed., *Topics and Opinions* (London: Macmillan, 1960), 19.

18 R. H. Tawney, *The Acquisitive Society* (London: G. Bell, 1921), 3, 6, 181.

19 Hugh Trevor-Roper, 'How Spain kept out of the war', *Sunday Times*, 7 June 1953; 'Lost Generation', *Sunday Times*, 1 November 1959.

20 Sir Richard Rees, *For Love or Money: Studies in Personality and Essence* (London: Secker & Warburg, 1960), 149-58; Hugh Trevor-Roper, introduction to Burnett Bolloten, *The Grand Camouflage: The Spanish Civil War and Revolution, 1936-39* (London: Pall Mall Press, 1968), 1-3; Christopher Hobhouse, *Oxford: As It Was and as It Is To-Day*, 2nd edn revised by Marcus Dick (London: Batsford, 1952), 105-6.

21 EUL 113/3/1/R, Hugh Trevor-Roper to A. L. Rowse, 17 January 1951; Trevor-Roper, 'Missing the Point', *Sunday Times*, 9 June 1963; Peter Ghosh, 'Hugh Trevor-Roper and the History of Ideas', *History of European Ideas*, vol. 37 (2011), 490-1.

22 Hugh Trevor-Roper, 'Historical Imagination', *Listener*, 27 February 1958; Lord Dacre of Glanton, foreword to Ernst Klee, Willi Dressen and Volker Riess eds, *'The Good Old Days': The Holocaust as Seen by its Perpetrators and Bystanders* (New York: Konecky, 1991), x, xvi; Trevor-Roper, *One Hundred Letters*, 412.

23 J. I. M. Stewart, *Full Term* (London: Gollancz, 1978), 63-4.

24 Hugh Trevor-Roper, foreword to Ewen Montagu, *Beyond Top Secret U* (London: Peter Davies, 1977), 9; Hugh Trevor-Roper, *The Secret World: Behind the Curtain of British Intelligence in World War II and the Cold*

War, ed. Edward Harrison (London: I.B. Tauris, 2014), ix, 7, 8; Nigel West ed., *The Guy Liddell Diaries*, vol. 1 (London: Routledge, 2005), 156; Edward Harrison, *Secret Service against the Nazi Regime: How our Spies Dealt with Hitler* (Barnsley: Pen & Sword, 2022), 112–54.

25 Bodleian, MS Berlin 256, Stuart Hampshire to Isaiah Berlin, 9–11 March 1945; Hugh Trevor-Roper, 'The liberal tide', *Spectator*, 22 December 1990; Trevor-Roper, introduction to Andrew Lawson, *Discover Unexpected London* (Oxford: Elsevier-Phaidon, 1977), 7.

26 J. I. M. Stewart, *The Guardians* (London: Gollancz, 1955), 14; Ghosh, 'Trevor-Roper', 484.

27 Worcester College archives, Woodward papers box 1, E. L. Woodward to Lord Strang, 4 July 1961; Storm Jameson, *A Cup of Tea for Mr Thorgill* (New York: Harper, 1957), 68.

28 Dacre papers 17/1/1, Hugh Trevor-Roper to Xandra Howard-Johnston, 7 November 1953.

29 Ernest Gellner, *Words and Things: A Critical Account of Linguistic Philosophy and a Study in Ideology* (London: Gollancz, 1959), 237, 241–2; Hugh Trevor-Roper, 'Time for a New Game', *Sunday Times*, 11 October 1959; Dacre papers 17/1/1, Hugh Trevor-Roper to Xandra Howard-Johnston, 27 June 1953, misquoting a remark of Charles Fisher (Senior Censor, 1910–14; killed in the naval battle at Jutland, 1916) given in Sir Charles Tennyson, *Life's All a Fragment* (London: Cassell, 1953), 20.

30 Gellner, *Words and Things*, 33, 39, 63; Gilbert Ryle, *The Concept of the Mind* (London: Hutchinson, 1949), 56, 58.

31 Text of Stuart Harris's interview with Peter Herbst, Bells Creek, New South Wales, 21 February 1994 (I owe this reference to Michael Cremer).

32 Christ Church Library, Dundas papers, ms 580/5; Dacre papers 1/3/28, Hugh Trevor-Roper to Charles Stuart, 23 December 1956.

33 Text of Stuart Harris's interview with Peter Herbst; BL Add ms 72766, Quintin Hailsham to Roy Harrod, 20 October 1959.

34 J. I. M. Stewart, *The Last Tresilians* (London: Gollancz, 1963), 14; Stephen Spender, *New Selected Journals, 1939–1995*, ed. Lara Feigel and John Sutherland (London: Faber & Faber, 2012), 242; *The Complete Works of W. H. Auden: Poems, 1940–1973*, ed. Edward Mendelson (Princeton: Princeton University Press, 2022), 491, 991.

35 Sir Maurice Powicke, *Modern Historians and the Study of History* (London: Odhams, 1955), 166, 229, 232; Powicke, 'The School of Modern History', *Oxford Magazine*, 27 February 1930. Hugh Trevor-Roper, 'Making History', *Sunday Times*, 26 June 1955.

36 Bodleian, Berlin papers 246, Maurice Bowra to Isaiah Berlin, 20 October 1936, and Berlin papers 241, Noël Annan to Berlin, 12 November 1953;

Hugh Trevor-Roper, *Letters from Oxford: to Bernard Berenson*, ed. Richard Davenport-Hines (London: Weidenfeld & Nicolson, 2006), 163–4, 244; BLPES, Economic History Society papers 0/1A, Habbakuk to Trevor-Roper, 6 March 1951; Sisman, *Trevor-Roper*, 209; Sir Rupert Hart-Davis ed., *The Lyttelton–Hart Davis Letters*, vol. 1 (London: John Murray, 1978), 65, and vol. 4 (London: John Murray, 1982), 57; interview with Alan Macfarlane, 18 November 2021; María Jesús González, *Raymond Carr: The Curiosity of the Fox* (Brighton: Sussex Academic Press, 2013), 64, 159.

37 Kenneth Rose, *Who's In, Who's Out: Journals, 1944–1979*, ed. D. R. Thorpe (London: Weidenfeld & Nicolson, 2018), 318, 376, 389; information from Kenneth Rose, 12 August 2009.

38 M. W. Rowe, *J. L. Austin: Philosopher and D-Day Intelligence Officer* (Oxford: Oxford University Press, 2023), 373.

39 Murdoch, *Living on Paper*, 44; Dacre papers 6/34, quoted Allan, 'Historian as Public Intellectual', 263.

40 NA KV 2/3941, serial 70a, report by Detective Sergeant Viveash of Hill's speech to Reading branch of CPGB, dated 4 April 1950; KV 2/3943, 'Professor Christopher Hill', 8 February 1954; KV 2/3944, serial 198a, Christopher Hill, biographical statement, n.d. [1950].

41 EUL 113/1/2/4/4, A. L. Rowse, 'Christopher Hill'; Trevor-Roper, *Historical Essays*, 293; Hugh Trevor-Roper, 'Communism in Europe' and 'Communism in France', *Observer*, 14 and 21 September 1947; Christopher Hill, *Lenin and the Russian Revolution* (London: Hodder & Stoughton, 1947), 236–7; Trevor-Roper, *Why I Oppose Communism: A Symposium* (London: Phoenix, 1956), 7–8.

42 Trevor-Roper, *Historical Essays*, 295, 298.

43 Hugh Trevor-Roper, 'Ex-Communist v. Communist', *Manchester Guardian*, 10 July 1950; Hugh Trevor-Roper, 'The Future of Communism' [review of James Burnham's *The Coming Defeat of Communism* in unidentified magazine], 1950; Sir David Cannadine ed., *A Question of Retribution? The British Academy and the Matter of Anthony Blunt* (printed for the British Academy by Oxford University Press, 2020), 14; Richard Davenport-Hines, 'Fellows Pro and Con', *Times Literary Supplement*, 7 August 2020.

44 Trevor-Roper, *Historical Essays*, 7, 10.

45 University of Utrecht, Hugh Trevor-Roper to Pieter Geyl, 24 May 1955; Richard Evans, *Eric Hobsbawm: A Life in History* (London: Little Brown, 2019), 384–5; Hugh Trevor-Roper, *The China Journals*, ed. Richard Davenport-Hines (London: Bloomsbury, 2020).

46 Trevor-Roper, *Letters from Oxford*, 35; Lord Wyatt of Weeford, *The Journals of Woodrow Wyatt*, vol. 1, ed. Sarah Curtis (London: Macmillan, 1998), 246; Gilmour papers, Hugh Trevor-Roper to Ian Gilmour, 7 May 1986;

Trevor-Roper, 'The liberal tide', *Spectator*, 22 December 1990.

47   Trevor-Roper, *One Hundred Letters*, 28; Trevor-Roper, *Letters from Oxford*, 73; Trevor-Roper, 'Is Franco a Fascist?', *Sunday Times*, 14 June 1953.

48   Trevor-Roper, *One Hundred Letters*, 41; Dacre papers 17/1/2, Hugh Trevor-Roper to Xandra Howard-Johnston, 5 and 10 April 1956.

49   Hugh Trevor-Roper, introduction to Jacob Burckhardt, *Judgements on History and Historians*, trans. Harry Zohn (Boston: Beacon Press, 1958), 15–16.

50   Trevor-Roper, 'Wrack and Crumbling'.

51   Worcester College Library, Masterman papers, PRO 10/1/45, Masterman memorandum of March 1947; EUL 113/3/1/W, E. L. Woodward to A. L. Rowse, 5 October 1955. For Galbraith's historical credo, see his article 'Diplomatic', *Oxford Magazine*, 27 November 1930.

52   Private conversation with one of the gentlest, wisest and most scrupulous of Oxford medievalists, 2 December 2011; EUL 113/1/2/4/3, Rowse notes on 'Ernest Fraser Jacob', c. 1964; Southern, *History*, 180-1.

53   Trevor-Roper, *One Hundred Letters*, 58–9; University of Utrecht, Geyl papers, Hugh Trevor-Roper to Pieter Geyl, 2 June 1964; Trevor-Roper, 'Namierana'; Trevor-Roper, 'The Namier Method', *Sunday Times*, 15 May 1955; cf. J. P. Cooper, 'Recollections of Namier', *Oxford Magazine*, 3 November 1960, 65–7.

54   Gooch, *History and Historians*, xxiii; Trevor-Roper, *Letters from Oxford*, 110.

55   University of Utrecht, Geyl papers, Hugh Trevor-Roper to Pieter Geyl, 28 January 1953; Pieter Geyl, *Encounters in History* (London: Collins, 1963), 55, 340, 342, 401.

56   Pieter Geyl, *History of the Low Countries: Episodes and Problems* (London: Macmillan, 1964), 2; Hugh Trevor-Roper, 'Heavy Meal', *Sunday Times*, 27 June 1954; Trevor-Roper, 'Toynbee System', *Sunday Times*, 17 October 1954; Trevor-Roper, 'Historians' Failures', *Sunday Times*, 21 August 1955; Trevor-Roper, 'New Lamps for Old', *Sunday Times*, 26 February 1956; Trevor-Roper, 'Arnold Toynbee's Millennium', *Encounter* (June 1957), 14–27; Trevor-Roper, 'A. J. P. Taylor, Hitler, and the War', *Encounter* (July 1961), 88–96; Trevor-Roper, 'E. H. Carr's Success Story', *Encounter* (May 1962), 69–76.

57   Trevor-Roper, 'Human Nature in Politics', *Listener*, 10 December 1953.

58   Geyl, *Encounters*, 355–7; University of Utrecht, Geyl papers, Hugh Trevor-Roper to Pieter Geyl, 9 September 1958. For an overconfident representation of Trevor-Roper's views, see Finn Fuglestad, 'The Trevor-Roper Trap, or the Imperialism of History', *History in Africa*, vol. 19 (1992), 309-26.

59 Hugh Trevor-Roper, 'Introduction', in Dennis Stock ed., *This Land of Europe: A Photographic Exploration* (Tokyo: Kodansha International, 1976), 9.

60 Trevor-Roper, *Historical Essays*, v.

61 Dacre papers 17/1/3, Hugh Trevor-Roper to Xandra Howard-Johnston, 17 December 1954; Trevor-Roper, *Letters from Oxford*, 43, 60, 237; Trevor-Roper, foreword to Giorgio de Santillana, *Reflections on Men and Ideas* (Cambridge, Mass.: MIT Press, 1968), v; Trevor-Roper, *Historical Essays*, 273, 276, 277.

62 Trevor-Roper's introduction to Jacob Burckhardt, *Judgements on History and Historians* (London: George Allen & Unwin, 1959), 14, 16, 18.

63 Trevor-Roper, 'Apologia transfugae'.

64 Trevor-Roper, *Letters from Oxford*, 74; Lewis Namier, *Facing East* (London: Hamish Hamilton, 1947), 25; Hugh Trevor-Roper, 'Tyrant', *Sunday Times*, 9 November 1952.

65 Hugh Trevor-Roper, 'The Mind of Adolf Hitler', in *Hitler's Table Talk, 1941–1944* (London: Weidenfeld & Nicolson, 1953), xi, xiii. See also Mikael Nilsson, 'Hugh Trevor-Roper and the English Editions of Hitler's *Table Talk* and *Testament*', *Journal of Contemporary History*, vol. 51 (2016), 788–812.

66 Worden, 'Trevor-Roper', 262; Dacre papers 17/1/1, Hugh Trevor-Roper to Xandra Howard-Johnston, 4 December 1954; Hugh Trevor-Roper, 'Contradictions', *Sunday Times*, 23 October 1955; 'Apologia transfugae'.

67 BLPES, Gellner papers 24/1, Hugh Trevor-Roper to Ernest Gellner, 26 September 1959; Hugh Trevor-Roper, 'Time for a New Game', *Sunday Times*, 11 October 1959; Gellner, *Words and Things*, 246, 253–4.

68 Keith Thomas, 'The Changing Family', *Times Literary Supplement*, 21 October 1977; Thomas, 'The Ferment of Fashion', *Times Literary Supplement*, 30 April 1982; Richard J. Evans, *In Defence of History* (London: Granta, 1997), 122.

69 Worcester College archives, Masterman papers, PRO 10/1/45, Neale to Masterman, 28 June 1951; Sir Keith Hancock, *Country and Calling* (London: Faber & Faber, 1954), 200; BLPES, Economic History Society 0/1A, Michael Postan to H. J. Habbakuk, 2 November 1950.

70 Lawrence Goldman, *The Life of R. H. Tawney: Socialism and History* (London: Bloomsbury, 2013), 237; Ghosh, 'Trevor-Roper', 484; Sisman, *Trevor-Roper*, 190–1.

71 BL Add ms 71197, Hugh Trevor-Roper to Roy Harrod, 10 June 1951.

72 www.alanmacfarlane.com/autobiography/Oxford postgraduate; Trevor-Roper's foreword to Felix Raab, *The English Face of Machiavelli: A Changing Interpretation, 1500–1700* (London: Routledge & Kegan Paul, 1974), viii.

73 Sisman, *Trevor-Roper*, 188–9, 192; EUL 113/3/1/R, Hugh Trevor-Roper to

A. L. Rowse, 28 October 1950; BLPES, EcHS 0/1A, Michael Postan to Lawrence Stone, 2 November 1950.

74 Worcester College archives, Woodward papers, E. L. Woodward to Lord Strang, 25 January 1953.

75 Dacre papers 6/12, Hugh Trevor-Roper to John Masterman, 4 May 1951.

76 EUL 113/3/1/R, Rowse memoir, 'Hugh Redwald Trevor-Roper'; V. H. Galbraith, 'Austin Lane Poole', *Oxford Magazine*, 9 May 1963, 288–9.

77 Brown, *Journeys of the Mind*, 168.

78 Dacre papers 6/12, Hugh Trevor-Roper to Nicholas Thompson, 11 May 1951.

79 Worcester College archives, Masterman papers, PRO 10/1/45, John Masterman to J. E. Neale, 26 June 1951; Trevor-Roper, 'Namierana'.

80 Worcester College archives, Masterman papers, PRO 10/1/45, J. E. Neale to John Masterman, first and second letters of 28 June 1951.

81 Worcester College archives, Masterman papers, PRO 10/1/45, Hugh Trevor-Roper to John Masterman, 3 July 1951.

82 Dacre papers 6/12, Robin Dundas to Hugh Trevor-Roper, 20 July 1951. Emphasis in original.

83 Dacre papers 1/3/17, Hugh Trevor-Roper to Patrick Trevor-Roper, 29 March 1957; Elliott, *Spain, Europe*, 25.

84 Masterman papers 10/1/45, Asa Briggs to John Masterman, 13 December 1956.

85 Dacre papers 1/2/3, Isaiah Berlin to Hugh Trevor-Roper, 15 March 1957; Isaiah Berlin, *Enlightening: Letters 1946–1960*, ed. Henry Hardy and Jennifer Holmes (London: Chatto & Windus, 2009), 575.

86 Bodleian, MS Berlin 273, Hugh Trevor-Roper to Isaiah Berlin, 16 March 1957, and MS Berlin 241, Noël Annan to Berlin, 25 July 1957.

87 Hugh Trevor-Roper, *Men and Events: Historical Essays* (New York: Harper Brothers, 1959), 320; University of Utrecht, Geyl papers, Hugh Trevor-Roper to Pieter Geyl, 29 January 1958.

88 Hugh Lloyd-Jones, Valerie Pearl and Blair Worden eds, *History and Imagination: Essays in Honour of H. R. Trevor-Roper* (London: Duckworth, 1981), 8, 11, 12, 13.

Chapter 12: Robert Blake: The Busy Hum of Rumour and Intrigue

1 Robert Jackson, 'The division between young university Conservatives', *The Times*, 20 January 1969.

2 Lord Acton, *Historical Essays and Studies* (London: Macmillan, 1907), 424.

3 Robert Blake, 'Anthony Eden', in John Mackintosh ed., *British Prime*

Ministers in the Twentieth Century, vol. 2 (London: Weidenfeld, 1978), 105, 115; Robert Blake, 'Late Deceiver', *London Review of Books*, 17 September 1981, where the quip about the intelligentsia is attributed to Baldwin.

4 Kenneth O. Morgan, 'Robert Norman William Blake', *The Queen's College Record* (December 2003), 71.

5 William Waldegrave, *The Binding of Leviathan: Conservatism and the Future* (London: Hamish Hamilton, 1978), 45.

6 Andrew Roth, *Heath and the Heathmen* (London: Routledge, 1972). Neither *Burke* nor *Debrett* blazoned or illustrated the armorial bearings that were granted to Blake in 1973 so it seems right to describe them here. *Arms*: Quarterly Argent and Gules on a Bend Sable between two Billets three Garbs Or a Chief Vair. *Crest*: On a Wreath of the Colours an Heraldic Tyger sejant Argent gorged with a Coronet Or and supporting with the dexter forepaw a Tower Sable masoned Or. *Supporters*: On either side an Eagle Gules wings elevated and addorsed Argent and charged on the underside with a pierced Mullet Gules in the beak a Penner and Inkhorn Or. *Motto*: none. The bend and the chief on the shield indicate him to be a man of Norfolk. The eagles were adapted from the coat of arms of the Queen's College, of which he was Provost.

7 For Blake's grievances against Cooper, see BL Add ms 71182, Robert Blake to Roy Harrod, 26 December 1952.

8 Mary Gordon ed., *The Letters of George S. Gordon, 1902–1942* (Oxford: Oxford University Press, 1943), 37–8; E. H. W. Meyerstein, *Of my Early Life (1889–1918)*, ed. Rowland Watson (London: Neville Spearman, 1957), 118.

9 Sir Desmond MacCarthy, 'George Gordon', *Sunday Times*, 5 September 1943; James Patrick, *The Magdalen Metaphysicals: Idealism and Orthodoxy at Oxford, 1901–1945* (Macon, Georgia: Mercer University Press, 1985), xi–xii.

10 M. W. Rowe, *J. L. Austin: Philosopher and D-Day Intelligence Officer* (Oxford: Oxford University Press, 2023), 113.

11 Gilbert Ryle, 'T. D. Weldon', *Oxford Magazine*, 19 June 1958, 527–8; L. W. B. Brockliss ed., *Magdalen College, Oxford: A History* (Oxford: Magdalen College, 2008), 617–19.

12 Rowland Watson ed., *Some Letters of E. H. W. Meyerstein* (London: Neville Spearman, 1959), 290, 310; R. W. Johnson, *Look Back in Laughter: Oxford's Post-war Golden Age* (Newbury: Threshold Press, 2015), 48–9.

13 David Cannadine ed., *A Question of Retribution? The British Academy and the Matter of Anthony Blunt* (printed for the British Academy by Oxford University Press, 2020), 43, 46–7, 50, 62; Lord Blake, 'British Academy of

Cowards', *Daily Mail*, 8 August 1980; Richard Davenport-Hines, 'Fellows pro and con', *Times Literary Supplement*, 7 August 2020.

14 Richard Shannon, 'Robert Norman William Blake, 1916–2003', *Biographical Memoirs of Fellows of the British Academy*, vol. 7 (Oxford: Oxford University Press, 2008), 70.

15 Dacre papers 1/2/12, Robert Blake to Hugh Trevor-Roper, 29 December 1968.

16 Dacre papers 17/1/1, Hugh Trevor-Roper to Xandra Howard-Johnston, 7 July 1953.

17 Robert Blake, 'A dull but close election?', *Illustrated London News*, 20 June 1964.

18 Dacre papers 1/2/2, Robert Blake to Hugh Trevor-Roper, 2 October 1951, and 1/2/qv, Blake to Trevor-Roper, 16 April 1960.

19 Dacre papers 1/2/qv, Robert Blake to Hugh Trevor-Roper, 12 January 1958; Dacre papers 1/2/4, Blake to Trevor-Roper, 5 April 1961; House of Lords debates, 18 May 1977.

20 BL Add ms 71182, Robert Blake to Roy Harrod, 26 December 1952; Dacre papers 1/2/6, Blake to Hugh Trevor-Roper, 31 December 1962; Dacre papers 172/7, William Gladstone to Trevor-Roper, 4 January 1963.

21 BL Add ms 71197, Robert Blake to Roy Harrod, 6 August 1956; House of Lords debate, 5 February 1975.

22 Dacre papers 1/2/8, Robert Blake to Hugh Trevor-Roper, 24 December 1964.

23 BL Add ms 71609, 18 June 1954, Robert Blake to Roy Harrod, 18 June 1954, 2 and 16 April 1955.

24 Christopher Hobhouse, *Oxford: As It Was and as It Is To-Day*, 2nd edn revised by Marcus Dick (London: Batsford, 1952), 106–7; BL Add ms 71618, Marcus Dick to Billa Harrod, 9 March 1949; Add ms 72744, Robert Blake to Roy Harrod, 2 April 1959. On Dick, see also Balliol College Library, diary of Harold Nicolson, 27 June 1953.

25 Dacre papers 1/2/6, Robert Blake to Hugh Trevor-Roper, 6 August 1962.

26 J. I. M. Stewart, *The Madonna of the Astrolabe* (London: Gollancz, 1977), 52–3.

27 Dacre papers 1/2/6, Robert Blake to Hugh Trevor-Roper, 1 September 1961.

28 Dacre papers 1/2/15, Robert Blake to Hugh Trevor-Roper, 6 April 1971.

29 Ryle, 'T. D. Weldon', 1958; Dacre papers 1/2/15, Robert Blake to Hugh Trevor-Roper, 31 August 1956, and Blake to Trevor-Roper, 16 April 1960.

30 Vivian Ridler, *Diary of a Master Printer: A Year in the Life of the Printer to the University, Oxford* (Oxford: Perpetua Press, 2022), 182.

31 Robert Blake, 'The Future of Education', *Illustrated London News*, 1 August

1964; Blake, 'The effects of Robbins on Oxford', *Oxford*, May 1964, 62; Robert Bridges, 'Poor Poll', *New Verse* (Oxford: Clarendon Press, 1925), 6.

32 Blake, 'Future of Education'.

33 Robert Blake, *The Private Papers of Douglas Haig* (London: Eyre & Spottiswoode, 1952), 30–1.

34 Blake, *Haig*, 42; Robert Blake, *The Conservative Party from Peel to Major* (London: Heinemann, 1997), 195–7.

35 Dacre papers 1/2/2, Robert Blake to Hugh Trevor-Roper, 15 September 1951; G. M. Young, 'Testament of faith', *Sunday Times*, 3 December 1950.

36 Robert Blake, *The Unknown Prime Minister: The Life and Times of Andrew Bonar Law, 1858–1923* (London: Eyre & Spottiswoode, 1955), 86–7, 461.

37 Ibid., 121, 179; Dacre 1/2/6, Robert Blake to Hugh Trevor-Roper, 6 August 1962.

38 Robert Blake, 'The 14th Earl of Derby', *History Today*, vol. 5 (December 1955), 850–9.

39 Robert Blake, 'Baldwin and the Right', in John Raymond ed., *The Baldwin Age* (London: Eyre & Spottiswoode, 1952), 43, 47–8.

40 Robert Blake, 'Anthony Eden', in Mackintosh ed., *British Prime Ministers in the Twentieth Century*, vol. 2, 75–6, 86.

41 Dacre papers 1/2/15, Robert Blake to Hugh Trevor-Roper, 10 January 1957; Robert Blake, 'Baldwin and the Right', in John Raymond ed., *The Baldwin Age* (London: Eyre & Spottiswoode, 1952), 42; Robert Blake, 'A dull but close election?', *Illustrated London News*, 20 June 1964.

42 Robert Blake, 'Westminster Scene', *Illustrated London News*, 23 July 1966.

43 Dacre papers 1/2/2, Robert Blake to Hugh Trevor-Roper, 16 April 1960.

44 BL Add ms 72757, Robert Blake to Roy Harrod, 21 October 1957.

45 Robert Blake, 'Conservative Unity', *Illustrated London News*, 29 August 1964, and 'Westminster Scene', *Illustrated London News*, 15 January 1966.

46 Robert Blake, 'Lessons of Disraeli for today's Tories', *Sunday Telegraph*, 19 April 1981; Robert Blake, *Disraeli* (London: Eyre & Spottiswoode, 1966), 765–6.

47 Blake, *Disraeli*, 477, 713, 714. An informative review of the book is Noël Annan, 'Making It', *New York Review of Books*, 6 April 1967.

48 Blake, *Disraeli*, 562–3.

49 Robert Blake, 'What sort of Little England?', *Sunday Telegraph*, 21 January 1968.

50 Murray Kempton, 'A Letter from the Wasteland', *New York Review of Books*, 23 October 1969.

51 Robert Blake, 'The Conservatives in search of a policy', *Illustrated London News*, 9 October 1965, and 'Westminster Scene', *Illustrated London News*, 9 April 1966.

52   Blake, *Conservative Party from Peel to Major*, 300, 309; Roth, *Heath and the Heathmen*.

53   Robert Blake, 'Mr Wilson, Ulster and the Lords', *Illustrated London News*, 10 April 1965; Blake, 'Westminster Scene', *Illustrated London News*, 28 May 1966; Blake, 'Reflections on the Heath era', *Illustrated London News*, 28 April 1979.

54   Simon Leys [Pierre Ryckmans], *The Hall of Uselessness: Collected Essays* (New York: New York Review of Books, 2013), 463.

55   J. I. M. Stewart, *The Gaudy* (London: Gollancz, 1974), 238.

56   Karl Löwith, *The Meaning of History: The Theological Implications of the Philosophy of History* (Chicago: University of Chicago Press, 1949), 25, 190.

57   Pierre Nora, 'Between Memory and History: *Les Lieux de Mémoire*', *Representations*, no. 26 (1989), 7, 17; Peter Brown, *Journeys of the Mind* (Oxford: Princeton University Press, 2023), 156.

58   Ferdinand Mount, 'How bad can it get?', *London Review of Books*, 15 August 2019.

59   Philip Rieff, *Fellow Teachers* (London: Faber & Faber, 1975), 200.

60   *The Complete Works of W. H. Auden: Poems, 1940–1973*, ed. Edward Mendelson (Princeton: Princeton University Press, 2022), 675; Michael Oakeshott, *Notebooks, 1922–1986*, ed. Luke O'Sullivan (Exeter: Academic Imprint, 2014), 512–13; Louis Namier, *Conflicts: Studies in Contemporary History* (London: Macmillan, 1942), 195.

61   Nora, 'Between Memory and History', 8, 9, 10, 14.

62   David Rieff, *In Praise of Forgetting: Historical Memory and its Ironies* (New Haven: Yale University Press, 2016), 63–4, 108–9, 117, 144; Wisława Szymborska, *Map: Collected and Last Poems* (New York: Houghton Mifflin Harcourt, 2015), 287.

63   C. M. Woodhouse, 'Highbrows and the Party', *Times Literary Supplement*, 20 November 1959.

64   Arthur Hugh Clough, 'Amours de Voyage', canto I, verse XII; Elie Kedourie, *Perestroika in the Universities* (London: Institute of Economic Affairs, 1989), 44.

Index